Global Stage

Teacher's Book 2

Dave Tucker

macmillan education

Macmillan Education
4 Crinan Street
London N1 9XW
A division of Macmillan Education Limited

Companies and representatives throughout the world

Teacher's Book ISBN 978-1-380-00225-9
Teacher's Blended Pack ISBN 978-1-380-00222-8

Written by Dave Tucker

First published 2019

Designed by emc design ltd
Front cover design and concept by 3CD
Cover adaptation by Roberto Martinez

The authors and publishers would like to thank the following for permission to reproduce their photographs: Matthew Hayes (p. 16), Lina Acosta Sandaal (p. 18)

The authors and publishers are grateful for permission to reprint the following copyright material: p. 11 Extract from 'Framework for 21st Century Learning' © 2017 Partnership for 21st Century Skills. Reprinted with permission; p. 17 Extract from 'Collaborative for Academic, Social, and Emotional Learning' © 2017 CASEL. Reprinted with permission.

Full acknowledgements for illustrations and photographs in the facsimile pages can be found in the **Language Book** ISBN 978-1-786-32349-1 and **Literacy Book** ISBN 978-1-786-32348-4.

Printed and bound in Mexico
by Compañía Editorial Ultra, S.A. de C.V.

2021 2020
10 09 08 07

Contents

macmillan education

Unit	Vocabulary	Explore Language	Global Citizenship
Language Review	**Vocabulary** *Animals, Activities, Clothes, Family, Food, Home, Places in a Town* **Grammar** *Question Words, Possessive Adjectives and Pronouns, There Is/Are, Present Progressive, Simple Present*		
1 What Does It Do? page 10	**Gadgets** *alarm clock, cell phone, computer, keyboard, laptop, mouse, radio, screen, tablet, TV, video game* **Places and Objects in School** *bookcase, cafeteria, classroom, gym, hallway, language lab, playground, projector, whiteboard* **Song** *Living in a Modern World*	Simple Present: Adverbs of Frequency *How often … ?* *always / often / sometimes / rarely / never* Present Progressive Review	How is technology in schools different around the world? **Listening Skills** Listening for gist and details.
2 Thank You page 22	**Food** *cherry, chicken, corn, cupcake, eggplant, fruit, peas, pineapple, rice, sausage, spinach, tomato* **Containers, Food and Drink** *a bag of, a bottle of, a bowl of, a box of, a can of, a carton of, lemonade, potato chips, soup* **Song** *It's Market Day!*	Quantifiers: *a lot of, much, many* Quantifiers with questions: *How much …? How many … ? Some / Any*	How is fruit different around the world? **Listening Skills** Listening for gist and details.
Put It Together	**Review Units 1 and 2** *Lemonade for Everyone*		
3 It Keeps Changing page 36	**Nature** *beach, desert, forest, glacier, island, lake, ocean, mountain, river, valley, waterfall* **Animals** *bear, chameleon, duck, feathers, fur, penguin, scales, snake, swan* **Song** *It's a Wonderful World*	Simple Past: *be* statements Simple Past: *be* questions	How do animals change? **Listening Skills** Listening for gist and details.
4 What Happened? page 48	**Action Verbs 1** *bake, carry, clap, compete, dance, drop, start, study, trip* **Action Verbs 2** *bounce, finish, learn, move, pack, play, practice, smile, travel, wait* **Song** *It's OK*	Simple Past: Regular verb statements Simple Past: Regular verb questions	What is special about a first day at school? **Listening Skills** Listening for gist and details.
Put It Together	**Review Units 3 and 4** *Explore the Island*		
5 Let's Go Back page 62	**Parts of the Body and Adjectives** *body, claws, dangerous, dinosaur, huge, scary, slow, tail, tiny, wings* **Fossils and Ruins** *bones, broken, build, dig, find, fossil, jug, pottery, skeleton* **Song** *King of the Dinosaurs*	Simple Past: Irregular verb statements Simple Past: Irregular verb questions	Where can we learn about the past in different countries? **Listening Skills** Listening for gist and details.

Speaking	Writing	International English	Literacy Book
			Phonics Review: *Long vowel sounds; Blends and Digraphs, CVC words*
Presentation Describing Technology **Pronunciation** /eɪ/ and /e/	**Punctuation** Periods and question marks **Product** A Technology Survey	**US** *cell phone; rarely; hallway* **UK** *mobile phone; hardly ever; corridor*	**Story** *The After-School Inventor* **Instructional Text** *My Good Ideas Book* **Reading Skill** Identifying a Sequence of Events
Conversation Making Suggestions, Discussing Needs **Pronunciation** /l/ and /r/	**Punctuation** Capital letters and commas **Product** A Description of My Kitchen	**US** *eggplant; cupcake; potato chips* **UK** *aubergine; fairy cake; crisps*	**Informational Text** *Chuseok: Korea's Harvest Festival* **Science Fiction** *First Harvest* **Reading Skill** Understanding the Setting
Conversation Showing Enthusiasm **Pronunciation** /ɑr/ and /ʌ/	**Sentence Building** *and, but* **Product** A Postcard		**Poem** *The Bear and I* **Informational Text** *Clean Cars* **Reading Skill** Comparing and Contrasting Information
Presentation Describing an Important Event **Pronunciation** /d/ and /t/ or /ɪd/	**Spelling** Regular verb endings **Product** A Description of an Event	**US** *practice* **UK** *practise*	**Informational Text** *Where Is She?* **Story** *The Angry Mountain* **Reading Skill** Identifying Cause and Effect
Presentation Describing a Dinosaur **Pronunciation** /oʊ/ and /ɔr/	**Sentence Building** *because* **Product** A Diary		**Fantasy** *The Time Book* **Informational Text** *Time Capsules* **Reading Skill** Identifying the Main Idea and Details

Speaking	Writing	International English	Literacy Book
Presentation Giving Instructions **Pronunciation** /g/ and /k/	**Spelling** Comparative and superlative endings **Product** A Personal Profile	**US** *jewelry; mustache; clean* **UK** *jewellery; moustache; tidy*	**Story** *The Superstar* **Informational Text** *Visit Gaudí's World* **Reading Skill** Identifying Fact and Opinion
Conversation Deciding What to Do **Pronunciation** /n/ and /ŋ/	**Sentence Building** Imperatives **Product** Team Game Instructions	**US** *horseback riding, biking; trade* **UK** *horse-riding, cycling; swap*	**Informational Text** *Great Teamwork* **Story** *It's Mine* **Reading Skill** Predicting Endings
Conversation Taking Turns and Playing Games **Pronunciation** /oʊ/ and /aʊ/	**Sentence Building** *I think, because* **Product** A Hero Profile	**US** *track and field; math* **UK** *athletics; maths*	**Biography** *In First Place* **Play** *A New Hero* **Reading Skill** Understanding Characters
Presentation Describing Your Dream House **Pronunciation** /s/ and /ð/	**Sentence Building** Sequencers **Product** A Picture Story	**US** *stove, bathtub* **UK** *cooker, bath*	**Fable** *The Clever King* **Informational Text** *Amazing Castles* **Reading Skill** Scanning for Specific Information
Conversation Buying a Ticket **Pronunciation** /r/ and /w/	**Text Type** Emails **Product** An Amazing Journey Email	**US** *country; round-trip* **UK** *countryside; return*	**Story** *Young Nicholas* **Biography** *The Thirty-Year Journey* **Reading Skill** Identifying the Sequence of Events

Unit	Reading 1	Reading 2	Reading Skill	Content Area	Social and Emotional Learning	Key Concept	Language Book
Phonics Review	Long vowel sounds, blends and digraphs, CVC words						
1 What Does It Do? page 8	**Fiction** *The After-School Inventor* Story *cl*– blend	**Nonfiction** *My Good Ideas Book* Instructional Text	Identifying a Sequence of Events	Science Technology	Self- Awareness Accurately recognize own strengths and limitations	Why do people invent things?	**Vocabulary** gadgets, places and objects in school **Grammar** simple present with adverbs of frequency present progressive review
2 Thank You page 24	**Nonfiction** *Chuseok: Korea's Harvest Festival* Informational Text	**Fiction** *First Harvest* Science Fiction –*st* blend	Understanding the Setting	Social Studies Communities	Self-Awareness Identify what triggers emotions	Why do we celebrate harvests?	**Vocabulary** food, containers, food and drink **Grammar** quantifiers with statements and questions
3 It Keeps Changing page 40	**Fiction** *The Bear and I* Poem –*ng* blend	**Nonfiction** *Clean Cars* Informational Text	Comparing and Contrasting Information	Science Environmental Science	Social Awareness Evaluate others' emotional reactions	How can we make good changes in our world?	**Vocabulary** nature and animals **Grammar** simple past: *be*
4 What Happened? page 56	**Nonfiction** *Where Is She?* Informational Text	**Fiction** *The Angry Mountain* Story –*nd* blend	Identifying a Cause and Effect	History World Events	Self-Awareness Label and recognize emotions	How do events change our lives?	**Vocabulary** action verbs **Grammar** simple past: regular verbs
5 Let's Go Back page 72	**Fiction** *The Time Book* Fantasy	**Nonfiction** *Time Capsules* Informational Text –*nt* blend	Identifying the Main Idea and Details	History Civilizations	Social Awareness Understand other views and perspectives	How can we find out about the past?	**Vocabulary** parts of the body, adjectives, fossils, and ruins **Grammar** simple past: irregular verbs

Unit	Reading 1	Reading 2	Reading Skill	Content Area	Social and Emotional Learning	Key Concept	Language Book
6 Look What I Made page 88	**Fiction** *The Superstar* Story *wh–* digraph	**Nonfiction** *Visit Gaudí's World* Informational Text	Identifying Fact and Opinion	Science Architecture	Self-Management Set plans and work towards goals	Why do people make things?	**Vocabulary** art, physical characteristics, and short adjectives **Grammar** comparatives: short adjectives superlatives: short adjectives
7 We're a Team page 104	**Nonfiction** *Great Teamwork* Informational Text	**Fiction** *It's Mine* Story *–ck* blend	Predicting Endings	Science Symbiotic Relationships	Relationship Skills Exhibit cooperative learning and working towards group goals	What is good about teamwork?	**Vocabulary** activities and working with others **Grammar** telling the time modal verbs: *can* for permissions, requests, and offers
8 You're My Hero page 120	**Nonfiction** *In First Place* Biography	**Fiction** *A New Hero* Play *tr–* blends	Understanding Characters	History Important People	Responsible Decision-Making Identify problems when making decisions and generate alternatives	What makes a hero?	**Vocabulary** sports, long adjectives, and attributes **Grammar** comparatives: long adjectives superlatives: long adjectives
9 Do You Live Here? page 136	**Fiction** *The Clever King* Fable	**Nonfiction** *Amazing Castles* Informational Text *br–* blend	Scanning for Specific Information	Science Architecture	Self-Management Regulate emotions such as impulses, aggression, and self-destructive behavior	Why did people build castles?	**Vocabulary** around the home and emotions **Grammar** simple past review *there was / there were*
10 Are We There Yet? page 152	**Fiction** *Young Nicholas* Story *sw–* blend	**Nonfiction** *The Thirty-Year Journey* Biography	Identifying the Sequence of Events	History Important People	Self-Management Display grit, determination, or perseverance	Why do people travel?	**Vocabulary** journeys and weather **Grammar** future plans: *going to* prepositions of movement

Welcome to *Global Stage*

You have in your hands a complete language and literacy course that will support you and your students in developing their English skills, and their love of reading and the English language.

The **Language Book** contains the building blocks of language skills and systems. Students will focus on learning the language and how it works. Beautiful picture dictionary scenes, lively songs, and contextualized grammar sections support them in working out and learning new language. Photos and texts about children around the world will inspire them to explore thought-provoking questions about what it means to be a Global Citizen. Live-action videos will expose learners to other children using the language they are learning before they take their turn.

The **Literacy Book** contains a variety of fiction and nonfiction texts, as well as activities for learners to explore literacy concepts, develop reading skills, and respond to the texts they have read. As they work through the course, students will further develop their thinking skills, and they will build self-reflection skills, which will allow them to become increasingly more effective and independent learners.

Together, the **Language** and **Literacy Books** explore topics across the curriculum while exposing students to differences in American and British English through the International English feature.

How to Use the Books Together

The **Language Book** and **Literacy Book** units are designed to provide a complete English language learning experience. There is no prescribed order for teaching the books: You may start with either book. You can choose to work through a whole unit and then move to the other book. Alternatively, you can start with the first **Literacy Book** reading, then move to the **Language Book**, then back to the second **Literacy Book** reading.

Used together, the two books cover the four skills, provide a solid foundation in vocabulary and grammar, and help train your learners to become competent users of English and independent thinkers.

Pedagogical Philosophy

The goal of ***Global Stage*** is to support children in becoming competent and confident English speakers while also developing as self-directed, inquisitive learners and responsible global citizens.

Global Stage starts with the child and looks out towards the world.

Global Stage assumes that every learner comes to school with a wealth of knowledge, thoughts, and opinions about their lives and the world, and that this is the starting point for their continued learning. All units include moments for students to consider and share their experiences, as well as consider others' points of view. This not only validates their thoughts, priming them to be open to learning, but is also the basis for learning empathy, which is one of the goals of our Global Citizenship lesson.

We know that children learn best when they feel safe to express their emotions. This is why we have carefully interwoven a social and emotional learning strand into the course. When you read the texts with your class, you will find opportunities to pause and reflect on how the characters feel and why, as well as opportunities for the students to think about how they feel in their lives when they encounter similar situations. Building and strengthening the ability to reflect will support students in becoming considerate, thoughtful citizens of the world.

Global Stage encourages self-reflection and a growth mindset to support children in increasing their academic achievement.

Every child has strengths they can build on, as well as areas they should develop and strengthen. We also know that what students and their teachers believe about intelligence influences academic achievement. A growth mindset is the belief that intelligence is not fixed, but rather can grow and continue to develop. Carol Dweck, who coined this term, and her colleagues demonstrated that a growth mindset empowers children to increase their academic achievement.

Global Stage supports students by helping them learn to reflect on their learning. Teachers can further support their students by focusing their praise on children's effort and improvement from where they start on their learning journey. This kind of feedback that focuses on growth reinforces the notion that children have the power to make progress by working toward it, encouraging students to view their progress and skills as something they can improve, rather than purely the result of their static abilities.

Global Stage includes various forms of review to support children in improving self-reflection skills: Our **Language Book** reviews, the Think It Over pages, are always open-ended, prompting students to think about what they have learned, how they have learned it, how they think they might learn better, and what they think they should continue to work on. When you do these lessons in class, you can take advantage of this social moment for students to hear from each other. One child may mention that they learned the most with the unit song, while another might recall a game or a story. Children will benefit from considering what has worked for them and for others, while also planning for how to continue to learn. These are also moments for you to praise the class for their effort, pointing out where they've made progress.

Our **Literacy Book** includes Think Together pages, a space for students to get used to reflecting on how they respond to texts, and how working with those texts might have enriched what they think about the Key Concept questions at the top of the page.

Finally, our **Student's App** on **Navio** allows learners to review the language and skills they have studied and receive instant feedback, as well as increasing challenges as they progress. Students will be supported in learning and improving their English, while having fun and working at their own pace.

Helping children notice where they are making progress will help them build their self-reflection skills and also encourage them to seek further challenge.

Global Stage helps you teach beyond the test.

In ***Global Stage*** you will find a robust and engaging course. With its dual book approach to language and literacy, and its focus on engaging the students and allowing them to develop their thinking and self-management skills, ***Global Stage*** supports children in learning beyond the language needed for doing well on tests.

Students are challenged to learn at a stimulating pace. They encounter a variety of topics and language points, as well as texts and ideas. But you and they have strong support every step of the way. Whether it is the way the **Language Book** sets up a speaking or writing task in incremental steps so the learner knows what to work on and the teacher can see where they need help, or the way thinking opportunities are woven into the two books, encouraging children not only to learn information but also get better at analyzing it, ***Global Stage*** supports students' long-term development. For example, throughout the six levels of ***Global Stage***, learners will be developing the ability to work out the meaning of Words in Context. They will learn that words have many layers of meaning, and they will learn to develop strategies to work out aspects of the meaning themselves, from the context in each text. Their goal won't be to learn the word, but rather to understand the overall meaning of the text, and to make an educated guess about what the word may mean in that context. This skill will help them become better readers, learners, and test takers throughout their academic lives in English and in whatever other language they happen to be studying.

Global Stage supports children in developing 21st Century Skills.

In their widely accepted *Framework for 21st Century Learning*, which outlines their vision for student success in the new global economy, the Partnership for 21st Century Skills says that:

> *Learning and innovation skills increasingly are being recognized as the skills that separate students who are prepared for increasingly complex life and work environments in the 21st century, and those who are not. A focus on creativity, critical thinking, communication, and collaboration is essential to prepare students for the future.*

Global Stage infuses these important skills into every unit in a way that challenges the children and enhances the learning objective in each lesson. Students are consistently given opportunities to think and discuss everything from readings and skills to grammar points and writing mechanics. This ensures they are actively communicating to form a solid and personalized understanding of English. Our Think Together lesson, in the **Literacy Book**, includes a cooperative learning activity where learners can practice collaborating in a structured way, building the skills to listen to others, participating responsibly, and contributing equally to the activity outcome. Finally, lessons like Take the Stage and Write About It encourage creativity as students plan and produce individual presentations, conversation role-plays, and texts and critical thinking as they are supported to organize their thoughts.

Course Components

Language Book

The **Language Book** contains seven lessons per unit:

- Two vocabulary lessons. One includes a song and the other is linked to Global Citizenship themes and includes listening activities.
- Two Explore Language lessons with grammar presentation and practice.
- A speaking lesson (Take the Stage / Talk About It) that presents either a presentation or conversational skill and includes pronunciation practice.
- A writing lesson (Write About It) that explores writing mechanisms such as spelling and punctuation.
- A Think It Over lesson that focuses on self-reflection. This Assessment for Learning approach gets students involved in their learning and helps the teacher tailor future lessons to the needs of the students.

Throughout ***Global Stage***, students are exposed to a simplified inductive approach to grammar, vocabulary, and skills. They are guided to look at language in context to discover patterns and extrapolate meaning. When students are given an opportunity to work out a concept for themselves, they are much more likely to develop a deeper understanding, appreciation, and retention of knowledge.

In addition, opportunities to review and recycle what they have learned are built into the course with the review lessons (Put It Together) after every two units. These communicative games help students enjoy revisiting and practicing target language. There is also a mid-year and an end-of-year play, so students can use the language they've learned in a practical context. The first play, *Adventures on Purple Mountain*, uses vocabulary and grammar structures from Units 1–5. The second play, *King Grandpa's Treasure*, recycles vocabulary and grammar structures from Units 6–10.

Literacy Book

There are two texts in each unit of the **Literacy Book**, which are fully explored in a series of lessons.

- A Get Ready to Read lesson introduces the unit topic and creates interest. It also includes a pre-reading exercise and the reading skill focus.
- A Reading lesson presents a fiction or nonfiction text.
- An Explore the Reading lesson includes post-reading comprehension and analysis activities, and one of the texts is the vehicle for the phonics activity.
- Each unit ends with a Think Together lesson that draws the two readings together and explores the Key Concept for each unit.

In each unit, students encounter a reading skill and learn the use of the skill through practice in context. Learning these skills helps students read more quickly and effectively and gives them greater confidence, which in turn means they get more enjoyment from reading.

Each text includes a Words in Context feature where students are encouraged to work out the meaning of words from their context, rather than learn the words as vocabulary.

The **Literacy Book** develops Social and Emotional Learning (SEL) and Content and Language Integrated Learning (CLIL), while also including Visible Thinking Routines (VTR) and opportunities for Critical Literacy. Students are encouraged to work collaboratively by discussing and exploring ideas through Cooperative Learning Routines.

Three-Stage Reading Approach

The goal of the reading lessons is to get students reading for pleasure and to absorb information, rather than focusing on the mechanics of language in the text. The teaching notes suggest a three-stage approach to achieve this:

- Stage 1 **Listen and Engage.** This stage should be purely about reading for enjoyment and might include a prediction question to keep students motivated to find the answer.
- Stage 2 **Analyze the Text and Features.** In this stage, students read the text once again, while you help them analyze the text through the embedded callout questions. These questions will strengthen students' ability to make sense of the text and encourage them to begin thinking critically about what they are reading.
- Stage 3 **Interact with the Text.** This stage is about encouraging students to become actively involved in the learning process. They are asked to act out or perform the reading in some way. Alongside developing reading fluency, this allows students to think about the characters, setting, and concepts more deeply.

The Phonics Approach

The **Literacy Book** uses some elements of the "whole word approach" to reading (such as listening and following the text), combined with phonics practice. Research suggests that these approaches both possess merit and are more effective when used together.

The Review Unit at the start of the level reviews initial sounds, end sounds, short vowel sounds, and consonant-vowel-consonant (CVC) words that students will be familiar with from pre-primary courses. Each subsequent unit contains a Phonics section in one of the Explore the Reading lessons. In Level 2, the focus is mainly on consonant blends.

The phonics strand in ***Global Stage*** provides additional support for young readers and offers a jumping-off point for you to take this further with your class, if you choose.

Phonics *wh–*

Listen and say.

whale wheel where whisper why

Now find more words starting with *wh–* in the reading.

Together, the two books lay the foundation for an inductive approach to learning, encouraging students to recognize patterns and think critically through ordering, analysis, and categorization tasks.

The Unit 1 Walkthrough notes give more in-depth information about the purpose and learning outcomes for each activity, as well as further guidance on addressing core features such as visualization, inductive grammar, international English, reading skills, Words in Context, and learning reflections.

Student's App on Navio

The **Student's App** on **Navio** is where children all find their practice activities for the course. It expands on the topic and objectives found in the **Language Book** and **Literacy Book**. It includes automatically graded interactive exercises for each unit, which can be done in class or for homework, so that children receive immediate feedback. These exercises cover reading and listening skills, phonics practice, speaking skill and pronunciation practice, extended writing practice, as well as grammar and vocabulary.

The digital practice world also provides support and guidance for more introspective objectives such as reading comprehension, SEL and CLIL activities.

The **Student's App** on **Navio** transforms the classroom-based lessons found in the **Language Book** and **Literacy Book** into an immersive, self-directed, game-like experience that students can do alone.

Using the **Student's App** on **Navio** with your students can take different forms:

Classroom study with **Language** and **Literacy Books** and Tap & Teach Lessons (TTL).

- Study and practice alone in a computer lab with **Student's App**.
- Study and practice alone at home with **Student's App**.
- Study and practice with parents with **Student's App**.

Each gameplay produces data which is then sent to the teacher's gradebook, providing deeper insight into each student's strengths and weaknesses, and concrete data that can be quickly accessed to create more insightful feedback.

The activities on the **Student's App** on **Navio** are benchmarked to Cambridge English online practice, ranging from *Starters* for the lower levels to *Preliminary for Schools* for Level 6. This benchmarking covers both content and web app functionality, preparing students academically and equipping them for the practical experience of online testing.

Teacher's Book

This Teacher's Book provides all the steps you need to bring each lesson of the **Language** and **Literacy Books** to life, including lesson objectives, warm up and cool down activities, and full answer keys. Audio and video scripts are at the back of the book, and Unit 1 contains a comprehensive walkthough, with clear explanations of the purpose of each activity and tips on how to make the most of them in class.

The notes also remind the teacher of the additional support available through the Tap & Teach Lessons (TTL) for heads-up learning, the supplementary printouts in the Resource Bank, and extra practice students can do in class or at home.

Teacher's App on Navio

The **Teacher's App** on **Navio** is your primary source for classroom resources and supplements, and is designed to work on both laptops and tablets. It includes Tap & Teach Lessons (projectable classroom lessons), the Resource Bank, the Test Generator, Student's Progress Tracker, the Enhanced Teacher's eBook as well as access to the **Student's App** on **Navio**.

Tap & Teach Lessons (TTL)

Tap & Teach Lessons (TTL) are the course projectables. They contain tools for delivering dynamic and stimulating lessons, including class audio, videos, and interactive activities. If you use the TTL with an interactive whiteboard, you will be able to use all the standard features, such as highlighting and hiding content.

There are three different types of video in ***Global Stage***:

- **Song Videos** (optional). These appear in Lesson 1 of the **Language Book** and may be used to practice some of the set 1 vocabulary as well as features of rhythm and stress patterns in English.
- **Speaking Videos** (essential). These appear in Lesson 5 of the **Language Book** and feature a child or children modelling a presentation or conversation, which includes functional language. Students will analyze the language and use the video as a model when planning and preparing for their own presentation or conversation.
- **Reading Videos** (optional). These accompany in one reading text of the **Literacy Book** per unit to engage students visually and aurally. This method of digital storytelling helps students make connections to past experiences and apply critical thinking to the new information they are being given.

Videos at Home: The Flipped Classroom Approach

If you are unable to watch the videos in class or you want to provide students with additional support, consider asking them to watch the videos at home before the lesson. This allows students to engage with the content in a way that suits them and allows them to pause and rewatch as many times as they want. It also offers parents the opportunity to watch the video with their child and support their learning.

If they watch the song or reading videos at home, give students a question or task to think about while they are watching. They will come to class feeling relaxed, confident, and prepared with ideas and observations to share. If students watch the speaking video at home, you could also have them do activities A and B from Take the Stage / Talk About It before the lesson. Watching the videos at home also frees up class time for collaborative and communicative activities.

Resource Bank

The **Resource Bank** is where you can find:

- **Phonics Support**. Phonics printouts provide extra practice of the sounds covered throughout the course.
- **Differentiated Writing Support**. Attractive writing templates for the Write About It pages in the **Language Book**. These include "Support" and "Challenge" options for students that need them.
- **Review Unit Support**. Extra practice for the review units at the start of each student book. These cover grammar, vocabulary and phonics.
- **Grammar Printouts**. Extra practice for each grammar lesson in the **Language Book**.
- **Tests**. Unit, mid-year, and end-of-year tests.
- **Cambridge English Exam Materials**. Practice for students preparing for *Starters*, *Movers*, and *Flyers*.
- **Letters to Parents**.
- **Other Printouts**. Graphic organizers to aid Visible Thinking Routines and reading skills in the **Literacy Book**, as well as extra materials for Put It Together games and extension activities in the **Language Book**.
- **Videos and audio tracks** to support the course.
- **Curricula and Framework mapping documents**.

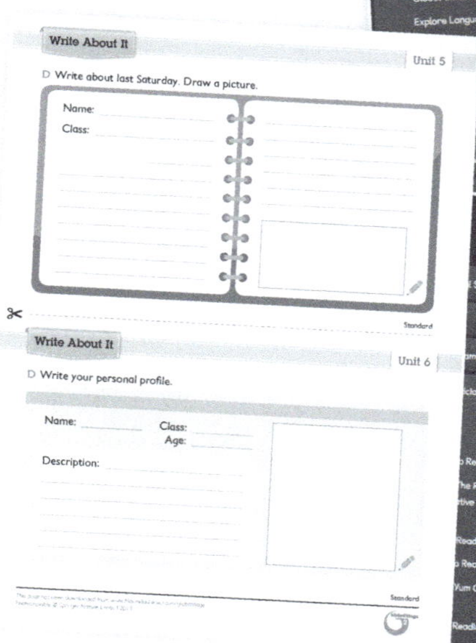

Test Generator

The Test Generator contains the pre-written unit, mid-year, and end-of-year test activities, as well as extra activities that allow teachers to generate and edit new tests.

Student's Progress Tracker

The Progress Tracker is an interactive gradebook that allows you to track your students' progress within ***Global Stage*** and the **Student's App** on **Navio**.

Student's App on Navio

As the teacher, you have full access to the **Student's App** on **Navio** so you can assign homework and activities for your students, and explore the digital world yourself.

Enhanced Teacher's eBook (ETB)

The digital **ETB** is an extended version of this **Teacher's Book**. In addition to teaching notes, it provides classroom management tips; ideas for differentiating activities; projects to support the Global Citizenship lessons. In addition, there are a range of activity and lesson extension ideas, such as further exploitation of Social and Emotional Learning (SEL), Discussion, Genre, Video Focus, Critical Thinking, Creative Thinking, and Collaboration. The ETB also highlights key links between the **Language Book** and the **Literacy Book**.

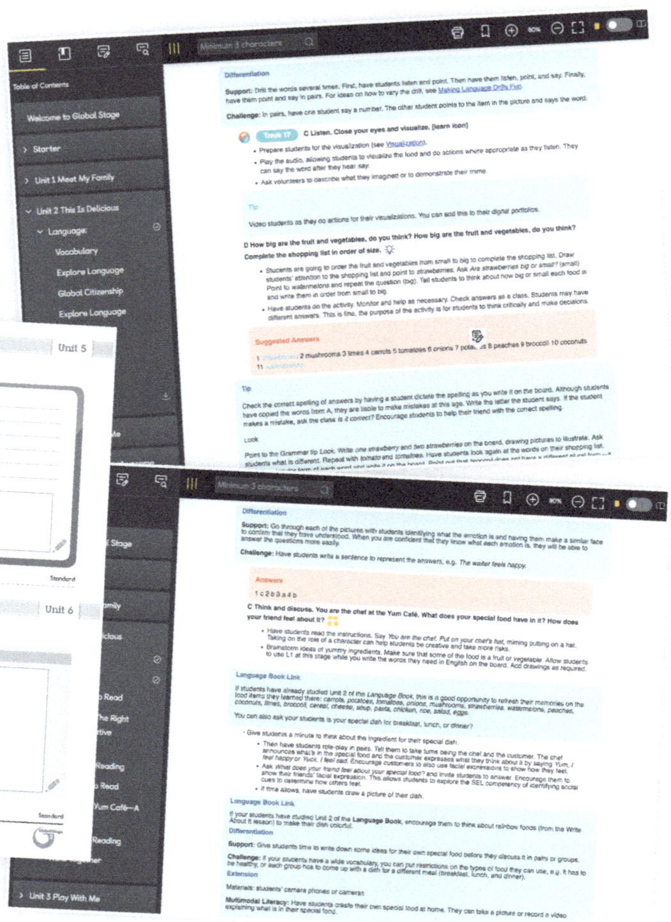

Holistic Learning

While the success of students and schools may be measured in terms of tests and grades, ***Global Stage*** believes in taking a holistic approach by developing the whole child and preparing him/her to take on the challenges of global living. Through its subject matter and in its activity types, the course encourages students to develop thinking skills, engage in cooperative learning activities, develop social and emotional learning (SEL) skills, and gain an awareness of global citizenship.

Global Citizenship

> *Global Citizenship Education (GCE) aims to empower learners to assume active roles, to face and resolve global challenges, and to become proactive contributors to a more peaceful, tolerant, inclusive and secure world.*
>
> —United Nations Educational, Scientific and Cultural Organization

The **Language Book** includes a Global Citizenship lesson in each unit, which has been designed to teach students about the lives of other children through the context of a listening activity. Discussion questions help them explore ideas and make connections to their own lives. The long-term objective is to prepare students for experiences outside of their everyday world and to fulfil aspirations to travel and study abroad.

In Level 2, lessons raise awareness about other countries through topics that students will be familiar with, such as different kinds of fruit around the world; what is special about a first day at school; and heroes around the world. The Unit 1 Walkthrough notes for the **Language Book** provide guidance for teaching Global Citizenship lessons.

Matthew Hayes is a doctoral researcher at the Institute of Education in London under Douglas Bourn, Professor of Development Education. His research concerns Global Citizenship Education in English language textbooks.

What is GCE?

What does the future hold for your students, many of whom will graduate well into the 2030s? From the environment to the economy, poverty to jobs, challenges abound. But whatever the future holds, there is one thing we can be certain of: the biggest challenges facing humanity are not constrained by national borders or language but are truly global in scale and character. These are global problems requiring global solutions, and those of us working in education have a unique responsibility and opportunity to prepare the next generation for these challenges. GCE offers a solution to these challenges and has emerged in recent years as a high-profile policy agenda in education systems all over the world.

With this in mind, GCE can be an effective toolkit for teachers wishing to prepare their students for the challenges and opportunities of the 21st century. The skills and values it espouses are essential if our students are to successfully navigate all the future holds. GCE is too important to languish on the fringes of the curriculum, competing for space as an arbitrary additional subject in an already overcrowded timetable or sandwiched into one-off school events. Just as Digital Literacy is moving beyond ICT and into every corner of the curriculum, GCE thrives best where it is embedded in mainstream curriculum subjects. Few subjects better provide the context and aspiration called for by GCE than the teaching of English as a second language.

There is much scope for creativity too. Although GCE is a declared target of the United Nations' Sustainable Development Goals, one of its virtues is that it is not owned or prescribed by any supranational organisation. There is no mandated curriculum and no accreditation body. The core concepts underpinning GCE have been traced back to some of our earliest history and are not only to be found in Western culture and philosophy. Arab scholars, for example, have written of the influence of medieval Muslim thinkers on GCE theory.

This democratic quality to GCE enables a wide variety of policy and practice, as GCE can be adapted to local contexts and cultures, and to your classroom. There are three broad themes in current GCE thinking and practice and as you work through this textbook, you will see these throughout the exercises and subject matter.

Global orientation: Often referred to as cosmopolitanism, this area of GCE cultivates a student's awareness of the world—its structures, cultures and politics—with a positive "orientation". Its focus is on tolerance and understanding, developing citizens that can comfortably and successfully navigate the world in all its variety.

Global skills: This area is about the competencies aspired to by global citizens. You may recognize it as closely related to "21st Century Skills" and "Life Skills", and it cultivates skills such as collaboration, creativity, critical literacy, and communication. This not only prepares students for success in a competitive global knowledge economy, but for lives as contributing global citizens able to identify and solve problems that are both local and global.

Global conscientiousness: This third theme runs through all aspects of GCE and is its most distinguishing feature. It is signalled through the word "citizenship"; denoting an individual's legal status as a member of a given community, with this status granting them certain rights and responsibilities. While historically this community has been restricted to the nation-state, *global* citizenship looks beyond the national to the global community of which we are all a part. Its rights and responsibilities are global in nature, calling each of us to action. This can take many forms and there should be no universal prescription of actions to be taken. It is being an *active* global citizen which is required of us. This means listening to our conscience and, when it identifies global injustice, being motivated by this to act.

Your selection of this high level English language textbook means English is a leading subject in your curriculum and timetable. No doubt you acknowledge the English language as the *lingua franca* of the modern era, enabling your students to participate on a global scale—whether in work or life. As educators, then, what better context in which to use GCE to encourage your students to think beyond their immediate community, and be globally oriented, competent and conscientious. The English language may have an historical affinity to the West, but GCE recognises that it should not be a pedestal to promote one culture and education above any other. On the contrary, through embedding GCE in English language teaching we can encourage our students to question an unjust world and its imbalanced perspectives.

By using this textbook to teach English in a creative, forward-thinking and global way you will be providing your students with the skills and values to go out into the world and be truly active global citizens.

Social and Emotional Learning (SEL)

> *Social and emotional learning (SEL) is the process through which children and adults acquire and effectively apply the knowledge, attitudes, and skills necessary to understand and manage emotions, set and achieve positive goals, feel and show empathy for others, establish and maintain positive relationships, and make responsible decisions.*
>
> —Collaborative for Academic, Social, and Emotional Learning

Research shows that SEL can positively affect students' connection to school, promote positive behavior, and lead to academic achievement. Helping students develop social and emotional skills lays the foundation for behaviors that will lead to positive personal development and professional success.

The five SEL areas are shown below.

Self-Management

The ability to recognize emotions, thoughts, strengths and weaknesses. This includes having confidence and optimism.

Self-Awareness

The ability to regulate emotions, thoughts and behaviors in different situations. This includes managing stress and working toward goals.

Responsible Decision-Making

The ability to empathize with others, to understand social norms, and to recognize resources and support in family, schools, and community.

Relationship Skills

The ability to establish and maintain healthy relationships. This includes active listening, cooperating, and handling conflict well.

Social Awareness

The ability to make good choices based on ethics, safety, and social norms. This includes considering the well-being of oneself and others.

SEL is integrated into the **Literacy Book**, and a key concept area is addressed throughout the fiction text in each unit. As part of the reading strategy, students are guided to make connections between the SEL concept and the people and events in the text and, ultimately, to their own lives.

Lina Acosta Sandaal, MA, LMFT is the founder of Stop Parenting Alone, a parenting and therapy center in Miami in the USA. She is the parenting expert of a national morning show, and consults for MomsRising, a lobbying organization for family rights.

What is SEL?

Your mouth is dry, and your heart is in your ears. Some of your students look frozen, while others wiggle in their chairs. No one is truly into the day's well-planned discussion. What is happening? Why is the lesson failing? The lesson is suffering the effect of emotions, social awareness, and self-judgment in the classroom. In every moment of a teacher's day, the mind, brain, and body flow through the interactions between the external information and the internal understanding and reflecting of the environment. So when I am asked what is SEL and why do we need it, my response is whether you intentionally teach it or not, you have been a model for SEL from the first day you stepped into a classroom.

The goal of integrating and implementing social and emotional learning into the curriculum is to build students' ability for self-awareness, self-management, social awareness, relationship skills, and decision making. Students attain these competencies by practicing ways to understand and manage emotions, build and manage relationships, and show care and concern for others. The Fetzer Group coined the term, and the word "learning" was intentional. Social emotional skills and development are not stagnant; they continue to grow and expand with each experience students have with caregivers, teachers, friends, and the culture/community at large. If you hold this in mind, that your students are learning through repetition how to be self-aware, how to manage emotions and focus, how to continue to build and manage relationships and practice decision making, then the task of social and emotional learning in your curriculum will not feel so difficult.

Why SEL Is Important to Your Classroom

It is an absurd task to attempt to separate what happens socially and emotionally to a student from what they are cognitively learning from your lesson. When you ignore how SEL and academic achievement work together you are only teaching a percentage of your student, and not the whole child. A majority of teachers understand that their students walk into the classroom full of emotions, thoughts, and experiences that hinder their academic achievement. Deficits in social and emotional development hamper students' ability to learn, which leads to them disrupting the classroom. A student who cannot manage their emotional state will become overwhelmed with fear and embarrassment if you ask them to speak to you in a language in which they are not fluent. Focus, cognitive flexibility, and decision-making are impacted when we have low self-awareness and management of our emotional states.

Recall the difficulty of writing emails at work when you have just had a fight with a loved one on the phone. When we have a strong emotional and social response, it is hard to focus on the task at hand. If it is difficult for an adult, imagine a young student. If your curriculum includes social and emotional learning, your students will be practicing skills to make those daily stressors less intrusive to their learning. Research supports this. Children in the HighScope Perry Preschool Study showed how social and emotional skills attained in preschool continued to bring positive outcomes to those students through age 40. HighScope moved "non-cognitive" skills to the forefront of their curriculum. Conversely, the Adverse Childhood Experiences Study (ACEs) showed that children who suffer adverse experiences and do not process those emotions fare poorly both in their mental and physical health. Social and emotional learning helps students thrive throughout their entire lives.

What Well-Accomplished SEL Looks Like

Now, stop and imagine your classroom in a group discussion: one of the students is playing with his lip while rocking slightly, another student is raising her hand as high as possible, hoping you will see that she wants to speak next, and another student is mumbling in response to the story you just read together. In a classroom that prioritizes SEL, all of these examples of self-management and relationship skills are accepted. Why? Because you understand that the student who is playing with his lips and rocking regulates his emotional and physical states this way, instead of standing up and disrupting the class. The student who knows to raise her hand and contain her emotions is making a responsible, self-aware decision in managing her excitement as to not interrupt her friend who is speaking.

Finally the student who is speaking slowly, quietly and under his breath is at last risking to discuss in a group because you have spoken to your students about what it means to feel scared, how to tolerate that fear, and how to work through it. Today you reap the benefit of that continued social-emotional message. How amazing that your quiet, observant student has made the decision to speak, experiences the safety to manage his fear and the opportunity to strengthen his relationships with his friends and you, his teacher.

Content and Language Integrated Learning (CLIL)

Research has shown that content-based learning increases motivation as students see language being used in real-life contexts. The nonfiction texts in the **Literacy Book** include content from a range of different subject areas. They feature engaging topics and provide opportunities for thinking and discussion.

In Level 2, students will learn through technology, social studies, science, history, and architecture.

Competencies

Global Stage incorporates five competencies that have been identified and linked to outcomes such as better academic performance and positive peer relationships. Relevant icons appear in the footers of each lesson, and the teaching notes in the TB and ETB highlight which activities are connected to each competency to allow for further exploration in the classroom.

Me	Activities that develop social and creative skills, and consider lifestyle choices.
Act	Activities that help develop a sense of social responsibility, mutual understanding, tolerance and ethical behavior.
Think	Activities that develop thinking skills to explain, infer, classify, discuss, notice, and discover.
Learn	Activities that foster learning autonomy and help develop learning strategies.
Communicate	Activities that promote interpersonal and collaborative skills to develop teamwork, leadership, empathy, and responsibility.

Self-Reflection

Self-reflection is an important part of any learning process. Research shows that without regular review and reflection time, much of a lesson can be forgotten. Self-reflection increases students' understanding of how they learn best, making future learning more effective and leading to improvements in achievement.

Self-reflection is a critical feature of ***Global Stage***. Students are asked to reflect on their performances and written work in the Speaking and Writing lessons in the **Language Book** and to reflect more deeply about their learning in the end-of-unit lessons in the **Language Book** and **Literacy Book**.

The Think It Over lesson in the **Language Book** provides graphic organizers for students to respond to questions such as *What did I do? How did I learn?* and *What did I learn?* The purpose of these questions is to get students into the habit of self-reflection from an early age, helping them begin to learn how to learn.

In the My Reading Journal section of the Think Together lesson in the **Literacy Book**, students are asked to give a personalized response to the readings and reflect on the unit as a whole. They are encouraged to think critically about what they enjoyed and why, what they would like to learn more about, and to identify strengths and weaknesses.

In Levels 1 and 2, both the **Language Book** and **Literacy Book** ask students to start making connections between what they enjoyed and what they learned. This prepares them for higher levels where they will be expected to understand how successes were achieved, how less successful experiences can be turned into learning experiences, and to find strategies for working through activities they find less enjoyable.

The Unit 1 Walkthrough notes for both books provide more information on making these lessons a valuable and successful experience.

Learning Techniques

Visible Thinking

Visible Thinking is a flexible research-based framework developed out of Harvard University for enriching classroom learning and fostering students' intellectual development. Some of its key goals are:

- To develop deeper understanding of content.
- To encourage greater motivation for learning.
- To develop learners' thinking and learning abilities.
- To develop learners' attitudes toward thinking and learning and their alertness to opportunities for thinking and learning.
- To create a shift in classroom culture toward a community of enthusiastically engaged thinkers and learners.

Visible Thinking employs thinking routines—short, easy-to-learn strategies that help extend and deepen students' thinking. These routines make it easier for you to see how the students are thinking and interpreting content: *Are students explaining things to one another? Are they offering creative ideas? Are they brainstorming and debating plans?* Visible Thinking encourages students to develop discussion skills and to find personal meaning in the content. This stimulates their continued interest and commitment to their own learning in the classroom.

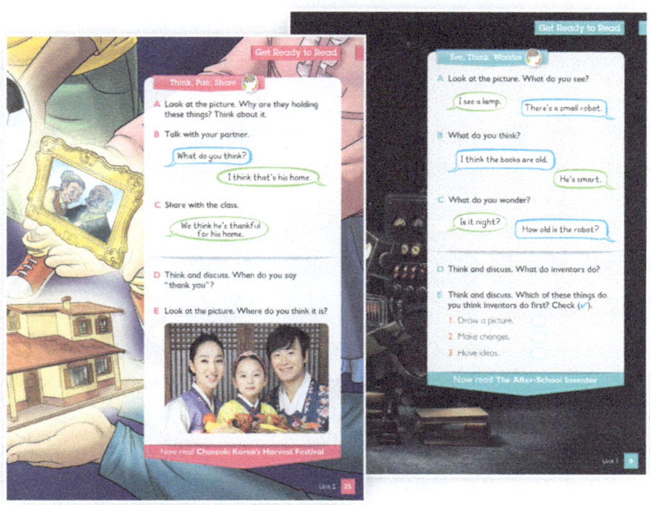

In Level 2, each opening lesson in the **Literacy Book** features either a See, Think, Wonder or a Think, Pair, Share Visible Thinking Routine (VTR). These routines stimulate their curiosity and encourage them to make predictions, observations, and interpretations about the pictures. They provide an opportunity for students to think about the overarching theme/topic of each **Literacy Book** unit and tie in with a pre-reading activity to prepare students cognitively for what they are about to read.

See, Think, Wonder

For See, Think, Wonder students are asked what they see in the picture, then what they think about it, and finally what they wonder about it (or any questions they have about it).

This routine works best when students are given time to think of ideas individually before discussing these ideas in small groups and then sharing them with the class. In this way, students begin to use English language meaningfully, although it is acceptable for them to use L1 to express more complex ideas.

Think, Pair, Share

This routine encourages individual participation and can be used with all abilities and class sizes. Students think through questions using three distinct steps:

Step 1 **Think**. Students are given time to think independently about the question that has been posed, forming ideas of their own.

Step 2 **Pair**. Students are grouped in pairs to discuss their thoughts. This step allows students to articulate their ideas and to consider those of others.

Step 3 **Share**. Student pairs share their ideas with the whole class.

The benefit of using this routine for discussion questions is that students get to practice and learn through repetition, their ideas become more refined at each stage of the process, and they often feel more comfortable presenting ideas to a group with the support of a partner.

For both routines it is important to scaffold student responses by asking follow-up questions, e.g. *What makes you say that?* Example dialogues are provided in the teaching notes to help you do this. Make sure you record students' thinking visible by noting down and displaying their ideas to return to in the Think Together lesson at the end of the unit.

VTRs are a great way to engage learners at the start of a topic, but they can also be used halfway through the unit to keep students connected to the topic. It can also be used at the end of the unit to allow students to apply what they have learned about the topic in a meaningful way.

Cooperative Learning Routines

Teachers who use Cooperative Learning Routines can make a huge difference in achievement and engagement by providing opportunities for multiple students to participate and answer a question, instead of calling on just one student for the answer. Along with higher academic achievement, you will see a reduction in the gap between high- and low-achieving students, improved social skills, higher self-esteem, more enthusiasm for learning, a happier classroom climate, and decreased discipline problems. You will also see the emergence of leadership and conflict-resolution skills.

The following routines are used in Level 2 in both the **Literacy Book** and **Language Book**:

A **Round Robin** is where groups of students take turns brainstorming as many different answers to a discussion question as they can within a limited time frame (one minute is recommended). A **Rally Robin** works the same way, but with pairs of students brainstorming answers.

The **Three-Step Interview** takes the place of the traditional group discussion because each person in a group must produce and receive information. In the first two steps of this routine, students work with a student from a different group. They interview each other about a topic. Then, in the third step, students return to their original groups and take turns sharing what they have learned from their partners. You can also have them share ideas with the class.

Numbered Heads Together is a cooperative learning strategy that holds each student accountable for learning some material. Students are placed in groups and each person is given a number (from one to the maximum number in each group). The teacher poses a question and students "put their heads together" to figure out the answer. The teacher calls out a specific number to respond as spokesperson for the group. This strategy ensures that each member of a group knows the answer to a problem or question asked by the teacher. Because no one knows which number will be called, all team members must be prepared.

Inside-Outside Circle. You will need to make some space in the classroom for this routine. Students stand in concentric circles facing each other. Students in the outside circle ask questions, and those who are inside answer the questions. On a signal, students rotate to create new partnerships. On another signal, students trade inside/outside roles. Talking one-on-one with a variety of partners gives extensive practice in speaking and active listening skills. Interactions can be structured to focus on specific skills and/or target language.

Chalk Talk. Write different words on large sheets of paper and have groups of students brainstorm everything they can think about that word, e.g. Pirate: has a parrot, wears a black patch, sails a boat, has a black flag. This is a chance to generate new ideas, review language, and bring a topic into focus.

Option Explosion. Students discuss and share ideas to think of solutions to a problem, e.g. how to get water into an empty pool. List obvious ideas, such as filling a bucket from a faucet, and then encourage students to think of more unusual options, such as getting an elephant to squirt water with his trunk! At the end of the discussion, ask students what they feel they have learned, and have them vote for the best solution. This routine develops creative thinking and decision-making skills by encouraging students to explore hidden options.

Tips for Setting Up Class Discussions

- Write the question(s) on the board, and give students a minute to reflect in silence.
- If there is more than one discussion question, deal with each in turn, giving students time to think and discuss in pairs or small groups. Help with new words and allow the use of L1 (mother tongue) for more complex ideas.
- Help students structure their discussions by providing appropriate graphic organizers on the board or handing out templates for the groups to fill in.
- You will not always be able to ask everyone for their ideas. Be sure you choose different students each time, so no one feels left out.
- You could have students share their ideas in teams. If students sit together at a table, have table teams. Have each team choose a name or color. During each lesson or activity, one person will give the team's answers and responses. Record who the speaker is for each activity so everyone gets a turn.
- Give the speaker an object, such as a cardboard microphone, to remind students who will speak.
- The Cooperative Learning Routines can be used as mechanisms for structuring the discussions and sharing information discussed.
- When sharing ideas as a class, Circle Time can provide a relaxed atmosphere, which may encourage students to contribute more. Have a regular schedule for Circle Time discussions so students know when to expect them, e.g. at the start of every Explore the Reading lesson in the **Literacy Book**. See the **Circle Time** box for more suggestions.

Circle Time

Designate a particular area of the classroom for Circle Time, free from distractions. If possible, provide cushions laid out in a circle, so students are comfortable sitting on the floor. You could also use a particular sound, such as a drum beat, to call students to Circle Time.

During Circle Time, ask open-ended questions and encourage students to give reasons for their answers. Pass an object around, so it is clear who is speaking, and tell students to listen to each other. Encourage everyone to join in the discussion, but give students a safe word to use, such as *pass*, if they need more thinking time. Let them know it's OK to need time to think and that you will come back to them.

At the end of the Circle Time discussion, praise students and have them give themselves a pat on the back.

Visualization

Visualizations are used in the vocabulary lessons of each unit to encourage students to create mental images of the new words, using their senses combined with previous experiences. Visualizations provide a different way for students to engage personally with the language and help them learn new words.

To set up a visualization activity, take several deep breaths with students, slowly saying *breathe in, breathe out*. Count down slowly from ten to one using a calm voice. Say *Close your eyes and visualize*, pointing to your temples with both hands to demonstrate *imagining*. If students prefer to keep their eyes open, that's fine, too. The key is for them to feel calm and relaxed, so avoid using phrases like *You must keep your eyes closed* or *Don't Look!* which will restrict students.

Play the audio track and encourage students to imagine or act out as prompted. Pauses have been included in the audio to give students time for reflection. They then repeat the word.

After the visualization activity, give students time to share their images. They can do this through drawing, miming, or by describing their thoughts to a partner using L1. Emphasize that everyone's visualizations will be different and that all ideas are valuable.

Students may need additional support the first time you try this technique. You can play the audio track through twice to give them a second chance to create images in their mind. When they share images, students will learn from one another and get ideas for the next time you do this activity. The more regularly you do this, the more students will understand what is expected and the more they will get out of the activity. A second optional visualization track is available in the **Tap & Teach Lessons (TTL)** for the vocabulary in the Global Citizenship lesson.

Multimodal Literacy

To become fully literate in today's world, students must become as proficient with the new literacies of search engines, web pages, email, instant messages, blogs, podcasts, e-books, wiki pages, digital photos, videos, and apps as they are with the traditional literacies of paper, pencil, and books.

However, students also need to learn new skills to enable them use each of these technologies effectively, e.g. searching for key words and navigating a nonlinear reading pathway via hyperlinks. Students also need to develop and utilize critical-thinking skills for online reading. In an age when anyone may publish anything on the internet, it is more important than ever to equip students with the tools to critically evaluate source material.

Both the **Language Book** and the **Literacy Book** provide opportunities for developing higher-order thinking skills through activities that teach students to analyze, question, and to foster thoughtful discussion.

In addition, the digital ETB includes Multimodal Literacy ideas for taking lessons beyond the pages of the book and integrating them with the students' own technologies. An example of this is a research project, where students are asked to find more information about a topic using both print and digital resources. Projects can be researched at home with parental support, or teachers can provide opportunities for small groups to collaborate together, culminating in a class presentation.

Students can also be encouraged to create using different technologies (including digital cameras, videos, apps) and to choose work to upload to their digital portfolios, which can be shared with parents.

Ideas for Introducing Multimodal Literacy Skills and Concepts

- **Encourage students to use *Global Stage's* digital resources.** The **Student's App** on **Navio** provides important early experiences of navigating an online interface in a controlled and safe environment.
- **Show how putting precise keywords into search engines can help you find better information.** If you have access to computers and are able to get online in school, give students a question to answer in pairs, but tell them they can only use one keyword. Discuss how successful they were, then have them repeat the activity with two and then multiple keywords. Elicit that using more keywords helps you be more specific and gives you better information to answer the question.
- **Highlight the importance of scanning for key information.** When you're teaching students how to scan reading texts for relevant information, explain how this is also a useful skill for finding key information online. Every time you ask students to research something online, elicit what they need to look out for to scan effectively.
- **Have struggling readers teach more confident readers.** When you introduce a new technology or skill in class, differentiate by teaching it to struggling readers first so that they become the experts, and then empower them to teach more confident readers. That way everyone is given the chance to be good at something and no one gets left behind.
- **Use digital portfolios in your classroom.** Digital portfolios replace traditional folders as a way to capture and store students' work. You can put students in charge of what gets included in their portfolio as a way to encourage independence, responsibility, and reflection. They enable you to:
  - Demonstrate oral skills through videos and audio recordings, alongside on-paper tasks.
  - Empower students struggling with writing and reading by giving them alternative ways to express themselves and demonstrate learning.
  - Share students' learning easily and frequently with parents, without organizing a time for them to come into class, and without risk of the work getting mislaid at home.

Digital portfolios also allow students to view their learning journey and become a valuable tool for self-reflection. The **ETB** provides suggestions for digital portfolios.

Classroom Management

Making Language Drills Fun

The **Language Book** audio contains language drills to practice the new language presented in each Vocabulary and Explore Language lesson. Drilling helps familiarize students with the language and encourages them to notice the correct pronunciation and rhythm. It also allows you to see which words or phrases will need further practice.

Drilling works by being repetitive, so it is important to add some variations to make it fun and keep students engaged. You can do this by having students say the words or phrases in different ways:

- **Volume**. Have students whisper and then get progressively louder, and then quieter again.
- **Emotion**. Have students use a happy voice and then repeat with sad, angry, tired, and excited voices.
- **Speed**. Have students speak very slowly, then get progressively faster, and then slower again.
- **Voices**. Have students imagine they are a lion, then have them repeat by imagining they are a mouse, a robot, a bird, and a frog. Even when speaking in these different styles, students should be encouraged to use the correct pronunciation and intonation.

Try not to overload students by asking too much at once. The first time you play the audio, have them focus on pronunciation. When you feel they are comfortable with this, encourage them to notice and replicate the correct intonation.

For grammar drills, focus on rhythm and chunks of language, not just individual words. After practicing the recorded sentences, you can extend it further by encouraging students to make new sentences with the target structure. Have the students build a substitution drill on the board starting with the original questions or sentences. Write the sentences on the board, leaving a line for the words you want to change and encourage them to call out suggestions, e.g. *How often do you use this* ________. Students could suggest *cell phone*, *laptop* or *video game*. Then have them practice saying the new sentences in pairs.

Role-play in the Classroom

Performing role-plays in class is a great way for students to interact with the new language or stories and gain confidence using the language in a more informal way. Both the **Language** and **Literacy Books** offer many opportunities for role-play. For example, students can role-play the presentation dialogues in the Explore Language lessons, and they can role-play the stories in the **Literacy Book**. Some of the Talk About It lessons in the **Language Book** require students to plan and write a role-play conversation.

Five Stepping Stones to Performance

- **Step 1** Put students into groups according to how many parts there are in the dialogue or story you are going to role-play. Don't always allow students to work in the same pairs or groups; rather, encourage students to work with classmates they don't normally work with. Pair confident students with less-confident classmates. Allow students to assign themselves roles within their groups, as this will practice valuable negotiating skills.
- **Step 2** If the conversation or story you wish to role-play is on audio or video, then play it first for students to follow. Discuss how the characters' voices differ, and encourage them to think about how the characters are feeling at key moments in the story. You could also have students notice sound effects and ask them what these add to the overall effect.

  Play it again, this time encouraging students to say their lines out loud along with the audio/video.

  If you have time, play it again, and have students focus on reproducing the intonation.
- **Step 3** Now, give students time to practice their role-play without multimedia. They can use the dialogue or the story in the book to help them remember their part. Encourage students to speak with expression and to try to think about intonation. Where appropriate, have them think about the type of voice their character has, e.g. a deep voice or a high, squeaky voice. Tell them to think about how their character is feeling and to include some suitable facial expressions and actions.

  You can challenge stronger students to continue the conversation or add embellishments to their character.
- **Step 4** When they are ready, pairs or groups can come to the front and perform their role-play for the class. With large classes, you won't have time for everyone to perform in a lesson, so make sure everyone gets a chance at some point during the course. Encourage students to video record each other's performances. These videos can be uploaded to their digital portfolios.
- **Step 5** You could organize an open event at the end of the term for parents. Have groups of students prepare and act out different stories from the **Literacy Book** or the plays from the **Language Book**. You will need to give students extra practice time to give them confidence to perform in front of an audience. Encourage them to think about suitable sound effects to use in their performance (e.g. rustling paper for rain), or to source these through sound-effect apps. You could also get students and families involved in providing costumes and making props.

Tip Get students to vote on their favorite song from the **Language Book** and have them perform it together at the beginning of the open event. This will help dispel a lot of nerves and ensure a smoother performance when students come to act out the stories.

Words in Context

The Words in Context feature focuses on helping students apply strategies for dealing with words they do not know. The goal is not for children to learn the full meaning of a word, but rather understand what the word means in that particular context. Students discover that words have many layers of meaning, and that they will build knowledge of words over time. Every time they encounter a word, they learn one aspect of the meaning of the word.

It can be helpful to gradually introduce the following strategies into lessons:

- Look at each sentence containing a target word, encouraging students to **look at the pictures to guess the meaning**.
- **Use comparison to guess the meaning of new words**. Have students look at pictures representing the two words. Ask *How are they different? Can you guess what they mean?*
- **Use the words around the new words to guess their meaning**. Tell students to be logical and think about what would *make sense* in this context? Use L1 (mother tongue) to explain this idea.
- Remind students to **look for clues in sentences near the new word**. For example, does it seem like the word has a *positive* or a *negative* connotation?
- **Use actions in the video to help discover meaning**. Ask students to put their hands on their heads when they hear one of the new words. On their cue, pause the video, and encourage students to look at the image on screen to figure out the meaning of the new word.
- **Use the story itself to establish meaning**. Ask students if they have already figured out the meaning of any of the words from the context of reading the story once.

- **Use storytelling to establish meaning.** If you read the story aloud to students, ask them if your storytelling helped them understand any of the new words. Ask them what you did that helped. (You pointed to things, you used intonation to highlight important words, and you used gestures.) Read the story again if necessary, making sure you do all of these things, particularly in relation to the new words.
- **Use L1 knowledge to establish meaning.** Have students try to guess the meaning of each word individually. Tell them to start by trying to find similar words in their own language. They can then discuss their ideas in pairs.

Differentiated Learning

Even across one class, students differ in many ways; from age, energy, interests, adaptability, experience, and familiarity with the world outside the home, to emotional maturity, linguistic aptitude, and physical development. As a way of targeting learning to meet individual students' needs, lessons include below-level *Support* differentiation ideas to help students achieve the activity goal and above-level *Challenge* ideas to extend activities.

Activity-specific *Support* and *Challenge* differentiation ideas are provided in the digital **ETB**. For print users, the following are ways you can differentiate activity types:

Songs

Support: Some students may not feel confident enough to sing and do actions at the same time. In this case, split the class into two and have some students as actors and others as singers.

Challenge: With students' books closed, project the song words using the **TTL** and then mask one or two words at a time. Have students sing the song, trying to remember the words that you have masked. Increase the number of hidden words until they are singing large parts of the song from memory.

Conversations

Support: Write a model conversation on the board and underline the words that students need to change to personalize it.

Challenge: Encourage students to create a longer exchange than is provided on the page by adding additional questions and suggestions.

Writing

Support: Have students use the text in Activity A as a template. You can project it onto the board and underline the parts that they should change.

Challenge: Have more-confident students include additional information and language in their writing and make sure they don't feel restricted by their plan.

Think It Over: What did I learn?

Support: Students can make a colorful word cloud with all the new vocabulary words they recall.

Challenge: Students can write I can statements to show what they learned. Brainstorm some ideas on the board, e.g. *I can sing a song about …; I can ask people about …; I can give a presentation about …; I can use …; I can write about … .*

Visible Thinking Routines

Support: Encourage students to ask you for new vocabulary. Write a simple question like *How do you say … in English?* on the board for them to use.

Challenge: Encourage students to ask another student *What do you think?* after they have made their point so that gradually the discussion becomes less teacher-centered.

Discussions

Support: Write possible beginnings of the answers on the board for students to finish as a class. Then have students discuss in pairs and choose their favorite answers or add a new idea.

Challenge: Challenge confident students to extend their answers and give a reason for why they make each suggestion. Also remind them to react to their partner's ideas, to make the conversation flow naturally.

Reading Fiction

Support: To help students follow the story and focus on the key information, play the audio while they read and have them raise a hand every time there is an action.

Challenge: Encourage students to join in with the audio every time they see or hear the phrase *says* (character) or *asks* (character). This will raise their awareness of how to include direct speech in a story.

Reading Nonfiction

Support: To help students follow the text, support them to identify a theme for each page and write the themes on the board. Call out the themes in random order and have students turn to the right page and point. Making a "mental map" of the text in this way helps students find what they need more efficiently.

Challenge: Read some of the phrases from the pages in a random order and have students say the heading of the section the phrase is from.

Role-plays (in the Literacy Book)

Support: Allow students to look at their books as they act out the story. If you are playing the video while they do this, pause at regular intervals to allow them to catch up.

Challenge: Turn off the video and have students improvise the story however they wish.

Games Bank

Alphabet Game
Write the alphabet vertically in three or four columns on the board, with space next to each letter to write a word. Divide the class into two teams. Teams brainstorm words related to a topic starting with each letter of the alphabet (or as many as they can think of). Teams then take turns to say a word (give a 10 second time limit). Write each team's word in a different color next to the letter it starts with on the board. Letters cannot be repeated. If a team can say no more words, move on to the next team, until no one can say a word. Count the words in the different colors to see who scored the most.

Apple Tree
Practice target vocabulary and spelling with this game. Draw an apple tree on the board with eight apples on it. Think of a word and draw a dashed line for each letter in the word. Students call out letters to try and guess the word. If the letter is in the word, write it in the correct position; if the letter is not in the word, erase one of the apples in the tree and re-draw it on the ground, containing the incorrectly guessed letter. The first student or team to guess the word wins a point. If all the apples fall before the word is guessed, no one wins.

This game can also be extended to complete sentences. Write each word of the sentence with gaps for each of the letters and fill in all the letters that the students guess as they go along. The sentence fills out very quickly!

Board Race
Divide the class into two teams and divide the board vertically in two halves. Give a board pen to one of the students on each team. Tell them the theme and give them two minutes to write as many words connected to that theme as they can. Each word must be written by a different student and only one student is allowed to be standing from each team at any time. When finished, have the teams check each other's spelling and count how many correct words each team had.

Chain Game
Use chain memory games to practice the target language. Have students sit in a circle. One student says a sentence using the target language, e.g. *In my kitchen, I have (a bottle of lemonade).* The next student repeats the first sentence and adds another sentence, e.g. *In my kitchen, I have a bottle of lemonade and a bag of potato chips.* The next student remembers all of the previous sentences and adds his/her own.

You can vary this game to suit your class, e.g. by having students only remember the sentence said by the previous student, or by having them make a chain in small groups.

Correct the Teacher
Call out lines from songs, stories, dialogs, or writing texts, but make mistakes. When students hear a mistake, they raise their hands and call out *No!* Choose a student to correct the mistake.

Disappearing Sentences
Choose four reasonably simple sentences from a reading text. Write the sentences on the board and have students read them aloud. Then erase two or three words from each sentence and have students say them again, including the missing words. Erase more words and repeat until students are saying the complete sentences from a (nearly) empty board.

Disappearing Words
Ask students to choose what they consider to be the most important words in a text and write them on the board (up to about 15 words). Have them turn away and then erase one word from the board. Have students turn back and identify which word is missing. Ask them how the word was used in the text. Continue until you have an empty board.

Draw It!
Have a volunteer come to the front, and show him/her a word from the vocabulary set you wish to practice, or whisper it into his/her ear. The student draws the word on the board. Have students raise their hands and guess.

Find Someone Who
Have students go around the class asking questions using the target language to find students who answer yes for each one. Alternatively, make a vocabulary game by preparing word cards with the target vocabulary. Hand out one card per student, randomly. Students will stand up and try to find more students with the same word as him/her. When he/she finds someone, he/she should stand next to that student.

How Many Words?
Read out some sentences and have students count the words in each sentence. (Point out that contractions, e.g. *wasn't* count as one word in this game.) When students think they know the number of words, they raise their hands. Invite a student to say the number, ask if the others agree, and then count the words together to see if they were correct.

I Spy …
You can play *I Spy …* with objects around the classroom or within the pages of the **Language Book** and **Literacy Book** (ideally projected on the board). Say *I spy with my little eye something beginning with (A)*, and have students guess what you are looking at, then have them continue the game. Alternatively, play with colors: *I spy with my little eye something (red).*

Kim's Game

Write target vocabulary words (up to eight items) on the board, and have students look at them for one minute. After the minute is up, clear the board and have students work as a group to list as many words as they can remember. Give two points per correctly spelled word and one point if there is a spelling mistake.

You can play a variation, with students memorizing words or pictures from spreads of the **Language Book** and **Literacy Book**.

Matching Halves

Write two columns of words from a reading text next to each other on the board. Tell students they can match parts of the left and right columns to make a short phrase from the story. Give a little thinking time and then invite students to come and draw a line to make a match. Ask if everyone agrees and ask if they can remember how the phrase was used in the story.

Mime It!

The same as *Draw It!* but students act out the word you give them.

Missing Vowels

Write sentences on the board with the vowels missing. Have students work in pairs to complete the sentences by inserting the letters *a, e, i, o,* and *u* in the correct places. When most pairs have finished most of the sentences, invite students to come to the board and write two words each. Ask if everyone agrees with the finished sentences. Leave these sentences on the board to refer to later in the lesson.

Pass the Whisper!

Have students stand in a line. Whisper a sentence or question using the target language to one student and have him/her pass it on until it reaches the student nearest the door. That student says the sentence or question aloud. Repeat as required.

Physical Spelling

Read out a key word. Have students spell out the word and do actions at the same time: they should raise their arms for letters with stalks going up (e.g. b); fold arms for words with no stalk (e.g. c), and lower arms to sides for letters with stalks going down (e.g. p).

Running Sentences

Divide the class into two teams. Give a board pen to the first student in each team. Read out a sentence from or about the readings. After hearing the sentence twice, the students with the pens run to the board and write the first word of the sentence on the board and then pass the pen to the next student, who writes the next word. Both teams stop writing when one team finishes the sentence. Check the sentence to see how many correct words they had. Then play again with a different sentence. The team with the most correct sentences at the end of the game wins.

Running Spelling

Divide the class into two teams and give one student in each team a board pen. Divide the board in two. Say a word twice. The students with the pens then run to the board and write the first letter of the word. They then hand the pen to the next student in their team who writes the next letter. Both teams stop writing when one team finishes the word. Check the spelling. Then play again with a different word. The team with the most correctly spelled words at the end of the game wins.

Simon Says

Use this game to practice actions and imperatives. Give an instruction. If you say *Simon says* before the instruction, students should do it. If you don't say *Simons says*, students should stay still.

Silly Sentence

Have students work in pairs to make a silly sentence with the target phonics sound. They should choose three or four words from the words you have already written on the board from the phonics activity. Do an example, e.g. *For our first harvest we're having a feast and AuGust is eating last!* The sillier or more nonsensical the better. Students can then perform their silly sentence in front of the class.

Spell It

Spell out a selection of key words quite fast. Repeat as necessary until the majority of students recognize the word and have their hands raised. Invite students to say the word and remember how it was used.

Stand Up, Sit Down

Call out statements that practice the target language, e.g. *My mom is tall.* If the statement is true for students, they stand up. If it is not true, they stay sitting down. Alternatively, you can have students put their hands on their heads for true statements and keep their hands by their sides for false ones. You can play this game for any true/false statements. You can also play this game as a way for students to express likes/dislikes: students stand up if they like something and stay seated if they don't.

Versus

Have students stand in a line in the middle of the classroom or in the corridor. Call out a series of two option questions using words from the vocabulary set you want to practice, pointing to the left or right for each option. Students choose their favorite by stepping to the left or right, according to their preference. Alternatively, use actions instead of movements. Demonstrate as you call out, e.g. *Do you prefer ... the moutains?* (hands on head) or the beach (hands behind back)

What's the Next Word?

Divide the class into small groups. Read out sentences from the story and stop before key words. Have students decide in their groups what the next word is and raise their hands to answer.

What Was the Last Word?

Divide the class into two teams and give each team a board pen. Play the audio and stop after key vocabulary. One member of each team runs to the board and writes the last word heard.

Who Said It?

Review dialogue and characters from readings. Make handwritten cards with a quotation from the reading. First, check that students remember the names of the characters in the target reading. Then hold up one of the cards, saying *What does it say?* and have the students read it aloud all together. Ask *Who said it?* When they have answered for each sign, play the reading video or audio again to check answers.

Word Tennis

In this game, pairs of students will pass words or sentences between them. Encourage them to say the words quickly, like a ball between tennis players. Version 1: Students take turns to change an adjective in a sentence, e.g.

Student A: *A tall bed*
Student B: *A small bed*
Student A: *A big bed*
Student B: *A beautiful bed*

Version 2: Students take turns making verb/noun collocations, e.g.

Student A: play
Student B: soccer
Student A: watch
Student B: TV

Yes/No Game

Write a big *Yes* on the left of the board and a big *No* on the right. Tell the students you will say sentences. If they agree with the sentence or think it is true, they point left and say *Yes!* If they disagree or think it is false, they point right and say *No!*

Alternatively, make the game into a Total Physical Response (TPR) game by assigning *Yes* to one side of the room and *No* to the other and having students move from one side to the other as you say each item.

Language Review

Vocabulary

Lesson Objectives

- to review and practice vocabulary of family, clothes, animals, food, activities, home, and places in a town

Materials

Audio Track 1

A TRACK 1 TB p. 213 **Listen and number. Who's Frank?**

- Have students say what they can see on p. 6. Ask *Where are they? What is happening? What family members can you see? What food can you see? Are they happy?*
- Tell students they are going to listen to a conversation about a family. Ask the gist question *Who's Frank?* and have students guess who Frank might be. Play the audio and have students listen. Then elicit answers.
- Tell students to listen again and write numbers next to the words in the picture. Play the audio again, pause after *grandparents*, and point out the example number 1. Play the rest of the audio and have students number the words in the order they hear them. Check answers as a class.

Answers

Frank is Sam's pet frog.
1 *grandparents* 2 hat 3 sweater 4 parents
5 jacket 6 boots 7 shorts 8 twins 9 sneakers
10 pet

B **Look and write. What can you see?**

- Draw or project the table on the board. Have students look at the picture again and find one more item for each column in the table. Write them on the board.
- Have students work individually to find other animals and food to write in the table.
- To check answers, invite students to come to the board and write a word each. Ask if the others agree and have them correct any spelling if necessary.

Answers

Animals: *frog*, giraffe, elephant, penguin, hippo, parrot
Food: *carrots*, pasta, strawberries, watermelon, peaches, mushrooms

C **Look, unscramble, and write.**

- Ask students what they can see in the pictures. Ask what they all have in common. (they are all free-time activities)
- Do the first item together. Have students look at the picture, then direct their attention to the second word, *TV*. Then ask what verb is used with TV.
- Have students complete the rest of the activity individually then check as a class.

Answers

1 *watch TV* 2 read comic books 3 do ballet
4 paint a picture 5 make cookies 6 play soccer
7 go surfing 8 go swimming

D **Think and write.**

- Project the crossword on the board or have students look in their books. Check students' understanding of the terms *across* and *down*.
- Elicit the answer to the first clue (3 across) and have students notice that it has already been written in the grid as an example.
- Ask a volunteer to read the second clue (5 across) and say the answer.
- Have students work in pairs to complete the crossword.
- To check answers, invite students to come to the board and write a word into the correct space if you have it projected, or just write it on the board if not, so everyone can check their spelling.

Answers

Across: 3 *sports center* 5 yard (or park) 6 kitchen
8 hotel
Down: 1 hospital 2 bedroom 4 bathroom 7 café

Practice Resource Bank: Language Review Vocabulary Printout

Explore Language

Lesson Objectives

- to review and practice question words, possessive adjectives and pronouns, the present progressive, *there is* / *there are*, and the simple present with *can*, *have*, and *be*

Materials
Audio Track 2

A TRACK 2 TB p. 213 **Listen and choose.**

- Have students look at the picture and say what they can see.
- Tell them they are going to listen to some questions and answers. They should circle the correct option for each.
- Play the first dialogue and have them notice the example answer.
- Play the rest of the audio and have students complete the activity individually. Stop between questions if you think students need extra time to find and complete their answer.
- Give students time to compare answers with a friend.
- To check answers, have a pair read a completed dialogue, then play the audio to confirm.
- Drill each question and answer.

Answers
1 *How many* 2 Where's 3 What are 4 Whose 5 When

B Read and match.

- Refer students to the example sentence and answer. Ask a student to read them aloud.
- Have students complete the rest of the activity individually, then compare answers with a friend.
- To check answers, ask students to read pairs of sentences. Ask if everyone agrees.

Answers
1 c 2 b 3 a 4 d

C Look at A. Read and choose.

- Have students look back at the picture in A. Write or project sentence 1 on the board and have students notice the example answer circled. Have them point to where they can find this answer in the picture.
- Have students complete the activity individually and compare with a friend.
- To check answers, ask volunteers to read the completed sentence aloud and come to the board and point to where in the picture they found the answer.
- Ask students if we use the present progressive to talk about things that happened yesterday or things that are happening now. (things that are happening now)

Answers
1 *aren't* 2 is 3 sitting 4 isn't 5 is

D Look at A. Read and complete with *is*, *isn't*, *are*, or *aren't*.

- Refer students to the example sentence and ask if they can see soup in the picture. (no) Ask them to look for hippos, flowers, a café, and a lake. Then have them complete the activity.
- Check answers by asking for volunteers to read completed sentences aloud. Ask if everyone agrees.

Answers
1 *isn't* 2 aren't 3 are 4 isn't 5 is

E Read and complete. Then match.

- Tell students that 1–3 are descriptions of animals. They have to complete the descriptions using the words in the box, then draw a line to match the description to the animal (a–c) it describes.
- Before they begin, point out the verbs in the box. Ask *What do we use "has" and "have" for?* (possession; e.g. I have a red bike.) *What do we use "can" for?* (ability; e.g. I can swim.) *What do we use "be" for?* (to describe things; e.g., He's a boy. I'm her sister.) *Which verbs in the box are be verbs?* ('m and 're)
- Refer students to the example description and animal. Ask *Can a tiger swim?* (yes) *Is it gray?* (no— it's black, orange, and white) *Can zebras swim?* (yes) *Are they gray?* (no— they're black and white) So b must be correct—a hippo can swim and is gray.
- Have students complete the other descriptions and use the same process to decide on the animal to match them to.
- To check answers, ask pairs of students to read a description and say the animals. Ask if everyone agrees.

Answers
1 *'m; b* 2 're; can; c 3 has; eat; a

Practice Resource Bank: Language Review Grammar Printout

Long Vowel Sounds

Lesson Objectives

- to review long sounds *a, e, i, o, u*
- to review basic vocabulary

Materials

Audio Tracks 1 to 5

A TRACK 1 TB p. 227 **Listen and say. Then look at the pictures and write the words with the long *a* sound.**

- Ask students what they can see in each picture. Don't correct them—they will hear the answers in the audio.
- Play the audio and have students listen and repeat. Ask what sound all the words have.
- Refer them to the example answer and have them repeat the word again.
- Have them complete the other words. (remind them they must all have the long *a* sound) Check answers as a class.
- Then ask volunteers to come to the board and underline the different spellings that can make the long *a* sound. Make sure one *a_e* and one *ai* word is underlined.

Answers

1 *cake* 2 plane 3 rain 4 table 5 grapes 6 paint
7 baby 8 plate

B TRACK 2 TB p. 227 **Listen and say. Then choose the words with the long *e* sound.**

- Play the audio and have students listen, read, and repeat.
- Ask what sound the circled word makes. Is it different from the other two words? (it's the only one with a long e)
- Have students find and circle the word with the long e sound for each group. Check answers as a class.
- Have students suggest a word that demonstrates each of the possible spelling combinations for the long e: *ea, e_e,* and *ee.* Drill the three words.

Answers

1 *tree* 2 teeth 3 green 4 sweet 5 eat 6 bee
7 these 8 leaf

C TRACK 3 TB p. 227 **Listen and say. Then complete the words with the long *u* sound.**

- Play the audio and have students listen and repeat. Ask what sound all the words have.
- Play the audio again and have students listen and complete the words—point out that there is a *u* in all the words except one. Write answers on the board for students to check their spelling.
- Elicit the different spelling combinations that make the long *u* sound: *ue, ui, oo, ou* and *u_e*. Have four students come to the board to write one word for each. Drill for pronunciation.

Answers

1 *glue* 2 cute 3 juice 4 Tuesday 5 blue 6 fruit
7 soup 8 room

D TRACK 4 TB p. 227 **Listen and say. Choose the letters that make the long *i* sound. Then complete the table.**

- Ask students to say the words chorally and then confirm the pronunciation with the audio.
- Point out the *i* in *Friday.* Elicit that *i* also makes the long *i* sound in *kind.* Then ask students which letters make the same *i* sound in number 3. Point out the e at the end of the word *nine*, which makes the short *i* into a long *i*. Have students circle both letters because it is the combination of the two that makes the sound.
- Ask students to write *kind* and *nine* in the table.
- Have students circle the letters that make the *i* sound in numbers 4 to 8 and complete the table. Check answers.

Answers

1 *Friday* 2 kind 3 nine 4 bike 5 ice 6 lion
7 climb 8 drive
Column 1: 1; 2; 6; 7 Column 2: 3; 4; 5; 8

E TRACK 5 TB p. 227 **Listen and say. Then complete the sentences using a word with the long *o* sound.**

- Play the audio and have students listen, read, and repeat.
- Have students complete the activity individually. Check answers.
- Have students suggest a word that demonstrates each of the possible spelling combinations for long *o*: *oa, ow, oe,* and *o*. Drill the four sounds and example words.

Answers

1 *boat* 2 goat 3 bowl 4 yellow 5 soap 6 hippo
7 sofa 8 toe

F **Match the words to the correct long vowel sound.**

- Look at the example and ask students which other word has the long e sound. Have them draw a line.
- Have students match the other words.
- Check answers and have students repeat all the words.

Answers

long **e**: *green*, teach
long **a**: way, main
long **i**: line, five
long **u**: oops, you
long **o**: cold, toe

Practice Resource Bank: Literacy Review
Phonics Printouts

Blends and Digraphs

Lesson Objectives

- to review blends *st*, *pl*, *fl*, *pr*, and *fr* and digraphs *sh* and *ch*
- to review vocabulary

Materials

Audio Tracks 6 to 8

A TRACK 6 TB p. 227 **Listen and choose the correct word with sh.**

- Refer students to the example sentence. Ask where we normally find a shell (on the beach) and a shirt (on a person or in a bedroom).
- Give students a little time to read each sentence and decide the probable answer before listening. Then play the audio and have students circle the correct words.
- Check answers. Then ask students to repeat the completed sentences.

Answers

1 *shells* 2 fish 3 shoes 4 wash 5 shut 6 shirt
7 brush 8 short

B TRACK 7 TB p. 227 **Listen and say. Use *st* or *ch* to complete the words. Then match.**

- Play the audio and have students listen and repeat.
- Refer students to the example and point out the *st*. Then point out the line matching the word to the picture. Elicit the word and picture for number 2. Use numbers 1 and 2 to remind students that *st* and *ch* are the only two options to complete the words.
- Project the activity or write numbers 1–8 on the board and invite students to come and complete a word. Ask if everyone agrees. If you project the activity, different students can draw lines to match the words. Alternatively, call out the words and have students point to the pictures in their books.

Answers

1 *stick* 2 chair 3 strawberries 4 check 5 star
6 chicken 7 storm 8 child
a *1* b 2 c 5 d 7 e 8 f 4 g 6 h 3

C **Unscramble these words starting with *pl* or *fl*.**

- Have students say and spell the example word. Point out the initial letters *pl*. Elicit the answer for number 2 and point out the initial *fl*.
- Have students unscramble and write the other words. Remind students all the words start with *pl* or *fl* and that the initial blend will always be followed by a vowel sound.
- Have students work in pairs to say and spell the words together. Check answers.

Answers

1 *plant* 2 flap 3 fly 4 plum 5 float 6 plane
7 flower 8 play 9 plate

D TRACK 8 TB p. 227 **Listen and say. Then listen again and write the words starting with *pr* or *fr*.**

- Play the audio and have students listen and repeat.
- Ask how many of the words they can remember. Play the audio again and have students write the words starting with *pr* or *fr*.
- Write numbers 1–9 on the board and invite students to come and write a word each. Ask if everyone agrees.
- Tell students they have one minute to come to the board and suggest an alternative spelling if they think they see a mistake on the board. Check with the class if they agree with each proposed alternative, then remove the incorrect spelling.

Answers

1 *prize* 2 free 3 prince 4 front 5 pretty
6 friend 7 present 8 frog 9 fries

E **Find the words with blends and digraphs.**

- Have students look at the word search and point out the example word. Then ask students to raise their hands as soon as they see another word. Have them circle it on the board or point to it in your book, then cross it off in the word box.
- Have students find and circle the words, then compare with a friend.
- Drill all the words in the box.

Answers

plate; pretty; fries; chair; float; stand; shirt

F	C	H	E	S	S	S	P
R	S	T	A	N	D	L	L
I	W	F	G	P	W	U	A
E	P	L	C	Y	S	G	T
S	X	O	H	C	H	B	E
R	X	A	A	Z	I	M	F
E	L	T	I	F	R	U	X
B	W	P	R	E	T	T	Y

Practice Resource Bank: Literacy Review
Phonics Printouts

UNIT 1

What Does It Do?

Unit Overview

Themes

Technology

Inventors and inventions

Synopsis

In this unit, students will explore how and why people invent things, how technology impacts on our lives, and how children learn in different ways around the world. They will plan and prepare a presentation about technology and write a technology survey using target vocabulary and grammar from the unit.

Language Book

Vocabulary

alarm clock, cell phone, computer, keyboard, laptop, mouse, radio, screen, tablet, TV, video game

p. 35

Explore Language

Simple Present with Adverbs of Frequency: *How often …? Always, Often, Sometimes, Rarely, Never*

p. 37

Global Citizenship

How is technology in schools different around the world?

bookcase, cafeteria, classroom, gym, hallway, language lab, playground, projector, whiteboard

p. 39

Explore Language

Present Progressive Review

p. 41

Take the Stage

Presentation: describing technology

p. 43

Write About It

A Technology Survey

Punctuation: periods and question marks

p. 45

Think It Over

Review and Reflection

p. 47

Literacy Book

Think Together
Why do people invent things?

p. 61

Visible Thinking
VTR: See, Think, Wonder

p. 49

Nonfiction
Creative Nonfiction: *My Good Ideas Book*

Words in Context: problem, solution, hexagon, improve, parachute

p. 57

Fiction
Story: *The After-School Inventor*

Words in Context: invent, try again, change, mirror, mess, invention, machine

p. 51

Reading Skill
Identifying a sequence of events

p. 55

Phonics
cl–

p. 53

Language and Literacy Connections

The connecting theme in Unit 1 is technology and how we use it.

	Language	Literacy
Vocabulary	**Set 1:** gadgets **Set 2:** places in school	**Fiction:** *alarm clock* **Think Together:** *computer, projector, TV*
Grammar	Simple Present with Adverbs of Frequency: ***How often …? Always, Often, Sometimes, Rarely, Never*** We sometimes watch movies. How often do you use this tablet? Present Progressive Review I'm talking to Luis. Are you talking to me?	Fiction I always try again. It's changing all my clothes. Nonfiction My pencil always rolls off the table.
Skills	Pronunciation: /eɪ/ and /e/	**Reading:** identifying the sequence of events **Phonics:** *cl–*
International English	*cell phone / mobile phone; rarely / hardly ever; hallway/corridor*	*eraser/rubber; clean/tidy; favorite/favourite*

Lesson 1 Walkthrough: Vocabulary

This lesson introduces the theme of the unit, and presents and practices the first vocabulary set.

Warm Up

Warm Up activities are either language or topic-based. Their purpose is not to pre-teach new vocabulary, but to engage students, activate prior knowledge, and prepare students cognitively for the lesson ahead.

The digital **Enhanced Teacher's eBook (ETB)** also contains Two-Minute Review activities to recall previously taught language or skills. These activities are quick to do, so time is not taken away from the rest of the lesson, and are easy to integrate into a classroom routine. You can choose to do both the Two-Minute Review and the Warm Up, or just one or the other, to suit the needs of your class.

Activity A Contextualized Presentation: Picture Dictionary Scene

Activity A contextualizes the first lexical set (eight to twelve words) in an illustrated scene. This scene is designed to support learning by providing word-picture association. Alongside this, its purpose is to get students thinking about the unit topic, reviewing language, and making connections to their own world. It includes key characters from the corresponding **Literacy Book** unit and the previous unit of the **Language Book** for students to identify. This is to help students make connections between the two books, between units, and between the topics and characters showing how communities are made up. **Literacy Book** Links are highlighted in the digital **ETB**. The picture can be exploited through VTR to activate schema (see **TB p. 19**).

The new language is contextualized aurally in a dialogue or monologue. The audio includes at least six of the target vocabulary items to encourage students to explore the image and develop discrimination skills. Students should be encouraged to point to the pictures or words as they hear them mentioned. The process of listening, searching for, and finding vocabulary items helps students to engage with the target language.

There is always a gist or comprehension question to focus students and help them understand the general meaning of the dialogue. The digital **ETB** provides further comprehension check questions to explore the picture and audio in more detail.

International English

See **TB p. 35**.

Activity B Drill & Controlled Vocabulary Practice

Activity B is a drill and provides initial practice of all the target vocabulary. Pausing the audio will give all students enough time to say the words and enable you to give immediate feedback on pronunciation. For ideas on how to make drills fun, see **TB p. 22**.

The listen and number task asks students to write numbers next to the vocabulary items in the picture in the order they hear them mentioned. This gets students thinking about the target language, which will help them to learn it. Make sure you pause the audio to give students enough time to think and write.

Activity C Visualization

Activity C is a visualization activity and offers a different pathway for students to interact with the target language. The audio prompts students to create their own mental images of the vocabulary and to do actions where appropriate. This personalized approach makes learning more meaningful and therefore more memorable. Students are not expected to articulate (in English) what they have visualized because sometimes this may be harder than the target word. However, a variety of pair work, class work, and exchanging ideas have been provided to give students a means for creative output. See **TB p. 21** for how to set up the visualization activity.

Activity D Controlled Practice & Critical Thinking

Activity D provides further language practice by getting students to interact with the picture dictionary. Critical thinking skills are developed as students complete a categorization task such as a Venn diagram, graphic organizer, or table, and sometimes more than one answer is possible.

Activity E Song

Activity E is always a song connected to a unit theme and provides additional context for the target language: any words not in the dialogue in Activity A will be included here. The song allows students to have fun with the language and helps them to learn through rhythm, rhyme, and repetition. There is usually a link to a Social and Emotional Learning (SEL) competency.

The song is supported by an animated video with the lyrics displayed to encourage heads-up participation. When the song lends itself to it, students can invent actions or movements to do while singing; a Total Physical Response (TPR) approach will help them to learn and retain the new language. Additional Video Focus ideas are provided in the digital **ETB**.

Cool Down

The Cool Down is a final game or activity that provides an opportunity to wrap up the lesson. It reviews and reinforces the lesson objectives.

Language

Vocabulary

Lesson Objectives

- to learn vocabulary of gadgets: *alarm clock, cell phone, computer, keyboard, laptop, mouse, radio, screen, tablet, TV, video game*
- to sing a song about the benefits of gadgets in the modern world

Materials
Audio Tracks 3 to 6; Video

Warm Up

Play *Stand Up, Sit Down* with sentences about gadgets (see TB p. 26). Suggested sentences: *Stand up if … you like watching TV / you like playing games / there are two TVs in your house / there are two computers in your house / you use a phone every day / you don't listen to music.*

A TRACK 3 TB p. 213 **Listen and find. Where's Luke?**

- Have students say what they can see in the picture on pp. 10–11. Ask *Where are they?* (in a house) *What are they doing?* Ask students if they recognize anyone in the picture. (the girl with the laptop is Zara from the Review unit)
- Tell students they are going to listen to a conversation about Zara's family. Play the audio and have students point to the words or pictures they hear as they listen. Note: not all the words are on the audio.
- Ask the gist question *Where's Luke?* Have students point to him in the picture. Ask a student to say where he is, and ask if the others agree. Play the audio again for students to check.

Answer
Luke is under the table.

B TRACK 4 TB p. 213 **Listen, say, and number the pictures in A.**

- Play the audio and have students point to the pictures and say the words.
- Tell students to listen again and number the pictures in the order they hear them. Look at the example together first. (*computer*)
- Then check answers.

Answers
1 *computer* 2 TV 3 cell phone 4 tablet 5 mouse 6 video game 7 keyboard 8 alarm clock 9 screen 10 laptop 11 radio

International English

Say *Can you find the flags? Point to the US flag. Point to the British flag. Do you know what a cell phone is called in the UK?*

Point to the words *mobile phone* and ask students if they know why it has this name. (*mobile* means it can move around)

Point out that although both *cell phone* and *mobile phone* are correct, it's a good idea to choose one type of English and always use that. Ask *Which word do we use?*

C TRACK 5 TB p. 213 **Listen. Close your eyes and visualize.**

- Prepare students for the visualization. (See TB p. 21)
- Play the audio, allowing students to visualize the gadgets and situations as they listen. Make sure students know not to speak until they hear the word *say*. Put your finger to your lips if necessary.
- Get feedback from some students by asking the questions again and having volunteers share their ideas.

D **Look and write.**

Students are going to classify the vocabulary into two columns. This encourages critical thinking.

- Have students look at the picture, or project and enlarge it using the Tap & Teach Lessons (TTL). Ask them to find the cell phone in the picture and point at the screen. Then ask students to find and name a gadget that doesn't have a screen. Have them complete the table individually.
- To check answers, draw or project the table on the board. Invite students to write the gadgets in the correct columns. Discuss any incorrect answers.

Answers
Has a screen: *cell phone*, TV, computer, laptop, tablet
Doesn't have a screen: *keyboard*, alarm clock, radio, mouse, video game

E TRACK 6 TB p. 213 **Listen and sing. Then watch and sing.**

- With books closed, write or project the song title on the board. Ask *Is the song about our world today or about the past?* and elicit answers.
- Play the song and have students listen and raise their hands every time they hear an item from B.
- Have students open their books. Give them a moment to look at the lyrics. Play the song again and stop after each line for students to repeat.
- Play the song again without pausing and encourage students to sing along.
- Play the song video and encourage students to sing as they watch. They can move to the music or invent actions or a dance.

Cool Down

Play *Draw It!* (see TB p. 25) using the technology items in this lesson.

Practice **Student's App:** Vocabulary Practice; Video

Lesson 2 Walkthrough: Explore Language

The grammar lessons present and practice the target structures using a simplified inductive approach. This encourages the students to think about the patterns of language and to make and test assumptions through carefully staged and scaffolded activities. By laying the groundwork for the kinds of tasks they will do in higher levels, they are supported to become independent thinkers from the very beginning.

Activity A Contextualized Presentation

Activity A presents the lesson's grammar focus through the context of a dialogue or story. Students listen and read, but the target language is not highlighted at this point. The gist question gives students a reason to listen and supports them to understand the story. The digital **ETB** provides questions to check students' comprehension. If you don't use the **ETB**, try to think of simple comprehension questions to ask your students to help them make connections with prior knowledge and personalize the scenario.

International English

This feature exposes students to differences in vocabulary, language, and spelling between American English (US) and British English (UK). Point to the box with the flags. Ask students if they know which countries the flags represent. Tell them that the flag with stars and stripes is for the USA (United States of America) and the flag with crosses is for the UK (United Kingdom). Ask students if they know which language is spoken in these countries. (English) Tell them that in both countries people speak English but that some words are different and some words are pronounced the same, but spelled differently. Equally, some words are spelled the same and pronounced differently! Tell students that they will see American English words used in this course, but that British English is also correct. It is important that while they are aware of the differences, you and they choose one variety to use, especially in exams.

To make the most of this feature, build up a display of British and American English words throughout the year. One way to do this is to print out or draw the two flags and create word cards that students stick around the relevant flag.

Activity B Grammar Analysis Table

Activity B is a grammar table with sections for students to fill out, focusing on form. Most of the sentences come from the dialogue in Activity A; if they are not there, the answers will be filled in, with the key word(s) highlighted. Students need to identify the sentences and copy the missing words, thereby drawing their attention to the grammar structure and to language patterns. This task is heavily scaffolded for the first three units. After this, the level of challenge is increased, as students are expected to identify and write more missing words. This task can be done initially as a whole class activity. Once students feel more confident, encourage them to complete it in pairs or small groups.

Attached to the table is a language tip, pointing out additional information related to the grammar point that needs further support. There are three types of tip:

- **Remember** when students have most likely already seen this language feature, e.g. contractions.
- **Look** a new, additional piece of information about the grammar, e.g. a spelling pattern or anomaly.
- **Watch Out** highlights typical mistakes learners make.

Activity C Inductive Analysis

Activity C is a continuation of the language analysis, as students are asked to focus on the meaning and usage of the grammar structure. Concise concept statements are given to explain how the language is used. Students have to think critically to choose between different options, which helps them to interact with the language. Encourage students to discuss their ideas in pairs before checking answers as a class. First language (L1) can be used to support this task when language in the concept statements is above level.

Activity D Drill: Sentence Level

See **TB p. 40**.

Activity E Controlled Practice: Written

See **TB p. 40**.

Activity F Freer Practice: Communication

See **TB p. 40**.

Explore Language

Lesson Objectives

- to learn to make simple present statements with adverbs of frequency
- to talk about how often people do things

Materials
Audio Tracks 6 to 8; (optional) Video

TRACK 6 TB p. 213 **Warm Up**
Sing ***Living in a Modern World*** again (audio or video).

A **TRACK 7** TB p. 213 **Listen and read. Who does Grandpa email?**

- Project the story or have students look in their books. Ask students what they can see happening in the pictures. Ask *Who is the man?* (Grandpa from the previous lesson) *Who do you think the boy is?* (his grandson)
- Play the audio and have students follow in their books.
- Ask the gist question *Who does Grandpa email?* and elicit the answer. Play the audio again for students to check. Ask further comprehension questions (see **ETB**) and play the audio again.

Answer
his friend, Sidney

International English

Have students find *rarely* in the story. Ask them to say the same sentence using *hardly ever*. Ask if they can remember hearing either version before. Ask *Which do we use?*

B **Look at A. Complete.**

- Write or project the table on the board. Point to the example answer in the table. (How often) Have students find it in the story in A. Ask *Who says it?* (the boy)
- Point to the blank after *How often* and ask students to go back to the story to find the word. (do) Elicit the word and write it in the table on the board.
- Have students work in pairs to complete the table. Point out that all the sentences with the answers are in the story.
- Complete the table on the board, and have students check or correct their answers. Highlight the auxiliary verbs *do* and *does* and ask students to tell you which pronouns we use with each one.
- Have students look at the Grammar tip *Remember.* Ask them to find and explain the differences in the two sentences (*I/she, use/uses*). Remind students we use the *s* on the verb when we talk about one person.
- Still looking at the *Remember* box, ask students where in the affirmative sentence they would put *always, never,* or *rarely*. Look at the table for examples. Point out the order of subject + adverb + verb.

Practice **Resource Bank:** Grammar Printout; **Student's App:** Grammar Practice

Answers
How often; do; use; rarely

C **Think and discuss. Then choose and complete.**

- Read the two options and ask students to circle which they think is correct. Refer students to the sentences in the table in B to help. Have them compare ideas with a partner.
- Read the options again and have students raise their hands for the one they chose.
- Elicit the adverbs of frequency to complete the line from *never* to *always*. Invite students to come and write the missing words on the board in the correct place.

Answers
1 how many times 2 (never) rarely; sometimes; *often* (always)

D **TRACK 8** TB p. 214 **Listen and say.**

- Play the audio and have students tell you how many technology items they heard mentioned. (five: tablet, video games, TV, radio, alarm clock)
- Play the audio again and have students listen and repeat.
- For ideas on how to vary the drill, see TB p. 22.

E **Put the words in order.**

- Highlight the example answer for number 1, and use this to reinforce the word order (subject-adverb-verb).
- Have students complete the activity individually and then compare answers with a friend. Check answers together.

Answers
1 *My dad never watches TV.*
2 I rarely play video games on a tablet.
3 My grandparents often listen to the radio.
4 I sometimes watch movies on my dad's laptop.

F **Write questions about your friends. Then ask and answer.**

- Write a *How often* question on the board about a student and say, e.g. *How often does Jess use her cell phone?* Invite students to tell you how to ask that question directly. (*How often do you use your cell phone?*)
- Have students think of *How often* questions they would like to ask their friends. Brainstorm examples on the board. Then have students write *How often* questions for three friends not sitting next to them, using third-person pronouns.
- Next, have students turn their questions into direct, first-person questions. Have students walk around the classroom, asking and answering the questions and recording answers in their notebooks.
- Have students report back their findings to the person sitting next to them.

Cool Down
Play *Pass the Whisper!* (see TB p. 26) with sentences from this lesson (E and F).

Lesson 3 Walkthrough: Global Citizenship

This lesson presents and practices the second vocabulary set, practices listening for gist and specific details, and gives students the opportunity to learn about the lives of other children around the world and to make connections with their own lives.

Opening Question

The **opening question** takes the place of the Warm Up and is designed to activate interest and curiosity in the Global Citizenship topic by helping students to make connections to prior knowledge. Don't correct students at this point or give too much feedback. The lesson is structured so that they develop ideas to discuss at the end of the class.

Activity A Contextualized Vocabulary

Activity A presents the new vocabulary through eye-catching photos or pictures, to provide a real-world context. There is a contextualized listening activity which presents at least six of the target vocabulary items through a dialogue or monologue. This listening activity provides an introduction to the Global Citizenship part of the lesson on the facing page. Students will be able to make connections between this audio and the audio for D and E.

Activity B Drill & Controlled Vocabulary Practice

See **TB p. 34**.

Activity C Vocabulary Practice: Game

Activity C is a game. This is a chance for students to communicate and collaborate while using and practicing the target language. Students learn more by working with different people, rather than the same friend each time. One way to achieve this is by giving students a word or picture card and asking them to find another student with the same card. Students with matching cards will work together in the activity.

Visualization

There is a visualization audio track for this vocabulary set on the TTL. See **TB p. 34**.

Activity D Listening for Gist and Main Idea

Activity D provides input for the Global Citizenship discussion at the end of the lesson. There are usually two speakers for each lesson (or one speaker explaining differences, e.g. Unit 4) who explore the Global Citizenship theme in connection to different countries around the world. Students listen for the main idea of the audio topic and answer a gist question.

Before they listen, give students some time to look at the pictures. You could let them find the countries mentioned on a world map and ask them what they already know about these countries to activate prior knowledge. Tell students to listen out for key vocabulary they recognize. Explain that thinking about these words in order will help them to understand what the listening is about and answer the gist question. Some of the new vocabulary from Activity A is always recycled here.

Activity E Listening for Detail

Activity E encourages students to listen out for specific details and ignore anything that is not relevant. Ask them how many of the questions they can answer from information they have remembered from D, but reassure them that this is not a memory test and that it doesn't matter if they don't remember. Then play the audio again, so they can listen and check their answers and answer any questions they missed.

Discussion Questions

The discussion questions address the key holistic learning concepts that run through the unit. The discussion can be done in pairs with some whole-class input at the end. The Global Citizenship strand at this level raises students' awareness of the world around them. It asks them to compare themselves with other children from around the world, and think about how they fit into it.

There is usually one personalization question and one question that asks students to look further and see the bigger picture. Deal with each one in turn, giving students time to think and discuss in their pairs or small groups. Allow use of L1 for new words and more complex ideas as this will enable students to express themselves and develop a clearer understanding of the key concepts. You can also challenge students to provide sentences beyond their ability by translating words and phrases from L1 into English.

Bring the class together to discuss the conclusions they have reached. Use graphic organizers on the board to present students' ideas. Revisit the opening question and see if students answer it differently now. In-depth ideas to help you structure the discussion can be found in the digital **ETB**.

Global Citizenship

Lesson Objectives

- to learn vocabulary for places and objects in a school: *bookcase, cafeteria, classroom, gym, hallway, language lab, playground, projector, whiteboard*
- to explore similarities and differences between different schools
- to think about the uses of technology in a school
- to practice listening for gist and details

Materials

Audio Tracks 9 to 11; (optional) Audio Track A

Opening Question

Ask the opening question: *How is technology in schools different around the world?* Elicit ideas and encourage students to think about how other schools are similar to or different from yours. Don't correct them or give much feedback. Focus on activating students' prior knowledge and awakening curiosity; students will find out more about the topic during the lesson.

A TRACK 9 TB p. 214 **Listen to Teddy talk to Olivia about his school. Does Teddy's school have technology?**

- Tell students they are going to listen to a dialogue about two different schools. Have students listen to decide if their school is more like Teddy's or Olivia's.
- Ask the gist question *Does Teddy's school have technology?* and elicit the answer. Play the audio again to check.

Answer

Yes, it does.

B TRACK 10 TB p. 214 **Listen, say, and number the pictures in A.**

- Play the audio and have students listen, point, and repeat.
- Play the audio again and have students listen again and number the pictures in the order they hear them. Point out the example answer. (whiteboard)
- Check answers as a class.

Answers

1 *whiteboard* 2 playground 3 bookcase
4 language lab 5 gym 6 classroom 7 hallway
8 cafeteria 9 projector

International English

Have students look at the two words and ask if they can remember which was used in the dialogue. (Olivia says the hallway is long.) Point out that both are correct and ask *Which do we use?*

TRACK A TB p. 214 **Visualization**

The TTL has a visualization audio track for this vocabulary set (see TB p. 21).

Practice Student's App: Vocabulary Practice; Listening Comprehension Practice

C Play *Word Tennis* with a friend.

- Point out that some of the new vocabulary items are made of two words; for example, *book* + *case*; *white* + *board*. Elicit these words and write them on the board. (*bookcase, language lab, hallway, classroom, whiteboard, playground*)
- Say the first part of a word and have the whole class recall the second part. Repeat this a few times and then have students continue in pairs, taking turns to say the first parts. (See *Word Tennis*, TB p. 27)

D TRACK 11 TB p. 214 **Now listen to Olivia and Akash. Number the pictures. Who uses technology at school?**

- Listening for gist: tell students they are going to hear two children—one from the UK and one from Bangladesh—talking about their families. The first time they listen, students should number the pictures. Play the audio. Then check answers.
- Ask the gist question *Who uses technology at school?* Play the audio again to check.

Answers

a 2 b 1 Akash uses technology.

E Listen again. Write *True* or *False*.

- Listening for detail: play the beginning of the audio again, up to ... *projector and a big screen.* Point out the example answer (*True*) next to number 1.
- Have students look at the other sentences and see if they can remember any answers. Play the rest of the audio and have students complete the activity individually.
- To check answers, ask pairs of students to read a sentence—one student reads the sentence, and the other says *true* or *false*. Ask if everyone agrees and discuss why the false sentences are false.

Answers

1 *True* 2 True 3 False 4 True 5 False

Discussion Questions

- Draw students' attention to the discussion questions: *What technology do you like using? Do people need technology to learn? Why?* Have students discuss the questions in pairs or small groups (see **ETB**).
- At the end, you can make a list of the technology students like using to learn and create a bar graph on the board to show the results.
- Return to the opening question to ask again *How is technology in schools different around the world?* Discuss the differences and similarities students have discovered in this lesson. Ask *Are there more similarities or differences? Are you surprised by anything?*

Cool Down

Play the *Yes/No Game* (see TB p. 27) with sentences about technology, e.g. *There's a projector in my classroom.*

Lesson 4 Walkthrough: Explore Language

This lesson presents and practices the second grammar structure(s) and has the same structure and purpose as Lesson 2.

Activity A Contextualized Presentation

See **TB p. 36**.

Activity B Grammar Analysis Table

See **TB p. 36**.

Activity C Inductive Analysis

See **TB p. 36**.

Activity D Drill: Sentence Level

Activity D is a drill of four to five sentences/questions to allow students to familiarize themselves with the new language. Drills give students intensive practice in hearing and saying new phrases.

The first time you play the audio, focus on pronunciation. Then play it again, this time encouraging students to concentrate on intonation. Using different activities will help you to keep drills fun and stop them from becoming repetitive. See **TB p. 22** for a variety of drill ideas.

Activity E Controlled Practice: Written

Activity E is a controlled practice activity and gives students some heads-down time to use the new grammar structure. Encourage students to do this as independently as possible, using the table in Activity B, so that they can process what they have learned and you can assess their level of understanding.

Activity F Freer Practice: Communication

Activity F allows students to practice the target language through a freer, more communicative activity or game. Where there is text inside speech bubbles, this provides a model, but make sure students understand that they can choose what to say.

Throughout the digital **ETB** there are ideas to differentiate lesson content in a mixed ability class. *Support* ideas suggest a simpler pathway for completing an activity or provide scaffolding to enable less confident students to complete the activity. *Challenge* ideas encourage more confident students to use additional language to take activities further. For more activity specific differentiation ideas, see **TB p. 24**.

Competencies

Icons throughout the teaching notes highlight which activities are connected to one of the five competencies: Me, Act, Think, Learn, and Communicate.

See **TB p. 19** for more information.

Explore Language

Lesson Objectives

- to review the present progressive for actions happening now
- to ask and answer about what people are doing

Materials
Audio Tracks 12 and 13

Warm Up

Play a Total Physical Response (TPR) game. Call out different activities and have students act them out, e.g. *You're using a cell phone; you're playing on the playground; you're using a laptop.*

A TRACK 12 TB p. 214 **Listen and read. Who sends Dad a message?**

- Ask students what they can see happening in the images on p. 16. Ask *Who is the boy?* (Luis, who was helping his grandpa in Lesson 2) *Who do you think the other two people are?* (his mom and dad) *What gadgets can you see?* (two cell phones, two laptops, and a mouse)
- Play the audio and have students follow in their books.
- Ask the gist question *Who sends Dad a message?* and elicit the answer. Play the audio again for students to check. Ask further comprehension questions (see **ETB**).

Answer
Luis

B Look at A. Complete.

- Write or project the table on the board. Tell students that the sentences they need are all in the dialogue.
- Look at the first sentence in the table and the example answer in blue. (talking) Have students find it in the dialogue in A. Ask *Who says it?* (mom)
- Point to the blank before *talking* and ask students to go back to the story to find the word. ('m) Elicit the word and write it on the board. Elicit that *I'm* is short for *I am*.
- Have students work in pairs to complete the other blanks in the table.
- Complete the table on the board and have students check or correct their answers.
- Ask students how we make the present progressive. (subject + *be* + verb + *–ing*) Ask for an example. (e.g. I am walking, she is listening)
- Ask students how we make a negative sentence in the present progressive. (add *not/n't* to *be*)
- Have students look at the Grammar tip *Remember* and ask them what happened to make the *–ing* form of the verb. (removed the e) Ask two students to come to the board and make the *–ing* form of *make* and *live*. Explain that all verbs that end in e follow this rule.

Practice **Resource Bank:** Grammar Printout; **Student's App:** Grammar Practice

Answers
'm; *ing*; 's; ing; Are; I'm not

C Think and discuss. Then choose.

- Read both options aloud to the class, and then give students some time to decide their answers on their own.
- Write *PAST* on the left of the board and *NOW* on the right. Read the options to the students again and have them point left or right to show their choice. Check that everyone agrees and confirm which answer is correct.

Answer
1 happening now

D TRACK 13 TB p. 214 **Listen and say.**

- Play the audio track and have students listen for how many *–ing* verbs they hear mentioned. (five: talking, using, doing, sitting, playing)
- Play the audio again and have students listen and repeat.
- For ideas on how to vary the drill, see TB p. 22.

E Read and complete in present progressive.

- Have students scan the text and find all the activities in it. Ask them to raise a hand to say an activity they found.
- Point out the example answer in number 1 to students. Elicit whether it is positive or negative. (positive) Have students continue the activity individually. Remind them they can look at the table in B.
- To check answers, ask students to read a sentence each. Ask if everyone agrees.

Answers
1 *'m writing* 2 're playing 3 isn't listening 4 Are; using

F Play a guessing game. Mime. Then ask and answer.

- To help students remember the vocabulary they will need, call out a word from the box and have them find an image of it in their books as quickly as they can.
- Have two students read the example dialogue aloud.
- Brainstorm all the different actions students do in the different places in your school and all the actions they use with different gadgets. Write the verbs they say on the board.
- Mime doing one of the actions, and have students guess what you are doing and where you are. Remind them of the form *Are you …–ing in the …?*
- Have students work in pairs to continue the game, taking turns to mime and guess.

Cool Down

Play *Running Sentences* (see TB p. 26) with present progressive sentences from this lesson (from A, E, or F).

Lesson 5 Walkthrough: Take the Stage / Talk About It

The first productive skills lesson is dedicated to speaking and functional language. Take the Stage lessons present and practice a presentation. Talk About It lessons present and practice a conversation. The productive task is modeled by a child or children in a video, which shows the students what they are going to do themselves and helps to bring the language alive. Ideally the video should be watched in class. However, if this isn't possible, use the Flipped Classroom Approach (see TB p. 15) and have students watch the video before the lesson.

Building students' confidence in speaking is a key part of the language learning classroom and the activities are carefully staged to help them analyze the language, brainstorm their own ideas, and plan what they will say. Performing successfully, in a conversation or a presentation, helps ensure learners are receptive to future learning.

Activity A Video Showcase

Activity A asks students to watch the video and answer a gist question. Ask some additional comprehension questions to make sure students understand the video. This is important because the video models the spoken practice students will do later on in the lesson. Comprehension questions have been provided in the digital **ETB**. The digital **ETB** also provides a Video Focus idea in every speaking lesson.

There is a *Watch* callout question, which encourages students to notice something about the model conversation/presentation in the video (e.g. body language). This feature is often picked up in the *Reflect* callout and serves as a reminder that communication is more than just the words you use. Notes for the *Watch* callout are provided in the **ETB**.

Activity B Functional Language

Activity B asks students to watch the video again, this time with their books open; the functional language is highlighted for students to notice. Students can try to do the activity from memory first and then check their answers when you re-play the video. Giving students a critical thinking task, such as analyzing and categorizing the key phrases, will help them to prepare for structuring their presentation or conversation later in the lesson.

Pronunciation

Pronunciation in the **Language Book** is <u>not</u> linked to the phonics work in the **Literacy Book**. While phonics focuses on helping students decode a combination of letters to read a word, the pronunciation activities are about communicating clearly and intelligibly.

Students will practice saying sounds and words accurately, first by watching and copying your mouth movements and then by listening to and repeating the audio. The sounds featured here have been chosen because they are difficult for many learners and may require additional practice.

Activity C Planning

Activity C is the planning stage of the presentation/conversation; it allows students to personalize their ideas using the functional language from the video. It is important to teach students to brainstorm ideas and plan before giving a presentation. C helps them prepare their ideas before organizing them in D.

Activity D Preparation

Activity D is where students use their ideas from C to prepare a presentation/conversation, guided by the template provided in the book. Students will prepare presentations individually and conversations in pairs. Often students are asked to choose one or two ideas to take forward from C. Encouraging students to make choices is an important part of this course, because it promotes engagement and critical thinking.

At this level it is a good idea for students to write their notes out in full, although you may feel that stronger students don't need to do this.

Activity E Practice and Production

Activity E is an opportunity for students to practice with a partner and perform/present. For the presentation lessons, choose a few students each lesson to perform to the class—keep a record so each student gets a chance to perform over the course of the year. If students don't perform to the whole class, have them perform to each other in small groups. At this age, it may not be appropriate to ask students to reflect on how their peers did, in order to avoid any negative comments; instead suggest ways of appreciating each other's efforts, e.g. by clapping or saying *Good job!* For the conversation lessons, it is enough that they have the conversation with a friend; they don't need to perform it. You can go round to monitor and offer praise and support.

The activity ends with a *Reflect* callout feature for students to think about how they did and circle. Encourage them to be honest here and tell them that it is easy to forget to do things when we are nervous, but that speaking gets easier with practice! Notes for the *Reflect* callout are provided in the digital **ETB**.

Take the Stage

Lesson Objectives

- to prepare and give a presentation about using technology
- to recognize and reproduce /eɪ/ and /e/

Materials
Video; Audio Track 14

Warm Up

Do a TPR activity. Say and mime the following actions. Then have students copy you.

Phrases: *Open the laptop case* [unzip]. *Take the laptop out of the case. Open the laptop. Press "on." Type your password* [look around to make sure no one is watching]. *Start to work!*

A TB p. 234 **Watch and listen. Why is a laptop useful?**

- Tell students they are going to watch a video of a girl talking about the technology she uses and why it is useful.
- Play the beginning of the video up to *my presentation is about laptops*. Ask students what the presentation is about. Ask what words they think they will hear, and write their ideas on the board. Play the video and then ask students which of their words she used.
- Ask students the gist question *Why is a laptop useful?* Play the video again to check the answer. Ask further comprehension questions (see **ETB**).

Answer
because it has a screen, a keyboard, and a mouse (because it has everything you need)

B **Watch again. Check (✔) the phrases you hear.**

- Have students read the phrases and draw attention to the example.
- Play the video again and have students check the other phrases they hear.
- Then check answers. If necessary, watch again to clarify.
- Have students analyze when to use the phrases. Ask *What does Grace say to introduce herself and her subject?* (1, 2—this is the beginning) *Which phrases tell us information about laptops and about how Grace uses laptops?* (3, 4, 5, 7—this is the middle, the main part of the presentation) *What does she say to finish?* (9—the end)
- Have students write *B* (beginning), *M* (middle), and *E* (end) after each of the phrases. Then have them add a letter after the two unused phrases, too. (both M)

Answers
1; 2; 3; 4; 5; 7; 9 (6 and 8 are not said)

- Ask students if they think Grace did a good presentation. Ask if they think she spoke clearly and was easy to understand. If necessary, play the video again.

Practice **Student's App:** Speaking Skill Practice; Video

Pronunciation /eɪ/ and /e/

TRACK 14 TB p. 216 **Listen and say.**

The long diphthong **/eɪ/** and the shorter **/e/** sound can be difficult for some students.

- Demonstrate the shorter, wider mouth position for the **/eɪ/** sound, as in *name*. Demonstrate the **/e/** sound, as in *help*, and encourage students to copy you.
- Play the audio and have students repeat each word under their breath after they hear it. Play the audio again and have them say the words aloud. Play it one more time and have students say the **/eɪ/** words loudly and the **/e/** words softly.
- Say *These words are used in the video. What other words do you know with these sounds?* Have students discuss in pairs, then elicit ideas (e.g. *radio, lesson*) and write them on the board in two sections. Drill all the words at the end.

C **Plan. Think about the technology you like. Choose (✔) two and complete.**

- Tell students that they are going to plan a presentation about technology, like Grace did. Have them choose two items they like from the box.
- Draw students' attention to the table, and to the example provided in the first row. Discuss each answer with students, ensuring that they understand how to form a sentence with each of the column headings. Complete one row of the table on the board by eliciting suggestions from students.
- Have students work individually to complete the table for their own choices.
- Have students compare their ideas with a friend.

D **Prepare your presentation. Use your ideas from C and phrases from B.**

- Play the video from A one more time to give students a model.
- Ask students to look at the plan they made in C and choose one gadget to talk about. Have them use this plan and phrases from B to complete the presentation notes. Remind them which phrases to use at the beginning, middle, and end of their presentation.

E **Practice with a friend. Then share with your class.**

- Have students practice their presentations with a friend as many times as they need to. Remind them to smile and speak slowly and clearly. Encourage them to pause after each phrase.
- Invite volunteers to come to the front of the classroom to give their presentation. Have the audience give a round of applause after each presentation.

Cool Down

Invite students to say one thing they liked about the presentations they listened to.

Lesson 6 Walkthrough: Write About It

The second productive skills lesson focuses on the mechanics of writing, e.g. punctuation and spelling, while laying the groundwork for a process-writing approach in higher levels. There is always a model text as well as a brainstorm/planning stage for the final production task. The structure of the lesson is similar to Lesson 5.

Activity A Contextualized Writing Mechanics

Activity A presents the lesson's writing focus through a model text. It is important to ask students comprehension questions to ensure they have understood the text, since they will be expected to produce their own writing based on this model by the end of the lesson. Some comprehension questions are provided in the digital **ETB**. The teaching notes take a simplified inductive approach, by encouraging students to look at the model and notice the mechanic.

Activity B Controlled Practice

Activity B builds on A by having students practice using the target writing mechanic. Encourage them to use the model in A as a guide.

Activity C Planning

Activity C teaches students to brainstorm and plan before writing by providing a graphic organizer to help students collate their ideas. Stronger students can be given the Challenge printout from the Resource Bank which has another column/section to complete.

Activity D Production: Writing Task

Activity D is the productive writing task. Encourage students to do a draft version, then either peer- or self-correct, before writing their final version. Research shows that feedback is more useful between drafts and it gets students into the habit of self-correcting.

As well as the Challenge printout mentioned for C, there are two other writing printouts which can be downloaded from the Resource Bank: the Standard template can be used by most of the students for their final written piece. Less confident students can have the Support printout which gives them more scaffolding to complete the same task as the rest of the class. Stronger students should be encouraged to expand on the model given in A by recycling language from previous lessons and giving more examples where relevant.

As with the Speaking lesson, there is a *Reflect* callout which relates to the mechanic explored in A and B. Focus on this callout before students write their final draft and give students time to self-correct their work where necessary. Notes are provided in the digital **ETB**.

Cool Down

Cool Down activities give closure to the lesson. They are designed to get students thinking about what they learned and might include a game to review new language/concepts, or provide an opportunity to share classwork completed during the lesson.

Write About It

Lesson Objectives

- to review the use of periods and question marks
- to plan and answer a technology survey

Materials
(Optional) Support, Standard, and Challenge writing printouts from the Resource Bank (one per student) (Activities C, D)

Warm Up

Play *Missing Vowels* (see TB p. 26). Write on the board the following sentences, which have the vowels removed:
_ _s_ _ t_bl_t _nd _ TV. / My f_v_r_t_ t_chn_l_gy _s my t_bl_t. / Sh_'s _s_ng _ l_pt_p.
(Solution: I use a tablet and a TV. / My favorite technology is my tablet. / She's using a laptop.)

A Read the survey and answers. Underline the question marks (?) and circle the periods (.).

- Have students scan the survey and count how many different types of technology they find. (there are four) Ask students why they think the student completed the survey. (To see how much technology is a part of his/her life.)
- Ask students what comes at the end of the first sentence in the survey. (a question mark) Ask them how many question marks they can find in the survey. (four) Have students underline them all.
- Ask students what other punctuation marks they can see in A. (there are periods, a comma, and two exclamation points; students might also mention apostrophes) Have them count the periods (six) and circle them.
- Refer students to the callout question: *When do we use question marks?* Check understanding of the word *question*, then have students find the questions in the table (column 1) and say what punctuation is used (question marks at the end).

Answers
There are four questions marks and six periods.

Let's Talk Technology!
What technology do you use?
How often do you use it?
What's your favorite technology?
Is your teacher using technology today?
I use a tablet and a TV. I often watch the TV and I sometimes use the tablet. My favorite technology is my tablet. I use it to play games. Today, my teacher isn't using her cell phone. She's using a laptop.
We use technology a lot!

B Write the question marks and periods.

- Refer students to the example sentence and ask why there is a period at the end. (It's the end of a complete sentence.)
- Have students continue the activity individually. While they are doing this, write or project the unpunctuated sentences on the board.
- To check answers, invite students to come to the board and place one punctuation mark each until all are complete. Ask if everyone agrees.

Answers
1 *My school has a cafeteria*
2 Do you use a laptop?
3 How often does your dad use his cell phone?
4 My grandma has a computer.
5 Are you doing your homework?

C Plan. Think about the survey questions. Complete.

- Tell students they are going to write their own answers to a technology survey like the one they read in A.
- Elicit one item of technology and discuss how often it is used. Have students then think about the technology they see and use during their own day and complete the table in their books with their own ideas. Tell students that at this stage they only have to write single words. Challenge printouts can be handed out now.
- Have them share their plan with a friend.

D Write your answers to the survey.

- Have students complete the survey using their ideas from C. Encourage them to use full sentences with correct punctuation.
- Have students write their final versions neatly on paper. Alternatively, hand out the Support and Standard printouts from the Resource Bank. Point out that a well-presented text is easier and more enjoyable to read. Display the finished surveys around the classroom.

Cool Down

Play *How Many Periods?* Read the first seven sentences from the script of Grace's presentation about laptops (see video script TB p. 236). Ask students to listen carefully and count the periods. They should raise their hands when they think they know how many there are.

Practice **Student's App:** Writing Practice

Lesson 7 Walkthrough: Think It Over

The final lesson in the **Language Book** encourages students to reflect on what they have learned and what they want to explore further. Students are not expected to articulate all their ideas in English. It is important that the students reflect for themselves rather than being told what they studied as this gives them another opportunity to develop as independent thinkers while also beginning to take responsibility for their learning and learning styles. At this level, their responses will help you to adapt future lessons to suit your learners' needs and to make targeted suggestions for further practice. This lesson also helps establish a home-school connection as parents can ask their children to explain their reflections.

What did I do?

This question focuses students on the activities they did during the unit, both in and outside of the **Language Book**. Help them to recognize that they are able to do a lot of different things, and bring in props to trigger memories.

Encourage students to make a personal and **roman** response to the question when choosing activities to draw or write about. This allows you to see what students found interesting and challenging, and what they feel they've achieved. Ask students to think about why they enjoyed certain activities and didn't enjoy others. Ask them how they felt when they were doing something they found hard and how they felt after they did it.

What did I learn?

The purpose of this question is to find out what students think they have learned, rather than what *you* think they have learned. Explain that ideas can be content-related, as well as to do with language. In early units, brainstorm ideas on the board and tell students they can either choose one idea to draw/write about, or think of their own idea. In later units, have students discuss their ideas in pairs, but be careful not to pair quieter students with dominant ones, as it is important for each student to have the opportunity to make a personal response. Try not to limit your students to think only about vocabulary and grammar; the reflection should take in all aspects of learning and be inclusive. The digital **ETB** provides differentiation activities to support this question.

How did I learn? / What was my favorite part?

These two questions alternate across the units. Their purpose is to help students to begin to identify personalized learning strategies.

How did I learn? Encourage students to think about what helped them to remember something, e.g. repeating something lots of times in a drill, through a cooperative learning routine, using the **Student's App** on **Navio** at home, or creating a mental picture of the vocabulary in their head.

What was my favorite part? At the end of the level you may be able to point out that our favorite part is often the way we learn best—that when we enjoy doing something we usually find it easier to learn. Encourage students to think about how they can make the learning more enjoyable for themselves. This helps them to start taking responsibility for their personal learning journey.

How well did I do?

This question asks students to evaluate their own progress. However, answers will only be valuable if students feel they can be honest. You may find it helpful to explain what it means to analyze ourselves and to provide some concrete examples to help them understand, e.g. *if you can remember 20 words color in the happiest face. If you can remember 15, color in the next happiest face. If you can remember one or two, color in the sad face.* Let them know that it's OK to color in the sad face, it just means they need to do more practice. You can suggest targeted practice to suit different students' needs, such as the grammar printouts or the practice on the **Student's App** on **Navio**.

What can I do next?

Encourage students to think of all the different ways they can continue their English learning journey outside of the classroom, including use of new media, e.g. apps, video games, vlogs. Brainstorm ideas as a class, using the suggested words as prompts. Make additional suggestions based on the things students identified as enjoyable, e.g. if they loved the Lesson 1 song, suggest they sing it at home. Make sure you follow up in the next lesson by asking questions, e.g. *What did your mom say when you sang the song? Tell me about the English movie you watched.*

Looking Forward

This features a teaser question about the next unit. To create excitement and interest in learning more, brainstorm possible answers and review these predictions in the first lesson of the next unit to see who was correct.

Further Review and Recycling

Regular recycling of new language helps increase exposure and build confidence and understanding.

Put It Together communicative games come after every two units, providing an opportunity to review and recycle the language learned in the previous lessons. These fun activities are designed to encourage students to use the language in context and to want to play again and again. Some of the games are based on Cambridge English exam activity types, thereby preparing them in an enjoyable way.

Plays review and recycle language from Units 1–5 and Units 6–10 in amusing contexts which could be used as a performance pieces mid-year or end-of-year.

Think It Over

Lesson Objectives

- to review what has been learned in the unit
- to reflect on the unit and their progress
- to think about learning strategies and how to continue learning at home

Warm Up

Play the *Yes/No Game* (see TB p. 27) for technology that appears in the unit.

Suggested items: *tablet* (Y), *spaceship* (N), *computer* (Y), *cell phone* (Y), *mouse* (Y), *projector* (Y), *time machine* (N), *printer* (N), *video game* (Y), *homework machine* (N)

Read the questions and draw or write your answers.

- Encourage review of the language and reflection on the ideas from the unit to help students make connections to past learning experiences. Give students time to think about and discuss activities in the unit before they complete the questions. Explain that they can choose to either write a few words or sentences, or to draw a picture. Allowing students to make a personal response will help them retain knowledge and engage with the learning.

What did I do?

- Give students a few minutes to look back through the unit at the different activities they did. Ask questions about the unit; for example, *What did you sing about? What activities and actions did you do? What did you talk about?*
- Encourage students to identify something in the unit that they found challenging but which they completed and feel proud of. Alternatively, ask them to choose something that was particularly memorable for them—either because it was interesting, or it was different, or even because it was noisy! You can use L1 to explain these ideas to students. Tell them they can draw or write about this activity.

What did I learn?

- Ask questions about the unit; for example, *What words do you know now? What sentences can you say? What do you know about different countries?* Brainstorm some ideas on the board.
- Encourage students to draw a picture or write sentences about the outcome of their learning.

How did I learn?

- Ask students how they learned the gadgets words in Lesson 1. Elicit ideas (e.g. by seeing the words next to the pictures, by doing the visualization activity, by hearing the words in a story, by doing a writing or a speaking activity). Encourage students to think about the pronunciation and spelling of the words they learned in this unit. Ask *What helps you remember how to say/spell these words?*
- Encourage students to draw a picture or write about some of the activities that helped them learn.

How well did I do?

- Tell students to color in the number of batteries that best expresses how well they have learned the unit content (i.e., the more they color, the more they feel they have learned). Ask *What do you remember? What do you understand? What do you need to practice more?* Encourage students to look back through the unit to see how much they remember, what they did well, and what they found difficult.

What can I do next?

- Brainstorm ideas with the class about what students can do to continue to learn (e.g. watch the videos again, play the game on p. 17 again, talk to a friend about technology).
- Encourage students to think about what they can do at home to improve their English, using the verbs in the box as a prompt, for example, read the stories to family members, sing the song to a family member, play English games on a tablet or phone, talk to a family member about technology, and so on.
- Ask students to choose one or more activities from the list (read, sing, play, talk) that they will do to practice their English.
- Once students have completed the page in their books, have them discuss with a friend what they drew or wrote. Did they choose the same activities or different ones?

Looking Forward

Draw students' attention to the character at the bottom of the page. Ask *Who's this?* and elicit what they remember about her. (she is Luis's mom in Lesson 4, p. 16) Ask students to think what foods she might like. Elicit ideas, then tell students that they will find out in the next unit.

Practice **Resource Bank:** Unit Test;
Student's App: Vocabulary and Grammar Review

Lesson 1 Walkthrough: Get Ready to Read

There are two sections to this lesson: Section 1 is always a Visible Thinking Routine (VTR). See TB p. 16 for more on VTRs. Section 2 contains pre-reading activities and previews a reading skill which will be explored in more detail in later lessons. The teaching notes on this page are flexible, so you can tailor lessons to suit your learners. You can either choose to do the VTR and pre-reading activities in one lesson, or alternatively spend longer developing the VTR discussion and start the next lesson with the pre-reading activities, then go straight into the reading. There is no Cool Down activity in the main teaching notes, but an extension activity provided in the digital **Enhanced Teacher's eBook (ETB)** may be used as a Cool Down.

Warm Up

Warm Up activities are designed to generate interest in the topic and activate schema to help students make connections between their own experiences and the readings. Activities are purposely not vocabulary-focused to give the **Literacy Book** a distinct first language (L1) feel. The digital **ETB** provides a quick Two-Minute Review activity for each Lesson 1, to review ideas generated by the previous unit. You can choose to do both the Two-Minute Review and the Warm Up or just one or the other, to suit the needs of your class.

Activities A, B, C Visible Thinking Routine: See, Think, Wonder / Think, Pair, Share

Activities A, B, and C are either a See, Think, Wonder or a Think, Pair, Share VTR. Each routine uses a striking image related to the unit's topic to foster thoughtful and constructive classroom discussions. For both routines, use the Visible Thinking Routine graphic organizer printout from the Resource Bank to help students formulate their ideas.

For See, Think, Wonder, allow students to think silently for one minute at each step of the routine. Then take ideas from the class. After the first flurry of ideas, encourage students to keep looking and to see more things. Explore the difference between students seeing on their own and seeing things together (group discovery). You can allow some discussion in L1 here, but try to re-formulate students' ideas into simple English. Avoid leading students to an answer by keeping supporting questions open, e.g. *What (else) do you see/think/wonder about the picture? What colors/shapes do you see?*

For Think, Pair, Share, give students a minute to look at the picture before you introduce the discussion question and encourage them to think about what they can see. Have them share their ideas and write useful words on the board. This provides students with a bank of vocabulary to draw on during the discussion part of the routine. When you introduce the question, make sure students have enough time to think about their own ideas before they discuss in pairs, as this will lead to a richer discussion.

The teaching notes include a list of vocabulary students will most likely find in the picture. Model conversations for the VTR are also provided. The parentheses are there as a reminder that students don't have to produce full sentences; the goal here is for them to communicate their ideas in whatever way they can. You may also find it helpful to have students express their ideas through drawing. Make sure you keep a record of students' ideas on construction paper or sticky notes, so you can revisit them later in the unit and see if opinions have changed.

Transition

The **Transition** is a discussion question designed to move you smoothly between the two sections of this lesson (VTR and pre-reading activities). This helps students make connections between the ideas they explored in the VTR and the reading. Alternatively, you can use this question as a Warm Up, if you decide to start the pre-reading activities in the next lesson.

Activity D Activate Schema

Activity D poses a discussion question for students to apply the work they did in the VTR even more closely to the unit's topic. Have students discuss the question in pairs before sharing their ideas as a class. You can write up their ideas and suggestions in graphic organizers on the board, to develop critical thinking skills.

Activity E Skill Preview

Activity E previews the unit's reading skill. This will be addressed fully in the second Get Ready to Read lesson. You are not expected to teach the skill actively in Lesson 1. The goal is to introduce the concept gently and attune students to look for and/or use it as they read.

Get Ready to Read

Lesson Objectives

- to activate prior knowledge about inventors and inventions
- to encourage students to observe and interpret through a See, Think, Wonder VTR
- to preview the reading skill of identifying the sequence of events

Materials

(Optional) VTR printout from the Resource Bank (Activities A, B, C)

Warm Up

- Use this activity to engage students in the topic.
- Write the word *invention* on the board. Ask students what they think it means. Tell them that an invention is the first one of something. Tell them that the first TV was made in 1927—it was invented in 1927.
- Ask students to think of all the important inventions they can—elicit one or two examples (e.g. the car, the computer) to start their ideas. Give students a minute to think of ideas. Then ask them to raise their hands to give their suggestions. Write some of their ideas on the board. Take a class vote to find out the most popular invention.

See, Think, Wonder

A Look at the picture. What do you see?

Students are going to do a See, Think, Wonder VTR to explore the image of a young boy who is a keen inventor.

- Ask students *What do you see?* and elicit answers.
- Give students one minute to look at the picture before sharing more answers in small groups or pairs. Then bring the groups together to share ideas as a class.
- Students will likely find: a boy, a lot of books, a robot, a machine for making tea, a (rocking) chair, a bookcase, a lamp, a cup, sugar.
- Students may also notice: a window, the boy's glasses, his shirt and overalls, a computer, a gold teapot.

Here's an example of this part of the routine.
Teacher: What do you see?
Student: I (can) see a boy.
Teacher: What else do you see?
Student: A lot of books.

B What do you think?

- Say *I think the boy likes reading. What do you think about the picture?* Give students one to three minutes to think about the picture silently. Then have students work in small groups to share their ideas, before sharing ideas as a class. Monitor and provide language help when needed.
- Answers will vary depending on students' opinions. Remind them to respect each other's thoughts and opinions.

Here's an example of this part of the routine.
Teacher: What do you think?
Student A: I think it's night.
Teacher: What makes you say that?
Student A: It's dark. There's a lamp.
Teacher: That's interesting. Anything else?

C What do you wonder?

- Say *I wonder if the chair is old. What do you wonder? What questions do you have?* Give students one to three minutes to think about the picture silently.
- Have students share their ideas in groups or as a class. Allow students to be creative and encourage them to share. There are no wrong answers. Language does not need to be perfect.

Here's an example of this part of the routine.
Teacher: What do you wonder?
Student A: What's the boy reading?
Teacher: OK, what else?
Student B: Do his robots work?
Teacher: Good question!

Transition

Ask students if the boy looks like an inventor. Ask *Where do inventors work? What do they use? Is it easy to be an inventor?*

D Think and discuss. What do inventors do?

- Have students read the question. Ask *Do inventors just wait for a good idea to come? How do they get their ideas?* Elicit from students one or two things that they think inventors do. Give students time to think and then have them share their ideas in pairs or small groups.
- When they have had time to discuss, ask students if they agreed on an answer. Have them share some of their answers with the class.

E Think and discuss. Which of these things do you think inventors do first? Check (✔).

This is a preview of the reading skill of identifying the sequence of events.

- Have students read the three actions and think about the correct order for inventors. They should check the action they think comes first.
- Elicit the action they think comes first, then ask which action comes second and which comes last. (suggested order: have ideas, draw a picture, make changes) Check everyone agrees, and discuss why these things are in this order.

Now read **The After-School Inventor**

Lesson 2 Walkthrough: Reading 1, Fiction

The reading lessons aim to support the development of literacy and to foster a love of reading, to encourage students to become lifelong readers.

There is one **fiction** and one **nonfiction** text in each unit. Fiction texts are laid out to emulate storybooks inspired by ESL/L1 materials and expose students to language in context which may be slightly above level. This is because research shows that with the right support, reading slightly above level can significantly improve overall reading skills.

Nonfiction texts give students a chance to learn new concepts and vocabulary, as well as broaden their view of the world. They also often appeal to reluctant readers. Nonfiction texts are laid out to look like nonfiction books, websites, and articles to give a realistic and aspirational feel to the book.

Warm Up

This Warm Up allows you to review the ideas generated at the end of the previous lesson in preparation for the reading. Alternatively, if you are carrying the lesson straight on from the previous page, use this activity to transition between the pre-reading and reading part of the lesson.

Warm Ups in the **Literacy Book** are about setting the scene for the upcoming lesson and activating students' memory, curiosity, and desire to learn. Don't correct language unless the students ask you to.

Reading Approach

First Reading: Listen and Engage

The purpose of the first reading stage is to engage students and help them become familiar with the text. This sets the scene for the comprehension and analysis work that will come next. Before they read, encourage students to identify things in the pictures that they find interesting, surprising, or unusual. Engagement is more important than vocabulary at this stage, so it's fine for students to point if they are unable to name what they see.

For this first exposure to the text, read it out loud or have students listen to the audio and follow along in their books. To help students feel comfortable and enjoy watching/listening to the story, have everyone seated in a circle at the front of the class. This is a great opportunity for students to see and hear how to read fluently and with expression, so if you are reading, do character voices and facial expressions where appropriate. Pause only to ask prediction questions, which can help to motivate students and encourage them to want to find out what happens next. Do not spend time analyzing the language at this point, full comprehension is not necessary for students to enjoy a text.

Words in Context

See **p. 58**.

Second Reading: Analyze the Text and Features

Ensure students get to explore the text in a variety of ways to keep them motivated and active participants in the learning process. If you read the text out loud in the first reading stage, have students read chorally in the second stage, or have them read silently with or without the audio.

The purpose of the second reading stage is to analyze the text and features using the callout questions from the colored boxes in the **Literacy Book**. The teaching notes tell you the purpose of the questions, e.g. gist, detail, text focus, making connections, personalization, and give ideas about how to exploit them.

International English

This feature exposes students to differences in vocabulary, language, and spelling between American English and British English. Point to the box with the flags. Ask students if they know which countries the flags represent. Tell them that the flag with stars and stripes is for the USA (United States of America), and the flag with crosses is for the UK (United Kingdom). Ask students if they know which language is spoken in these countries (English). Tell them that in both countries people speak English but that some words are different and some words are pronounced the same, but spelled differently. Tell students that they will see American English words used in this course, but that British English is also correct. It is important that while they are aware of the differences, you and they choose one variety to use, especially in exams.

To make the most of this feature, build up a display of British and American English words throughout the year. One way to do this is to print out or draw the two flags and create word cards that students stick around the relevant flag.

Third Reading: Interact with the Text

The third reading stage gives students the chance to interact with the text on a more personal level. With fiction texts students are encouraged to read aloud or role-play the text. This activity allows students to explore what characters are thinking and how they are feeling. They can also experiment with different voices and patterns of intonation. For ideas on setting up role-plays in class, see **TB p. 23**.

Fiction: *The After-School Inventor— A Story*

Lesson Objectives

- to read a rhyming story about an inventor
- to explore the SEL competency of self-awareness by accurately recognizing strengths and limitations
- to make a personal connection to the reading

Materials
Audio Tracks 9 and 10

Warm Up

Ask students to choose and hold up their favorite possession from their desk or backpack. Have students see if they can find any of their favorite items, or anything similar, on pp. 10–15 of the **Literacy Book**.

TRACK 9 TB p. 228 Reading Approach

First Reading: Listen and Engage

- Ask students to notice the title, the genre, the pictures, and the text on the page. Have them point to Clara.
- Tell students that the reading is about inventions. Ask them if there are any inventions they would like to make (e.g. something to put away toys).
- Play the audio while students read. Encourage them to move a finger along the text in time with the audio.
- Read the whole story before asking *Is Clara the same age as you? How is her life similar to yours? How is it different?*
- Then look at the Words in Context.

TRACK 10 TB p. 228 Words in Context

- Play the audio and have students repeat the words.
- Have a race to find the words in the reading.
- Tell students they can **use the pictures** to help establish the meaning of new words. Have them work in pairs to do this, using Language 1 (L1) as necessary.
- Then bring the class together and use these discussion points to confirm the meanings.

invent Students met this word in the previous lesson. Ask them to look at the sentence—*I invent things after school.* Ask for suggestions for the meaning of the word and confirm the correct ideas. (to think of or make something new)

try again Have students find the phrase *I always try again.* Look at the pictures. Ask what happened before and what she does next. Mime looking disappointed and then getting enthusiastic again.

change Have students find the word and sentence. Ask what happened before and what she does next. Mime drawing, erasing, and drawing again.

mirror Have students find the word and point to the mirror in the picture. Have them mime looking at themselves in a mirror.

mess Refer students to the sentence and picture. Ask *Why is Mom not happy?*

invention Students may remember this word from the previous lesson. Have them point to the sentence the word appears in and ask what the invention is. Have students point to other inventions in the story.

machine Have students point to the word and picture. Ask what machines they have in their homes. Give them an example if necessary (e.g. washing machine).

Second Reading: Analyze the Text and Features

- Read the rhyming story chorally. Encourage students to make each line feel rhythmic, to highlight the verse form.
- Ask some questions to check comprehension. Then have students discuss the questions in the green boxes using Think, Pair, Share. (see TB p. 20)
  - **Gist** (p. 10): *Are all of Clara's inventions good?* Ask students to look at the pictures, as well as the text, to decide. Ask for examples of inventions that are good / not so good. (the rain glasses, umbrella pen, and special mirror aren't so good)
  - **Detail** (p. 14): *Look at the buttons on the mirror. What can the mirror do?* (*small/big* makes the reflection smaller or bigger; *back/front* shows a reflection of the back or front of the person in the reflection)
  - **Personalization** (p. 15): *Which invention is your favorite?* Ask one student to name their favorite and have the others raise their hands if they agree. Ask another student for his/her favorite and continue until all students have voted.

International English

Point to the two boxes with flags and elicit which words are American English and which words are British English. Point out that all of these words are correct English, and ask *Which words do we use?*

Third Reading: Interact with the Text

- Listen to the audio again and have students join in with the rhyming words. Then have them repeat the lines of the poem with appropriate rhythm and intonation.
- Put students into pairs to practice saying the poem, taking turns to say pairs of lines.

Cool Down

Ask students what part of the story they liked best and why. Then ask if they think Clara will get better at inventing. Reinforce the idea that the more we practice, the better we get, and we can always learn from our mistakes.

Practice **Student's App:** Video

Lesson 3 Walkthrough: Explore the Reading

This lesson allows students to explore the previous text further with comprehension, analysis and discussion activities.

Activity A Reading Comprehension

Start this lesson with oral comprehension questions to remind students about the text. Arrange them in a circle and have a discussion about the story. The teaching notes suggest *Wh- questions* (who, where, what, when, why) you can ask to help students to remember the gist and details of the reading. Play the video to review the story if you don't want to read the text as a class again.

The lesson then moves on to a heads-down activity which allows you to check students' understanding of the reading. If there are areas that you find students don't understand, you can return to the text and address these before moving on to the analysis part of the lesson.

Activity B Text Analysis

Activity B is an age-appropriate analysis task, which asks students to begin to think critically about what they have read and to consider the causes, problems, solutions, or consequences. They will need to look back at the reading to answer questions. Help students find a strategy for doing this by encouraging them to look at the pictures and scan the text for key words, rather than re-reading the whole text again.

Activity C Post-Reading Discussion & SEL focus

The teaching notes for the fiction text include places to highlight the SEL competency of the unit. There are discussion questions to help students personalize the SEL competency and make connections between the text and their own knowledge and understanding of the world. There are often opportunities here for critical literacy, as students can be encouraged to consider the point of view of different characters. See **TB p. 17** for more on SEL.

Phonics

A phonics box is always attached to one Explore the Reading lesson in each unit. This features a high frequency sound from the previous lesson's reading, to help students decode the combination of letters to read words. Show students that the same sound in English can often be represented by different letters and encourage them to apply this skill of decoding to other unfamiliar words.

The phonics activity is supported by audio to help students recognize the sounds within the words, but the focus of the activity should be on reading and spelling rather than accurate pronunciation (there is targeted pronunciation work in the **Language Book**). See **TB p. 13** for more about the phonics approach in ***Global Stage***.

Explore the Reading

Lesson Objectives

- to understand and analyze *The After-School Inventor* through reading comprehension activities
- to explore the SEL competency of self-awareness by accurately recognizing strengths and limitations
- to make a personal connection to the reading
- to recognize and reproduce *cl–* blends

Materials
Audio Tracks 9 (Activity A) and 11

Warm Up

Play *What's the Next Word?* (see TB p. 27) with sentences from *The After-School Inventor.*

A Read and match.

- Before students open their books, find out what they remember. Use some of the five *W* words to ask questions: *What does Clara do after school?* (invent things) *Why does she do it?* (to make her life easier/better) *Who helps her?* (no one—she does it by herself) *What are her best inventions?* (students' own answers)
- Ask a student to read the first sentence and its pair in the right-hand column. Have students look back at the reading and find the clean-up machine (p. 15).
- Have students work individually to match the other descriptions with the inventions and find them in the reading.
- To check answers, play the audio (Track 9) again and have students raise their hands to ask you to pause when one of the answers comes up.

Answers
1 d 2 e 3 a 4 c 5 b

B Read and choose the answer.

- Read the first question and have the class read the example answer chorally. Have students find the information for the answer in the reading (p. 10).
- Have students choose the answers for the other questions on their own or in pairs.
- To check answers, nominate pairs of students to read a question and the relevant answer. Ask if everyone agrees.

Answers
1 *She invents things after school.* 2 She tries again.
3 She makes a plan. 4 The mirror doesn't work.
5 Her mom does. 6 It cleans her room.

C Think and discuss. Do you think it is easy or difficult to be an inventor? Why?

- Have students remember and say what an inventor does (they can look back at the reading for ideas). List their ideas on the board.
- Refer students to the question in C and give them some time to think of their answers.
- Ask the class for their opinions. Try to include as many students as possible. Encourage students to phrase their answers like the example given (*I think … because …*).
- Ask students if their opinion changed while listening to their friends' ideas.
- Use this discussion point to explore the SEL competency of self-awareness by accurately recognizing strengths and limitations.
- Ask students *What are Clara's goals?* (to invent new things) *How does she overcome problems to make progress?* (she keeps trying) *Do you think she likes solving problems?* (she is very happy with her inventions that help her) Point out that Clara is very independent and enjoys it. It helps her feel she can do anything she wants!

Phonics *cl*

TRACK 11 TB p. 228 **Listen and say.**

- Play the audio and have students look at the words in the box. Ask them what sound all the words have in common.
- Play the audio again and have students repeat the words. Ask a few individual students to repeat each word.
- Ask students to choose their favorite word from the list and to tell a friend.
- Have students find more words in the reading starting with *cl–*. Give a two-minute time limit. Ask volunteers to write a word they found on the board. Then invite students to read them out loud.

Answers
Clara; clock; click; clothes; clean

Cool Down

Play *Physical Spelling* (see p. TB 26) with vocabulary from the phonics section.

Practice **Resource Bank:** Phonics Printout;
Student's App: Phonics Practice; Reading Comprehension Practice

Lesson 4 Walkthrough: Get Ready to Read

This lesson provides pre-reading activities, including a reading skill focus, to prepare students for the second text.

Activity A Reading Skill Focus

Activity A practices the reading skill that was previewed in Lesson 1. It takes an inductive approach to learning, with students being encouraged to practice the reading skill and notice how it can help them understand the reading before the skill is named in the skills box. Where the reading skill involves pictures, you could do a See, Think, Wonder routine before the students answer the questions to help them make connections between the pictures and their own experiences. This will help them to make sense of the reading in the next lesson.

Activity B Reading Skill Practice

Activity B allows students to practice the reading skill from A and apply it to the forthcoming reading. When they have finished, discuss what students think and encourage them to say why they think it.

Activity C Pre-Reading Discussion

Activity C is a discussion question relating to the reading on the next pages. The discussion question personalizes the learning and encourages students to become active participants, by asking them either to connect the reading to their own lives or to think and express opinions. You can vary the activity by using a cooperative learning routine such as a Round Robin or a Chalk Talk (see TB p. 17 for more about cooperative learning routines).

Get Ready to Read

Lesson Objectives

- to practice the reading skill of identifying a sequence of events
- to activate prior knowledge about inventors and their notebooks

Warm Up

Do a mime sequence with students. Say and mime *Open your book. Read. Pick up your pen. Write the answer. Put down your pen. Raise your hand.*

Encourage students to join in with you, first with the mimes and then with the phrases. Then do the actions and say the phrases in a different, random order. Finally, have students say and do everything in the correct order, this time without your help.

A Look and read. Then write the instructions in order.

This lesson practices the skill of identifying a sequence of events. Students previewed this skill in Lesson 1.

- Ask students what they can see in the pictures. If you are using the TTL, enlarge the pictures on the board to help students focus.
- Have one student read the four answer options.
- Ask students which instruction they think goes with the first picture (Press on).
- Have them decide the order for the other instructions and write them under the pictures.
- To check answers, call out the numbers in the correct order and have students respond with the relevant instruction.
- Have students mime the sequence in the order they have proposed. Ask them *Does it work?* Check everyone agrees.
- Point out the skills box below the activity. Read it aloud to students. Ask them what another word for *sequence* is (order). Ask students why this order is important (some things, e.g. computer games, don't work if we don't do things in the right order).

Answers
1 Press on. 2 Type password. 3 Press play.
4 Play the game.

B Read and put in order.

- Point out to students that the words in the box are in the correct order. The sentences below the box are not.
- Ask students to decide which is the first instruction and take a class vote. When the correct answer is chosen, have them write *First* next to it.
- Have them work individually to decide which instructions are second, third, and last.
- To check answers, ask four volunteers to read the sequence of instructions, saying them in the order that they should be followed. After each sentence, ask the class *Is that correct?*

Answers
Third; First; Last; Second

C Think and discuss. Why do you think inventors have notebooks?

- Give students some time to think of their answers to the question.
- Ask students to work with a partner to discuss the question. Remind them to use phrases such as *Me, too* and *I don't think so* to respond to their partner's opinions.
- When they have had time to discuss in pairs, elicit some opinions from the class. Try to include as many students as possible in the discussion.
- Ask students if their ideas changed as they listened to their friends' ideas.
- Ask them *Where do inventors get their ideas from?* Give students time to think and then ask for suggestions.

Cool Down

Ask students a question about inventors. It can be a question they have already answered; for example, *Why do inventors have notebooks? What do inventors do with a new idea? What's the last thing that inventors do?*

Have students build an answer around the class, each student contributing one word to the answer until they make a complete sentence. If one student gets stuck, other students can help.

Then ask a new question until every student has contributed one word.

Now read **My Good Ideas Book**

Lesson 5 Walkthrough: Reading 2, Nonfiction

The structure of the reading lessons allows students to be exposed to the text multiple times. This helps them to connect oral and written forms, which is important for the development of reading skills. There is a focus on reading for analysis and pleasure, rather than simple mechanics. Students will gain independence with each reading as you progress through the course.

One reading lesson in each unit is supported by a video. Digital storytelling is helpful because it transcends language and culture by engaging students in a way that is both visual and auditory, as well as textual. Learners can make connections to previous experiences more easily, think critically about new information, and use their own knowledge to fill in any gaps in understanding.

Videos can be used as part of the overall reading strategy: as a way of engaging students with the text; as part of the process of analysis; and as a tool to help them interact with the text on a more personal level. The digital **ETB** provides extension activities for each video lesson. If you aren't able to play the video in class, have students watch it at home prior to the lesson. See **TB** p. 15 for more information about the Flipped Classroom Approach.

Warm Up

See **TB p. 50**.

Reading Approach

See **TB p. 50**.

Words in Context

Each reading lesson has a **Words in Context** box which pulls out certain key words from the text for students to explore in greater detail. It is recommended you look at these Words in Context after the students have read the text (or watched the video) at least once through. This is so that the first reading can be about enjoyment and engagement, rather than vocabulary learning. Don't pre-teach these words. It is more valuable to offer students strategies to help them decode the meaning for themselves. Different strategies are suggested in the notes, with more detail on **TB p. 15**.

Introduce a different strategy in each lesson and encourage pairs of students to use a combination of strategies to help them decode the words. It is fine for students to use L1 for this, to enable them to express their thoughts and ideas clearly.

Then ask questions (provided in the notes) to check understanding and clarify meaning. Effectively you are providing students with tools which will help them to work out the meaning of other unfamiliar words they encounter in the future. Review the meaning of all the Words in Context by having a student choose one, and the others point to the relevant part of the picture or make an appropriate gesture.

It should be noted that these words have been highlighted to help students' comprehension of the texts. They are not part of the course's key language and will not appear in any assessment material.

Nonfiction: *My Good Ideas Book—* An Instructional Text

Lesson Objectives

- to read an instructional text about inventions
- to make a personal connection to the reading

Materials
Audio Tracks 12 and 13; Video; access to an internet search engine (Warm Up, WU)

Warm Up

Have students look around the classroom and identify inventions, no matter how simple (e.g. the pencil, the ruler, the backpack). Have students guess how long ago each one was invented, and use the internet to find the answer (in English if possible) with the search query *When was the ______ invented?* The answer will usually come up in the first result.

TRACK 12 TB p. 228 Reading Approach

First Reading: Listen and Engage

- Have students look quickly at pp. 18–21 and predict what they will read about. (inventions)
- Play the video and ask students if their predictions were correct. Alternatively, play the audio and have students listen and follow in their books.
- Then look at the Words in Context.

TRACK 13 TB p. 228 Words in Context

- Play the audio and have students repeat the words.
- Have a race to find the words in the reading.
- Play the video again and tell students to **use the images and actions in the video to help establish the meaning of the new words** (see Words in Context on TB p. 23). Have them discuss their ideas with a partner, using L1 if necessary.
- Then bring the class together and use these discussion points to confirm the meanings.

problem / solution Have students find both words in the sentence on p. 18 of their books. Ask *What comes first, the problem or the solution?*

hexagon In this case the most useful tool for understanding the new word is the diagram next to it. Have students draw a hexagon of their own. Ask *How many sides does it have?*

improve Draw a basic stick person on the board and say *Hmmm, it's OK …* Then change it and say *Excellent! Now it's great! What did I do?* (improved it)

parachute Point to the pictures on the page and ask *Which is the parachute?* Have students mime using a parachute.

Practice Student's App: Video

Second Reading: Analyze the Text and Features

- Play the audio and have students listen and follow in their books. Alternatively, have them read silently.
- Ask students to think about the following question while they read: *Is this reading a story or real information?* (information)
- Ask some questions about the reading to check comprehension.
- Then use Think, Pair, Share (see TB p. 20) to discuss the questions and information in the green boxes.
    - **Making Connections** (p. 18): *Thomas Edison had thousands of notebooks.* Ask students what they think this fact tells us about Thomas Edison. (he probably had a lot of ideas and wrote them all down—even if they didn't seem like very good ideas at the time!) Ask students if they know what his inventions (movie projector, sound recorder, light bulb) do and which is the most important.
    - **Making Connections** (p. 19): *Where do new ideas come from?* Have students look at the pictures and captions and ask them if they can see where some ideas come from (e.g. from inventions already made, from nature, from old things used in a new way). Ask them where their own ideas come from.
    - **Personalization** (p. 21): *Do you like drawing or making new things?* Ask students to raise their hands if they like to do this. Point out that not everyone likes doing the same things—some people are good at making things, some people at using them, and some people at describing them!

Third Reading: Interact with the Text

- Play the video one more time, telling students to say the text aloud while they are watching. Tell them that after this, they will be the voice of the video so they should listen carefully to the timings.
- Mute the video and have individual students narrate the text, one page at a time. Have the others mime the actions that are in the phrase or around it.
- Alternatively, have one group of students read the text while another group of students mimes the actions alongside them.

Cool Down

Play *Mime It!* (see TB p. 26) using the inventions from pp. 18–21.

Lesson 6 Walkthrough: Explore the Reading

This lesson follows the same structure as the first Explore the Reading lesson with comprehension, analysis, and discussion activities to explore the second reading text. It also provides further practice of the reading skill.

Activity A Reading Comprehension

Before doing **Activity A**, have a Circle Time discussion (see **TB p. 21**) with books closed to check students' comprehension of the text. This can be a nice routine to have at the beginning of each Explore the Reading lesson.

Activity B Text Analysis and Practice

Activity B is a text analysis activity that usually involves practicing the unit reading skill. Have students answer the questions individually from memory first. Then they can look back on the reading in pairs to check their answers.

Activity C Post-Reading Discussion and CLIL focus

Activity C is a discussion question which encourages students to be active participants in the learning process. The question involves an element of personalization to help students make connections between the text and their own lives.

Have students discuss the question in pairs or small groups. Bring it together with a class discussion and write students' key ideas on the board in the style of a survey. Display results in a bar graph or tally chart to lay the foundations for reasoning skills and teaching students to analyze data.

There is a Content and Language Integrated Learning (CLIL) focus in every nonfiction Explore the Reading lesson to allow students to explore the texts through a real-world context. See **TB p. 18** for more on CLIL.

Competencies

Icons in the teaching notes highlight which activities in the **Literacy Book** are connected to one of the five competencies: Me, Act, Think, Learn, and Communicate. See **TB p. 19** for more information.

Cool Down

Cool Down activities give closure to the lesson. They are designed to get students thinking about what they learned and might include a game to review new concepts.

Explore the Reading

Lesson Objectives

- to understand and analyze *My Good Ideas Book* through reading comprehension activities
- to practice the reading skill of identifying a sequence of events
- to learn through CLIL (science): inventions and understanding how technology helps us
- to make a personal connection to the reading

Materials

(Optional) Video or Audio Track 12 (A); pictures of a parachute, a train, a pencil, and a light bulb (Activity C)

Warm Up

Play *Stand Up, Sit Down* using sentences about *My Good Ideas Book* (see TB p. 26).

Suggested sentences: *To get started, you need ideas, time, and a computer.* (False; You don't need a computer.) *When you have a problem, look for a solution.* (True) *Plants and animals can give you good ideas.* (True) *The fast train is shaped like a shoe.* (False; It's shaped like a kingfisher.) *If your idea isn't right, give up.* (False; Try again and again and again.)

A Read and put in order.

This activity reviews the reading skill of sequencing events.

- If more than a day has passed since students first read *My Good Ideas Book*, allow them some time to review the reading by themselves—or you could have them watch the video or listen to the audio.
- With books closed, find out what students remember about the reading. Use the five *W* words to ask questions: *Where can you write your ideas?* (in a notebook) *Who invented the light bulb?* (Thomas Edison) *Where can you get ideas from?* (nature, things we use every day, old objects) *Why is a drawing important?* (It can help you see your idea.) *Who can give us help and opinions?* (family and friends)
- In this activity, students will think about the process for inventing something. If you are using the TTL, project A. Ask students to look at the phrases in the box and then use the reading to decide which is the first in the sequence. Check everyone agrees and have students write it in the space.
- Have students work alone to decide on the correct order for the other phrases. Then ask them to compare their answers with a friend.
- To check answers, have students raise their hands to contribute one phrase each in the correct order. Ask if everyone agrees.

Answers

1 have a good idea 2 draw a picture
3 make a model 4 share your idea 5 *try again*

B Read and complete.

- Have students work in groups to decide on answers to the first part of the diagram by referring to p. 18.
- Have students work independently to complete the spaces in the other parts. While they are doing this, draw the diagram on the board (at child-friendly height) or project it on the board.
- To check answers, invite students to come and write an item each on the board. Ask if everyone agrees.

Answers

1 *ideas*; time; a notebook; *a pencil* 2 *a problem*; *objects you use*; animals; plants 3 *draw a picture*; make a model; *test your idea*; *improve your idea*; show it to friends/family

C Think and discuss. How are these inventions helpful?

This activity allows students to explore the science objective of understanding how inventions help us.

- If possible, show students a picture of each invention. Ask them to match each picture to the name in their book.
- Tell students they are going to have a discussion about why these four inventions are useful.
- Read the example answer about parachutes. Then ask students for more suggestions for why parachutes are helpful. (getting help, food, and water to places where cars can't go; entertainment—parachute jumping; getting to places quietly with no one seeing you— secret agents!)
- Have students think about all the possible ways the other items can help us. Tell them they can make notes if they want to, and they can ask you for help with vocabulary.
- Then give students time to discuss their ideas in pairs or small groups. While they are doing this, write the other three inventions on the board with a circle around each one and space to write around them.
- Ask students for suggestions about any of the inventions. Involve as many students as possible. For each suggestion, write a key word or phrase on the board extending from the circle around the invention.

Cool Down

Play *Find Someone Who*. Have students write down their favorite invention from the reading. Then ask them to mingle with the other students in the class, saying their choice and listening to the choices of others. When they find someone who likes the same invention as them, they sit down together and discuss why they chose it.

Practice Student's App: Reading Comprehension Practice

Lesson 7 Walkthrough: Think Together

This lesson brings the unit full circle to consider the key concept question. This acts as the thread for all the lessons related to the readings. The teaching notes support you to address this question.

Students are also encouraged to revisit the Lesson 1 VTR image to see if their perceptions have changed or shifted now that they know more about the topic. Review their initial ideas and see if students can offer more information or link the image more explicitly to the unit's topic.

Activity A Text Comparison

Activity A is a text-to-text comparison task which lays the foundations for more communicative comparison analysis in higher levels. Learning how to compare and contrast is an important skill which has been shown to: improve students' ability to memorize content; develop higher-order thinking skills; strengthen comprehension skills; and improve writing skills.

If you have not done the Two-Minute Review, it may be beneficial to have students brainstorm what they remember about both texts before you start.

Activity B Speaking Routine

Activity B has a text-to-world base which is explored through a cooperative learning routine, such as Round Robin, Three-step Interview, or Numbered Heads Together (see **TB p. 20**). Cooperative learning routines create opportunities for purposeful communication and collaboration which encourages students to become actively engaged in their learning.

See **TB p. 21** for more about setting up class discussions and speaking routines.

My Reading Journal

My Reading Journal allows students to give a personalized response to the readings and reflect on the unit as a whole. The goal is to foster self-reflection as a learning tool, to help students to see the importance of the learning process, to encourage them to think critically about texts and to express preferences, and motivate and empower them to want to learn more.

Think Together

Lesson Objectives

- to make connections between the readings
- to explore the key concept: Why do people invent things?
- to reflect on the unit and provide personal thoughts and opinions

Warm Up

Have students look at the key concept question at the top of the page: *Why do people invent things?* Give students two minutes to discuss the answer in pairs, then bring the class together and ask them for their best idea. Write the reasons on the board in a spidergram.

A Read and match the inventions to the inventors. Complete the Invention column.

- Ask students how many inventions they can remember from both readings—have them raise their hands when they remember one. Write the inventions on the board.
- Have students identify Clara Doodle's invention in the box and write it in the table.
- Have students identify and complete the table for the other inventions.
- To check answers, draw or project the table on the board and invite students to complete the *Invention* column. Ask if everyone agrees.

Answers
See answers in B

B Look at A. What is the reason for each invention? Complete the Reason column.

- Ask students to look in the box, find the reason for Clara Doodle's alarm clock pillow (*to wake up on time*), and write it in the table.
- Have them identify the reasons for the other inventions. They can refer back to the readings if necessary.
- To check answers, invite students to complete the *Reason* column on the board. Ask if everyone agrees.

Answers
Clara Doodle: the alarm clock pillow; to wake up on time
Karl Benz: the car; to travel quickly with no horses
Leonardo da Vinci: the parachute; to travel in the air
Thomas Edison: the movie projector; to show movies

C Think and share. Why are these inventions important? Give reasons. Do a Round Robin.

Students are going to make connections between what they know and what they have learned in the unit.

- Set the class up for a Round Robin cooperative learning routine (see TB p. 20).
- Elicit one or two ideas about why robots are an important invention. (they make work easier, they can do dangerous things or go to dangerous places for us, they can help people who can't do things for themselves, they can do things faster than people)
- Give students time to think about why each invention is important. Then put students in groups of four and demonstrate the Round Robin with one group. Ask *Why are robots important?* and point to each student in turn to give an answer.
- Have students do the Round Robin in their groups, focusing on one invention at a time. Then invite groups to share their ideas.

Practice Resource Bank: Unit Test;
Student's App: Key Concept Practice

My Reading Journal

Write three interesting things from this unit.

This task encourages students to review and remember what they learned. Tell the class one interesting thing that you learned from this unit; for example, *I learned that Leonardo da Vinci invented the parachute hundreds of years ago!* Have students look back at the readings to choose and write three interesting things they learned. Then have them compare with a friend. Ask some students to tell the class which three things they chose.

Example Answers
1 I learned that Thomas Edison invented the movie projector.
2 I learned that you can get ideas from animals and plants.
3 I learned that inventors make a plan.

What's an invention you want to know about? How can you learn about it?

This question focuses on personalization. Tell students about an invention you want to know more about (e.g. LED lights). Ask for suggestions about how you could learn about them. (use the internet, look in a book, ask someone who knows more than me about it)

Have students complete the sentences about the invention they'd like to learn more about. Help where necessary with vocabulary and phrasing. Then encourage students to compare with a friend. Invite students to share their ideas with the class.

Answers
Student's own answers

Cool Down

Have students look back at the unit opener picture on pp. 8–9 or project it on the board. Ask if they now have more ideas about what's happening in the picture. (perhaps the books are notebooks with his ideas and drawings; perhaps the tea-making machine is a first model and he needs to improve it; perhaps he is concentrating so hard because he is trying to find a solution to a problem)

UNIT 2

Thank You

Unit Overview

Themes

Food

Being thankful

Synopsis

In this unit, students will learn about different kinds of food, find out how and why communities celebrate harvest, and think about different ways we can express gratitude. They will plan and prepare a conversation about online shopping and write a description about food using target vocabulary and grammar from the unit.

Language Book

Vocabulary

cherry, chicken, corn, cupcake, eggplant, fruit, peas, pineapple, rice, sausage, spinach, tomato

p. 64

Explore Language

Quantifiers: *A lot of, Much, Many*

p. 65

Global Citizenship

How is fruit different around the world?

a bag of, a bottle of, a bowl of, a box of, a can of, a carton of, lemonade, potato chips, soup

p. 66

Explore Language

Quantifiers with Questions: *How much ...? How many ...? Some/Any*

p. 67

Talk About It

Conversation: making suggestions, discussing needs

p. 68

Write About It

A Description of My Kitchen

Punctuation: capital letters and commas

p. 69

Think It Over

Review and Reflection

p. 70

Literacy Book

Think Together
Why do we celebrate harvests?
p. 77

Visible Thinking
VTR: Think, Pair, Share
p. 71

Fiction
Science Fiction: *First Harvest*

Words in Context: pick, worried, grow, believe, stripes
p. 75

Nonfiction
An Informational Text: *Chuseok: Korea's Harvest Festival*

Words in Context: weave, cloth, contest, festival, harvest, ancestors
p. 72

Reading Skill
Understanding the setting
p. 74

Phonics
–st
p. 76

Language and Literacy Connections

The connecting theme in Unit 2 is food and where it comes from.

	Language	Literacy
Vocabulary	**Set 1:** food **Set 2:** containers, food and drink	**Nonfiction:** *rice* **Fiction:** *corn, fruit, peas, pineapple, tomato*
Grammar	**Quantifiers:** ***A lot, Much, Many*** You don't have many cherries. You have a lot of pineapples. I don't have much fruit. **Quantifiers with Questions:** ***How much …? How many …? Some/Any*** How much food do we have? We have some food. We don't have any lunch.	**Nonfiction** There are many kinds of food. Some people buy new clothes. **Fiction** There isn't much water. There is a lot of food.
Skills	**Pronunciation:** /l/ and /r/	**Reading:** understanding the setting **Phonics:** *–st*
International English	*eggplant / aubergine; cupcake / fairy cake; potato chips / crisps*	

Vocabulary

Lesson Objectives

- to learn vocabulary of food: *cherry, chicken, corn, cupcake, eggplant, fruit, peas, pineapple, rice, sausage, spinach, tomato*
- to sing a song about appreciating healthy food and treats

Materials
Audio Tracks 15 to 18; Video

Warm Up

Play *Stand Up, Sit Down* with sentences about food (see TB p. 26).

Suggested sentences: *I like / I don't like … pizza/apples/salad/ tomatoes/meat/chicken/eggs/vegetables/chocolate*, and so on.

A TRACK 15 TB p. 214 **Listen and find. What's Lucy making?**

- Have students say what they can see happening in the picture on pp. 22–23. Ask *Where is this? What can you see people doing? Does this look like your hometown? Can you see Erin from Unit 1?* (she is the woman holding the box)
- Tell students they are going to listen to a conversation happening in the market. Play the audio and have students point to the words or pictures as they listen.
- Ask the gist question *What is Lucy making?* and elicit the answer. Play the audio again for students to check. Have students share their answers with a friend before checking then check as a class.
- Look back at p. 21. Say *Can you answer Erin's question?* Play the audio again to check. (she likes peas)

Answer
Lucy is making orange juice.

B TRACK 16 TB p. 214 **Listen, say, and number the pictures in A.**

- Play the audio and have students point to the pictures and repeat the word.
- Tell students to listen again and write numbers next to the words in the picture. Do the example together. (tomato) Then check answers as a class.
- Have students repeat the words again, first under their breath and then aloud.

Answers
1 *tomato* 2 chicken 3 spinach 4 corn 5 fruit
6 eggplant 7 cupcake 8 sausage 9 pineapple
10 peas 11 cherry 12 rice

International English

Have students look at the words and elicit which are American English and which are British English. Ask if they've every heard them before. Drill the pronunciation (*aubergine* /ˈəʊbə(r)ˌʒiːn/) Ask *Which words do we use?*

C TRACK 17 TB p. 215 **Listen. Close your eyes and visualize.**

- Prepare students for the visualization (see TB p. 21).
- Play the audio, allowing students to visualize the food and do actions where appropriate as they listen. They can say the word after they hear *say*.
- Ask volunteers to describe what they imagined or to demonstrate their mime.

D **Look, unscramble, and write.**

- Students are going to reorder the letters to complete the words. Write the first scrambled word on the board. Ask students to look at the answer and spell the correct word. On the board, cross out each letter as students say it, so that they understand that they should use each letter once and that every letter must be used.
- Elicit the answer to number 2 and check whether their suggested answer works by having them spell it while you strike through each letter. Then have students continue the activity individually.
- To check answers, invite students to come to the board and write one word each. Ask if everyone agrees.

Answers
1 *fruit* 2 peas 3 rice 4 eggplant 5 sausage
6 spinach 7 tomato 8 corn 9 pineapple
10 cupcake 11 chicken 12 cherry

E TRACK 18 TB p. 215 **Listen and sing. Then watch and sing.**

- Write the title of the song on the board. Ask *What's a market?* If necessary, explain that some towns and countries have a market on a specific day each week. Ask *What do you usually buy in a market? What are the people buying in the market?* (food—mostly fruit and vegetables)
- Play the song, encouraging students to listen and enjoy the music. Have students raise their hands every time they hear an item from B.
- Give students a moment to look at the lyrics. Play the song again and stop after each line for students to repeat.
- Play the song again and encourage the class to sing.
- Play the song video encouraging students to sing as they watch. They can move to the music, invent actions or a dance.

Cool Down

Draw a smiley face on the left side of the board and a sad face on the right. Tell students you will say the names of some items of food. If they like the food, they point left and say *yes* and if they don't like it, they point right and say *no*. If they have never tasted the food, they can point to the middle. Use names of food from this lesson and any other foods students mentioned in the Warm Up.

Practice **Student's App:** Vocabulary Practice; Video

Explore Language

Lesson Objectives

- to learn to use quantifiers: *a lot of, much, many*
- to talk about quantities of food
- to practice using food vocabulary

Materials

Audio Tracks 19 to 20

Warm Up

Play *Disappearing Words* with the vocabulary words from Lesson 1 (see TB p. 25).

A TRACK 19 TB p. 215 **Listen and read. What fruit does Mr. Bell have?**

- Project the images from p. 24 or have students look in their books. Ask them what they can see happening and what they think the people are talking about.
- Play the audio and have students follow the dialogue in their books.
- Ask them the gist question *What fruit does Mr. Bell have?* and elicit answers. Play the audio again for students to check. Ask further questions to check comprehension (see **ETB**).

Answers

cherries and pineapples

B **Look at A. Complete.**

- Write or project the table on the board.
- Point to the first example answer in the table. (a lot of) Have students find the sentence in the dialogue. Ask *Who says it?* (Ling)
- Have students work in pairs to look at the dialogue to fill in the blanks and complete the table.
- To check answers, elicit the completed sentences, fill in the table on the board, and have students check or correct their answers in their books.
- Point out that in these sentences we use *a lot of* for positive sentences. and *much* and *many* for negative sentences.
- Have students look at the Grammar tip *Remember* and ask them if you can count cherries. Count with them to check, drawing cherries on the board as you say the words: *one cherry, two cherries, three cherries.* Ask a student to come to the front and draw apples and demonstrate the same thing. Say *Count nouns can be plural.* Then tell the student you want to count spinach. Ask if you can count spinach and try counting while a student tries to draw: *one spinach, two spinaches … no!* Say *There is no plural form for noncount nouns.* Elicit that fruit is also a noncount noun.
- Have students find *much* and *many* in the table. Ask *Do we use count or noncount nouns with "many"?* (count) Repeat the question for *much.* (noncount)

Answers

Count Nouns: many; *a lot of*
Noncount Nouns: much; a lot of

C **Think and discuss. Then choose.**

- Check understanding of the word *quantity* by saying *Quantity means how many there are—if I have two cherries, do I have a large or small quantity?* (small)
- Have students work in pairs to read and discuss the sentences. Tell them to look at the table and at p. 24 to help them. Have students circle the correct options. Then check answers as a class.

Answers

1 large quantities 2 small quantities

D TRACK 20 TB p. 215 **Listen and say.**

- Play the audio and have students tell you how many food items they heard mentioned. (four: cherries, fruit, pineapples, rice)
- Play the audio again, pausing after each question/sentence, and have students listen and repeat.
- For ideas on how to vary the drill, see TB p. 22.

E **Read and complete with *a lot of*, *much*, or *many*.**

- Have a volunteer read the first sentence of the dialogue out loud. Point out the example answer and ask *Is the sentence positive or negative?* (positive) *Is it talking about a large quantity or a small quantity?* (a large quantity)
- Have students continue the activity individually and then compare their answers with a friend.
- To check answers as a class, ask individual students to read aloud a line of the dialogue. Ask if everyone agrees.

Answers

1 *a lot of* 2 many 3 a lot of 4 much 5 a lot of

F **Play a game. Draw your lunch. Then guess.**

- Draw your lunch on the board, including some of the food items in the word box. Draw large quantities of some things and small quantities of others, to encourage students to use the new grammar.
- Say *Guess my lunch!* and encourage students to make guesses, using the food items in the box and the grammar from the lesson. Confirm whether they are right or not.
- Divide the class into pairs and have them play the game, taking turns to draw their lunch and guess their partner's lunch. Tell them that the lunch doesn't have to be realistic.

Cool Down

Play *Pass the Whisper!* (see TB p. 26) with sentences from this lesson.

Practice **Resource Bank:** Grammar Printout; **Student's App:** Grammar Practice

Global Citizenship

Lesson Objectives

- to learn vocabulary of food and containers: *a bag of, a bottle of, a bowl of, a box of, a can of, a carton of, lemonade, potato chips, soup*
- to think about how fruit around the world is different
- to think about the importance of fruit in our diet
- to practice listening for gist and details

Materials

Audio Tracks 21 to 23; (optional) Audio Track B

Opening Question

Ask the opening question: *How is fruit different around the world?* Elicit ideas and encourage students to think about the fruit they eat that doesn't grow in their country, as well as fruit they have in their country that is not found in other countries.

Don't correct or give much feedback. Focus on activating students' prior knowledge and awakening curiosity; students will find out more about the topic during the lesson.

A TRACK 21 TB p. 215 **Listen to Basilio talk to his mom about lunch. What does he have in his lunchbox?**

- Tell students they are going to hear a dialogue about a boy named Basilio and his school lunch. Ask *What fruit can you see in A?* (pineapple, lemon; some students may recognize dragon fruit or point out the orange on the carton of juice)
- Play the audio and have students point to the words or pictures as they listen.
- Ask the gist question *What does he have in his lunchbox?* and elicit answers. Play the audio for students to check.

Answers

salad and rice

B TRACK 22 TB p. 215 **Listen, say, and number the pictures in A.**

- Play the audio and have students listen, point, and repeat.
- Tell students to listen again and this time number the pictures. Point out the example answer (a box of).
- Then check answers.

Answers

1 *a box of* 2 a bag of 3 a bowl of 4 a bottle of 5 a can of 6 a carton of 7 lemonade 8 soup 9 potato chips

International English

Draw students' attention to the two ways of saying *potato chips / crisps*. Drill the pronunciation of both. Then ask *Which do we use?*

TRACK B TB p. 215 **Visualization**

- The TTL has a visualization audio track for this vocabulary set (see TB p. 21).

C Play *What's In It?*

- Write the six containers from the vocabulary list on the board (a bottle of, a can of, etc.) and have students brainstorm some items that can go in each one. Initially, they are likely to say the words in the pictures (e.g. lemonade), but encourage them to go beyond this lesson and think of other items (e.g. apple juice, milk).
- Then ask students to imagine they have each of the six containers in their backpack. Tell them to make a list of what is inside each container.
- Divide the class into pairs and have them take turns to guess what is in each person's backpack. They can guess up to three times for each item. If they guess correctly, they get a point. For example, Student A: *In my backpack, I have a can of …* Student B: *Tomatoes?* Student A: *No.* Student B: *Peas?* Student A: *Yes.* The student with the most points wins.

D TRACK 23 TB p. 215 **Now listen to Vania and Precious. Write the country. Who eats fruit for breakfast?**

- Listening for gist: tell students they are going to listen to two girls—one from Botswana and one from Indonesia—talking about a food from their country.
- Play the audio and have students listen and write the correct country below each name. Check answers as a class.
- Ask the gist question *Who eats fruit for breakfast?* Play the audio again to check.

Answers

a Vania Indonesia b Precious Botswana
Precious eats fruit for breakfast.

E **Listen again. Choose.**

- Listening for detail: play the beginning of the audio again, up to … *green outside and yellow inside.* Read the example sentence and have students notice the circled word.
- Have students look at the other sentences and see if they can remember any answers. Then play to the end of the audio and have students complete the activity individually.
- To check answers, ask volunteers to read the correct sentences. Ask if everyone agrees.

Answers

1 *green* 2 king 3 ice cream 4 green 5 fruit

Discussion Questions

- Draw students' attention to the discussion questions: *Do you have the same fruit in your country? Why is it important to eat fruit?* Have students discuss in pairs or small groups (see **ETB**).
- Return to the opening question to ask again *How is fruit different around the world?* Discuss the differences and similarities students have discovered in this lesson. Are they surprised by anything they have learned?

Cool Down

Play *Running Spelling* (see TB p. 26) with vocabulary from the unit.

Practice **Student's App:** Vocabulary Practice; Listening Comprehension Practice

Explore Language

Lesson Objectives

- to learn and practice using quantifiers in questions
- to practice using food and containers vocabulary

Materials
Audio Tracks 24 and 25

Warm Up

Ask students to tell a friend three things they will have for lunch today (they can guess if they don't know). The other students listen and draw what their friend says.

A TRACK 24 TB p. 215 **Listen and read. What food does Elena have?**

- Have students look at the pictures on p. 28. Ask *Where are they? What are they doing? How are the people feeling?* Ask students if they recognize any of the people. (in pictures 3 and 4, they should notice Ling from Lesson 2; she's with her family)
- Play the audio and have students follow in their books.
- Ask the gist question *What food does Elena have?* and elicit the answer. Play the audio again for students to check. Ask further comprehension questions (see **ETB**).

Answer
sandwiches and apples

B **Look at A. Complete.**

- If you are using the TTL, project the table on the board. If not, write the first example on the board. Point to the example answer (much). Have students find the sentence in the dialogue it comes from.
- Have students work in pairs to complete the table.
- To check answers, ask some students to read a completed question or sentence each and ask if the others agree.
- Ask students if we use *some* for positive or negative statements. (positive) Draw a bowl full of fruit and a bowl with not much fruit on the board. Elicit which shows *some* and which shows *a lot*.
- Have students look at the Grammar tip *Remember* and point out the sentence in the table "We don't have any lunch." Ask *Is this a positive of negative statement?* (negative) *How do we know?* (the word *don't*) *Is there food for lunch or not?* (no)

Answers
much; some; many; any

C **Think and discuss. Then choose.**

- Have students work in pairs to discuss the sentences. Tell them to look at the table and at p. 28 to help them circle the correct options.
- Then check the answers as a class.

Answers
1 how many 2 how much

D TRACK 25 TB p. 215 **Listen and say.**

- Play the audio and have students tell you what words from B they heard. (much, many, any, some)
- Play the audio again and have students listen and repeat.
- For ideas on how to vary the drill, see TB p. 22.

E **Look and complete.**

- Refer students to the example answer and ask why *how much* is used. (It's a question about food, which is a noncount noun.)
- Elicit the answer to number 2 and discuss why it is *some*. (It's a positive statement.) Then have students continue the activity individually.
- To check answers, ask volunteers to read aloud a sentence each. Ask if everyone agrees.
- For number 4, highlight that we can count the quantity of uncountable things such as water or lemonade when they are in a container. (This information will be useful for students in the next activity.)

Answers
1 *How much* 2 some 3 How many 4 How much
5 any

F **Play *That Makes Ten!* Choose how many. Then ask and answer.**

- Tell students they are planning a birthday picnic for ten people and they need to get together a lot of food.
- Refer students to the list of food items. Discuss what sort of container is required for each item (e.g. a can of soup—not a bowl, if they're carrying it to a picnic). Ask *Are the containers count or noncount nouns?* (count)
- Have students work individually to choose a number between 1 and 9 to write next to each food item. Tell them that it should be a secret. Explain that this is the number of, for example, soup cans they have.
- Have two students read the example dialogue. Then tell students to walk around the class, taking turns to ask questions to different students to try to find someone who can make one of their items add up to ten. The first pair of students to make an item add up to ten sits down and raises their hands.

Cool Down

Play *Running Sentences* with some of the sentences from the dialogue (see TB p. 26).

Practice **Resource Bank:** Grammar Printout;
Student's App: Grammar Practice

Talk About It

Lesson Objectives

- to prepare and role-play a conversation about buying food
- to recognize and reproduce /l/ and /r/

Materials
Video; Audio Track 26

Warm Up

Ask *Do you like shopping? What do you like to buy when you go shopping? Where do you go shopping?* Elicit responses and help with vocabulary as necessary.

A TB p. 234 **Watch and listen. What fruit does Rob want?**

- Tell students they will watch a video of a boy and his dad talking about shopping for food.
- Introduce the gist question *What fruit does Rob want?* Play the video to check the answer. Ask further comprehension questions (see **ETB**).

Answer
pineapple

B **Watch again. Check (✔) the phrases you hear.**

- Have students read the phrases and draw attention to the example.
- Play the video again and have students check the other phrases they hear.
- Then check answers.
- Ask students to think about when the phrases are used—to ask a question or to make a suggestion. Ask students to categorize them by writing Q (2, 3, 4, 8) or S (1, 2) next to the relevant phrases. Point out that one of the phrases will fit into both categories.

Answers
1; 2; 3; 4; 8 (5; 6; 7 are not said)

Pronunciation /l/ and /r/

TRACK 26 TB p. 216 **Listen and say.**

- For speakers of some languages, the sounds /l/ and /r/ are very difficult to distinguish. Contextualized practice and a specific focus help students hear and start to pronounce the difference. Do provide correction, but don't expect students to be able to do this perfectly the first time.
- Demonstrate the mouth and tongue position for the /l/ sound as in *let's* and encourage students to copy you. Then demonstrate the /r/ sound as in *Rob*.
- Play the audio for students to repeat the sounds and words. Repeat if students need more practice.
- Say *These words are used in the video. What other words do you know with these sounds?* Have students discuss in pairs, then elicit ideas (e.g. lunch, cherry) and write them on the board in two sections. Drill all the words at the end.

C **Plan. You need to go shopping. Write a list.**

- Tell students that they are going to plan a conversation about shopping like Dad and Rob.
- First, call out the names of some types of food and have students say what container they come in; for example, lemonade (bottle/can), milk (carton), cereal (box), carrots (bag), rice (bag). Then have students complete the shopping list with quantities of the items they wish to buy.
- Invite students to give examples of items and quantities on their list. Encourage them to use one of the phrases from the video; for example, *I need three bottles of lemonade.* Have the others respond with *Me, too!* if they have it on their list.

D **Prepare your conversation. Use your ideas from C and phrases from B.**

- Play the video from A one more time to give students a model.
- Project or write the conversation template on the board and complete it as you demonstrate.
- Ask students for a suggestion to complete the first green bubble; for example, *OK, we need … apples.* Then point to the first pink bubble. Have students choose one of the questions from B that will fit there; for example, *How many apples?* Encourage a confident student to suggest an answer. Continue, eliciting suggestions for the rest of the flow chart.
- Have students work in pairs to write their own the conversation in a notebook using their ideas from C and the phrases from B. Encourage them to use different ways to make suggestions. Monitor and help as needed.

E **Practice with a friend.**

- Have students practice their conversation as many times as they need to. Remind them to use gesture to acknowledge suggestions and to react to things their partner says with facial expressions, as well as words.

Cool Down

Do a pronunciation chant to practice the /l/ and /r/ sounds.

Run, run, run!
Yes, let's, let's, let's!
Let's run, let's run! Go, go, go!

Practice **Student's App:** Speaking Skill Practice; Video

Write About It

Lesson Objectives

- to review the use of capital letters and commas
- to plan and write a description about food in the kitchen

Materials

(Optional) Support, Standard, and Challenge writing printouts from the Resource Bank (one per student) (C, D)

Warm Up

Play a *Chain Game* to engage students' interest in the topic of food (see TB p. 25).

Start the chain by saying *In my kitchen, I have a bottle of lemonade.* Prompt the next student to say *I have a bottle of lemonade and …*

A Read the description. Underline the capital letters and circle the commas(,).

- Have students read the description individually. Tell them to concentrate on these two questions while they read: *Where is the food?* (in the cabinet, on the table) *What do the family members like?* (Dad likes peas, Mom likes mangos) Give them time to read the whole description, then elicit answers.
- Write a series of lowercase and capital letters on the board like this: a A g G J j M m s S Y y. Tell students to say stop when you point to a capital letter. Point to the first letter and then move your finger or pen slowly along the line. Stop when students tell you to and circle the capitals.
- Have students find and underline all the capital letters in the description.
- Write *I have a lot of carrots tomatoes and spinach.* on the board and ask students what's missing. (the commas)
- Have them skim the description and count and circle the commas. Ask how many they found. (there are six) Ask when we use commas. (to separate items in a list)

Answers

Our Kitchen

In the cabinet we have some rice, pasta, and cans of peas. Dad loves peas. We don't have many cupcakes, cookies, and bags of potato chips. On the table there's a bowl of fruit. There are some cherries, apples, and mangos. Mom eats a mango every day. We eat a lot of fruit and vegetables in my family.

B Write the sentences with capital letters and commas.

- Refer students to the prompt sentence and example answer.
- Have students complete the activity individually. While they are doing this, write or project the unpunctuated sentences on the board.
- To check answers, invite students to come to the board and correct the sentences. Elicit why the capital letters are needed in Mom, Dad, and Grandpa. (These are the family members' names.) Ask if everyone agrees.

Answers

1 *We eat fruit, rice, and pasta.*
2 Carlos likes mangos, pasta, and cherries.
3 I eat dinner with Mom, Dad, and Grandpa.
4 She has a lot of soup, rice, and water.

C Plan. Think about your kitchen and your family. Complete.

- Tell students they are going to write their own description, like the one in A. Discuss what a description is. Students may say that descriptions are for telling about things we can see, smell, taste, feel, and hear.
- Ask students to think about food they have and don't have at home. Ask who in their family likes the different food.
- Have students look at the table. Tell students to imagine they are in their kitchen. Tell them to think about what they have, what they don't have, and what foods their family members like.
- Elicit an item and person for each column as an example, and then have students complete their own tables individually. Challenge printouts can be handed out now.

D Draw your kitchen and describe it.

- Have students write their own description of their kitchen, using their plan from C. Support printouts can be handed out now.
- Have students write their final versions neatly on paper or hand out the Standard printouts from the Resource Bank. Allow them time to decorate their descriptions. Display the finished descriptions around the classroom.

Cool Down

Give students time to read and appreciate each other's descriptions. Ask them to say one thing they like about another person's description.

Practice **Student's App:** Writing Practice

Think It Over

Lesson Objectives

- to review what has been learned in the unit
- to reflect on the unit and their progress
- to think about learning strategies and how to continue learning at home

Warm Up

Play the *Yes/No* game with words from this unit (see TB p. 27). Tell students *yes* is if it is a food and *no* is if it isn't.

Suggested items: *chicken* (Y), *bottle* (N), *lemonade* (Y), *melon* (Y), *carton* (N), *can* (N), *eggplant* (Y), *bowl* (N), *spinach* (Y), *market* (N), *durian* (Y)

Read the questions and draw or write your answers.

- Encourage review of the language and reflection on the ideas from the unit to help students make connections to past learning experiences.

What did I do?

- Give students a few minutes to look back through the unit at the activities they did. Ask questions about the unit; for example, *What did you sing about? What activities and actions did you do? What conversation did you have? What did you write? What games did you play?*
- Tell students they can draw or write about activities they liked or found interesting, but encourage them not to choose their favorite activity yet. Instead, encourage them to identify something in the unit that they found challenging but which they completed and feel proud of. Alternatively, ask them to choose something that was particularly memorable for them—either because it was interesting, or it was different, or even because it was noisy! You can use L1 to explain these ideas to students.

What did I learn?

- Brainstorm some ideas on the board about what students remember from the unit—foods, containers, smells, tastes, food they liked and didn't like.
- Ask students what words they can find that they didn't know before. Ask if they can now make questions or answers that they couldn't before. Ask what new facts they learned, especially about fruit from around the world, and if they learned about eating healthily.
- Encourage students to draw a picture or write about what they learned.

What was my favorite part?

- Have students look back through the unit and decide what they enjoyed the most. Tell them it can be an activity they found fun, a story they enjoyed reading, a favorite character, or a favorite food. They should try to choose just one and draw a picture and/or write about it. Explain that when we like something, it is often easier to learn and remember.

How well did I do?

- In this activity, students evaluate their own progress. Tell students to color in the number of cupcakes that best expresses how well they have learned the unit content (i.e., the more they color, the more they feel they have learned). Ask *What do you remember? What do you understand? What do you need to practice more?* Encourage students to look back through the unit to see how much they remember.

What can I do next?

- Brainstorm ideas with the class about what students can do to continue to learn (e.g. watch the video about shopping online again, role-play the dialogues, play the game on p. 25 again).
- Encourage students to think about what they can do at home to improve their English using the verbs in the box as a prompt; for example, watch a TV show or video clips in English, practice talking to family members in English, share ideas about fruits with family members, look online to find out more about fruit from around the world, and so on.
- Ask students to choose one or more activities from the list (watch, practice, share, find out more) that they will do to practice their English.
- Once students have completed the page in their books, have them discuss with a friend what they drew or wrote. Did they choose the same activities or different ones?

Looking Forward

Draw students' attention to the character at the bottom of the page. Ask *Who's this?* and elicit what they remember about her (she is Elena, who shares her lunch in Lesson 4, p. 28). Ask *Where do you think Elena goes with her class?* and elicit suggestions. Tell students they will find out in the next unit.

Put It Together

To further review and recycle the language in Units 1 and 2, play the storytelling game, *Lemonade for Everyone*, on pp. 34–35. See TB p. 206 for teaching notes.

Practice **Resource Bank:** Unit Test; **Student's App:** Vocabulary and Grammar Review

Literacy

Get Ready to Read

Lesson Objectives

- to activate prior knowledge about thankfulness
- to do a Think, Pair, Share VTR
- to preview the reading skill of understanding the setting

Materials
(Optional) VTR printout from the Resource Bank (A, B, C); large piece of paper (WU)

Warm Up

Use this activity to create interest in the topic—thankfulness.

Point out that this unit is called *Thank You*. Have students imagine what the readings will be about. Write their ideas on a large piece of construction paper and display it on the wall.

Think, Pair, Share

A Look at the picture. Why are they holding these things? Think about it.

- Students are going to do a Think, Pair, Share VTR to explore the image of cupped hands holding important things.
- Start by asking students to say what they can see in the picture. Encourage them to use adjectives such as colors and shapes to describe what they see. Provide vocabulary where necessary.
- Students will likely find: a (soccer) ball, a home/house, hands, candy, a video game controller, a picture, grandparents, a shoe, the sun, various colors.
- Students may also notice: lollipops, round gumballs/gobstoppers, windows, people, fingers, buttons (on the video game controller), palms, gold picture frame, rays of light, various items of clothing.
- Then write the question *Why are they holding these things?* on the board. Mime holding something in your hands as you read the question. Give students one or two minutes to think independently about the question so that they form their own ideas. Tell them to place their hands on top of their heads when they are ready.

B Talk with your partner.

- Have students work in pairs to share ideas about why the people are holding these things and to think of possible answers together. Remind students that their ideas will vary and all answers are valid.
- Encourage students to listen to each other's opinions and use phrases such as *Me, too; Really?; I don't think so* and *Yes, I agree.*
- Circulate and encourage students to expand on their ideas by asking *What makes you say that?* They can use L1 for this if necessary.

C Share with the class.

- Bring the class back together and tell them that now they will complete the Share part of Think, Pair, Share. This third step helps students refine their ideas.
- Invite students to share their ideas with the class and encourage them to clarify their thinking. Remind them that they don't have to agree.

Here's an example of this part of the routine:

Teacher: (Student A), what do you and your friend think?
Student A: We think they are special things.
Teacher: How interesting. Why do you say that?
Student A: There's a yellow light.
Teacher: OK. How are they special?
Student A: These are her grandma and grandpa.
Student B: (We think) he likes soccer.
Teacher: OK. What else do you think?
Student B: (We think) these are (their) favorite things.
Teacher: OK, great. (Student C), what do you and your friend think?
Student C: We think they are gifts.

Transition

Ask students *Do you think the people in the picture are saying thank you for these things?* and elicit answers.

D Think and discuss. When do you say "thank you"?

- Ask students to recall all the times they said "thank you" yesterday and raise their hands to give a suggestion. Involve as many students as possible in the discussion.
- Ask students if they can group these occasions into general situations (e.g. when someone gives you something, when someone is kind, when someone helps you). Draw a spidergram on the board to show their ideas.

E Look at the picture. Where do you think it is?

This is a preview of the reading skill of understanding the setting.

- Ask students to look at the picture or project it on the board and have them say what they can see. (a family—mother, father, and daughter—wearing special or traditional clothes, smiling for a picture)
- Then ask *Where in the world do you think this is? Why do you think they are taking a picture? Why are they wearing special clothes?* Elicit the fact that it is probably a special occasion.
- Tell students that in the next lesson they will discover more about these people.

Now read **Chuseok: Korea's Harvest Festival**

Nonfiction: *Chuseok: Korea's Harvest Festival*— An Informational Text

Lesson Objectives

- to read an article about a harvest festival
- to learn about the Korean harvest festival
- to learn through CLIL (social studies): communities
- to make a personal connection to the reading

Materials

Audio Tracks 14 and 15; a world map or globe (First Reading, FR)

Warm Up

Write the word *celebration* on the board. Elicit things that happen at a celebration (e.g. *music, food, dancing, performances, singing*). Write students' ideas on one side of the board and leave them there to refer to during the lesson.

TRACK 14 TB p. 228 Reading Approach

First Reading: Listen and Engage

- Draw students' attention to the title of the reading in their books and ask them what they think it will be about. (Note: the pronunciation of Chuseok is /tʃuːsəʊ/).
- Ask students if they know where Korea is. Have a student find Korea on a map.
- Play the audio once straight through while students follow the text in their books.
- At the end, have students point to the king, a family, food, and dancing. Ask *Are the food, clothes, and dancing the same as in our country?*
- Then look at the Words in Context.

TRACK 15 TB p. 228 Words in Context

- Play the audio and have students repeat the words.
- Have a race to find the words in the reading. Ask *How many times can you find each one?* (weave: three; cloth: one; contest: one; festival: two; harvest: three; ancestors: one)
- Remind students to use pictures to help establish meaning and tell them they can also look for clues in sentences nearby.
- Then bring the class together and use these discussion points to confirm the meaning of each item.

weave Have students find the word (all three instances) and the images of weaving on p. 26. Use mime or draw a picture on the board to show how to weave threads.

cloth Have students find the word and images on p. 26. Ask if they can point to some cloth in the classroom. Ask *What do we make with cloth?* (clothes)

contest Refer students to the sentence on p. 26. Ask *What are they doing? What do we have at the end of a contest?* Encourage students to notice the words *wins* and *prize* in the second paragraph and ask if these help establish the meaning. Say *Contest is another word for a race or match.* Ask students what the race was about in this story. (making cloth) Ask if they have contests at school.

festival Have students find the word and sentence on p. 27. Encourage them to use the whole paragraph to help them establish the meaning. You could highlight words such as *holiday, families,* and *celebrate*. Ask them *Is a festival a happy time?* (yes) *What do people do in festivals?* (eat, dance, celebrate)

harvest Refer students to the picture of the family with the produce. Ask *Where do these things come from?* (They grow them.) Explain that a harvest is the time when you pick the things you have grown.

ancestors Have students find the word and sentence on p. 29. Point out that the word family/families appears twice in this paragraph. Ask *Does this help us understand the meaning?* Ask *Are ancestors part of our family? Our family now or in the past?* (past)

Second Reading: Analyze the Text and Features

- Have students read the whole text again, this time quietly by themselves. Ask them to think about which page they find the most interesting, while they read. Take a class vote.
- Then ask students to look at the blue boxes. Discuss each one as a class.
  - **Making Connections** (p. 27): *Why do people all around the world celebrate the harvest?* Ask students for their ideas. Point out that harvest is still important for everyone, even if we don't all take part as people used to.
  - **Personalization** (p. 29): *Is there a holiday like Chuseok in your country?* Ask students *What traditional holidays or festivals there are in your country? What do people do? When are they? Which is your favorite?*

Third Reading: Interact with the Text

- Listen to the audio again and have students mime all the actions they hear and see in the text.
- Students may enjoy reading the text out loud around the class (a small section each) when they are familiar with it. You can divide the class into two and have one half as readers and the other half as actors, then switch roles.

Cool Down

Return to the celebration-themed words that students brainstormed at the beginning of the lesson. Ask *Which of these happen in Chuseok?* Let them add new words.

Practice **Student's App:** Video

Explore the Reading

Lesson Objectives

- to understand and analyze *Chuseok: Korea's Harvest Festival* through reading comprehension activities
- to learn through CLIL (social studies): communities
- to make a personal connection to the article

Warm Up

Play *Stand Up, Sit Down* with sentences about the Chuseok festival (see TB p. 26).

Suggested sentences: *The beginning of Chuseok was a race to make food.* (False) *People go home for Chuseok.* (True) *They spend time with their friends and teachers.* (False) *They give thanks for the harvest.* (True) *People eat many kinds of food during the festival.* (True) *People wear old clothes.* (False) *Families remember their ancestors.* (True)

A Read and answer. How do people celebrate *Chuseok?*

- Before students open their books, have a Circle Time discussion about the reading (see TB p. 21). Ask some W questions, e.g. *Where is the festival?* (Korea) *Why is there a festival?* (to give thanks for the harvest and remember ancestors) *When does it happen?* (at the end of summer) *How long is Chuseok?* (three days) *Who do people spend time with during Chuseok?* (their families)
- Project the lesson page or copy the question and spidergram on the board. Ask students the question *How do people celebrate Chuseok?* and have them raise their hands to give a few suggestions. Write their answers on the spidergram in note form.
- Have students open their books and read the text again. Then have them raise their hands to give more answers. Add these to the spidergram. Ask which answers involve food, which involve activities, and which involve people.
- Have students choose ideas to write in the spidergram in their books.

Answers

buy new clothes; (the following may vary) dance and play games; have a big feast/meal; make rice cakes; have a special ceremony

B Read and complete. *Chuseok* is about being thankful. What are Korean people thankful for?

- Check the meaning of *thankful* with students: ask *Are we thankful for things we like or things we don't like?* (things we like) *What do we say when we are thankful?* (thank you)
- Have students look back at the reading and share ideas about what Korean people are thankful for with a friend.
- Invite students to raise their hands to suggest answers. Write their ideas on the board.
- Have students complete the sentences in their books.
- Ask students *Why is it important to show we are thankful?* Give some thinking time and then ask for suggestions. Lead students to conclude that people help more if we say thank you, and that knowing that others like what we do makes us feel happy.

Answers

their ancestors/family; the harvest (any order)

C Think and discuss. What holidays or traditions do you have to show thanks?

- Write the beginning of the sentence on the board: *I'm thankful for …* and tell students one or two things you are thankful for; for example, *I'm thankful for my friends. They're always there when I need them. I'm thankful for having a nice home. I can relax in my home.*
- Give students some time to think and then discuss in pairs what they are thankful for.
- Then move on to the social studies objective; communities. Ask students *Do you celebrate any holidays to show thanks with your family? What about with other people in the community?* (you could remind students that they are part of a school community) Ask *What do you do? What food do you eat?* If there isn't a big holiday, ask students to consider smaller ways they show gratitude, e.g. a hug or a thank-you card. Give students time to think and then discuss their ideas in pairs.
- Invite students to share what their family does to give thanks.

Cool Down

Tell students you will say some things you are thankful for. If they are also thankful for the same thing, they have to stand up and move to a different chair in the room and sit down.

To add a competitive edge to the game, the last person to sit down in a new chair has to make the next sentence.

Possible sentences to use: *I am thankful for … my family / chocolate cake / homework / my friends / having food to eat every day / rain / the sun.*

Practice **Student's App:** Reading Comprehension Practice

Get Ready to Read

Lesson Objectives

- to practice the reading skill of understanding the setting
- to activate prior knowledge about harvests

Warm Up

Play *Correct the Teacher* (see TB p. 25) by reading a version of the paragraph on p. 27 of *Chuseok: Korea's Harvest Festival.*

Possible phrases to use: Today, the festival of Chuseok is still an important sport (holiday) in Korea. It is at the end of homework (summer). It lasts 300 (three) days. People always go to the beach (home). They spend time with their phones (families). They want to sleep (celebrate) and give thanks for the internet (harvest).

A Look and complete. How does each place make the character act and feel?

This activity practices the reading skill of understanding the setting and its importance.

- Refer students to the pictures or project and enlarge them on the board. Establish who the girl is (Clara from *The After-School Inventor* in Unit 1) and what she is doing in each picture. (climbing, watching a cartoon on a tablet, and saying goodbye to someone at a station)
- Draw students' attention to the example answer in the first row (scared). Say the full sentence: *Clara feels scared.* Ask students why she feels scared in the first picture. (she thinks she might fall) Ask students if they would feel scared in this situation.
- Ask students to find the verb in the second box that describes what Clara's doing (climbing) and complete the first column of the first row.
- Have students complete the other two rows and compare with a friend. Draw or project the table on the board.
- To check answers, invite students to come and complete a word each in the table. Ask if everyone agrees.
- Have students look at the reading skill box about settings: *The setting is the time and place in the story. One story can have many different settings.* Ask them to think about how the different settings affect Clara's emotions. Discuss as a class. Point out how knowing the setting can help us understand a story better.
- Ask students how they feel in different settings (e.g. at home in bed, just before a race, on the last day of the holidays). Provide a model on the board: (At home in bed), I feel (tired).

Answers

1 climbing; *scared* 2 *laughing*; happy 3 crying; sad

B Look and complete. Compare and contrast the settings.

- Project and enlarge the two pictures on the board or have students look at them in their books. Tell them that these are pictures from the story they will read next. Elicit what they can see.
- Have students look at the Venn diagram and read the instructions. Check that they remember what *compare and contrast* means. Ask *What's the same? What's different?*
- Point out that *vegetables* is in the middle where the shapes overlap because it belongs to both pictures. The other spaces are for words that belong with just one picture. Elicit one word that belongs to each picture and then have students write the remaining words in the correct place in the diagram.
- To check answers, draw or project the diagram on the board and invite students to write a word each. Ask if everyone agrees.

Answers

In the Kitchen: inside; bowls
On the Farm: outside; plants
Both: *vegetables*, family, fruit

C Think and discuss. When is the harvest in your country? What foods are ready? How do people celebrate?

- Ask students to remember and say all the months of the year. Write them on the board. Ask students which months belong to which season and write the seasons next to the months.
- Give students some time to think of their answers to the questions.
- Have students discuss the questions in pairs. Remind them to use phrases such as *Me, too!* and *I don't think so* to create a natural conversation.
- Invite students to share their opinions with the class.
- Ask students if listening to their friends' ideas gave them any new thoughts.
- Ask students if they think harvests are different in different countries and why.

Cool Down

Have students do a visualization (see TB p. 21). Tell students to imagine they are helping with the harvest and to listen and mime:

You're with your family and you're picking vegetables! First, you take the potatoes from the ground—dig, dig, dig! Put the potatoes in a big bag. Now it's time for the apples. Take the apples from the tree—reach up high for the best ones! Put the apples in a basket. Pick up your basket or bag and carry it. It feels heavy. Put it down slowly and rest.

Now read First Harvest

Fiction: *First Harvest—A Science Fiction Story*

Lesson Objectives

- to read and understand a sci-fi story about a family harvest
- to explore the SEL competency of self-awareness by identifying what triggers emotions
- to make a personal connection to the reading

Materials
Audio Tracks 16 and 17; Video

Warm Up

Ask *What do you know about harvests?* Have students do a Rally Robin to answer (see TB p. 20).

TRACK 16 TB p. 228 **Reading Approach**

First Reading: Listen and Engage

- Have students spend a minute looking at the title of the story, the genre, the text, and the pictures. Tell them to look at all six pages. Ask them if they can guess what the story might be about.
- Play the video all the way through. Alternatively, play the audio and have students follow the text in their books. Ask them if their predictions were correct.
- Ask some personalization questions: *Is their life like yours? What's similar or different about it? Does the food look good? Do you wear different clothes to play outside?*
- Look at the Words in Context.

TRACK 17 TB p. 229 **Words in Context**

- Play the audio and have students repeat the words.
- Play the video again and tell students they can **use the actions in the video to help establish the meaning of new words** (see TB p. 23). Pause after each word and have students discuss in pairs. Use these questions to confirm meaning.

  If you don't have access to the video, ask students to use the pictures to establish meaning.

pick Point out Mom in the back of the top picture on p. 32. Ask *What's she doing?* (picking fruit) Reinforce the action using mime and ask students to show you how they pick fruit.

worried Ask students *Why is Dad worried?* (because it's hard for plants to grow) Ask *How do you look when you're worried?* and get students to show you a worried face.

grow Ask students to mime a plant growing. Ask *Why does Dad say it's hard for plants to grow there?* (there isn't much water)

believe Write *I believe* and *I don't believe* on the board. Say *Which means you think something is true?* (I believe) Point out that we often say *I don't believe it* when we are surprised that something is true. Ask *Why does Dad say I don't believe it?* (he is surprised the carrots are beautiful because he didn't think they would grow)

stripes Ask students if they can see stripes anywhere else in the reading (August's sweater has stripes) or in the classroom.

Second Reading: Analyze the Text and Features

- Play the audio and have students follow the text in their books.
- Then discuss the questions in the blue boxes as a class.
  - **Making Connections** (p. 32): *What do you think the setting is?* Ask students for their ideas. Elicit that they are on a different planet and ask how we know this. (the pictures show this and also the children have to wear space suits to go outside) See if anyone can tell you which planet they are on. (Mars—it says so the children's helmets)
  - **Making Connections** (p. 33): *Why is the family so happy about the harvest?* (They were worried that the plants wouldn't grow, but they worked hard and the harvest is good.) Ask students how they think the family feels after their excellent harvest. Explore the SEL competency of identifying what triggers emotions. *What made the family feel happy? If the harvest hadn't gone well, how would they have felt?*
  - **Personalization** (p. 37): A space suit is the clothing astronauts wear in space. Ask students if they think a space suit is comfortable to wear? Would they like to play in one?

Third Reading: Interact with the Text

- Listen to the audio or watch the video again and have students repeat key phrases of dialogue between the family. Ask students how they think each character is feeling and have them say the phrases again, trying to show that emotion.
- Ask students how they think the setting of the story makes the characters feel. (maybe more worried and more emotional—they are millions of miles from their home planet, and it may be dangerous)

Cool Down

Play *I Spy* … on Mars (see TB p. 25). Have students look at the pictures from the story for the clues, e.g. *I spy something beginning with 'p'.* (purple apple, p. 35)

Explore the Reading

Lesson Objectives

- to understand and analyze *First Harvest* through reading comprehension activities
- to explore the SEL competency of self-awareness by identifying what triggers emotions
- to focus on the reading skill of understanding the setting
- to recognize and reproduce the –*st* final blend

Materials

(Optional) Video; Audio Track 18; (optional) pictures of Mars (B)

TB p. 236 **Warm Up**

Play *Who Said It?* (see TB p. 27). Play the video to check answers.

Then play the video again, this time on mute, and have students say the dialogue for a character of their choice at the correct time. Allow them to use their books for this. Remind them to think of the emotions the person is feeling when they are speaking.

A Look and read. Answer the questions.

- Do a quick review of the story by asking questions; for example, *Who are the characters?* (Mom, Dad, Ruth, and August) *Where are they in the story?* (Mars) *What are they doing?* (their first harvest) *Why are they so happy?* (the harvest is successful)
- Focus students on the example and have them find the information in the reading (p. 32 "The family works hard on the farm and also in the images). Ask them what key word they would look for to find the answer to question 1. (grow)
- Have them write full-sentence answers for the other questions and compare with a friend.
- Then check answers with the class.

Answers

1 *They grow it on the farm.*
2 One vegetable the family grows is carrots/peas/tomatoes/corn/potatoes.
3 The story is set on Mars.
4 August and Ruth go outside to play.
5 Mom/She asks the children/them to check their space suits.

B Think, write, and discuss. Why is it hard to grow food on Mars?

- Ask students what they know about Mars. (e.g. dry, rocky, red planet; second-closest planet to Earth after Venus; no life; very cold) You could show some pictures.
- Ask what information they can find from the reading (there isn't much water; there isn't any air). Build a very basic list on the board, with the title Mars.
- Ask what things you need to make plants grow (oxygen, water, good soil, warmth, sunlight). Tell students that farms have insects and animals, many of which also help the plants grow. Build a second list on the board of these suggestions, with the title *Vegetables*.
- Have students look at the two lists and notice how different they are. Ask *Why is it hard to grow food on Mars?* and have the students complete the graphic organizer in B using the ideas on the board.

Suggested Answers

There are a lot of rocks. There isn't much water. It's too cold. There are no insects. There are no animals. Everything has to be inside because there is no air outside.

C Imagine you live on Mars. What's different? How does it make you feel? Draw the setting. Draw yourself.

This activity relates to the reading skill of understanding the setting.

- Ask students for some ideas about what life on Mars must be like and start making a drawing on the board.
- Once you have a detailed picture, say *Imagine you live here. How does it make you feel?* Give students time to think and then elicit adjectives to describe how this makes them feel. They can use L1 if necessary. Encourage them to give reasons for why they think they would feel this way to explore the SEL competency of identifying what triggers emotions.
- Have students draw a picture of themselves on Mars in their notebooks, which can be different from yours.
- Have students show their drawing to a friend and explain the features of the picture. Remind them to refer back to the questions in C as they talk to their partner. Invite them to share and discuss their drawings with the class.

Phonics –*st*

TRACK 18 TB p. 229 **Listen and say.**

- Play the audio and have students listen and look at the words in the phonics box. Ask them what sound all the words have in common. (they have –*st* at the end)
- Play the audio again and have students repeat the words.
- Ask students to choose their favorite word from the list.
- Have students find more words in the reading ending with –*st* and invite them to read them out loud.

Answers

harvest; August; feast; first

Cool Down

Play *Silly Sentence* (see TB p. 26); e.g. *For our first harvest, we're having a feast, and August is eating last!*

Practice **Resource Bank:** Phonics Printout; **Student's App:** Phonics Practice; Reading Comprehension Practice

Think Together

Lesson Objectives

- to compare and contrast between the readings
- to make connections about thankfulness
- to explore the key concept: Why do we celebrate harvests?
- to reflect on the unit and provide personal thoughts and opinions

Warm Up

Ask students to think about the question at the top of the page: *Why do we celebrate harvests?* Write or project this question on the board. Elicit ideas from students based on what they have read and discussed.

A Think and write. Compare and contrast the two harvest stories in this unit.

- Elicit the names of the two readings from the unit. Have students tell each other one thing they remember about each text.
- Give students some time to look at the readings to find as many similarities and differences as they can and make notes in their books.
- While they are doing this, draw or project the table on the board.
- To check answers, invite students to come to the board and write something in the table on whatever side they choose. Ask if everyone agrees. Extend the table if necessary.
- Have students copy additional answers if needed so that their table is full.

Suggested Answers

What's the Same?: *They both have families.* They both celebrate. They both have a feast. They are both happy times.
What's Different?: In space, they don't go home to join their family. In space, it's their first harvest. At Chuseok, they dance and buy clothes. At Chuseok, they remember their ancestors.

B Think and discuss. Imagine you are a farmer. Make a table about your harvest and your celebration. Do a Think, Pair, Share.

Students are going to explore further the key concept by making connections about what they know and what they have learned in the unit with a Think, Pair, Share learning routine (see TB p. 20).

- Ask students to imagine they are farmers who are going to celebrate their harvest. Ask some questions to encourage thinking skills: *What fruit and vegetables do you have? Who picks the fruit and vegetables? Where do you put all the food? Where do you have the celebration? Who is invited? Who cooks the feast?*
- Give students time to think and put together their ideas.
- Have students compare ideas in pairs and categorize them in a table with the headings *Our harvest has …* and *Our celebration has …*
- Ask pairs to share their ideas with the rest of the class.

Practice Resource Bank: Unit Test; Student's App: Key Concept Practice

My Reading Journal

Be the author. Choose *Chuseok: Korea's Harvest Festival* or *First Harvest*. Read the ending again. Write and draw what happens next.

This activity asks students to make predictions based on what they read and learned in the readings.

Ask students to turn to p. 29 in their books, look at the end of the *Chuseok* reading, and elicit a few suggestions of what might happen next. (e.g. washing the dishes after the feast, going back to their homes after the family celebration) Do the same for p. 37 and the end of *First Harvest*. (e.g. the children play outside, Mom makes an apple pie, Dad puts more seeds in the garden)

Have students choose one of the readings and write what they think happens next. Then they draw a picture that illustrates their idea.

Do you like this unit? How many golden apples do you give it? Circle.

This question focuses on personalization.

Give students some time to look back at all the pages of the unit (pp. 24–39) and decide how many golden apples they will give it. Make sure they understand that they are rating the unit, not their progress.

Have students compare their scores with a friend and say what they liked and didn't like about the unit.

Ask students what their favorite part of the unit was.

Answers

Students' own answers

Cool Down

Have students look back at the unit opener picture on pp. 24–25 or project it on the board. Ask if they now have any more ideas about why the people are holding these things. (perhaps the person holding the sun is thankful that it has allowed the fruit and vegetables to grow; perhaps all the items are things that make up a harvest celebration: family, home, games, food)

UNIT 3

It Keeps Changing

Unit Overview

Themes

The natural world

Climate change

Synopsis

In this unit, students will learn how animals can change, explore the effect climate change is having on our world, and find out about clean cars. They will plan and prepare a conversation about animals that change and write a postcard using target vocabulary and grammar from the unit.

Language Book

Vocabulary

beach, desert, forest, glacier, island, lake, mountain, ocean, river, valley, waterfall

p. 80

Explore Language

Simple Past: *Be* Statements

p. 81

Global Citizenship

How do animals change?

bear, chameleon, duck, feathers, fur, penguin, scales, snake, swan

p. 82

Explore Language

Simple Past: *Be* Questions

p. 83

Talk About It

Conversation: showing enthusiasm

p. 84

Write About It

A Postcard

Sentence Building: *and, but*

p. 85

Think It Over

Review and Reflection

p. 86

Literacy Book

Think Together
How can we make good changes in our world?
p. 93

Visible Thinking
VTR: See, Think, Wonder
p. 87

Nonfiction
Informational Text: *Clean Cars*

Words in Context: gasoline, energy, oil, noisy, air, electricity, expensive
p. 91

Fiction
Poem: *The Bear and I*

Words in Context: hole, twice, enemy, thin, trap, melting
p. 88

Reading Skill
Comparing and contrasting information
p. 90

Phonics
–ng
p. 89

Language and Literacy Connections

The connecting theme in Unit 3 is looking at changes in nature.

	Language	Literacy
Vocabulary	**Set 1:** nature **Set 2:** animals	**Fiction:** *bear, fur*
Grammar	**Simple Past: *Be* Statements** They were in the forest. They weren't scared. **Simple Past: *Be* Questions** Where was he yesterday? Were they green?	**Fiction** Its fur was the color of the snow. **Nonfiction** Most cars were gasoline cars.
Skills	**Pronunciation:** /ɑr/ and /ʌ/	**Reading:** comparing and contrasting information **Phonics:** *–ng*
International English		*color/colour, gasoline/petrol*

Vocabulary

Lesson Objectives

- to learn vocabulary of geographical features: *beach, desert, forest, glacier, island, lake, mountain, ocean, river, valley, waterfall*
- to sing a song that highlights important changes in nature

Materials
Audio Tracks 27 to 30; Video

Warm Up

Play the *Alphabet Game* (see TB p. 25) with nature words (e.g. places, animals, plants), to generate interest in the new topic.

A TRACK 27 TB p. 216 **Listen and find. Where's Ivan going?**

- Have students look at the scene and say what they can see happening. Ask *Where are they? What do you think the people are doing? Would you like to be here?* Draw students' attention to the girl with the blonde hair; they should notice that it is Elena from Unit 2.
- Tell students they are going to listen to a guide telling Ivan and Elena about a walk. Play the audio and have students point to the words or pictures as they listen.
- Ask students if their predictions about the picture were correct. Ask *What are the people doing?* (going for a walk)
- Ask students the gist question *Where's Ivan going?* and elicit the answer. Play the audio again for students to check. Ask if they think the guide has a good plan. Ask *Does Ivan agree?* (no, because he wants to go the quick way)
- Look back at p. 33. Say *Can you answer Elena's question?* Listen again to check. (She is on a school trip with her class, on an island.)

Answer
to the café

B TRACK 28 TB p. 216 **Listen, say, and number the pictures in A.**

- Play the audio and have students point to the pictures and say the words.
- Tell students to listen again and write numbers next to each geographical feature. Do the example together (river). Pause the audio after each word to give students time to find the item and write their answers.
- Then check answers as a class.

Answers
1 *river* 2 mountain 3 waterfall 4 valley 5 beach
6 ocean 7 glacier 8 desert 9 lake 10 forest
11 island

C TRACK 29 TB p. 216 **Listen. Close your eyes and visualize.**

- Prepare students for the visualization (see TB p. 21).
- Play the audio, encouraging students to visualize the nature words and do actions where appropriate as they listen. They can say the word after they hear *Say*.
- Have students draw pictures of some of the places they imagined and show their friend.

D **Look and write.**

Students are going to classify the vocabulary into two groups. This encourages critical thinking.

- Check understanding of *land* and *water* using the picture on p. 36–37. Say *Point to something made of water. Point to something not made of water.* Elicit that this is *land*.
- Have students notice the examples in the table, and the number of rows for each category. Have them work individually to classify the other words. While they are doing this, draw or project the table on the board.
- To check answers, invite students to come to the board and write a word each. Ask if everyone agrees.

Answers
Land: *mountain*, desert, island, beach, valley, forest
Water: *river*, ocean, glacier, waterfall, lake

E TRACK 30 TB p. 216 **Listen and sing. Then watch and sing.**

- With books closed, write or project the song title, *It's a Wonderful World*, on the board. Check students understand that *wonderful* means something really good. Ask students what words they expect they will hear and write 10–15 of their suggestions on the board.
- Play the song and have students raise their hands every time they hear an item from their list.
- Have students open their books and give them a minute to look at the lyrics. Play the song again and stop after each line for students to repeat.
- Play the song video and encourage students to sing as they watch. They can move to the music or invent actions or a dance.

Cool Down

Play *Running Spelling* with the new vocabulary (see TB p. 26).

Practice **Student's App:** Vocabulary Practice; Video

Explore Language

Lesson Objectives

- to learn to make statements in the simple past with *be*
- to practice using geographical features vocabulary

Materials

Audio Tracks 31 and 32; sentence cards (F)

Warm Up

Play *Correct the Teacher* with the song ***It's a Wonderful World*** (see TB p. 25). Sing, or say the lines from memory, without the audio or video.

A TRACK 31 TB p. 216 **Listen and read. Where's Ivan?**

- Project the story on the board or have students look in their books. Ask students what they can see happening in the pictures and what they think the people are talking about.
- Play the audio and have students follow the story in their books.
- Ask the gist question *Where's Ivan?* and elicit the answer. Play the audio again for students to check. Then ask further comprehension questions (see **ETB**).

Answer

behind the tree

B **Look at A. Complete.**

- Write or project the table on the board.
- Draw students' attention to the first example in blue (*was*). Ask *What kind of word is it?* (a verb) Have students locate the word in the story. *Ask Who says it?* (Ivan)
- Have students work in pairs to complete the rest of the table and raise their hands when they finish. Put pairs together to check one another's work and show where they found the answers in the story.
- When everyone is finished, elicit the answers, writing the missing words in the table on the board. Have students check or correct their answers in their books.
- Elicit when we use *was* and *were*. (*was* is used for I and he/she/it; *were* is used for you, we, and they) Ask *Which are the positive verbs?* (*was*/*were*) and *Which are the negative verbs?* (*wasn't*/*weren't*)
- Have students look at the Grammar tip *Look*. Point out that *ago* comes after the time phrase and is used with When questions. Ask some questions to have students produce more time phrases using ago; for example, *When was the start of this lesson?* (X minutes ago)

Answers

was; wasn't; were

C **Think and discuss. Then choose.**

- Have students work in pairs to discuss the statement and choose their answers. They can look at the table in B and the story in A to help them.
- Check answers as a class. Reinforce the concept by asking if the story in A is happening now, or before now—in the past. (before now)

Answer

1 past

D TRACK 23 TB p. 216 **Listen and say.**

- Play the audio track and have students tell you how many names of places they hear mentioned. (four: tree, mountain, island, beach)
- Play the audio again, pausing after each sentence, and have students listen and repeat.
- For ideas on how to vary the drill, see TB p. 22.

E **Read and complete.**

- Ask students what type of text they can see in the activity. (it could be a postcard, a letter, or an email)
- Point out the first blank with a smiley emoji and ask *Does this need a positive or a negative verb?* (positive) Then elicit that the sad emoji needs a negative verb. Look at the example answer together and ask why it is *was*. (😊 = positive, and *I* takes *was*)
- Have students continue the activity individually and then compare answers with a friend. Remind them to cross out the answers in the box as they use them.
- To check answers, ask volunteers to read a sentence (or part of a sentence) each. Write the numbered answers on the board so everyone can check.

Answers

1 *was* 2 was 3 wasn't 4 weren't 5 were

F **Play *Pass the Whisper!***

- Set up the class for the game (see TB p. 26).

  Suggested sentences: *The mountains were very big. The beach was very hot. My friends weren't at the beach. The water wasn't very cold. This wasn't a lake millions of years ago.*

Cool Down

Play a memory game to recycle prepositions of place with the new grammar structure. Invite three or four students to come to the front of the classroom and turn to face the board. Quietly have three or four other students move to a different place in the classroom. Have students at the front turn and see the new positions for five seconds and then turn away again. Now ask the moving students to all sit back in their original places and have the students at the front turn back and try to remember where the other students were (e.g. *José was next to Alda! Helena was under the desk!*).

Practice **Resource Bank:** Grammar Printout; **Student's App:** Grammar Practice

Global Citizenship

Lesson Objectives

- to learn vocabulary of animals and their bodies: *bear, chameleon, duck, feathers, fur, penguin, scales, snake, swan*
- to explore how and why animals change and whether change is positive
- to practice listening for gist and details

Materials
Audio Tracks 33 to 35; (optional) Audio Track C

Opening Question

Ask the opening question: *How do animals change?* Elicit ideas and encourage students to think of all the changes that occur in different animals. Guide their ideas by making comparisons with your own hair, skin, and growing from a baby to an adult.

A TRACK 33 TB p. 216 **Listen to Sebastian learn about animals. Who's losing hair and skin right now?**

- Tell students they are going to listen to a conversation between a boy and a woman who looks after animals about how animals change. Play the audio track and have students raise their hands every time they hear the name of an animal (penguins, birds, ducks, chameleons, lizards, snakes).
- Ask the gist question *Who is losing hair and skin right now?* and elicit the answer. Play the audio again for students to check.

Answer
Sebastian

B TRACK 34 TB p. 216 **Listen, say, and number the pictures in A.**

- Play the audio and have students point to the pictures and say the words.
- Play the audio again and have students number the items in the order they hear them.
- Check answers as a class. Encourage students to mime each animal.

Answers
1 *penguin* 2 swan 3 duck 4 bear 5 chameleon
6 snake 7 feathers 8 scales 9 fur

TRACK C TB p. 216 **Visualization**

The TTL has a visualization audio track for this vocabulary set (see TB p. 21).

C Play a game. Choose three animals. Describe and guess.

- Choose an animal and start describing it for students to guess. For example, *This animal is big. It has brown or black fur. It lives in the forest. It walks on four legs, but it can stand on two legs. It can catch fish. It's very scary!* (a bear)
- Encourage students to remember what information you gave and write some prompts on the board; for example, big/small, color, fur/feathers/scales, where it lives, body parts, abilities, adjective.
- Have students choose three animals and think about how to describe them.
- Divide the class into pairs to play the game. Help with vocabulary as necessary, but encourage students to also use the new words as much as possible.

D TRACK 35 TB p. 216 **Now listen to Ingi and Kulop. Write the country. Which animal is now red and blue?**

- Listening for main idea: tell students they are going to listen to two children from Thailand and Iceland talking about animals in their countries. Play the audio and have students write the country under the name of each speaker.
- Ask the gist question *Which animal is now red and blue?* and elicit the answer. Play the audio again for students to check.

Answers
a Iceland b Thailand Picture b, the betta fish

E Listen again. Check (✔).

- Listening for detail: Have students read the sentences before they listen again and see if they can remember any of the answers.
- Play the audio again and have students complete the activity individually.
- Ask students which country they would like to live in and why.

Answers
1 *a glacier* 2 brown 3 to hide 4 fish 5 scales

Discussion Questions

- Draw students' attention to the discussion questions: *Do animals in your country change their skin? Why do animals change?* Have students discuss the questions in pairs or small groups (see **ETB**).
- Return to the opening question to ask again *How do animals change?* Discuss the new information students have learned in this lesson. Are they surprised by anything they have learned?
- Elicit the conclusion that we all change and point out that some changes (such as brain development) are not visible.

Cool Down

Play *Disappearing Sentences* (see TB p. 25) with sentences from the audio track 33.

Suggested sentences: *They have brown fur in the summer. Iceland is cold and white in the winter. Their scales change color from baby to adult. We have some pet fish at home.*

Practice Student's App: Vocabulary Practice; Listening Comprehension Practice

Explore Language

Lesson Objectives

- to learn how to make questions in the simple past with *be*
- to practice asking and answering questions about animals and how they change

Materials
Audio Tracks 36 and 37

Warm Up

Ask students *Do you have a pet? What kind of pet do you have?* Have students call out their pets and make a list on the board. Count to find out the most popular pet. Take a class vote on the most unusual pet.

A TRACK 36 TB p. 217 **Listen and read. Why are the leaves brown now?**

- Ask students what they can see in the picture on p. 42. Ask if they recognize the characters. (Nita is from the story in the forest two lessons ago; Ravi is a new character) Ask *Where are they?* (in someone's house) *What's in the glass box?* (leaves and a branch) *How do you think they feel?* (They look worried.)
- Play the audio and have students follow the dialogue in their books.
- Ask the gist question *Why are the leaves brown now?* and elicit the answer. Play the audio again to check. Then ask further comprehension questions (see **ETB**).

Answer
They're old.

B **Look at A. Complete.**

- Write or project the table on the board.
- Draw students' attention to the example in blue. (was) Have students find the first sentence in the dialogue and elicit who says it. (Nita)
- Have students work in pairs to complete the other questions and answers in the table. Remind them that all the sentences are in the dialogue.
- To check answers, ask students to read aloud a completed question and answer, and ask if the rest of the class agrees. Complete the table on the board and have students check or correct their answers.
- Have students notice the word order of the questions. Elicit that the verb comes before the subject for questions and that the verb comes after *W* words (where, when, what, who, why). Point out the short answers and elicit which is positive and which is negative.
- Have students look at the Grammar tip *Look* and ask students what day it was yesterday. Ask them what the weather was like yesterday and where they were yesterday afternoon.

Practice **Resource Bank:** Grammar Printout; **Student's App:** Grammar Practice

Answers
was; Was; wasn't; Were; were

C **Think and discuss. Then choose.**

- Give students a minute to think about the answer and then have them compare their ideas in pairs. Read the options and have students raise their hands for the answer they chose. Have them circle the correct option.

Answer
1 the past

D TRACK 37 TB p. 217 **Listen and say.**

- Play the audio and have students listen for how many times they hear were/weren't (five) and how many times they hear was/wasn't (five). Tell them to make checkmarks in their notebook as they listen.
- Play the audio, pausing after each sentence for students to repeat.
- For ideas on how to vary the drill, see TB p. 22.

E **Look and complete.**

- Draw students' attention to the picture and the label: *Yesterday at the animal park*. Then have them look at the example answer and ask why *was* is used. (it was yesterday; the penguin/it = singular)
- Have students continue the activity individually. Remind them to look at the picture to help them.
- To check answers, ask pairs of students to read questions and answers aloud. Ask if everyone agrees. Write the answers on the board for everyone to check.

Answers
1 *was* 2 Was; wasn't 3 were 4 Were; weren't
5 Was; was

F **Play a memory game. Close your book. Ask and answer with your friend.**

- Have two students read the blue and green speech bubbles in the example dialogue. Tell students that the questions are about the animals in E.
- Then have students raise their hands to ask you a question about one of the animals; for example, *What color were the ducks?* Say *Were they black?* (no) Encourage students to say if they think you were right or not. Elicit another question and this time get it right.
- Divide the class into pairs and have them close their books. Tell them to continue the game by taking turns to ask a question about the animals while the other person makes a suggestion in response. You could tell them to note down all the suggestions and check in their books at the end to see who had the best memory.

Cool Down

Play *Running Sentences* (see TB p. 26) with sentences from the dialogue.

Talk About It

Lesson Objectives

- to prepare and role-play a conversation about animals at a safari park
- to recognize and reproduce /ɑr/ and /ʌ/

Materials

Video; Audio Track 38; (optional) pictures of animals as babies and adults, e.g. penguin, seal, swan, bear, cat, bird (WU, C)

Warm Up

Stick pictures of animals on different sides of the classroom: animal babies one side and the same animals as adults on the other. Say *Let's go on safari!* Have the students 'visit' the baby animals and describe them.

Later on in the lesson, (e.g. before Act C), say *Let's go on safari again!* and have students "visit" the adult animals. Elicit descriptions and how they're different from before.

A TB p. 234 **Watch and listen. What animals do Gus and Lara love?**

- Tell students they are going to watch a video of some friends visiting a safari park.
- Introduce the gist question *What animals do Gus and Lara love?* Play the video. Then play the video again and ask students if any of the wild animals they listed on the board were mentioned. Ask further comprehension questions (see **ETB**).

Answer

penguins

B **Watch again. Match.**

- Have students read the phrases and draw their attention to the example. Have them follow the line and say what they should hear next. (*Really?*) Play the video to confirm.
- Now play the rest of the video and have students match the phrases. Pause the video to give students time to find the answers and draw lines. Have them raise their hands to tell you when they want you to pause the video.
- Check answers with the class. Elicit that the words on the right are all ways of showing interest. Have students practice saying these words with meaning.

Answers

1 f 2 d 3 b 4 a 5 c 6 e

Pronunciation /ɑr/ and /ʌ/

TRACK 38 TB p. 217 **Listen and say.**

- /ɑr/ and /ʌ/ are very similar sounds and can be difficult to distinguish. Students should be aware that /ʌ/ is a short sound and /ɑr/ is a little longer.
- Demonstrate both sounds and encourage students to copy you.
- Play the audio for students to repeat the sounds and words, first quietly and then gradually louder.
- Say *These are all words used in the video. What other words or names do you know with these sounds?* Have students discuss in pairs, then elicit ideas (e.g. Charlie, duck) and write them on the board in two sections. Have students say where to write each one. Drill all the words at the end.

C **Plan. What animals do you see at the safari park. Complete.**

- Tell the students they are going to have a conversation like Gus and Lara. If you have done the Warm Up with pictures, do the second part now. If not, show pictures and elicit how the animals changed from babies to adults.
- Look at the example in the table. Brainstorm other animals on the board, and discuss if they change from babies to adults. Remind them of the animals from the unit (e.g. pp. 42–43).
- Have students complete the table individually with four animals of their choice.

D **Prepare your conversation. Use your ideas from C and phrases from B.**

- Play the video from A one more time to give students a model. Tell them to follow the prompts in D while they listen.
- Have students work in pairs to complete the conversation in a notebook by choosing two animals from their plan in C and the phrases from B. Elicit some possible statements and answers and encourage students to reply with enthusiasm.

E **Practice with a friend.**

- Have students practice their conversation as many times as they need to. Remind them to be enthusiastic! Tell them they can make changes if any parts don't feel natural.

Cool Down

Write some prompts on the board and have students practice saying them with enthusiastic intonation. Then invite students to choose and say a prompt and the other students to choose and say an appropriate response from the phrases in B. Have students speak all together first and then ask some individuals for their response each time.

Suggested prompts: *I love horses! Look at that tiger! I don't like snakes! I have a pet lizard. Look at the colors of that chameleon! Elephants can swim.*

Practice **Student's App:** Speaking Skill Practice; Video

Write About It

Lesson Objectives

- to focus on the use of *and* and *but*
- to plan and write a postcard

Materials

(Optional) Support, Standard, and Challenge writing printouts from the Resource Bank (one per student) (C, D)

Warm Up

Have students brainstorm the best places they can think of for a vacation—they can be places in their country or in a different country, named places or generic terms like "the beach," or even imaginary vacation destinations like "Mars." Write the places on the board then point at them and have students mime what they would like to do there.

A Read the postcard. Underline *but* and circle *and*.

- Tell students they are going to read a postcard. Ask *When do you write a postcard?* (usually when on vacation) Have students read the postcard quickly. Check comprehension: *Who is it from?* (Ana) *Where was she yesterday?* (at a river near the mountains)
- Have students find *but* and *and* in the postcard and underline and circle them. While they do this, project or write the text on the board.
- Ask how many they found. (there is one *but* and two *ands*) Then check answers by having some volunteers come up to the board and underline or circle the correct words.
- Ask students *How many ideas are there in each sentence?* (two) *Why do we use* and? *Why do we use* but? Have students discuss in pairs, then elicit that we use *and* to connect two similar ideas and *but* to connect two opposite ideas.

Answers

Thursday, June 3

Hi Sofia

I'm having a great time here. Yesterday, we were at a river near the mountains and it was really hot. This postcard shows you the river millions of years ago. The mountains were the same, but the river was different. It wasn't a river then. It was a glacier and it was clean!

See you soon,

Ana

B Join the sentences with *and* or *but*.

- Have students look at the example sentence and ask why it uses *and.* (it connects two parts of the same idea) Elicit the answer to number 2 and ask why it uses *but.* (hot and cold are opposites)
- Have students complete the rest of the activity individually.
- To check answers, ask students to read the complete sentences out loud. Ask if everyone agrees.

Answers

1 *I was at a lake and it was very beautiful.*
2 I was hot but the water was cold.
3 A baby duck is small but an adult duck is big.
4 A polar bear lives in the Arctic and it eats fish.

C Plan. Think about a place. Choose and complete.

- Have students look at the postcard in A. Say *Was the place the same or different millions of years ago?* (different—the river was a glacier) Tell students that they are going to write a plan for a postcard. The postcard is going to describe a place—how it was and how it is now. The place doesn't have to be real.
- Elicit that the box on the left contains places and the box on the right contains adjectives. Tell them that they can think of their own places and adjectives if they prefer.
- Draw or project the plan on the board and have students suggest a place and before-and-after adjectives for each column.
- Have students complete their plans individually in their notebooks by choosing two places and adjectives that describe what the places were like before and what they are like now. Encourage them to be imaginative. Challenge printouts can be handed out now.

D Write your postcard. Draw a picture.

- Have students choose one of the places from their plan and have them write their own postcard in their notebooks, using A as a model and their ideas from C. Remind them to include some detail to make it interesting and to join ideas using *and* or *but*. Support printouts can be handed out now.
- Ask students if they used *and* or *but* in their postcard. If they didn't, ask if they can find a way to include them, by putting similar or different ideas together in the same sentence.
- Have students write their final versions neatly on paper or hand out the Standard printouts from the Resource Bank. Allow them time to decorate their postcards. Display the finished postcards around the classroom.

Cool Down

Have students leave their finished postcards on their desks and circulate around the classroom, enjoying their friends' texts and pictures. Ask students to look for an interesting text, a good picture, or information they didn't know before. Before they leave, ask students to say one thing they liked about a classmate's postcard.

Practice **Student's App:** Writing Practice

Think It Over

Lesson Objectives

- to review what has been learned in the unit
- to reflect on the unit and their progress
- to think about learning strategies and how to continue learning at home

Warm Up

Play the *Yes/No Game* (see TB p. 27) for geographical features and animals/animal features that appear in the unit.

Suggested items: *mountains* (Y), *lake* (Y), *park* (N), *scales* (Y), *fur* (Y), *tiger* (N), *desert* (Y), *waterfall* (Y), *chameleon* (Y), *feathers* (Y), *teeth* (N), *valley* (Y), *kangaroo* (N), *island* (Y), *elephant* (N), *bear* (Y), *ducks* (Y), *penguins* (Y)

Read the questions and draw or write your answers.

- Give students time to think about and discuss activities in the unit before they complete the questions.

What did I do?

- Give students a few minutes to look back through the unit at the different activities they did. Then ask questions about the unit; for example, *What did you sing about? Who was in the stories? What animals did you learn about? What animals did Gus and Lara see at the safari park?*
- Encourage students to identify something in the unit that they found challenging but which they completed and feel proud of. Alternatively, ask them to choose something that was particularly memorable for them—either because it was interesting, or it was different, or even because it was noisy! You can use L1 to explain these ideas to students. Tell them they can draw or write about this activity.

What did I learn?

- Ask questions about the unit; for example, *What words do you know? What new sentences can you say? What do you now know about changes in animals and nature? What did you talk about in your conversation?* Have students discuss ideas in pairs.
- Encourage students to think of one or two things, among all the ideas just mentioned, that they are proud of or that they will remember because it was interesting or useful or unusual.
- Ask students to draw a picture or write about the thing or things they have chosen.

How did I learn?

- Ask students how they learned the nature words in Lesson 1. Elicit ideas. (e.g. by seeing the words next to the pictures, by doing the visualization activity, by hearing the words in a story, by doing a writing or a speaking activity) Then ask about other lessons and the activities they did to help them remember and understand. Ask *What helps you remember …?*
- Encourage students to draw a picture or write about some of the activities that helped them learn.

How well did I do?

- Tell students to color in the number of birds that best expresses how well they have learned the unit content (i.e., the more birds they color, the more they feel they learned). Ask *What do you remember? What do you understand? What do you need to practice more?* Encourage students to look back through the unit to see how much they remember, what they did well, and what they found difficult.

What can I do next?

- Brainstorm ideas with the class about what students can do to continue to learn (e.g. practice talking about how animals change, sing the song again, play the memory game on p. 43 again).
- Encourage students to think about what they can do at home to improve their English, using the verbs in the box as prompts; for example, read the stories with family members, watch the song video on a tablet or phone, sing the song to family members, practice vocabulary and grammar by doing activities on the **Student's App on Navio**.
- Ask students to choose one or more activities from the list (read, watch, sing, practice) that they will do to practice their English.
- Once students have completed the page in their books, have them discuss with a friend what they drew or wrote. Did they choose the same activities or different ones?

Looking Forward

Draw students' attention to the character at the bottom of the page. Ask *Who's this?* and elicit what they remember about him. (Ravi is looking for Charlie in Lesson 4, p. 42) Ask students if they can guess who he might be with at the school fair. Tell them they will find out in the next unit.

Practice **Resource Bank:** Unit Test;
Student's App: Vocabulary and Grammar Review

Get Ready to Read

Lesson Objectives

- to activate prior knowledge about climate change
- to encourage students to observe and interpret through a See, Think, Wonder VTR
- to preview the reading skill of comparing and contrasting information

Materials

(Optional) VTR printout from the Resource Bank (A, B, C)

Warm Up

Play *Versus* (see TB p. 27). Possible questions: *Do you prefer … a hot day or a cold day? / rain or sun? / a river or a forest? / cats or lions? / going by bike or going by car? / noisy places or quiet places?*

See, Think, Wonder

A Look at the picture. What do you see?

Students are going to do a VTR to explore the image of a man at the ocean.

- Ask students *What do you see?* Give them a minute to look at the picture before sharing in small groups or pairs.
- Then bring the class together and have a discussion about what they found.
- Students will likely find: (green) hills/mountains, (pink) water, sea/ocean/river, waves, rocks, a person/man, (blue) sky, grass, clothes (pants, shoes, white sweater), sunny day.

Here's an example of this part of the routine.
Teacher: What do you see?
Student A: (I see) water.
Teacher: Great, what colors do you see?
Student B: (I see) white and gray and pink.

B What do you think?

- Say *I think he's going to get wet. What do you think?* Give them one minute to think about the picture.
- Then have students work in small groups to share their ideas before bringing the class together. Answers will vary depending on students' opinions. Remind students to respect each other's thoughts and opinions.

Here's an example of this part of the routine.
Teacher: What do you think?
Student A: (I think) he's putting something in the water.
Teacher: What makes you say that?
Student A: He's holding a pink bottle.
Teacher: What else do you think?
Student B: (I think) he's painting the ocean.

C What do you wonder?

- Say *I wonder if he's cold. What do you wonder about the picture? What questions do you have?* Give students one minute to think about the picture silently.
- Have students share their ideas in groups or as a class.

Here's an example of this part of the routine.
Teacher: What do you wonder?
Student A: Why is he there?
Teacher: Good question. Why do you think?
Student A: (Because) he's doing an experiment.
Student B: He's an artist!
Teacher: Great. What else do you wonder?

Transition

Draw students' attention to the unit title and the word *changing*. Ask *What changes can you see here? Do you think they are good or bad changes?*

D Think and discuss. What good and bad changes in nature do you know about?

- Have students read the question and give them time to think about their answer. Prompt students to think about seasons, about things growing, and about how people change nature.
- Elicit ideas and write them on the board. Try to include as many students as possible in the discussion.

E Think and discuss. Look at this picture. Compare and contrast this setting to where you live.

This activity previews the reading skill of comparing and contrasting.

- Ask students to say what they can see in the picture and where in the world they think it might be. Ask *What's the same? What's different?*
- Give students some time to think of the differences between the picture and where they live and encourage them to also find some similarities. Have students compare their answers in pairs and then share ideas as a class.
- Ask students if they would like to live in this place and how life is different living in a place like this.
- Tell students that in the next lesson they will discover more about this place.

Now read **The Bear and I**

Fiction: *The Bear and I—A Poem*

Lesson Objectives

- to read a poem about a bear
- to learn about rhyme
- to explore the SEL competency of social awareness through evaluating others' emotional reactions
- to make a personal connection to the reading

Materials

Audio Tracks 19 and 20

Warm Up

Tell students to imagine they are walking in a forest. Have them mime reactions to the animals you say, e.g. *run away, stroke the animal(s), take a picture, scare it/them away* …

Say *Look, a bear! There are some bees. Can you see that snake? There's a horse eating grass.*

TRACK 19 TB p. 229 Reading Approach

First Reading: Listen and Engage

- Give students a minute to look at the title, the genre, the pictures, and the text. Then ask *Who do you think is the I in the title?* Don't give them the answer—tell them that they will discover by reading.
- Play the audio and have students follow in their books.
- After students have listened to the whole poem, ask *How does this story make you feel? Happy, sad, scared?*
- Then look at the Words in Context.

TRACK 20 TB p. 229 Words in Context

- Play the audio and have students repeat the words.
- Ask students to find each of the words in the reading. Note: *hole* and *enemy* are used twice.
- Tell students they can **use the words around the new words to guess their meaning** (see TB p. 23). Have them discuss this in pairs.
- Then use these discussion points to confirm the meaning of each word.

hole Ask *Where is the hole?* (in the ice) *What is it used for?* (to catch fish / for fishing) Have students mime digging a big hole and looking down into it.

twice Read the sentence *The polar bear was twice my size.* Put one hand about a meter from the ground and the other a meter above it. Repeat *twice my size!* Say *So the man is about two meters tall—how tall is the bear?*

enemy Ask *Are the bear and the man friends? Why not? If they aren't friends, what are they?*

thin Say *The ice on the sea was thin.* Draw a thin line and a thick line of ice on the board. Ask *Which is thin? Is the ice thin when it's very cold or when it isn't so cold?* (when it isn't so cold) *Is it safe to walk on thin ice? Why?* (no, it might break)

trap Ask *Was it easy to get out of the trap?* Ask if students can suggest some other types of traps. (people sometimes use traps to catch mice or other animals, police use traps to catch criminals!)

melting Ask *Does the ice melt when it's cold or warm? What other things melt?* (e.g. ice cream or chocolate)

Second Reading: Analyze the Text and Features

- Read the poem chorally together.
- Then discuss the questions in the green boxes as a class.
  - Text Focus (p. 42): *How many* ***stanzas*** *does this poem have?* Ask students what they think a *stanza* is. Confirm it is a group of lines in a poem, usually separated by a line of space. Ask them how many they can count in this poem. (eight)
  - Making Connections (p. 43): *What are the dangers for the man in the poem?* Ask students for their ideas from the reading. (the bear and falling in the sea through thin ice) Have them also think about other dangers that he might face, like getting very cold, falling on the ice, getting lost in a snowstorm, not having enough fish if the bear takes them.
  - Making Connections (p. 44): *Why do you think the ice was a trap?* Elicit what a trap is. Ask *Why does the man call it a trap?* (the ice stops them from getting out of the water)
  - Making Connections (p. 45): *Does the man change his mind about the bear?* This question relates to the SEL competency of evaluating others' emotional reactions. Ask students how the man feels when he first sees the bear (scared), when he sees it again (careful and angry—he says the bear is his enemy), and at the end (he misses the bear and wants to see it again). Ask why he wants to see the bear again. (it's part of his life, and he shares memories with it) Return to the question and ask if the man has changed his mind. (yes, he has)

International English

Highlight the different spellings of *color* and *colour* and show students that the pronunciation is the same. Ask *Which spelling do we use?*

Third Reading: Interact with the Text

- Listen again and have students mime the actions in the poem. Tell them that poetry is dramatic and creative, so they should be dramatic and creative with their actions.

Cool Down

Play *Rhyme It*. Call out one of a pair of rhyming words from the poem and have students find and say the other half of the pair. The pairs are: *snow – ago / there – bear / snow – go / enemy – me / thin – in / sea – enemy / by – I / old – cold.*

Practice Student's App: Video

Explore the Reading

Lesson Objectives

- to understand and analyze *The Bear and I* through reading comprehension activities
- to explore the SEL competency of social awareness through evaluating others' emotional reactions
- to make a personal connection to the reading
- to recognize and reproduce the *–ng* blend

Materials
Audio Track 21

Warm Up

Play *Man, Bear, or Place?* Write *Man* on the left side of the board, *Place* at the top, and *Bear* on the right. Tell students you will say adjectives connected to the characters and the setting of the story and they must decide who or what is being described and point left, right, or up. Sometimes they may point to more than one.

Suggested adjectives: *Snowy* (place), *giant* (bear), *scared* (man—and maybe bear when they are trapped under the ice), *white* (bear—and maybe place), *careful* (man), *hungry* (bear—and man?), *warmer* (place), *dangerous* (bear and place)

A Read and write *True* or *False*.

- Before students open their books, have a Circle Time discussion about the reading (see TB p. 21). Ask *Where is the story?* (a land of wind and cold) *Who is in the story?* (a bear and a man) *Why are they enemies?* (They were both hungry and wanted the fish.) *What happens to them?* (They fall through the ice into the water.) *How does the man feel about the bear then?* (That the bear is not his enemy.)
- Read the first sentence in A and ask students to say why it is false. (they were enemies) Ask them to find something in the poem that says this. (*The bear was my enemy.* p. 43)
- Have students read and decide if the other sentences are true or false and find something in the text to justify their answer.
- Read out the sentences and nominate students to say *True* or *False*. Check everyone agrees and ask students to give reasons for their answers.

Answers
1 *False* 2 True 3 False 4 True 5 False

B Read and answer. Then write the number of the stanza where you can find the answer.

- Look at the example with the class. Ask students to find the line in the poem that says this. (the first line, so stanza 1)
- Have students continue the activity individually and then compare with a partner. Then check answers as a class.

Answers
1 *a land of wind and cold; 1* 2 twice the man's size; 3
3 warm winters; 5 4 the ice broke; 5
5 he will see the bear again; 8

C Think and discuss. Are the man and the bear friends at the end of the poem? Why or why not?

This activity provides an opportunity to explore the SEL competency of evaluating others' emotional reactions.

- Ask students to say all the adjectives to describe the man's reactions to the bear in the different parts of the story and write them on the board. Tell them that these reactions allow us to understand his emotions—to know how he is feeling. In the same way, the man begins to understand how the bear is feeling. Explain that understanding how people feel helps us have a good relationship with them.
- Ask a confident student to read the last stanza of the poem. Ask *Do you think the man and bear are friends at the end of the poem? Why do you think that?* Do a Think, Pair, Share. Encourage students to justify their answers.

Suggested Answer
No, but they aren't enemies anymore. The man understands the bear now, and he hopes the bear is safe.

Phonics *–ng*

TRACK 21 TB p. 229 **Listen and say.**

- Introduce the *–ng* sound by saying *Sing a song*, encouraging students to imitate you. Allow students time to experiment with the sound.
- Play the audio and have students look at the words in the phonics box. Ask them what sound all the words have in common. (they have *–ng* at the end)
- Play the audio again and have students repeat the words. Ask a few individual students to repeat each word.
- Ask students to choose their favorite word from the list and to tell a friend.
- Have students find more words in the poem ending with *–ng* and invite students to read them out loud.
- Have students close their books. Play the audio of the poem once more. Have them raise their hands when they hear a word with *–ng* at the end and then repeat it.

Answers
young; fishing; morning; (things); changing; melting; getting; living

Cool Down

Play *Disappearing Words* (see TB p. 25) with the words from the poem.

Practice **Resource Bank:** Phonics Printout;
Student's App: Phonics Practice; Reading Comprehension Practice

Get Ready to Read

Lesson Objectives

- to practice the reading skill of comparing and contrasting information
- to activate prior knowledge about cars and how we use them

Materials

Audio Track 19

TRACK 19 TB p. 229 Warm Up

Play the audio of *The Bear and I* again and have students act out the story as it plays. You can choose if you want them all to be the man or if some should be the bear.

A Read and check (✔) the answers. Compare and contrast the bear and the man from the poem.

This lesson practices the reading skill of comparing and contrasting information.

- Refer students to the pictures and the example sentence. Ask *Does the bear eat fish?* (yes) *Does the man eat fish?* (yes) Point out the checks on each side.
- Have students continue the activity individually.
- To check answers, read the phrases and have students raise their left hand if they checked the bear, their right hand if they checked the man, and both hands if they checked both. Look for clarification in the text if students seem unsure about any of the answers.
- Refer students to the reading skills box under the pictures. Read it to them and then ask *Compare or contrast? The bear and the man both live in the arctic.* (compare) *The bear is big, but the man is small.* (contrast) Have students find one more thing from the list in A that is comparing (e.g. eats fish, falls in the water) and one more that is contrasting (e.g.. the man lives in a house, but the bear doesn't).

Answers

Bear and man: eats fish, lives in the arctic, is hungry, falls in the water

Bear only: is big and scary

Man only: lives in a house

B Look and read. Circle the things that are the same. Draw a line under things that are different. Compare with a partner.

- Focus students on the pictures of the cars. Ask *Are they the same or different?* Students are likely to say different. Say *Are you sure? Is there anything that's the same?* Draw two columns on the board, with the headings *Compare* and *Contrast.* Elicit ideas and write them in the correct column.
- Have students read the sentences to find things which are the same and different. Do an example with the class. Then have students continue the activity individually.
- Check answers as a class.

Answers

1 It's red and has (four wheels).
It's big, noisy, and (fast).
2 This car is small, (fast), and quiet.
It's white and has (four wheels).

C Think, write and discuss. What do we use cars for?

- Ask students to remember the last three or four times they were in a car and where they were going. Elicit some answers.
- Now give students some time to think of their answers to the question *What do we use cars for?* Encourage students not only to think of the everyday uses but also to think beyond this to less-frequent uses (e.g. *to travel to school/work, to get groceries, to go on a day trip, to go on vacation, to move things long distances*). Have them discuss their ideas in pairs and then as a class.
- Write their ideas on the board in a spidergram. Ask students if listening to their friends' ideas helped them think of new ideas, too.
- If there are still areas to explore, ask some questions to draw out more information: *What can we put in cars?* (luggage, shopping, friends) *What can we put behind cars?* (a trailer, a caravan, a broken-down car, bikes) *Can we have fun with cars?*
- Have students choose their five favorite answers from the class spidergram and write them in their books.

Cool Down

Do a visualization (see TB p. 21). Tell students to imagine they are going on a car journey and to follow your instructions. If you have space, they could do actions.

Suggested instructions: *Walk to the car, open the door, and get in. Fasten your seat belt! Now the car is moving—you're turning right and now left and now right and now left. The car stops! There's an animal in the road! Take a picture! What is it? Now the car starts again and you're going down and now up and now down and now up! Finally you arrive. Take off your seat belt and open the door. Get out of the car and close the door. Look around. Where are you?*

Now read **Clean Cars**

Nonfiction: *Clean Cars—An Informational Text*

Lesson Objectives

- to read a text about cars and the environment
- to learn through CLIL (science): exploring the environmental impact of different types of cars
- to make a personal connection to the reading

Materials

Audio Tracks 22 and 23; Video

Warm Up

Play *I Spy* (see TB p. 25) using the picture on pp. 48–49 to generate interest in the text.

TRACK 22 TB p. 229 **Reading Approach**

First Reading: Listen and Engage

- Play the video on mute and ask students what they think the text is about. Ask *Is it a story or real information?* (real information)
- Play it again with sound and ask them if their predictions were correct.
- Ask what words they heard e.g. cars, school, vacation, TV, lamp. This will help build their confidence noticing that they understood a lot of the text.
- Then look at the Words in Context.

TRACK 23 TB p. 229 **Words in Context**

- Play the audio and have students repeat the words.
- Have them race to find the words in the reading and how many times each word appears. (*gasoline*: six; *energy*: three; *oil*: one; *noisy*: two; *air*: four; *electricity*: one; *expensive*: three)
- Tell students that they can **use these multiple contexts to establish the meaning of the new words.** They can discuss the words with a partner, using L1 if necessary.
- Then use these discussion points to confirm the meaning of each word.

gasoline Say *A lot of cars use gasoline.* Ask students if they can see gasoline being put in a car in the pictures. (yes, into a truck at the bottom left of p. 49) Ask if their family car runs on gasoline.

International English

Elicit *gasoline* is American English and *petrol* is British English. Drill pronunciation of both. Ask students if they remember hearing either before. Ask *Which one do we use?*

energy Ask what energy does. (makes things work and move) Ask them where the cars' energy comes from. (fuel like gasoline or electricity)

oil Point out that the diagram on p. 49 is about oil. Ask students *What does oil look like?* Tell students that this oil was made over millions of years from tiny animals and plants that were buried underground.

noisy Say *Imagine you are in the street in the picture on p. 48. What can you hear? Is it nice? Is it noisy or quiet?* Ask students what other places are noisy. (airports, train stations, factories, school playgrounds!)

electricity Looking at the picture of the car that runs on electricity (on p. 51), say *This car uses electricity for energy.* Ask students *What's in the yellow tube?* (Point out that it isn't gasoline.) *Is there electricity in this classroom? Where? What do you have that works with electricity?*

expensive Read the last paragraph with students and point out that solar cars have a lot of positives—fast, not noisy, not dirty—so what's the negative? If they struggle, draw a lot of dollar (or other currency) signs on the board to indicate the cost of the car.

Second Reading: Analyze the Text and Features

- Play the audio and have students follow in their books.
- Then discuss the questions in the green boxes as a class.
  - **Gist** (p. 48): *What are good and bad things about cars?* Good: we use them to go to a lot of places. Bad: the reading says that cars make the air dirty and can be noisy, but students may also mention that cars can crash.
  - **Making Connections** (p. 49): *What does your body use for energy?* Ask students to remind you what different things the cars use for energy (gasoline, biofuel, air, electricity, and the sun). Ask them to tell you what they need for energy (food).
  - **Fun Fact** (p. 51): *Electric cars aren't new. The first car to go 100 km. per hour was an electric car in 1899.* Ask students to calculate how many years ago that was.
  - **Personalization** (p. 53): *Do you like cars? Why or why not?* Ask students to raise their hands first if they like cars and then if they do not. Have students talk to a friend about what they like or don't like about cars and then ask for suggestions. Ask each time if the others agree.

Third Reading: Interact with the Text

- Tell students they will provide a voice-over for the video. Put them in groups of five and assign each group member a different car to talk about in their own words.
- Play the video again and encourage students to think of some ideas.
- Then play the video with the sound muted and have students describe the cars they were assigned.

Cool Down

Do a Chalk Talk routine (see TB p. 20) with the five different types of cars, to see how much they can remember.

Explore the Reading

Lesson Objectives

- to understand and analyze *Clean Cars* through reading comprehension activities
- to learn through CLIL (science): exploring the environmental impact of different types of cars
- to practice the reading skill of comparing and contrasting information
- to make a personal connection to the reading

Materials
(Optional) Video

TB p. 236 Warm Up

Play the *Yes/No Game* (see TB p. 27) using sentences from the reading. Play the video to check answers.

Possible sentences: *We use cars a lot.* (yes) *Gasoline comes from oil in the air.* (no) *Some cars use air for energy.* (yes) *Dirty air is good for animals and people.* (no) *Biofuel makes the air very dirty.* (no)

A Look and read. Find words in the reading and label the cars.

- Before beginning the activity, recap other aspects of the reading by asking some questions: *What different cars are there?* (gasoline, biofuel, electric, air, and solar) *Why is dirty air bad?* (It changes the climate, and it's bad for animals, plants, and people.) *Why are electric cars better than gasoline cars?* (They are fast and quiet, and they don't make the air dirty.) *Where does biofuel come from?* (Plants like corn.)
- Have students read the instructions for the activity. Decide the word for the first car as a whole class. Tell students to look back at the reading to make sure they are spelling the word correctly. Then have students continue the activity individually.
- Check answers. Ask if everyone agrees.

Answers
1 solar 2 electric 3 biofuel 4 gasoline

B Read and complete the table using these words. Use some words more than once.

- Ask students what they remember about gasoline cars. Have them look back at p. 49 to help. Ask students what is good about gasoline cars (they're fast) and point out the word *fast* in the table. Ask them what words can go in the *Bad things* column and elicit the best answers from the options in the box.
- Have students continue the activity individually. Point out they can repeat words as often as they want, and write more than one thing for each car in each column but all the words must be used at least once.
- If you are using the TTL, project the table on the board. To check answers, invite students to come and fill in one cell each. Ask if everyone agrees.

Answers
gasoline; *fast*; noisy, dirty
biofuel: fast; noisy, dirty
electric: clean, fast, quiet; expensive
air: quiet, clean; slow, small
solar: quiet, clean; expensive

C What's the main idea of the article? Read and check (✔).

- Read the three phrases and have students say if they are true or false. (all true)
- Give students some time to look back at the text and decide what is the most important idea or the main idea of the article.
- Read the phrases again and have students raise their hands to vote for the one they think is the main idea.
- Ask for reasons why students chose the phrase they did.

Answer
2 (Possible reasons: all of the pages talk about this topic; the conclusion sentence is about this topic; the article talks about this more than the other two options)

D Think and discuss. Which clean car is your favorite? Why?

- This activity allows students to think about the environmental impact of different types of cars (CLIL science objective). Elicit the different types of clean cars from the class (biofuel, electric, air, and solar) and write them on the board with a circle around each.
- Give students time to look back at the text and also at the summary of the good and bad points in the table in B. Have them decide which is their favorite and to think about why.
- Have students discuss their answer in pairs. Remind them to follow the model and make a sentence with *because*.
- Ask some volunteers to tell the class which car they chose and why.
- Then take a class vote. Point out that there isn't one correct answer and all opinions are valid.

Cool Down

Pass a ball around the class and have the student holding the ball say one thing they would like to know about any of the cars. Make a list of all the questions students have and challenge them to find answers to some of them for homework.

Practice **Student's App:** Reading Comprehension Practice

Think Together

Lesson Objectives

- to make connections between the readings
- to explore the key concept: How can we make good changes in our world?
- to reflect on the unit and provide personal thoughts and opinions

Materials
large pieces of paper (one per group) and colored pens/pencils (A)

Warm Up

Ask students to think about the key concept question at the top of this lesson's page: *How can we make good changes in our world?* Write or project this question on the board. Elicit ideas from students based on what they have read and discussed in this unit. Remind students that there are no incorrect answers.

A Think and write. What problems does climate change make for people and animals?

- Have students look at the diagram in their books or project it on the board. Elicit an example for the *people* cloud and write it in the diagram (e.g. *dirty air*).
- Divide the class into an even number of small groups (it has to be an even number because they will join together later to swap ideas).
- Give each group a large piece of paper and some colored pens or pencils. Tell half of the groups to write *People* in the middle of the paper, and the other half to write *Animals*. Each group then brainstorms as many ideas as they can in a spidergram around their word. Tell them to look back at both readings and the image on the opening page for ideas. They can also use their own existing knowledge and include related issues, such as health problems and bad harvest, that are not mentioned in the readings. Monitor and help with vocabulary where necessary.
- When they have had time to complete their spidergrams, have two groups (with different categories) come together to tell each other what they wrote.
- When students have all had a chance to learn about both categories, put their spidergrams on the wall where they can still see them. Each student should choose their favorite three points from each poster and write them in their books.

Suggested Answers
People: dirty air, poor harvest, no food, dirty water, no water, they get sick, they die
Animals: no food, dirty water, their homes are destroyed (e.g. ice for the polar bears), it is too hot/cold/dry/wet for them, they get sick, they die

Practice Resource Bank: Unit Test; Student's App: Key Concept Practice

My Reading Journal

Now I know some new things about: polar bears; life in the Arctic; clean cars; climate change.

This question encourages students to identify things that they have learned.

Ask students to remember the important things, places, and ideas in each reading of this unit. They can look back at the readings to do this.

Have students think about the topics listed, consider if they learned something new about them, and circle *yes* or *no*. Ask them to think about exactly *what* they learned.

Call out each topic and ask students to raise their hands if they feel they learned something new about it. Ask some volunteers what they learned. You can also tell students what you learned.

How does this unit make you feel? Write and draw how you feel.

This question focuses on personalization.

Ask students how what they learned in the unit makes them feel. Start by eliciting some possible adjectives from students and add in extra ones in questions: *Do you feel happy? Scared? Positive? Worried? Calm? Interested? Bored?!*

Give an example and write it on the board; for example, *I feel interested, because I can learn more about how to keep our world clean.* Give students a minute to think about their feelings.

Have students write a sentence about how they feel and why. They can then draw a picture of themselves or of their favorite part of the unit.

Circulate and help by providing vocabulary as necessary.

Ask if any students would like to share their ideas with the class.

Answers
Students' own answers

Cool Down

Have students look back at the See, Think, Wonder picture on pp. 40–41. Ask them if they now have any more ideas about what the picture shows. Ask students if they think this situation will cause problems for the climate or for animals.

UNIT 4

What Happened?

Unit Overview

Themes

Important days in your life

World historical events

Synopsis

In this unit, students will learn about key historical events, look at how events can impact on our lives, and think about significant events in our own lives. They will plan and prepare a presentation about an important day and write an event description using target vocabulary and grammar from the unit.

Language Book

Vocabulary
bake, carry, clap, compete, dance, drop, start, study, trip
p. 96

Explore Language
Simple Past: Regular Verb Statements
p. 97

Global Citizenship
What is special about a first day at school?
bounce, finish, learn, move, pack, play, practice, smile, travel, wait
p. 98

Explore Language
Simple Past: Regular Verb Questions
p. 99

Take the Stage
Presentation: describing an important event
p. 100

Write About It
A Description of an Event
Spelling: regular verb endings
p. 101

Think It Over
Review and Reflection
p. 102

Literacy Book

Think Together
How do events change our lives?
p. 109

Visible Thinking
VTR: Think, Pair, Share
p. 103

Fiction
Story: *The Angry Mountain*
Words in Context: thunder, bark, ash, dream, sunrise
p. 107

Nonfiction
Informational Text: *Where Is She?*
Words in Context: plan, steal, lift, robbery, arrested
p. 104

Reading Skill
Identifying cause and effect
p. 106

Phonics
–nd
p. 108

Language and Literacy Connections

The connecting theme in Unit 4 is important events in the past.

	Language	Literacy
Vocabulary	**Sets 1 and 2:** action verbs	**Nonfiction:** *bounce, carry, move, pack, play, start* **Fiction:** *learn, wait*
Grammar	**Simple Past: Regular Verb Statements** We baked twenty-five cupcakes. She didn't carry any cakes. **Simple Past: Regular Verb Questions** Did Anna pack her backpack?	**Nonfiction** Peruggia waited for the guard to leave. He walked out the door. **Fiction** I played on the beach. I needed to find Mama and Papa.
Skills	**Pronunciation:** /d/ and /t/ or /ɪd/	**Reading:** identifying cause and effect **Phonics:** *–nd*
International English	*practice/practise*	*lined up / queued*

Vocabulary

Lesson Objectives

- to learn action verbs: *bake, carry, clap, compete, dance, drop, start, study, trip*
- to sing a song that highlights how every problem has a solution

Materials
Audio Tracks 39 to 42; Video

Warm Up

Tell students that in this unit they are going to learn some new action verbs. To activate their interest in the topic, play a game of *Simon Says* (see TB p. 26) with action verbs students already know; for example, *run, jump, climb, swim, play basketball, play video games, cook, eat,* and *sleep*.

A TRACK 39 TB p. 217 **Listen and find. Who wins the Spelling Bee?**

- Have students look at the scene and discuss with a partner what they can see. Ask *Where are they? What do you think they are doing?* Then explain that the students on the stage are not singing but taking part in a Spelling Bee—a competition to see who can spell the most words correctly.
- Draw students' attention to the boy in the yellow T-shirt in the bottom left corner and establish that he is Ravi from Unit 3.
- Play the audio and have students point to the words or pictures as they listen.
- Ask the gist question *Who wins the Spelling Bee?* and elicit answers. Play the audio again for students to check. Ask why they think Chen won. (because he studied)
- Look back at p. 47. Say *Can you answer Ravi's question?* Listen again to check. (He is with Alfred and Chen.)

Answer
Chen

B TRACK 40 TB p. 217 **Listen, say, and number the pictures in A.**

- Play the audio and have students point to the pictures and say the words.
- Play the audio again, this time pausing after each word if necessary for students to find it in the picture and write the number in the box.
- To check answers, have a volunteer name one of the actions and nominate another student to say the number. Repeat for all the words.

Answers
1 *dance* 2 clap 3 compete 4 bake 5 carry
6 trip 7 drop 8 start 9 study

C TRACK 41 TB p. 217 **Listen. Close your eyes and visualize.**

- Prepare students for the visualization (see TB p. 21).
- Play the audio, encouraging students to visualize the verbs and do actions where appropriate as they listen. They can say the word after they hear the word *say*.

D **Look and write.**

This activity practices visual discrimination and critical thinking.

- Draw students' attention to the sets of spaces and tell them that each of the new words fit into one of these shapes. Show students how the example *trip* fits into the first set of spaces—including the ups and downs of the letter stalks. Point out that, for example, *dance* doesn't fit—each shape works for only one word.
- Have students complete the activity individually. Suggest that they put a mark next to each word once they have used it so that they know which words they still have to use. While they are doing this, project the page or draw the other shapes on the board.
- Invite students to come to the board and write one word each. Ask if everyone agrees. Have all students say the words again and do an action for each word.

Answers
1 *trip* 2 carry 3 study 4 drop 5 start
6 compete 7 clap 8 bake 9 dance

E TRACK 42 TB p. 217 **Listen and sing. Then watch and sing.**

- Have students close their books. Tell them they are going to listen to a new song called *It's OK*. Say *Can you guess what the song is about?* and elicit suggestions.
- Play the song through once and have students raise their hands every time they hear one of the new verbs.
- Have students open their books. Play the audio again, this time stopping after each line for students to repeat.
- Play the song video and encourage students to sing and move to the music.

Cool Down

Play *Mime It!* with action verbs (see TB p. 26).

Practice **Student's App:** Vocabulary Practice; Video

Explore Language

Lesson Objectives

- to learn and practice using simple past regular verbs (positive/negative)
- to provide contextualized practice of vocabulary of action verbs

Materials

Audio Tracks 43 to 44

Warm Up

Brainstorm all the different competitions the students have taken part in. Ask *Do you like competitions? Why/Why not?* Then ask which new competitions they would like to try.

A TRACK 43 TB p. 217 **Listen and read. Who was lucky?**

- Ask students what they can see happening in the pictures on p. 50. Point to the boy and elicit that it's Alfred, who featured in the previous lesson.
- Play the audio and have students follow the dialogue in their books.
- Ask the gist question *Who was lucky?* and elicit the answer. Play the audio again for students to check. Ask *Why was he lucky?* (because some cupcakes didn't drop on the floor)

Answer

Alfred

B **Look at A. Complete.**

- Write or project the table on the board.
- Highlight the first sentence, which contains the example answer (baked). Have students look back at the dialogue in A to find where that sentence appears. Ask *Who says it?* (Alfred)
- Have students work individually to complete the table and raise their hands when they finish. Remind them that all the sentences appear in A.
- Ask students if the sentences are about the present or the past. (past) Ask which are positive verbs (on the left) and which are negative (on the right). Ask what differences they notice between the positive and negative verb forms. (past positive verbs end in *–ed* and past negative verbs have *didn't* + base verb form)
- Point out the double *p* in *dropped* and the negative *didn't drop*. Ask students if they can find another simple past verb in the story with a double *p*. (tripped) Elicit the negative. (didn't trip)

  Note: the spelling rules are covered in more detail in the Writing lesson.
- Have students look at the Grammar tip *Remember* and ask them if they know or can guess the reason why the *y* changes to an *i* in *carried* but not in *played*. (there is a consonant in *carry* but not in *play*)

Answers

baked; carried; dropped; didn't drop

C **Think and discuss. Then choose.**

- Have students work in pairs to read and discuss the sentence. Tell them they can look at the table and at p. 50 to help them circle the correct option. Then check the answer as a class.

Answer

1 –ed

D TRACK 44 TB p. 217 **Listen and say.**

- Play the audio and have students tell you what past verbs they hear. (baked, carried, didn't dance, didn't study)
- Play it again, pausing after each sentence for students to repeat.
- For ideas on how to vary the drill, see TB p. 22.

E **Read and complete in simple past.**

- Ask students to look quickly at the text and say what it is about. (it's an account of Alfred and the baking competition)
- Look at the example answer together and ask why it is the answer. (positive past = add *–ed* but in this case just add *d* because the e is already there)
- Have students continue the activity individually and then compare answers with a friend.
- To check answers, ask five volunteers to read a sentence each. Ask if everyone agrees. Write the verbs on the board so everyone can check.

Answers

1 *competed* 2 didn't bake 3 baked 4 carried
5 didn't carry 6 dropped

F **Play a chain game. Then write.**

- Ask two students to read the example dialogue. Point out that the second student remembers what the first student said and adds another activity.
- Tell students they will now play the same game and add an activity of their own. Ask a student at one side of the room to start and have the others remember what went before and add their own activities. If they are having difficulty remembering, the other students can help!
- If you have a large class, divide the class into groups of seven or eight to play the game—this reduces the memory load, the length of the game, and the time they have to wait to play!

Cool Down

Play *Pass the Whisper!* (see TB p. 26) with sentences from this lesson (see A, E, and F).

Practice **Resource Bank:** Grammar Printout; **Student's App:** Grammar Practice

Global Citizenship

Lesson Objectives

- to learn more action verbs: *bounce, finish, learn, move, pack, play, practice, smile, travel, wait*
- to explore why the first day at school is important
- to practice listening for gist and details

Materials
Audio Tracks 45 to 47; (optional) Audio Track D

Opening Question

Ask the opening question: *What is special about a first day at school?* Check students understand *special* means something that is important, different, and really good. Elicit ideas about the people, places, activities, and feelings associated with this event.

A TRACK 45 TB p. 217 **Listen to Kadir talk to his brother about his first day at school. When does Kadir start school?**

- Tell students they are going to listen to Kadir talk to his brother about his first day at school. Ask students what they can see in the pictures and how they think the children in the pictures are feeling.
- Play the audio and have students point to the words or pictures as they listen.
- Ask the gist question *When does Kadir start school?* and elicit the answer. Check the answer by listening again.

Answer
in September

B TRACK 46 TB p. 218 **Listen, say, and number the pictures in A.**

- Play the audio and have students listen, point to the pictures, and say the words.
- Play the audio again and have students write the numbers next to the words in the pictures. Listen to the example together (travel). If necessary, pause the audio after each verb to give students time to write their answers.
- Check answers as a class.

Answers
1 *travel* 2 pack 3 practice 4 learn 5 bounce
6 play 7 wait 8 smile 9 finish 10 move

International English

Ask students to notice the difference between the verbs *practice* and *practise*. Model the pronunciation, highlighting that it is exactly the same for both words, it is just the spelling of the verb that is different. In British English, *practice* is the noun.

TRACK D TB p. 218 **Visualization**

- The TTL has a visualization audio track for this vocabulary set (see TB p. 21).

C Play a game. Choose five actions. Mime and guess.

- Choose one of the new verbs (e.g. *bounce*) and mime bouncing a ball. Have students raise their hands when they know what verb it is you are miming.
- Have students choose five of the new verbs and decide how to mime them. They can do more than one action.
- Divide the class into pairs and have students take turns miming the verbs and guessing.

D TRACK 47 TB p. 218 **Now listen to Hiroko and Wati. Write the country. Who starts school in July?**

- Listening for main idea: tell students they are going to listen to two girls from Indonesia and Japan talking about school.
- Play the audio and have students write the country below each name. Check answers.
- Ask the gist question *Who starts school in July?* and elicit the answer. Play the audio again to check.

Answers
a Hiroko Japan b Wati Indonesia
Wati starts school in July.

E Listen again. Choose the correct name.

- Listening for detail: give students time to read the sentences before they listen again and see if they can remember any of the answers. Tell students that the answers will not appear in this order.
- Play the rest of the audio and have students complete the activity individually then check as a class.

Answers
1 *Hiroko* 2 Wati 3 Hiroko 4 Hiroko 5 Wati

Discussion Questions

- Draw students' attention to the discussion questions: *Was your first day at school the same or different? Did it feel special? Why?*
- Do a Think, Pair, Share. Give students some time to remember their first day at school and think about their answers. Have students discuss the questions in pairs or small groups (see **ETB**).
- Elicit the conclusion that the first day of school is a new phase in their lives. Everyone has a first day at school but everyone's experience can be different. We can all help to make a first day special. There will be other "first days" as they get older.
- Return to the opening question to ask again *What is special about a first day at school?*

Cool Down

Play *Running Spelling* (see TB p. 26) with the new vocabulary.

Practice **Student's App:** Vocabulary Practice; Listening Comprehension Practice

Explore Language

Lesson Objectives

- to learn how to make questions in the simple past with regular verbs
- to practice using action verbs in the past

Materials
Audio Tracks 48 and 49

Warm Up

Ask students to think of situations where they might need to pack a backpack, e.g. for school, to go on vacation, to move house. Take a class vote to see how many people have moved house. Ask *How did you feel before you moved? How did you feel after?*

A TRACK 48 TB p. 218 **Listen and read. Where do Anna's friends live?**

- Ask students what they can see in the pictures on p. 54. Ask *What are they doing?* (packing boxes into a truck—they're moving)
- Play the audio and have students follow the story in their books.
- Ask the gist question *Where do Anna's friends live?* and elicit the answer. Play the audio again for students to check. Ask further comprehension questions (see **ETB**).

Answer
Here! (near their new home)

B **Look at A. Complete.**

- Write or project the table on the board.
- Point out the example answer (didn't), then ask students to find that sentence in the story (picture 2).
- Have students work in pairs to fill in the blanks and complete the table. Check answers as a class.
- Elicit the main verb in each question, and highlight *did* as the auxiliary. Point out the word order: *did* + subject + verb. Then draw attention to the short answers that can be used after *Did* questions.
- Have students look at the Grammar tip *Watch Out*. Point out that *did* indicates the past in questions. The other verb (in green) doesn't change. *Did* does all the work!

Answers
Did; did ; ride; *didn't*; didn't

C **Think and discuss. Then choose.**

- Have students work in pairs to read and discuss the sentence. Tell them they can look at the table and at p. 54 to help them circle the correct option.
- Then check the answer as a class. Elicit that we use *do* in the simple present.

Answer
1 did

D TRACK 49 TB p. 218 **Listen and say.**

- Play the audio and have students count how many times they hear *did* (six) and *didn't* (two). Tell them to make a mark in their notebook each time.
- Play the audio again and have students listen and repeat.
- For ideas on how to vary the drill, see TB p. 22.

E **Put the words in order. Then answer for you.**

- Refer students to the example question and have them identify the subject and main verb. Ask some students the question until you get both answers—*Yes, I did* and *No, I didn't.* Point out that they should write the answer that is true for them each time.
- Have students continue the activity individually. Remind them to refer back to the table in B for help.
- Then have students work in pairs to ask and answer.
- To check answers, ask pairs of students to read a question and answer aloud.

Answers
1 *Did you ride your bike yesterday? Yes, I did*
2 Did you study in your bedroom? (Yes, I did. / No, I didn't.)
3 Did your mom bake a cake last week? (Yes, she did. / No, she didn't.)
4 Did your friends practice basketball yesterday? (Yes, they did. / No, they didn't.)

F **Guess about your friends. Then ask and answer.**

- Tell students they are going to guess what three friends did yesterday. Have two students read the examples on the page. Help them make the connection between the sentences on the piece of paper (the guesses) and the text in the speech bubbles.
- Then write two example guesses on the board:
  Yesterday (student 1's name) watched TV.
  Yesterday (student 2's name) didn't climb a tree.
- Elicit how you build the questions: *Did you watch TV yesterday? Did you climb a tree yesterday?* When the students answer, put a check or a cross next to the sentences to show whether or not your guess was correct.
- Elicit some more action verbs and write them on the board. Give students three minutes to write three or more guesses about things their friends might have done yesterday, using the verbs as a prompt.
- Then ask everyone to stand up and walk around the room to ask their friends and check their guesses.

Cool Down

Play *Pass the Whisper!* (see TB p. 26) with simple past yes/no questions, e.g. *Did you go to the park last weekend?* Have the last student in the line answer the question.

Practice **Resource Bank:** Grammar Printout; **Student's App:** Grammar Practice

Take the Stage

Lesson Objectives

- to prepare and give a presentation about an event or experience
- to recognize and reproduce the simple past regular verb endings /d/ and /t/ or /ɪd/

Materials
Video; Audio Track 50

Warm Up

Ask *Where do you usually go on vacation? What do you usually do?* Elicit responses and help with vocabulary where necessary. You could create a bar chart on the board to find out which activities are the most popular or the least common.

A TB p. 234 **Watch and listen. Where did Gus go?**

- Tell students they will watch a video of a boy talking about a vacation.
- Introduce the gist question *Where did Gus go?* and elicit suggestions. Play the video to find out and ask if any of the places they thought of were mentioned. Ask further comprehension questions (see **ETB**).

Answer
France

B Watch again. Check (✔) the phrases you hear.

- Have students read the phrases and draw their attention to the example.
- Play the video again, pausing for students to check the phrases they hear. Two phrases are not said (6 and 7). Check answers as a class.
- Have students analyze the phrases, categorizing them as follows: beginning, Gus introduces the talk (1, 2); and middle, Gus talks about his vacation (3, 4, 5). Ask students if they can remember what Gus says to end his presentation. ("Thank you for listening.") Play the video again to check if necessary.

Answers
1; 2; 3; 4; 5

Pronunciation /d/ and /t/ or /ɪd/

TRACK 50 TB p. 218 **Listen and say.**

- Demonstrate the **/d/** sound as in *traveled*, the **/t/** sound as in *practiced*, and the **/ɪd/** sound as in *started* and encourage students to copy you.
- Play the audio and have students repeat each verb.
- Highlight *started*, *visited*, and *wanted* and ask students if they can see why the *–ed* ending is pronounced **/ɪd/**. (If the verb ends in a **/t/** sound, the *–ed* is pronounced **/ɪd/**. This is also true for verbs that end in a **/d/** sound, like *end—ended*.)
- Write three columns on the board titled **/d/**, **/t/**, *and* **/ɪd/**. Ask *What other past verbs do you know from this unit that end with these sounds?* Elicit suggestions and write them on the board under the appropriate heading (e.g. *learned*, *dropped*, *waited*). Drill all the words at the end.

C Plan. Think about an important event in your life. Choose (✔) and complete.

- Say *In the video, Gus talked about an event that was important to him. Now you're going to plan a presentation about an important event in your life.* Ask students to look at the options and think about which one of these events they could talk about. Have them check their favorite.
- Draw students' attention to the box below and have them use the prompts to write notes about their important event. Remind students that for this section they don't have to write in complete sentences. Help with vocabulary as necessary.

D Prepare your presentation. Use your ideas from C and the phrases from B.

- Play the video from A one more time to give students a model.
- Have students use the plan they made in C and phrases from B to complete their notes. Remind them to look at how they classified the phrases in B into beginning and middle, and what to say at the end of a presentation.

E Practice with a friend. Then share with your class.

- Have students practice their presentation with a friend as many times as they need to. Tell them to try and use their notes less as they practice more. Remind them to look at the audience and speak slowly and clearly. Encourage them to pause after each phrase. This is an opportunity for them to look up and smile.
- Invite volunteers to come to the front of the classroom to give their presentation. Have the audience give a round of applause after each presentation.

Cool Down

Invite students to say one thing they liked about the presentations they listened to.

Practice **Student's App:** Speaking Skill Practice; Video

Write About It

Lesson Objectives

- to focus on the spelling of simple past regular verbs
- to write a description of an event

Materials

(Optional) Support, Standard, and Challenge writing printouts from the Resource Bank (one per student) (C, D)

Warm Up

Play *Board Race* (see TB p. 25) with the theme *sports*.

A Read the event description. Circle the regular verb endings.

- Read the description to students while they follow in their books. Ask *What was the event?* (a race) *What bad thing happened?* (She tripped.) *What good thing happened?* (Her friend stopped to help.) Ask *Do you have a good friend like this?*
- Have students find the first regular verb in the text (happened), which is already circled. Write it on the board and underline the *–ed*. Then have them find all the other verbs ending in *–ed* and ask how many they have. (there are seven including *happened*)
- Read the description again and have students say *stop* each time you say a regular *–ed* verb. Have them repeat the verb.

Answers

Last week something awesome happened! I was in a race at school. I started at the front of the race, but I tripped. My friend was next to me. She stopped and helped me. She was really kind. We didn't finish first, but we finished the race together. I learned that she's a really good friend!

B Look at A and the regular verbs in the box. Complete.

- Write or project the table on the board. Highlight the main verbs in the box and the headings in yellow at the top of the table. Explain these are the letters at the end of regular simple past verbs.
- Explain that for most regular verbs we can add *–ed* to the main verb to form the simple past. (point out *happened* in column 2) Ask students if they can tell you why *competed* is in the first column. (*compete* ends with e, so we only need to add d) Look at the third column and point out the double consonant + ed in *tripped*. Ask *Can you see another verb in A with a double consonant + ed?* (stopped) Have students write it in the table. Underline the last three letters in trip and stop and explain the rule (when short verbs end in a consonant, vowel, and consonant, we add another consonant + ed). Finally, elicit why *carried* is in the last column. (the *y* in *carry* gets changed to *–ied*)
- Have students complete the activity individually using A as a guide, and then compare with a friend.
- Write the answers into the table on the board for students to check their spelling.

Answers

\+ *d*: *competed*, bounced
\+ *ed*: *happened*, learned
\+ consonant + *ed*: *tripped*, stopped
y + *ied*: *carried*, studied

C Plan. Think about something you learned from an event. Choose and complete.

- Tell students they are going to write an event description. Ask what information they can include.
- Brainstorm an example on the board; for example, *What happened? Something good. Where? At school. When? In a show. Who were you with? My teacher. Actions: was nervous, counted, read a poem. I learned that: counting helps you feel calm.* Point out that everything they need to describe the event is there but not in full sentences yet—these are notes.
- Have students remember a time when they learned something. It can be something simple at home or something with more people in a different place. Have them complete the notes. Circulate and help with vocabulary as necessary. Challenge printouts can be handed out now.
- When students have finished, have each student compare their plan with a friend. Encourage them to give feedback to their friend about the story.

D Write your event description.

- Have students write a description of their important event in a notebook, using their notes from C. Remind students that they can use the same order as their notes. Support printouts can be handed out now.
- Have students write a clean, corrected version on a piece of paper or hand out the Standard printouts from the Resource Bank. Allow students time to decorate their descriptions and display them around the classroom.

Cool Down

Enjoy each other's work: have students circulate around the classroom, reading their friends' descriptions (and pictures). Ask students to look for an interesting text, an event similar to theirs, or something important to learn. Before they leave, have them say one thing they liked about another student's work.

Practice Student's App: Writing Practice

Think It Over

Lesson Objectives

- to review what has been learned in the unit
- to reflect on the unit and their progress
- to think about learning strategies and how to continue learning at home

Warm Up

Play *Mime It!* with the verbs from pp. 48–49 and 52 (see TB p. 26).

Read the questions and draw or write your answers.

- Explain to students that they can choose to either write a few words or sentences or draw a picture.

What did I do?

- Give students a few minutes to look back through the unit at the different activities they did. Ask questions about the unit; for example, *What did you sing about? What activities and actions did you do? What did you talk about? What stories did you read or listen to?*
- Tell students they can draw or write about activities they found interesting, but encourage them not to choose their favorite activity yet. Instead, encourage them to identify something in the unit that they found challenging but which they completed and feel proud of. Alternatively, ask them to choose something that was particularly memorable for them—either because it was interesting, or it was different, or even because it was noisy! You can use L1 to explain these ideas to students.

What did I learn?

- Ask questions about the unit; for example, *What new words do you know now? Can you make new questions or answers? What new things did you learn about other countries and people?* Have students discuss ideas in pairs.
- Encourage students to draw a picture or write sentences about what they learned.

What was my favorite part?

- Have students look back through the unit and decide what they enjoyed the most. Tell them it can be an activity they found fun, a story they enjoyed reading, a favorite character, or a favorite action. They should try to choose just one and draw a picture and/or write about it. Explain that when we like something, it is often easier to learn.

How well did I do?

- Tell students to color in the number of children that best expresses how well they have learned the unit content (i.e., the more they color, the more they feel they have learned). Ask *What do you remember? What do you understand? What do you need to practice more?* Encourage students to look back at the text to see how much they remember.

What can I do next?

- Brainstorm ideas with the class about what students can do to continue to learn (e.g. play the game on p. 55 again to guess what friends did last weekend, sing the song again).
- Encourage students to think about what they can do at home to improve their English, using the four verbs as prompts; for example, share what they have learned with family members, play the games on p. 51 and p. 53 with family members, talk to family members in English, find out more about their parents' first days at school, and so on.
- Ask students to choose one or more activities from the list (share, play, talk, find out more) that they will do to practice their English.
- Once students have completed the page in their books, have them discuss with a friend what they drew or wrote. Did they choose the same activities or different ones?

Looking Forward

Draw students' attention to the character at the bottom of the page. Ask *Who's this?* and elicit what they remember about her (Anna is the girl who was moving to a new house in Lesson 4, p. 54). Ask students to guess what she might see at the museum. Then tell them they will have to wait and find out in the next unit.

Put It Together

To further review and recycle the language in Units 3 and 4, play the game, *Explore The Island*, on pp. 60–61. See TB p. 207 for teaching notes.

Practice **Resource Bank:** Unit Test;
Student's App: Vocabulary and Grammar Review

Get Ready to Read

Lesson Objectives

- to activate prior knowledge about world historical events
- to encourage students to observe and interpret through a Think, Pair, Share VTR
- to preview the reading skill of identifying cause and effect

Materials

(Optional) VTR printout from the Resource Bank (A, B, C); (optional) picture of the Statue of Liberty in New York; pictures of statues or monuments in your country (C)

Warm Up

Play *Stop!* to generate interest in the topic of the lesson. Nominate one student to say the alphabet under their breath. Another student says *Stop!* and the first student says the letter they were on. In groups, students try to think of a famous person (first or last name) and a famous place (monument, city, country) starting with the chosen letter. The first group to finish says *Stop!* and the students compare answers. Start again with a new letter.

Think, Pair, Share

A Look at the picture. Why is it in the park? Where is it now? Think about it.

Students are going to do a Think, Pair, Share routine to explore the picture of the head of the Statue of Liberty in a park in Paris in 1883. Don't give students this information until after they've done the routine.

- Start by asking students to say what they can see.
- Students will likely find: a monument, a statue, a crown, trees, a building, the sky, a face, hair, a tunic, a plaque, writing, triangles, the colors black and white.
- Then write the questions *Why is it in the park? Where is it now?* on the board. Give students one or two minutes to think about the questions so that they form their own ideas.

B Talk with your partner.

- Have students work in pairs to share ideas. Remind them that their ideas will vary and all answers are valid.
- Circulate and encourage students to expand on their ideas by asking *What makes you say that?* They can use L1 if necessary.

C Share with the class.

- Bring the class back together and tell them that now they will complete the Share part of Think, Pair, Share. This third step helps students refine their ideas.
- Invite students to share their ideas with the class and encourage them to clarify their thinking. Elicit, if not already mentioned, that there's a similar statue in New York, USA. You could show a picture of the Statue of Liberty so they can compare and contrast the two.

Here's an example of this part of the routine.

Teacher: (Student A), what do you and your friend think?
Student A: (We think it's in the park because) the person is important.
Teacher: How interesting. Why do you say that?
Student A: There's a sign and she's wearing a crown.
Teacher: OK. (Student B), what do you and your friend think? Why is it in the park?
Student B: (We think) it's a gift.
Teacher: OK. What else do you think?
Student C: (We think) it's from America.
Teacher: OK, great. Why do you think that?
Student C: It's like the Statue of Liberty.
Teacher: Great. Where do you think it is now?
Student D: Maybe it's in a museum (because) it's old!

Transition

Have students begin to think about the importance of learning about historical events. Ask students if there are any statues or monuments of people in their town or country. Find out if they know who they are and why there is a statue of them. Ask *Do they live now or are they from history?* You could show some pictures of statues and monuments and tell students something about them.

D Think and discuss. What famous events in history do you know?

- Start with the famous events in students' own country's history, which they will probably know best. Give students some time to think and then ask for suggestions.
- Ask if any students know about famous events in world history or in other countries. Ask if they know where or when the first modern Olympic Games were (1896, Greece), when the first man walked on the moon (1969), when the first airplane flight was (1903), or when the first man climbed Mount Everest (1953).

E Think and discuss. Look at the museum at the beginning and end of the story. What changes can you see?

This is a preview of the reading skill of identifying cause and effect.

- Have students look at the pictures of the museum at the bottom of p. 57. If you can, use the TTL to enlarge each picture on the board. Ask what students can see in the first picture.
- Now have them compare and contrast with the second picture (saying what is the same and what is different). Elicit ideas for why there is extra protection and the crowds of people in the second picture, but don't reveal the story.

Now read **Where Is She?**

Nonfiction: *Where Is She?*—An Informational Text

Lesson Objectives

- to read an informational text about a famous event
- to learn about world history: exploring the history of the *Mona Lisa* and understanding how the past can impact the world today
- to learn through CLIL (history): understanding how journalism helps us to capture famous events
- to make a personal connection to the reading

Materials

Audio Tracks 24 and 25; Video; (optional) pictures of famous paintings (Second Reading)

Warm Up

Play *Simon Says* (see TB p. 26) with famous events from history, e.g. *Simon says … you're walking on the moon / … you're climbing Mount Everest* and so on.

TRACK 24 TB p. 229 Reading Approach

First Reading: Listen and Engage

- Have students look quickly at pp. 58–63 and predict what they will read about today. (a story of someone who stole a painting) Tell students to look at the title, the pictures, the text, and the genre. Ask *Do you think the story is set now or in the past?* (in the past) *Where is the setting?* (a museum)
- Play the video or the audio and have students follow in their books. Ask them if their predictions were correct.
- Ask *Is this an invented story or a real story?* (real) *Does the story have a happy ending?* (yes) Point to the title in the book and ask who "she" is. (*Mona Lisa*—the name of the painting and the person in the painting)
- Then look at the Words in Context.

TRACK 25 TB p. 229 Words in Context

- Play the audio and have students repeat the words.
- Have them race to find the words in the text.
- Remind students to **look for clues in sentences near the new word.** Students can discuss the words with a partner, using L1 if necessary.
- Then use these discussion points to confirm the meaning of each item.

plan Ask students to look at the sentence *plan* is in and the next paragraph. Ask *What was his plan? Do you have a plan for after school today? Do you have a plan for the weekend?*

steal Remind students of Peruggia's plan—ask students if they can see him doing it in the pictures. Look shocked. Ask *Is it OK to steal things?* and elicit that stealing is bad.

lifted Ask students to imagine Peruggia taking the painting. Say *How did he take it from the wall?* Ask students to mime the action. Then invite a student to lift up his/her book.

robbery Refer students to the sentence on p. 61. Ask *What did the people read about? Is this word a person or an action?*

arrested Refer students to the sentence and the picture on p. 62. Ask *What's happening? Where is the policeman taking Peruggia?* Clarify that if you arrest someone, you take them to the police station because they have done something bad.

Second Reading: Analyze the Text and Features

- Play the audio and have students follow the text in their books.
- When students have read in the whole text, discuss the questions in the red boxes.
  - **Making Connections** (p. 59): *Why is the* Mona Lisa *famous?* This question asks students to consider how past events in world history can impact the world today. One obvious answer is that it's an excellent painting by a famous artist. Encourage them to also find the answer given in the reading—that it only became very famous after it was stolen. Both answers are correct.
  - **Personalization** (p. 63): *What other famous paintings do you know?* Ask students if they can remember any other famous paintings they have seen and what's in them. You could project some paintings on the board and ask them if they know or like them.

International English

Elicit that *lined up* is American English and *queued* (**/kjuːd/**) is British English. Drill the pronunciation of both. Ask *Where did the people line up or queue in the reading?* (in front of the wall where the *Mona Lisa* was) *When did you line up or queue recently? Which one do we use?*

Third Reading: Interact with the Text

- Have students read the text silently.
- Ask some discussion questions to encourage students to think critically about why the story happened: *Why do you think Peruggia wanted to steal the painting? Why did people line up to see the empty space on the wall? Why didn't the other man want to buy the painting?*
- Ask them if they have any *Why* questions about the reading. Answer them if you can, or encourage students to research the answer.

Cool Down

Play *Who Said It?* with phrases from the story (see TB p. 27).

Practice **Student's App:** Video

Explore the Reading

Lesson Objectives

- to understand and analyze *Where Is She?* through reading comprehension activities
- to learn through CLIL (history): understanding how journalism allows us to capture famous events
- to make a personal connection to the reading

Materials
Video; Audio Track 24; colored pens or crayons (C)

TRACK 24 TB p. 229 **Warm Up**
Play the video or audio of *Where Is She?* again and have students mime the story.

A Read and choose the answer.

- Before students open their books, ask some quick-fire questions: *Where did the robbery happen?* (the Louvre Museum / Paris, France) *What did the man steal?* (the painting named the *Mona Lisa*) *When did he do it?* (in 1911) *How did the police catch him?* (He tried to sell it.)
- Have students open their books and look at A. Ask two students to read the example question and answer in number 1 and ask the class to find the part of the story that shows this. (p. 58, last sentence)
- Have students read and decide the answer for the other questions and find something in the reading to justify their answer. Tell them to look for key words in the story rather than rereading the whole story.
- To check answers, read the questions and answer options out in the style of a quiz master and have students call out their answers. Check everyone agrees and invite students to show where in the text they found the answer.

Answers
1 b 2 b 3 c 4 a 5 b

B Think and discuss. Do you think someone can steal a painting from a museum today? Why or why not?

- Ask students to recall how Peruggia stole the painting from the museum. (he dressed like a museum worker, put the painting under his clothes, took it out of the frame, and walked out the door) Ask *Is this possible today?*
- Give students time to think. Then ask them to compare ideas with a friend. Remind them that there is no correct or incorrect answer to this question—the important thing is to try to explain *why* they think what they do.
- Ask students if they have seen any movies about people who try to steal things from museums. Ask *What ways are there to stop them now? In the movie, do they stop the thief? Do you think they would have stopped Peruggia?*

C Imagine you work at a newspaper. The *Mona Lisa* is missing. Draw the museum worker's face when the painting is missing and when it is found.

- Ask students to imagine they are journalists working at a newspaper. Tell them they are going to interview the museum worker who discovered the painting was missing. Ask students how they think the museum worker feels. They should draw his expression in the *Missing* box.
- Now tell students they are going to interview the museum worker after the painting is found. Ask students to imagine how he feels now. They should draw his expression in the *Found* box.
- Give students time to think of three questions they would like to ask the museum worker for a newspaper article about the *Mona Lisa* (either lost or found). Then have them imagine they are the museum worker and write the answers they think he would give. Have students pass their questions to a friend to answer, so that no one answers their own questions. This allows students explore the history objective of understanding how journalism helps us to capture famous events.

Cool Down

Do a visualization activity. Tell students to imagine they are helping to catch the man who stole a painting from your museum. They must stand up and follow your instructions with actions and emotions, like this:

You're a worker at the museum. You look at the wall—the painting is gone! Oh, no! You look around, but you can't see anyone. You go downstairs and look out the door—there is a man running away. You run after him! You think he has the painting! The painting is very special—you run even faster. You catch the man, and he gives you the painting. The museum gives you a special prize to say thank you. You feel great!

Practice **Student's App:** Reading Comprehension Practice

Get Ready to Read

Lesson Objectives

- to practice the reading skill of understanding cause and effect
- to explore the SEL competency of self-awareness through labeling and recognizing emotions
- to activate prior knowledge about storms and how they make people feel

Warm Up

Play *Which Story?* Have students reflect on some stories they have read recently. Write *Clara* on the left side of the board, *Bear* on the right, and *First Harvest* at the top. Ask students if they remember the stories they read about these characters or events (*The After-School Inventor*, p. 10; *First Harvest*, p. 32; *The Bear and I*, p. 42). Tell them you will say sentences about the stories—they have to decide which story each sentence is about and point left, right, or up to indicate.

Suggested sentences: *She's an inventor.* (C) *They live on Mars.* (FH) *It happens in the Arctic.* (B) *They are enemies.* (B) *There is an alarm clock pillow.* (C) *They have pink potatoes.* (FH) *There isn't much water.* (FH) *There is a lot of ice.* (B) *The bedroom is a mess.* (C)

A Look at the pictures. Match what happened and why.

This lesson practices the reading skill of identifying cause and effect.

- Have students look at the pictures. Enlarge them if you're using the TTL. Ask students what they can see. Check they remember the girl in picture 1 (Clara Doodle, the after-school inventor). Ask if they can find a sentence about her on the right (b).
- Have students suggest how the other pictures should be matched.
- Direct students to the reading skill box and have them read the sentences about cause and effect. Ask *What comes first, cause or effect?* (cause first, effect after)
- Then ask *What's the cause with Clara?* (Her bedroom is a mess.) *And what's the effect?* (She invented a clean-up machine.) Have students identify the causes and effects of the other two pictures and sentences.

Answers

1 b 2 a 3 c

B Look at these pictures. Write *Cause* or *Effect*.

- Tell students that the two pictures are from the story they will read in the next lesson. Ask what they can see in each picture. Encourage students to compare and contrast the pictures, noticing the colors in the sky and on the ground. Again, you could enlarge them if you are using the TTL.
- Ask students to say which picture is first and is the cause, 1 or 2, and which picture is second and is the effect. (the cause is the volcano erupting; the effect is the island covered in ash) Allow students to use L1 for this discussion.
- Have students write *Cause* and *Effect* under the correct pictures.

Answers

1 Effect 2 Cause

C Think and draw. Are you scared sometimes? What makes you scared? Draw the cause and the effect.

- Give an example of what makes you scared (e.g. talking to a big group of people). Draw a picture on the board of you about to do the scary thing (e.g. standing in front of a group of people), and then draw another picture of your face looking scared. Ask students which is the cause and which is the effect.
- Have students think of something that makes them scared and draw the situation (cause) and how they feel (effect).

Cool Down

Play a mime game to combine the SEL competency of this unit (identifying emotions) and the reading skill of identifying cause and effect. Tell students that you are going to say some causes—some situations—and they have to decide what the effect is and mime how they feel.

Suggested situations: *You just ate a very, very big chocolate ice cream. You are spending the day with your grandparents. Your parents tell you that you are going on vacation. You hear that your favorite TV show is ending. You are moving to a new town. But the new house is big and beautiful. And your best friend also lives in the new town.*

Now read **The Angry Mountain**

Fiction: *The Angry Mountain—A Story*

Lesson Objectives

- to read a story about a scary event
- to explore the SEL competency of self-awareness through labeling and recognizing emotions
- to make a personal connection to the reading

Materials

Audio Tracks 26 and 27

Warm Up

Play *Stand Up, Sit Down* (see TB p. 26). Students stand up if the sentence is true for them.

Possible sentences: *I'm not scared of … spiders / crossing the road / volcanoes / tall buildings / tigers / monsters /* and so on.

TRACK 26 TB p. 229 Reading Approach

First Reading: Listen and Engage

- Organize students for Circle Time (see TB p. 21) and read them the story. Use a lot of gesture and movement as you read, point to things as you mention them, and use dramatic intonation to highlight important words and plot points.
- When you have read the whole story, have students find and point to Mount Tambora, the cloud, Mama and Papa, and the ship.
- Ask students *Is this a happy or a sad story?* (sad because she loses her home, but happy because they are alive and safe) *Is her life similar to or different from yours? How?*
- Then look at the Words in Context.

TRACK 27 TB p. 230 Words in Context

- Play the audio and have students repeat the words.
- Have students race to find the words in the reading.
- Tell students that they can **use L1 knowledge to establish meaning** (see TB p. 23). They can discuss their ideas with a partner, using L1 if necessary.
- Then use these discussion points to confirm the meaning of each word.

thunder Ask *Is thunder something you see or hear? What words tell you this?* (hear; loud noises, sounded) *Is it a quiet or loud sound?* (loud) Say *Look at the picture. Do you have thunder when the weather is good?* (no) Elicit that in the story, there wasn't any thunder; it was the volcano.

bark Say *What things do dogs do when they're scared? Do dogs shout like people?* (no, they bark)

ash *What comes out of a volcano?* (fire, ash, lava) *Look at the sentence* (p. 68): *Are ash and stones the same? What color is ash, do you think?* (gray)

dream Refer students to the sentence on p. 69: Ask students *What is the girl doing when she has dreams?* (sleeping) *What can be scary when you're sleeping?* (dreams) *Are dreams good or bad?* (They can be both, but the girl here is having bad dreams.)

sunrise Refer students to the first sentence in the second paragraph on p. 69: Ask *Is it morning or evening?* (morning) *Is the sun going up or down?* (up) *What are you usually doing at sunrise?*

Second Reading: Analyze the Text and Features

- Have students read the story again, and this time play the audio while they follow in their books.
- Discuss the questions in the red boxes as a class.
  - **Critical Thinking** (p. 66): *How did people's lives change?* Ask students what people's lives were like before and after the volcano. Ask *How did their home change? How did they change?*
  - **Making Connections** (p. 67): *Some mountains are volcanoes, like Mount Tambora.* Ask students if they know the names of any famous volcanoes. Do they have any volcanoes in their country?
  - **Making Connections** (p. 68): *In 1815 the explosion of Mount Tambora in Indonesia was the largest in history.* Ask students if they know of any other famous big volcanic eruptions. (Some suggestions: Mount Vesuvius, Italy, A.D. 79; Krakatoa, Indonesia, 1883; more recently, Mount St. Helens, USA, 1980)
  - **Personalization** (p. 69): *Why do you think the girl has bad dreams?* Ask students if they ever have bad dreams. Are their dreams about something they are scared of? Ask them how they think the girl feels and what her dreams are about.
- Utilize the story to explore the SEL competency of labeling and recognizing one's own and others' emotions. Ask students *How does the girl feel at the beginning of the story?* (interested, curious) *How do she and the other people feel in the middle?* (scared, confused) *How does she feel at the end?* (sad because her home is gone, but happy to be safe)

Third Reading: Interact with the Text

- Listen to the audio again and have students mime the actions and emotions of the story.

Cool Down

Play *Disappearing Sentences* with four sentences from the story (see TB p. 25).

Explore the Reading

Lesson Objectives

- to understand and analyze *The Angry Mountain* through reading comprehension activities
- explore the SEL competency of self-awareness through labeling and recognizing emotions
- to give a personal reaction to the story
- to recognize and reproduce the *–nd* blend

Materials
Audio Track 28

Warm Up

Play *Matching Halves* (see TB p. 26). Possible sentences:
Column 1: 1 *It sounded* / 2 *There was* / 3 *We must* / 4 *Ash* / 5 *full of* / 6 *Nothing* / 7 *We were*
Column 2: a. *leave.* / b. *scary things.* / c. *fire everywhere.* / d. *finally safe.* / e. *like thunder.* / f. *and stones* / g. *was left.*

Answers
1 e 2 c 3 a 4 f 5 b 6 g 7 d

A Read and answer.

- Before students open their books, have a Circle Time discussion to see what students remember about the story (see TB p. 21). Ask *When does the story happen?* (1815) *Where are the people?* (Mount Tambora, Indonesia) *Why do they run to the boats?* (to leave) *What happens to their homes?* (They are gone.) *How will their lives change?*
- Ask two students to read the example question and answer. Ask the class to find where this information is in the story. (p. 66)
- Have students continue the activity individually and then compare answers in pairs.
- Check answers by having pairs of students read out the questions and answers. Encourage them to show where they found the information in the story. Check that everyone agrees.

Answers
1 *The mountain's name is Mount Tambora.*
2 She's playing on the beach.
3 She climbs the tree to see the mountain.
4 Ash and stones fell down from the sky.
5 They leave on their boat.

B Think and discuss. Why do you think some people went inside and locked their doors?

- Refer students to the paragraph on p. 67. Read it to students while they follow along.
- Give students some time to think about why people went inside and then elicit suggestions. Help with vocabulary as necessary.

Possible Answers
People feel safe in their own houses. They wanted to stop the volcano coming into their house. They didn't understand what a volcano could do—this was before most people had science lessons—and they just wanted to ignore what was happening.

C Think, choose, and write. Imagine you lived near Mount Tambora in 1815. How do you feel?

- Expand on the SEL competency of labeling and recognizing your own and others' emotions. Give students some time to look at the pictures again and to notice the people's faces. Ask students to identify the different emotions. Call out the adjectives and have students mime feeling that way.
- Tell students to imagine they are in the story. Say *How do you feel?* and encourage them to choose two adjectives.
- Say *I feel sad because I liked our house and now it's gone. I feel hot because there is fire all around us.*
- Write the structure *I feel … because …* on the board. Give students time to write their own sentences to express how they feel using the adjectives they chose, then have them compare ideas with a friend.
- Ask if any students would like to share their ideas with the class.

Phonics *–nd*

TRACK 28 TB p. 230 **Listen and say.**

- Play the audio and have students look at the words in the phonics box. Ask them what sound all the words have in common. (they all have *–nd* at the end)
- Play the audio again and have students repeat the words, first in a whisper and then loudly. Ask a few individual students to repeat each word.
- Ask students to choose their favorite word from the list and to tell a friend.
- Have students find more words in the story ending with *–nd*, and invite students to read them out loud.

Answers
and; sound (as *sounded* and *sounds*); ground; island

Cool Down

Ask *Did you enjoy this story? Why or why not?* Encourage students to discuss in pairs and invite some students to share their answers with the class.

Practice **Resource Bank:** Phonics Printout;
Student's App: Phonics Practice; Reading Comprehension Practice

Think Together

Lesson Objectives

- to make connections between the readings
- to identify causes and effects
- to explore the key concept: How do events change our lives?
- to reflect on the unit and provide personal thoughts and opinions

Warm Up

Have students look at the key concept question at the top of p. 71: *How do events change our lives?* Ask how the events they have read about in this unit changed people's lives. (in *Where Is She?*, Peruggia goes to prison, and the picture becomes very famous; in *The Angry Mountain*, the girl and her family don't live in the same place after the volcano, and nor do hundreds of other people)

Encourage students to also think about how those events changed their lives. (they have heard of the *Mona Lisa*, and perhaps they wouldn't have if it hadn't been stolen; our planet is a little bit warmer because of the Mount Tambora volcano, and we also understand how dangerous volcanoes can be)

A Read and complete. Both readings have causes and effects. Complete the table.

- Ask students what main events they can remember in each reading. Elicit three or four from each—these should act as a general summary of the plot.
- Elicit that the cause of something is *why* it happens and the effect is *what* happens or what changes.
- Refer students to the first cause in the table (Peruggia steals the *Mona Lisa*) and ask what happened after that—what was the effect?
- Have students complete the table and then compare with a friend.
- Ask pairs of students to read the causes and effects. If there are different ideas, ask what the main or important effect was.

Answers

1 (Any one of:) the museum worker calls the police, people are surprised and shocked, the painting is missing for a long time and people can't see it, and the *Mona Lisa* becomes famous.
2 Peruggia tries to sell the *Mona Lisa*.
3 The girl / She climbs a tree.
4 Ash and stones fall down from the sky.

B Think and discuss. What were some important events in your life? Do a Three-Step Interview.

Students are going to make connections between the readings and their own life.

- Say *An important event in my life was when I started teaching.* Ask students to think about some important events in their own lives and to make a list in their notebooks.
- Set up the class for a Three-Step Interview cooperative learning routine (see TB p. 20).
- Write the question *What was an important event for you?* on the board and invite students to ask you it. Answer, and encourage them to ask the follow-up question *What else?*
- Then have students pair up with a student from a different group, and tell them to ask and answer the question on the board. Point out that they should listen carefully, because they'll share the information they hear.
- After students have reported back to their original group, invite students to share some of the things they have learned about other students.

My Reading Journal

Choose your favorite character from *The Angry Mountain* or *Where Is She?* Think of three questions you want to ask him or her.

This question asks students to make a personal connection to the characters in the stories they read.

Have students look back at the readings in the unit and decide on their favorite character. Give an example of your favorite character; e.g. *I like the Mona Lisa herself! She's powerful and calm and interesting.* Tell students questions you would like to ask her, e.g. *Do you like being famous? Were you scared when Peruggia stole you? Are you happy in the museum?*

Have students write three questions they would like to ask their favorite character and then discuss their choices with a friend. Invite students to share their ideas with the rest of the class. Ask if they can imagine the answers to the questions.

Answers

Students' own answers

Think of someone who would like to read this unit. Why did you choose him or her?

This question allows students to think about other people's reactions to what they read.

Tell students who you think would like to read this unit, e.g. *I choose my dad because he likes good stories, especially about crime and the police!*

Have students complete the sentence, then share their answer with a friend.

Answers

Students' own answers

Cool Down

Have students look back at the VTR picture on pp. 56–57. Ask if they have any more ideas about the picture. Say *Do you think the monument was made for a famous event in history? Do you think there was a newspaper article about it?*

Practice **Resource Bank:** Unit Test; **Student's App:** Key Concept Practice

UNIT 5

Let's Go Back

Unit Overview

Themes

Dinosaurs and learning about the past

How people lived in the past

Synopsis

In this unit, students will find out how life in Ancient Egypt was different from today, what we can learn about people from time capsules, and where we can go to learn about the past. They will plan and prepare a presentation about an imaginary dinosaur and write a diary entry using target vocabulary and grammar from the unit.

Language Book

Vocabulary
body, claws, dangerous, dinosaur, huge, scary, slow, tail, tiny, wings
p. 112

Explore Language
Simple Past: Irregular Verb Statements
p. 113

Global Citizenship
Where can we learn about the past in different countries?
bones, broken, build, dig, find, fossil, jug, pottery, skeleton
p. 114

Explore Language
Simple Past: Irregular Verb Questions
p. 115

Take the Stage
Presentation: describing a dinosaur
p. 116

Write About It
A Diary
Sentence Building: *because*
p. 117

Think It Over
Review and Reflection
p. 118

Think Together
How can we find out about the past?
p. 125

Visible Thinking
VTR: See, Think, Wonder
p. 119

Literacy Book

Nonfiction
Informational Text: *Time Capsules*
Words in Context: future, objects, newspapers, spacecraft, disc, Earth
p. 123

Fiction
Fantasy: *The Time Book*
Words in Context: strange, pharaoh, chariot, surprised, scared, ancient
p. 120

Reading Skill
Identifying the main idea and details
p. 122

Phonics
–nt
p. 121

Language and Literacy Connections
The connecting theme in Unit 5 is finding out about the past.

	Language	Literacy
Vocabulary	**Set 1:** parts of the body and adjectives **Set 2:** fossils and ruins	**Get Ready to Read:** *dinosaur* **Fiction:** *huge* **Nonfiction:** *dig, find* **Think Together:** *fossil*
Grammar	**Simple Past: Irregular Statements** I saw it there. We went to the dinosaur exhibition. **Simple Past: Irregular Questions** What did you see? Did you dig? Yes, we did. No, we didn't.	**Fiction** Then Jannah saw the huge chariot. Did I do something wrong? **Nonfiction** People put time capsules in two spacecraft. Voyager 1 and Voyager 2 went into space in 1977.
Skills	**Pronunciation:** /oʊ/ and /ɔr/	**Reading:** identifying the main idea and details **Phonics:** *–nt*

Vocabulary

Lesson Objectives

- to learn and practice vocabulary of parts of the body and adjectives: *body, claws, dangerous, dinosaur, huge, scary, slow, tail, tiny, wings*
- to sing a song about a dinosaur

Materials
Audio Tracks 51 to 54; Video

Warm Up

Introduce the lesson topic by playing a game of *Simon Says* (see TB p. 26) with parts of the body.

A TRACK 51 TB p. 218 **Listen and find. What's David's favorite dinosaur?**

- Have students look at the scene. Ask what they can see happening in the picture. Ask questions to guide them: *Where are they?* (a museum) *What dinosaurs do you recognize?* (students' own answers) Draw students' attention to the girl looking at the diplodocus and ask if they remember her (it's Anna, who moved to a new house in Unit 4).
- Play the audio and have students point to the words and pictures as they listen.
- Ask the gist question *What's David's favorite dinosaur?* Elicit the answer and play the audio again for students to check.
- Look back at p. 59. Say *Can you answer Anna's question?* Listen again to check. (She sees a lot of different dinosaurs.)

Answer
T-Rex

B TRACK 52 TB p. 218 **Listen, say, and number the pictures in A.**

- Play the audio and have students point to the pictures and say the words.
- Play the audio again and, if necessary, pause after each item to give students time to find it on the page and write the number in the box.
- To check answers, nominate students to say the number and the word.
- Have all students repeat the words aloud one more time, this time with a mime for each one.

Answers
1 *wings* 2 dinosaur 3 huge 4 tiny 5 body
6 claws 7 slow 8 dangerous 9 tail 10 scary

C TRACK 53 TB p. 218 **Listen. Close your eyes and visualize.**

- Prepare students for the visualization (see TB p. 21).
- Play the audio, encouraging students to visualize the words as they listen. Make sure students know not to speak until they hear the word *say*.
- Have students share their ideas by asking volunteers to describe what they imagined or to act it out.

D Look and write.

- Tell students that they are going to categorize the new vocabulary into two sets. Have a student read the names of the two categories (the table headings).
- Refer students to the examples—ask them to do a mime for *wings* and point out that it is an animal word (part of an animal in this case). Have them do a mime for *dangerous* and point out it *describes* animals.
- Have students complete the table individually with the new words. While they are doing this, draw (or project) the table on the board.
- To check answers, invite students to come to the board and write one word each in the table. Ask if everyone agrees.

Answers
Animal Words: *wings*, body, claws, dinosaur, tail
Descriptions: *dangerous*, slow, huge, tiny, scary

E TRACK 54 TB p. 218 **Listen and sing. Then watch and sing.**

- Project the song title *King of the Dinosaurs* on the board (but mask the lyrics) and ask students if they remember which dinosaur David said was the king of the dinosaurs (T-Rex). Tell them this is what the song is about.
- With books closed, play the song all the way through and have students raise their hands every time they hear one of the new words. Then ask them which words they heard.
- Have students open their books and give them a minute to look at the lyrics. Play the song again and stop after each line for students to repeat.
- Then play it again and have students sing along.
- Play the song video and encourage students to watch and sing. Then they can make up actions to do as they sing.

Cool Down

Play *Mime It!* with the new vocabulary (see TB p. 25).

Practice Student's App: Vocabulary Practice; Video

Explore Language

Lesson Objectives

- to learn to make irregular simple past statements
- to practice vocabulary of parts the body and adjectives

Materials
Audio Tracks 55 and 56; Video

TRACK 54 TB p. 218 **Warm Up**
Sing *King of the Dinosaurs* again and encourage students to do actions.

A TRACK 55 TB p. 219 **Listen and read. Did the dinosaur eat meat?**

- Project the story or have students look in their books. Ask students what they can see happening in the images. Guide them with some questions: *Where are they?* (at the movie theater) *What are they doing?* (watching a movie about T-Rex) *Are they having fun?* (at the beginning, yes, but they're scared at the end!) *Do you recognize the boy?* (It's David from previous lesson.)
- Tell students to listen and see if their predictions were correct. Play the audio and have students follow in their books.
- Ask them the gist question *Did the dinosaur eat meat?* Elicit answers then play the audio again for students to check. Ask further questions to check comprehension.

Answer
Yes, it did.

B Look at A. Complete.

- Tell students that in this lesson they will look at making simple past statements using irregular verbs. Check that they remember how to make regular statements (by adding *–ed*). Then project or write the table on the board.
- Have a student read aloud the first statement, including the example answer (saw). Ask another student to point to where in the story that answer can be found. Tell students to go through the other sentences in the table in the same way. Check answers as a class.
- Ask students if the sentences are about the present or the past (past). Ask how they are different from the regular past verbs they learned in Unit 4 (these don't end in *–ed*). Elicit which are the positive and which are the negative sentences (positive on the left, negative on the right). Point out the words in red: in the negative sentences, *did* is doing all the work again, just as it did with the regular verbs.
- Elicit the infinitives for each of the simple past verbs. Point out that sometimes it isn't obvious (e.g. *go* > *went*), so they should use the context of the sentence to figure out the meaning.
- Draw students' attention to the Grammar tip *Remember.* Elicit when they need to add an *–s* to a verb (3rd person singular in the present simple).

Practice **Resource Bank:** Grammar Printout; **Student's App:** Grammar Practice

Answers
saw; went; ate; didn't eat

C Think and discuss. Then choose.

- Check students understand *before* and *after*—point back over your shoulder and ask *Before now or after now?* (before) Do the same for *after*, pointing forward.
- Have students work in pairs to discuss the sentences. Encourage them to look at the table in B and the story in A and circle the correct options. Check answers as a class.

Answers
1 before 2 Irregular

D TRACK 56 TB p. 219 **Listen and say.**

- Have students practice saying the new structures. Play the audio, pausing after each sentence for students to repeat. For ideas on how to vary the drill, see TB p. 22.

E Read and complete in simple past.

- Ask students to look quickly at the text and say what it is about (a visit to a museum).
- Highlight the example answer and tell them they can find the past verbs they will need either in the story or in B.
- Have students continue the activity individually and then compare answers with a friend.
- To check answers, ask students to read a sentence each. Ask if everyone agrees. Write the verbs on the board so everyone can check spelling.

Answers
1 *went* 2 saw 3 had 4 didn't have 5 ran
6 didn't eat

F Play *Tic Tac Toe*.

- Draw the grid from F on the board and ask students if they know the game and how to win (the winner is the player who gets three in a row). Point out in this version they need to make a correct sentence to mark a space.
- Point to the bottom right square (Two years ago / go). Ask what *go* changes to in the past (went). Invite a student to read the example sentence in the speech bubble, and put an X or a circle in the square.
- Divide the class into two teams. Ask the first team to choose a square and give them 10–15 seconds to make a sentence using the words. If it is correct, mark the team's square with a circle or an X. Then the other team takes a turn. If an answer is incorrect, move on to the next team without marking a square. The first team to get three squares in a row wins.
- Have students play again in pairs or small groups.

Cool Down

Play *Pass the Whisper!* (see TB p. 26) with sentences from A or E.

Global Citizenship

Lesson Objectives

- to learn fossils and ruins vocabulary: *bones, broken, build, dig, find, fossil, jug, pottery, skeleton*
- to explore how and where we can learn about the past
- to practice listening for gist and details

Materials
Audio Tracks 57 to 59; (optional) Audio Track E

Opening Question

Ask the opening question: *Where can we learn about the past in different countries?* Elicit ideas and ask students to think about places, books, and people we can learn with or from.

Don't correct them or give much feedback; students will find out more about the topic during the lesson.

A TRACK 57 TB p. 219 **Listen to Paz talk about a museum near her town. What was very dirty there?**

- Have students look at the biggest picture (top left). Ask *Where is the girl? What do you think she is doing?* Play the audio for students to check their predictions. (she's in a museum, digging)
- Play the audio again and have students point to the words or pictures as they listen.
- Then ask the gist question *What was very dirty there?* Play the audio again for students to check the answer.

Answer
a bowl

B TRACK 58 TB p. 219 **Listen, say, and number the pictures in A.**

- Play the audio and have students point to the pictures and say the words.
- Play the audio again, this time pausing after each item, if necessary, for students to find it and write the number in the box.
- To check answers, play the audio again but stop after each number and have students say the word.

Answers
1 *find* 2 skeleton 3 jug 4 broken 5 bones
6 fossil 7 dig 8 build 9 pottery

TRACK E TB p. 219 **Visualization**

- The TTL has a visualization audio track for this vocabulary set (see TB p. 21).

C **Play *Back Spelling*. Guess the words your friend is spelling.**

- Students are going to write words, letter by letter, on each other's backs with their finger. As an example, call out a word from A and have students hold up their index finger and write it in the air as you spell it out (e.g. jug, j-u-g). Then have students write the word on their friend's back.
- Have students take turns choosing a word and writing it on their friend's back. If their friend guesses incorrectly, have them write the word again.

D TRACK 59 TB p. 219 **Now listen to Karol and Rashid. Number the pictures. Who lives in an old city?**

- Listening for the main idea: tell students that they will listen to two children from Pakistan and Poland talking about the places they live.
- Play the audio and have students number the pictures. Then check answers.
- Ask the gist question *Who lives in an old city?* and elicit the answer. Play the audio again for students to check.

Answers
a 2 b 1 Rashid lives in an old city.

E **Listen again. Write *True* or *False*.**

- Listening for detail: have students look at the sentences before they listen again and see if they can remember any of the answers. Then play the audio again and have students write the answers.
- Read each sentence aloud and have students stand up for *True* and sit down for *False*. Ask if they can correct the false sentences.

Answers
1 *True* 2 False; he saw a model of a very old town
3 False; he said the museum was fantastic
4 False; it is very old 5 True

Discussion Questions

- Draw students' attention to the discussion questions at the bottom of the page: *Which place do you want to visit? Why? Where can you learn about the past in your country?* Have students discuss the questions in pairs or small groups (see **ETB**).
- Return to the original opening question to ask again *Where can we learn about the past in different countries?* Discuss the information students have learned in this lesson. Ask if they now have any new ideas.

Cool Down

Play *Chain Game* (see TB p. 26) using the vocabulary from this lesson; for example, *I went to the museum, and I saw a skeleton … and some pottery.*

Practice **Student's App:** Vocabulary Practice; Listening Comprehension Practice

Explore Language

Lesson Objectives

- to learn to make irregular simple past questions
- to practice fossils and ruins vocabulary

Materials
Audio Tracks 60 and 61

Warm Up

Play *I Spy* (see TB p. 25) with pictures on p. 68.

A TRACK 60 TB p. 219 **Listen and read. What were the interesting shapes?**

- Ask students what else they can see in the pictures on p. 68. To guide them, ask *Where are they?* (in the country, in a science laboratory near a digging site) *Who is the girl?* (Jannah from Lesson 2, p. 64, and from The Time Book story in the **Literacy Book**) *What do you think their relationship is?* (father and daughter) Don't correct students—instead, tell them that now they will read the dialogue to discover if their predictions are correct.
- Play the audio and have students follow the dialogue in their books.
- Ask the gist question *What were the interesting shapes?* and elicit answers. Play the audio again for students to check.
- Ask students to think of a place where they could use the digital scanner and encourage them to think about what they'd like to find.

Answers
three cans and an old plate

B **Look at A. Complete.**

- Write or project the table on the board. Tell students that this lesson they will look at making simple past questions using irregular verbs.
- Have a student read aloud the first question, including the example answer (did). Ask another student to point to where in the dialogue that answer can be found. Have students complete the rest of the table, finding the answers in the story in A. Check answers as a class.
- Ask students *Are these questions about the present or the past?* (past) *What word tells us this is the past?* (did) Highlight the verbs in red and ask *Is the main verb in the question in the past?* (no, infinitive). Point out *did* does all the work in simple past questions.
- Point out to students that, because the verb doesn't change, questions in the simple past are exactly the same for regular and irregular verbs. Have them create some regular verb questions to confirm this; for example, *Did / listen to / music / yesterday?* (Did you listen to music yesterday?) *What / did / listen to?* (What did you listen to?) Point out that the short yes/no answers in the table are also the same as for regular verbs.

- Have students look at the Grammar tip *Remember.* Highlight the two questions in the table: *What did you see?* and *Did you dig?* Ask *Which question asks for specific information?* (the first one) Point out that the word order is the same as for simple present *W* questions. Have students think of some questions starting with *What* and ask you (using past or present verbs, irregular or regular).

Answers
Did; Did; Yes; didn't

C **Think and discuss. Then choose.**

- Have students discuss the sentence in pairs and circle the correct option in their books.
- To check answers, read the options and have them raise their hands for the answer they chose.

Answer
1 past

D TRACK 61 TB p. 219 **Listen and say.**

- Play the audio and have students tell you how many times they hear *did* (five) and *didn't* (one).
- Play the audio again, pausing after the question or answer for students to repeat.
- For ideas on how to vary the drill, see TB p. 22.

E **Put the words in order.**

- Refer students to the example sentence and point out the following order: question word + did + subject + verb.
- Have students continue the activity individually and then compare with a friend.
- Ask pairs of students to read questions and answers to the class. Ask if everyone agrees.

Answers
1 *What did you find* 2 Where did you find
3 Did you find it 4 Did you know

F **Play *Back to the Board*. Say the answers for your friend to guess the question.**

- Choose one student to come to the front and stand with their back to the board. Write a question on the board and encourage the other students to give the student standing some possible answers to that question. He/she must then guess what the question was.
- When the student has guessed correctly, another student can stand with his/her back to the board and the first student can write the question. The other students provide possible answers as clues, as before.

Cool Down

Play *Running Sentences* (see TB p. 27) with key sentences from the dialogue.

Practice **Resource Bank:** Grammar Printout; **Student's App:** Grammar Practice

Take the Stage

Lesson Objectives

- to prepare and give a presentation about a fictional dinosaur
- to recognize and reproduce /oʊ/ and /ɔr/

Materials
Video; Audio Track 62

Warm Up

Ask *What's your favorite dinosaur?* Elicit responses and encourage students to say why. They can look back at Lesson 1 and point to one in the picture if they can't remember all the names.

A TB p. 234 **Watch and listen. What did Flo's dinosaur eat?**

- Tell students they will watch a video of a girl named Flo talking about a dinosaur. Before playing the video, ask students *What different things did dinosaurs eat?* and elicit answers. (plants, meat, or both)
- Introduce the gist question *What did Flo's dinosaur eat?* Tell them to watch and find the answer.
- When the video is finished, ask *Were your ideas about what dinosaurs eat the same as Flo's dinosaur? Do you think this is a real dinosaur?* (No, Flo invented it.) *What makes you say that?* (Its name is based on hers.) Ask further questions to check comprehension (see **ETB**).

Answer
other dinosaurs

B Watch again. Check (✔) the phrases you hear.

- Have students read the phrases and draw their attention to the example.
- Play the video again and have students check the phrases they hear.
- Ask students to read a sentence each and say *yes* or *no*. Ask if everyone agrees.

Answers
1; 2; 3; 5; 6; 8

Pronunciation /oʊ/ and /ɔr/

TRACK 62 TB p. 219 **Listen and say.**

- Demonstrate the /oʊ/ sound as in *nose* and the /ɔr/ sound as in *Ecuador* and encourage students to copy you.
- Play the audio for students to repeat the sounds and words. Repeat if students need more practice.
- Say *These are all words Flo says in her presentation. What other words do you know with these sounds?* Elicit ideas (e.g. bones, short) and write them on the board in two sections. Drill all the words at the end.

C Plan. Invent your dinosaur. Write and choose (✔).

- Tell students that they are going to plan a presentation about an imaginary dinosaur like Flo did. Say *Let's look at the plan. What information did Flo include in her presentation?* (dinosaur's name, where it lived, when it lived, and what other animal it was like) See if students can remember what Flo said for each heading.
- Say *Now think about your dinosaur. What does it look like?* Tell students they can be as imaginative as they like. Have them complete the graphic organizer with their own ideas and check the words they want to use to describe their dinosaur. Point out the name can be based on their name if they want, like Flo's *Floraptor* was.

D Prepare your presentation. Use your ideas from C and phrases from B.

- Play the video one more time to give another model for students.
- Then have students complete their presentations from their plan, using their ideas in C and the phrases in B. Circulate and help as necessary.
- Allow students time to draw a picture of their dinosaur so they can point to its key features in the presentation.

E Practice with a friend. Then share with your class.

- Have students practice their presentation with a friend as many times as they need to. Remind them to smile and speak slowly and clearly. Remind them also to point to the picture to show important parts. The picture will act as a prompt and will allow them to be less reliant on their notes.
- Invite volunteers to come to the front of the classroom to give their presentation. Ask the others to listen and say how similar their own dinosaur is to the one presented. Tell them to rate each one on a scale of 1 (very different) to 5 (very similar).

Cool Down

Invite students to say one thing they liked about the presentations they listened to.

Practice **Student's App:** Speaking Skill Practice; Video

Write About It

Lesson Objectives

- to focus on the use of *because*
- to write a diary about last Saturday

Materials

(Optional) Support, Standard, and Challenge writing printouts from the Resource Bank (one per student) (C, D)

Warm Up

Ask students to remember a school trip they went on. Ask a volunteer *Where did you go? What did you do there? What was your favorite part? Did you buy anything to remember the trip?* Have students compare their memories in pairs and then ask them to share what they discussed with the class.

A Read the diary. Underline *because* and the phrase after it.

- Have students read the text. Establish that it is a diary. Ask *What event was it?* (a Kids' Dig Camp) *What did they do in the morning?* (They saw a video about Mexico.) *What did they do in the afternoon?* (They walked to a beach for their dig.) Ask students if they would like to do something like this.
- Have students find the first example of *because* in the text and ask them what is underlined after it. (*it was about Mexico*) Have them find the other examples of *because* and underline the phrases that follow. Ask how many others they found. (there are two more)
- Point out the question to the right of the diary—*When do we use* because? Ask *What do* because *and the phrase after tell us?* (why the thing mentioned before *because* happened) To clarify, ask students *Why did the writer like the video? Why did they dig slowly? Why were the bowls broken?* and have them answer using the underlined phrases.

Answers

because it was about Mexico; because the pottery was very old; because they were 200 years old

B Match.

- Have students look at the example matched for the first phrase. Point out that all the phrases in the second column start with *because*, and that without this word, they are just a lot of separate sentences.
- Have students complete the rest of the activity individually.
- To check answers, have students read out the whole sentence. Ask if everyone agrees.

Answers

1 d 2 c 3 e 4 b 5 a

Practice Student's App: Writing Practice

C Plan. Think about last Saturday. Complete.

- Tell students they are going to plan their own diary page about what they did last Saturday.
- Do an example together. Project (or draw) the table on the board. Point to the first cell and ask *What did you do?* Have students suggest an activity (e.g. rode a bike). Then have them suggest a possible answer for the *Why?* cell (e.g. it was sunny). Make sure they realize there is no right or wrong answer. Challenge printouts can be handed out now.
- Give students some thinking time to imagine their own experience last Saturday and then have them complete the the table with their ideas.

D Write about last Saturday. Draw a picture.

- Have students write their diary in a notebook, using their notes from C. Support printouts can be handed out now.
- Have students write out a clean, corrected version on paper or hand out the Standard printouts from the Resource Bank. Remind them to include the date at the top of the page. Allow students time to decorate their description with the things they did. Display the finished diaries around the classroom.

Cool Down

Enjoy each other's work: have students circulate around the classroom, enjoying their friends' diary pages (and pictures). Ask students to look for something interesting or an activity that was similar to theirs. Before they leave, have them say one thing they liked about another student's work.

Think It Over

Lesson Objectives

- to review what has been learned in the unit
- to reflect on the unit and their progress
- to think about learning strategies and how to continue learning at home

Warm Up

Play *Apple Tree* (see TB p. 25) with key vocabulary from this unit.

Suggested words: *dangerous, dinosaur, claws, scary, wings, skeleton, bones, fossil, broken, pottery*

Read the questions and draw or write your answers.

- Allowing students to make a personal response will help them retain knowledge and engage with the learning.

What did I do?

- Give students a few minutes to look back through the unit at the different activities they did. Ask questions about the unit; for example, *What did you sing about? What activities and actions did you do? What did you talk about? What stories did you read or listen to?*
- Encourage students to draw or write about activities they remember well or found interesting.

What did I learn?

- Ask questions about the unit; for example, *What new words do you know now? Can you make new questions or answers about the past? What new things did you learn about other countries, people, and dinosaurs?* Have students discuss ideas in pairs.
- Encourage students to think of one or two things, among all of the things that were mentioned, that they are proud of or that they will remember because it was interesting or useful or unusual.
- Ask students to draw a picture or write about the thing or things they have chosen

How did I learn?

- Ask students *Did you learn with pictures? With actions? By listening, reading, or writing? By discussing ideas? With your friends? With videos? With computers? How do you like learning best?* Ask students how they learned the new words in Lesson 1. Elicit ideas (e.g. by seeing the words next to the pictures, by hearing the words in a story, by visualizing the words).
- Encourage students to think about the pronunciation and spelling of the words they learned in this unit. Ask *What helps you remember how to say and spell these words?*
- Encourage students to draw a picture or write about some of the activities that helped them learn.

How well did I do?

- Tell students to color in the dinosaur that best expresses how well they have learned the unit content (i.e., the older the dinosaur, the better they learned). Ask *What do you remember? What do you understand? What do you need to practice more?* Encourage students to look back through the unit to see how much they remember, what they did well, and what they found difficult.

What can I do next?

- Brainstorm ideas with the class about what students can do to learn more (e.g. play the games on pp. 65–67 again, watch the song video again).
- Encourage students to think about what they can do at home to improve their English, using the four verbs as prompts; for example, read storybooks in English, practice their dinosaur presentation again, play video games on a tablet in English, use English websites to find out more about dinosaurs.
- Ask students to choose one or more activities from the list (read, practice, play, find out more) that they will do to practice their English.
- Once students have completed the page in their books, have them discuss with a friend what they drew or wrote. Did they choose the same activities or different ones?

Looking Forward

Draw students' attention to the character at the bottom of the page. Ask *Who's this?* and elicit what they remember about him. (he is Jannah's dad, Harold, from Lesson 4, p. 68) Ask students if they can guess what he sees in Art Class. Elicit predictions, then tell students they will find out when they study the unit.

Play 1

To further review and recycle the language in Units 1, 2, 3, 4, and 5, have students practice and perform the play, *Adventures on Purple Mountain*, on pp. 140–141. See TB p. 211 for teaching notes.

Practice **Resource Bank:** Unit Test; Mid-year Test; **Student's App:** Vocabulary and Grammar Review

Get Ready to Read

Lesson Objectives

- to activate prior knowledge about history and the past
- to encourage students to observe and interpret through a See, Think, Wonder VTR
- to preview the reading skill of identifying the main idea and details

Materials

(Optional) VTR printout from the Resource Bank (A, B, C)

Warm Up

Describe a dinosaur for students to draw. Draw it on your paper at the same time (but don't let them see what you're drawing): *It has two long legs and two short legs. It is standing on the long legs. It has a big head and a big nose. It has a big body, a long tail, and big teeth. It has small eyes.* (a T-Rex)

Show students your picture and have them hold up their own pictures. Ask who they think has a picture most like yours.

See, Think, Wonder

A Look at the picture. What do you see?

Students are going to do a See, Think, Wonder VTR to explore the picture of the dinosaurs.

- Ask students *What do you see?* Give students a minute to look at the picture before sharing their ideas in small groups or pairs. Bring the groups back together and have them share ideas as a class.
- Students will likely find: dinosaurs; cows; houses; grass; trees; mountains; colors green, white, and black; various body parts including legs, head, long neck, and tail.
- Students may also notice: mist/fog, farm, fence, field, roofs.

Here's an example of this part of the routine:
Teacher: What do you see?
Student A: (I see) dinosaurs.
Teacher: OK, tell me more about the dinosaurs.
Student B: They're really big!
Teacher: Great. What else do you see?

B What do you think?

- Have students read aloud the two examples on the page. Then give them one minute to think about the picture.
- Have students work in small groups to share their ideas before bringing the class together.

Here's an example of this part of the routine:
Teacher: What do you think?
Student A: (I think) the dinosaurs aren't real.
Teacher: What makes you say that?
Student A: They look like models.
Teacher: How interesting! What else do you think?
Student B: I think the cows aren't scared.

C What do you wonder?

- Have students read aloud the two examples on the page. Give them one minute to think of questions they have about the picture.
- Have students share their ideas in groups or as a class.

Here's an example of this part of the routine:
Teacher: What do you wonder?
Student A: (I wonder) why the dinosaurs are with the cows.
Teacher: Why do you think they are there?
Student B: Maybe it's a show?
Teacher: Maybe. What else do you wonder?
Student C: (I wonder) if the cows can see the dinosaurs.

Transition

Ask *Do you know how long ago dinosaurs lived?* (65–200 million years ago) *Did people live at the same time as dinosaurs?* (No, dinosaurs died millions of years before the first people.) *Would you like to travel back to the time of the dinosaurs?* (students' own answer)

D Think and discuss. You can travel into the past. How far back do you go?

- Give students two examples of periods of time they could travel back to—one in recorded history and one prehistory; for example, *I'd like to go back and see what this country was like in the year 1! And then I'd like to go back and see when people lived in caves.*
- Ask students what they'd like to see and have them think about how far back they would need to go (if they know). Have them discuss their ideas in pairs.
- Invite some students to share their ideas with the class, and decide who is going the furthest back in time.

E What do you think *The Time Book* is about? Read the summary and choose the main idea.

This is a preview of the reading skill of identifying the main idea and details.

- Tell students they will be reading a story called *The Time Book*. Ask them what ideas the title gives them about the topic of the story. Elicit some suggestions.
- Have students read the story summary and give them time to choose the main idea. Call out numbers *1, 2, 3* and have students raise their hands with their answers.

Answer

1 Jannah explores ancient Egypt with her book.

Now read The Time Book

Fiction: *The Time Book—A Fantasy Story*

Lesson Objectives

- to read a fantasy text about a girl in Ancient Egypt
- to learn about ancient Egypt
- to explore the SEL competency of social awareness through understanding others' views and perspectives
- to make a personal connection to the reading

Materials
Video; Audio Tracks 29 and 30; a world map (WU)

Warm Up

Write *Egypt* on the board and elicit everything students know about it. Show a world map and have students find Egypt on the map. Point out Cairo.

Ask if students know anything about *ancient* Egypt and write any ideas on the board.

TRACK 29 TB p. 230 Reading Approach

First Reading: Listen and Engage

- Have students look quickly at pp. 74–79 and say what they think they will read about today. (a girl who reads a book and it takes her exploring) Tell students to look at the title, the pictures, the text, and the genre. Ask *Do you think the story is set now or in the past?* (both)
- Play the video. Alternatively, play the audio and have students follow in their books. Ask students if their predictions were correct.
- Ask students *Is Jannah the same age as you? Do you like to read like her? Do you think this was a dream or was it real?*
- Then look at the Words in Context.

TRACK 30 TB p. 230 Words in Context

- Play the audio and have students repeat the words.
- Have them race to find the words in the reading. Ask *Which word is used three times?* (strange)
- Play the video again. Remind students they can **use the actions in the video to help establish the meaning of new words** (see TB p. 23).
- Bring the class back together and use these discussion points to confirm meaning.

strange Ask students to find the word on p. 74 and look at the sentence it is in and what comes before. Ask *How do you think Jannah feels when she sees a girl like her in the picture? Is it normal/usual?* Explain that in this context, *strange* means the opposite of *normal*.

pharaoh Have students find the word on p. 78. Have them point to the pharaoh in the picture. Ask *Is the pharaoh important?* Elicit what words are used for *pharaoh* in other countries or times in history (e.g. king, emperor).

chariot Ask *Can you see the chariot in the picture* (on p. 76)*? Do people still use chariots today? Do you want to sit in a chariot?*

surprised Pointing to the picture on p. 77, ask *How do you think the woman feels? Why is she surprised?* Have them demonstrate a surprised expression.

scared Have students think about what happened in the video up to the point where *scared* is used. Ask *How do you think Jannah feels? What would you do if someone said "Run!"?*

ancient Establish that this word is used to describe the city. Ask students if they can find another way of saying *ancient* in the reading (*very old* on p. 75). Ask students if the city is the same or different from the one they live in. Ask *What's the same? What's different?*

Second Reading: Analyze the Text and Features

- Play the audio and have students follow in their books.
- Stop and discuss the questions in the green boxes as a class when they appear in the reading.
  - **Gist** (p. 74): *Why is* The Time Book *special?* Ask students what happened when Jannah read *The Time Book*. (she traveled to the time in the picture)
  - **Making Connections** (p. 77): *The ancient Egyptians made glass, but they didn't have eyeglasses yet.* Elicit the woman didn't know the glasses would help her see. Ask students why they think the ancient Egyptians didn't have eyeglasses if they already had glass—students may need to use L1 to answer. (eyeglasses were only invented thousands of years later when more people started to read books)

Third Reading: Interact with the Text

- To help students get more involved in the story, divide the class into five groups: one group for Jannah, one for the old woman, one for the pharaoh, one for the guard, and one for Jannah's mother.
- Play the audio again and have students join in with the lines for their character. They have to follow the text very carefully to be able to join in at the right time.
- Play the audio again and this time have students add some actions (see TB p. 23 for further ideas).

Cool Down

Play *Correct the Teacher* (see TB p. 25).

Possible phrases to use: *It was time for Jannah to go to school.* (bed) / *I don't remember this book. It looks scary.* (interesting) / *Look! The teacher is coming.* (pharaoh) / *Put them in front of your nose.* (eyes) / *The streets were cold and dark.* (hot) / *Suddenly, there was a hand on her finger.* (shoulder)

Practice Student's App: Video

Explore the Reading

Lesson Objectives

- to understand and analyze *The Time Book* through reading comprehension activities
- to explore the SEL competency of social awareness through understanding others' views and perspectives
- to explore the theme of the reading and think about differences in the situations and times

Materials
Audio Track 29; (optional) Video (A)

TRACK 29 TB p. 230 **Warm Up**
Play *What's the Next Word?* (see TB p. 27) with the audio of the story from the previous lesson.

A Read and write *True* or *False*.

- Before students open their books, find out what they remember from the story. Use some of the five *W* questions (but don't give the answers yet—see the next instruction): *Where did the story happen?* (in Egypt) *Why was Jannah different from the ancient Egyptians?* (She wore glasses and different clothes.) *When did the story take place?* (in ancient Egyptian times) *Who shouted at Jannah?* (a guard)
- Play the video again to bring the story firmly back into focus for all students. If they struggled with any of the questions above, ask them again once they have watched the video.
- Focus students on the activity in the book and do the example together. Ask if they can find something in the reading (in the pictures or in the text) that shows this. (the picture on p. 74 shows Jannah's home is in the present, not the past)
- Have students read and write *true* or *false* for the other sentences and find something in the story to justify their answers. Remind them to look for key words rather than rereading the whole text. When they have finished, give them time to compare answers in pairs.
- To check answers, read the sentences and have students call out *True* or *False*. Invite students to show the part of the story that made them think that.

Answers
1 *False* 2 True 3 False 4 True 5 False

B Read and answer the questions.

- Ask two students to read the example question and answer.
- Have students work individually to find and write the other answers, using complete sentences like the example. Then have them compare their answers with a friend.
- To check answers, ask pairs of students to read their questions and answers. Ask if everyone agrees or if there is an alternative version of the answer.

Answers
(Students' wording may vary.)
1 *Jannah is in bed when the story starts and ends.*
2 She looked different because she had glasses and she was wearing pajamas / modern clothes.
3 She ran because she was scared.
4 Her mom's hand was on her shoulder.
5 The old woman had glasses, and the girl wasn't there. / It didn't look the same as at the beginning of the story.

C Think and discuss. Which of these things did ancient Egyptians <u>not</u> have? How did that make their lives different from yours?

- Use the first item *chariot* as the example. Ask students to look back at the reading and the pictures to see if the ancient Egyptians had chariots. (they did)
- Have students work in pairs to discuss whether they think the ancient Egyptians had the other items. They will find evidence in the reading and pictures to support their decision for some of the items, but will need to use prior knowledge and critical thinking skills for others. Tell them that if they can't see an item in the reading, they should think about whether it is likely the Egyptians would have had it or not and to give reasons for their answer.
- Note: they did have writing—the symbols on the wall above the pharaoh on p. 75 are representations of ancient Egyptian writing. They also had (invented) the earliest form of paper, called papyrus. It wasn't much like our paper these days, but it served the same purpose—it could hold ink and could therefore be written on.
- Explore the SEL competency of understanding others' views and perspectives. Ask students if they can think of things ancient Egyptians would find strange if they visited your school. Ensure that students name simple things such as notebooks, windows, and paved roads, as well as more obvious things such as technology. Ask *Do you think life was easier or more difficult then? How is life different now?*

Answer
They didn't have glasses.

Cool Down

Ask students if they would like to travel back to ancient time to visit. Have them discuss their ideas in pairs, then take a class vote.

Practice Student's App: Reading Comprehension Practice

Get Ready to Read

Lesson Objectives

- to practice the reading skill of identifying main ideas and details
- to think about important things from our time
- to activate prior knowledge of time capsules

Materials

Audio Track 29; a picture of a time capsule (B)

TRACK 29 TB p. 230 **Warm Up**

Play the audio of *The Time Book* again and have students act out the story.

If you use the TTL, use the Story Player in "Listen" mode with the volume muted to show the story without the sound and elicit what's happening (or the dialogue) in each frame.

A Read the paragraph. What's the main idea? Underline the answer.

This lesson practices the reading skill of identifying the main idea and details, which was briefly introduced in the first lesson of the unit.

- Project the paragraph on the board or have students look at it in their book. Tell students that this is a summary of *The Time Book*.
- Read the paragraph aloud or have a confident student do so. Ask students to listen to decide what the main idea is. When they have heard it once, ask them to read it again themselves and discuss with a partner what they think is the main idea.
- To check answers, have a volunteer come to the front and underline his/her chosen sentence on the board. Ask if everyone agrees. Then have everyone underline the confirmed sentence.
- Have students read the reading skill box about main ideas and details. Ask them to tell you the sentences from the paragraph that contain details (1, 3 and 4).

Answer

With her special book, she explored Cairo in ancient Egypt.

B Read the paragraph. Then write *Main Idea* or *Detail* for each sentence.

- Write the word *time capsule* on the board and ask if anyone has heard of this word. Hold up the picture you have brought in (or project it on the board) and explain as simply as possible: *A time capsule is a box or container we fill with things from now, for people to find in the future.*
- Project the paragraph on the board or refer students to it in their books. Have them read about time capsules. Ask them if they think it is an interesting idea.
- Point out the small numbers in red for each sentence and clarify that these relate to each of the bigger red numbers below the paragraph. Have students decide for each number whether it is the main idea or detail. Read each sentence and have students raise both hands for the main idea or just one for details. Where differences of opinion exist, discuss, asking students for their opinions and using L1 as necessary to ensure comprehension of this important idea.
- Have students write the agreed answers into their books.

Answers

1 Main idea 2 Detail 3 Detail 4 Main Idea

C Think and discuss. Name things you want to put in a time capsule.

- Tell students that they should imagine the school is putting together a time capsule. Ask them to imagine what they would like people in the future to see about how they live now.
- Give students one or two examples of your own for a time capsule (e.g. a photo of your family, a copy of today's newspaper for people to see what was important in this time, and a photo of your computer to show what technology was like). Point out that the items can be personal (like the first example) or more general (like the second and third).
- Give students some time to think about what they would like to put in their time capsule and then share ideas with a friend.
- Ask if any pairs would like to share their ideas with the class.

Cool Down

Play *Chain Game* (see TB p. 25). Start the chain by saying *In our time capsule, there's a photo.* Encourage the next student to say *In our time capsule, there's a photo and …* (some music).

Now read **Time Capsules**

Nonfiction: *Time Capsules—An Informational Text*

Lesson Objectives

- to read an informal text about time capsules
- to learn through CLIL (history): looking at ways we can find out about civilizations

Materials

Audio Tracks 31 and 32

Warm Up

Play *I Spy* (see TB p. 25) with the items pictured on pp. 82–83 to generate interest in the reading. Afterward, discuss any items that students don't recognize (e.g. the floppy disk).

TRACK 31 TB p. 230 Reading Approach

First Reading: Listen and Engage

- Give students time to look through the whole reading, to notice the types of pictures used, the title of the reading, and the genre. Ask them *Is it a real story, or is it imaginary?* (real) *How do we know?* (the marker saying Nonfiction, and there are photographs)
- Play the audio while students follow the reading in their books.
- At the end, ask the following gist question: *Do only scientists make time capsules?* (No, scientists, kids, anyone can!) Encourage students to suggest an answer, then read the text again to check.
- Then look at the Words in Context.

TRACK 32 TB p. 230 Words in Context

- Play the audio and have students repeat the words.
- Have them race to find the words in the reading. Remind them that some words are used more than once (*future* x 2, *spacecraft* x 2, *disc* x 3, *Earth* x 2).
- Remind students they can **use the pictures** to help establish the meaning of new words (see TB p. 23).
- Then use these discussion points to confirm the meaning of each word.

future Ask students what they know about time capsules and when people will see the information in them (not in the past, and not now, but in the future). Draw a timeline on the board and label it with *past*, *now*, and *future*. Call on different students to tell you something they are going to do in the future.

objects Ask them which of the items on p. 82 are objects (i.e. not letters or pictures).

newspapers Have students identify the picture of the newspaper. Ask *Does anyone in your family read the newspaper? Do you know the name of some of the newspapers in your country? Are all newspapers made of paper?* (No, there are now online newspapers.)

spacecraft Looking at the third page of the story, ask students *Where is the spacecraft on this page? Do all spacecraft look like this?* Point out the singular and plural of *spacecraft* are the same word with no s for plural (there is one singular and one plural in the reading).

disc Ask *What color is the disc?* (gold) *Can you see it in the picture? What shape is a disc?* (a circle)

Earth Ask students if they think we live on Earth or on Mars. Ask if they know the names of any other planets. Point out that names of planets have a capital letter, like cities and countries.

Second Reading: Analyze the Text and Features

- Give students time to read the text again individually for a better understanding. Ask which time capsule is the most interesting to them. Then take a class vote to decide which one the class likes best.
- Read the text again and stop and discuss the questions in the green boxes as a class when they appear in the reading.
  - **Gist** (p. 82): *What is a time capsule?* Have students discuss with a friend to make a definition of a time capsule in 12 words or fewer. Ask if anyone would like to share their definition with the class.
  - **Detail** (p. 83): *How many years did it take to find the time capsule?* Have students find the date the time capsule was put in the ground and when it was found. Have them do the math or do it with students on the board to find how many years it took to find it (219 years).
  - **Personalization** (p. 84): *How many languages can you say hello in?* Brainstorm different ways with the class and build a list on the board.
  - **Making Connections** (p. 85): *These are real photographs on the gold disc. Do they look old or new?* Draw students' attention to the photos and have them raise their hand if they think they look old and put their hand on their head if they think they look new. Ask volunteers why they chose their answer. Encourage them to find the answer in the reading. (old—they are more than 40 years old)

Third Reading: Interact with the Text

- Listen to the audio again. Then have individual students be the narrators of the text, with each student reading one phrase at a time.

Cool Down

Play *Matching Halves* (see TB p. 26).

Column 1: 1 *a present* / 2 *inside a* / 3 *under* / 4 *40 years* / 5 *55* / 6 *sounds of* / 7 *photos*

Column 2: a. *different languages* / b. *a building* / c. *of people* / d. *from the past* / e. *ago* / f. *time capsule* / g. *the sea*

Answers

1 d 2 f 3 b 4 e 5 a 6 g 7 c

Explore the Reading

Lesson Objectives

- to understand and analyze *Time Capsules* through reading comprehension activities
- to practice the reading skill of identifying the main idea
- to learn through CLIL (history): looking at ways we can find out about civilizations
- to recognize and reproduce the *–nt* blend

Materials
Audio Track 33

Warm Up

Project or write the title of the reading from the previous lesson on the board: *Time Capsules*. With books closed, ask students to remember all the items they can that were in time capsules in the reading and make a list on the board. (*letters, pictures, coins, newspapers, music, movies, video games, clothes, toys, sounds, songs, words* [*hello*]).

A Read and choose the answer.

- Have a Circle Time discussion (see TB p. 21) to find out what students remember from the reading. Ask *Why do people make time capsules?* (for people in the future to learn about the past) *Where do people put them?* (in the ground—or in space!) *What was in the capsule they found in 2014?* (coins and newspapers) *What would you like to put in a time capsule?* (students' own answers)
- Read the first question in A together and discuss why the answer is *future*. Have students look back in the reading and find somewhere that confirms their answer.
- Have students continue the activity individually, checking back to find something in the reading that confirms their answer each time. Then have students compare answers with a friend.
- To check answers, ask students to read correct sentences and ask if everyone agrees.

Answers
1 *future* 2 newspapers 3 forty 4 a lot of languages 5 in space

B Read and think. Then match. What's the main idea of each page?

- Write or project on the board the reading skill tip from the Get Ready to Read lesson, to remind students what the main idea is (and what details are, for comparison).
- Have students decide as a whole class what the main idea for p. 82 is.
- Then have students continue the activity individually.
- To check answers, say the number of each page and then *a, b, c, d*. Have students raise their hands for the answer they chose. Check that everyone agrees and go back to the reading to resolve any disagreements.

Answers
1 d 2 a 3 b 4 c

C Check (✔) two things to tell people in the future about. Write a message.

- Say *I want to tell people from the future about transportation and this school.* Elicit a short message on these topics from students and write it on the board; for example, *Many people use cars, but they make the air dirty. Our school is great—we have a computer in every room.*
- Have students choose two things to talk about and write their own short message to people in the future. Help with language if necessary. Tell students that by doing this, they are creating their own little bit of history for children in the future to learn from.
- Have students share their messages in small groups. Ask them what they think people in the future might learn from these messages (e.g. how children in their country lived, what they enjoyed doing, what they considered to be important). This allows students to explore the history objective of looking at ways we can learn about civilizations.

Phonics *–nt*

TRACK 33 TB p. 230 **Listen and say.**

- Play the audio and have students listen and look at the words in their book. Ask them what sound all the words have in common (they all have *–nt* at the end).
- Play the audio again and have students repeat each word, first in a whisper and then loudly. Ask a few individual students to repeat each word.
- Ask students to choose their favorite word from the list and to tell a friend.
- Have students find more words in the reading ending with *–nt*, and invite students to read them aloud.

Answers
want; present; different; went

Cool Down

Ask students *Do you think it's more fun to make a time capsule or to find one?* Have them discuss their answers in small groups, then have each group share with the class.

Practice Resource Bank: Phonics Printout;
Student's App: Phonics Practice; Reading Comprehension Practice

Think Together

Lesson Objectives

- to make connections between the two readings
- to explore the key concept: How can we find out about the past?
- to reflect on the unit and provide personal thoughts and opinions

Warm Up

Ask students to look at the question at the top of p. 87: *How can we find out about the past?* Ask if the readings in this unit helped them find out about the past. Ask if they would like to know more about the subjects of dinosaurs, ancient Egypt, and time capsules. Ask where they could go to find out more. Elicit ideas such as the library, the internet, a history teacher, and books they have at home.

Encourage students to also think about why it is important to find out about the past—how the past shapes the present. Discuss how today, too, will be history someday, and have them imagine what people will read about their lives. *What will be interesting to them? What will be the same, and what will be different?*

A Read, think, and check (✔).

- Refer students to the sentences and point out or elicit that items 1 to 6 are all ways to find out about the past. Discuss whether there are any they didn't mention during the Warm Up.
- Refer students to the example sentence and ask them if they can remember what picture Jannah saw in the book. (herself in an old street, an old lady wearing glasses) Point out the checkmark in the column for *The Time Book*.
- Have students continue the activity individually.
- To check answers, refer back to the readings if necessary to resolve disagreements.

Answers
1 *The Time Book* 2 Time Capsules 3 The Time Book
4 Time Capsules 5 The Time Book 6 Time Capsules

B Take the quiz. What do you do to learn about the past?

- Ask students if they like to learn about the past.
- Do the first question as a whole class. Ask students to raise their hands if they read nonfiction books. Not everyone will, so point out this is just one way to learn.
- Have students circle *yes* or *no* for the questions and then compare answers with a friend.
- Bring the class back together and find out who had the most circles for *yes*.

Answers
Students' own answers

Practice **Resource Bank:** Unit Test; Mid-year Test; **Student's App:** Key Concept Practice

C Think and discuss. Share your ideas for learning about the past. Do an Inside–Outside Circle.

- Tell students they are going to share ideas about how they can learn about the past. Set the class up for an Inside–Outside Circle cooperative learning routine (see TB p. 20).
- Tell the class that students on the outside will ask questions about ways to learn about the past. Point out they can ask follow-up questions: *When? / Why? / How do you do that?* Students on the inside will answer using their ideas from B and the Warm Up.
- Clap your hands to have students swap roles. Call out *Change!* to have students on the outside rotate one place to the left. They will then share with a new friend.

My Reading Journal

Find five words that are interesting or new to you. Write.

This question focuses on personalization.

Tell students some words that you found interesting in the readings (e.g. *ancient, capsule, Voyager*) and explain why you like them (you could talk about their sound, their meaning, if they are similar to a word in L1, etc.).

Ask students to look back at the readings and choose five words that they think are interesting. Have students compare with a partner to see if they have any words in common and discuss why they think these words are interesting.

Answers
Students' own answers

What person or event from history do you want to find out about?

This question focuses students on how they can continue to learn.

Say *I want to learn about the Voyager spacecraft. What do you want to learn about?*

Give students time to think about someone or something from history that they want to find out more about. Tell them it doesn't have to be something connected to this unit. Have them write their own sentence about it.

Invite students to share their sentence with the rest of the class.

Answers
Students' own answers

Cool Down

Have students look back at the VTR picture on pp. 72–73. Ask them if they now have any more ideas about the picture. Ask students where they think they can find a picture like this. (maybe a book or a website about dinosaurs) Ask them what they think is the best way to find out more information about dinosaurs. (books, internet, museums, models) Ask if they would like for this situation to be real. Say *Is it scary or exciting?*

UNIT 6

Look What I Made

Unit Overview

Themes

Being creative

Sculptures and architecture

Synopsis

In this unit, students will learn about amazing places around the world, find out about a famous architect, and think about where people get their ideas from. They will plan and prepare a presentation about making a collage and write a personal profile using target vocabulary and grammar from the unit.

Language Book

Vocabulary

box, drawing, jewelry, mask, painting, sculpture, beard, curly, mustache, straight

p. 128

Explore Language

Comparatives: Short Adjectives

p. 129

Global Citizenship

Which famous places in the world are amazing?

building, wall, clean, hard, messy, new, noisy, quiet, soft, thick

p. 130

Explore Language

Superlatives: Short Adjectives

p. 131

Take the Stage

Presentation: giving instructions

p. 132

Write About It

A Personal Profile

Spelling: comparative and superlative endings

p. 133

Think It Over

Review and Reflection

p. 134

Literacy Book

Think Together
Why do people make things?

p. 141

Visible Thinking
VTR: Think, Pair, Share

p. 135

Nonfiction
Informational Text: *Visit Gaudi's World*

Words in Context: architect, nature, coral, bench, cave

p. 139

Fiction
Story: *The Superstar*

Words in Context: superstar, assistant, fix, workshop, world

p. 136

Reading Skill
Identifying fact and opinion

p. 138

Phonics
wh–

p. 137

Language and Literacy Connections

The connecting theme in Unit 6 is what inspires us to make things.

	Language	Literacy
Vocabulary	**Set 1:** art and physical characteristics **Set 2:** short adjectives	**Get Ready to Read:** *jewelry* **Fiction:** *beard, curly, noisy* **Get Ready to Read:** *drawing, painting* **Nonfiction:** *building, new, wall*
Grammar	**Comparatives: Short Adjectives** The hair is curlier than Dad's. **Superlatives: Short Adjectives** They're the smallest buildings.	**Fiction** My brother's beard is longer and curlier. My son's arms and hands need to be bigger. **Nonfiction** The city of Barcelona in Spain has some of the world's greatest buildings.
Skills	**Pronunciation:** /**g**/ and /**k**/	**Reading:** identifying fact and opinion **Phonics:** *wh–*
International English	*jewelry/jewellery; mustache/moustache; clean/tidy*	

Vocabulary

Lesson Objectives

- to learn art and physical characteristics vocabulary: *box, drawing, jewelry, mask, painting, sculpture, beard, curly, mustache, straight*
- to sing a song exploring ways to be creative

Materials
Audio Tracks 63 to 66; Video

Warm Up

Introduce the unit topic by playing *Stand Up, Sit Down* (see TB p. 26).

Suggested sentences: *This week … I made my breakfast. / I made a picture. / I made a model. / I made my bed. / I made a phone call.*

A TRACK 63 TB p. 219 **Listen and find. What color are Mr. Pocassi's eyes?**

- Look at the picture on pp. 74–75. Ask *What can you see? What are they doing?* (making things) *Where are they?* (in a classroom)
- Draw students' attention to the man in a hat and glasses and ask if they remember him (he is Harold, Jannah's dad, from the previous unit).
- Ask *Who is holding a fossil?* (the teacher) Tell students that the teacher's name is Mr. Pocassi. Point out his name in the gist question in A.
- Tell students they are going to listen to George talking about things he made. Play the audio and have students point to the new words and pictures as they listen.
- Ask the gist question *What color are Mr. Pocassi's eyes?* and elicit the answer. Play the audio again for students to check.
- Say *What does Uncle Harold see?* Listen again to check. (He sees George's painting of some flowers, a drawing of his dad, a sculpture of his sister, and a mask of Mr. Pocassi.)

Answer
green

B TRACK 64 TB p. 219 **Listen, say, and number the pictures in A.**

- Play the audio and have students point to the items in the picture and say the words.
- Then play it again and have them number the items in order.
- Check answers by playing the audio again.
- Have all students repeat the words one more time, this time with a mime for each word.

Answers
1 *box* 2 drawing 3 curly 4 beard 5 straight
6 sculpture 7 mustache 8 painting 9 jewelry
10 mask

International English

Ask students to find *jewelry* and *mustache* on the page and point out that the spelling is different in American and British English. Explain that the pronunciation is the same and that this is true of many words. Ask *Which spelling do we use?*

C TRACK 65 TB p. 220 **Listen. Close your eyes and visualize.**

- Prepare students for the visualization (see TB p. 21).
- Play the audio, allowing students to visualize the descriptions and do actions where appropriate as they listen. They can say the word after they hear *say*.
- Divide the class into pairs or small groups, play the audio again, and have students share their ideas or do their mimes in pairs.
- Then ask students if they had similar answers.

D Look and write.

- Draw the first set of spaces on the board exactly as it appears in the book. Point out how the word *curly* fits into the spaces—including the ups and downs of the letter stalks. Show that, for example, *beard* doesn't fit.
- Have students analyze the other word shapes and complete the activity.
- Check answers as a class..

Answers
1 *curly* 2 straight 3 drawing 4 box 5 beard
6 jewelry 7 painting 8 mustache 9 sculpture
10 mask

E TRACK 66 TB p. 220 **Listen and sing. Then watch and sing.**

- Have students read the title of the song, *Get Creative*, and ask them what they think it will be about. Before they listen, have them look quickly at the lyrics and see if their prediction is correct.
- Have students close their books. Play the song and have students raise their hands every time they hear a word from B.
- Tell students to open their books. Play the song again, pausing after each line for students to repeat.
- Then play the song again and have students sing along. You could have half the class sing the first verse and half sing the second verse, then switch.
- Play the song video and encourage students to watch and sing.
- Ask *Is it good to get creative?* and elicit some responses. Encourage them to recognize that there are many ways to be creative, not just through arts and crafts.

Cool Down

Play *Draw It!* (see TB p. 25) with vocabulary from this lesson.

Practice **Student's App:** Vocabulary Practice; Video

Explore Language

Lesson Objectives

- to learn how to use comparatives with short adjectives
- to provide contextualized practice of art and physical characteristics vocabulary

Materials

Audio Tracks 67 to 68

Warm Up

Play *Mime It!* with the vocabulary from the previous lesson, pp. 74–75 (see TB p. 26).

A TRACK 67 TB p. 220 **Listen and read. Who did Lizzy paint?**

- Project the dialogue on p. 76 or have students look in their books. Ask who the boy is (George from the previous lesson). Ask if they recognize the girl (she's his sister Lizzy—there's a sculpture of her in the unit opener picture). Ask students what they can see happening in the images. Guide them with some questions: *Who made these pictures? Do you think they are good?*
- Tell students they are going to listen to George and Lizzy talking about their artwork. Play the audio and have students follow in their books.
- Ask the gist question *Who did Lizzy paint?* and elicit the answer. Play the audio again for students to check.

Answer

her/their dad

B Look at A. Complete.

- Write or project the table on the board.
- Highlight the first sentence to the class and have students find it in the dialogue in A. Draw students' attention to the example answer (bigger). Say *These are Dad's hands* and draw on the board the size of a normal hand. Ask *How big are the hands in the drawing?* and have a student draw a much bigger size.
- Have students work individually to complete the other sentences in the table. Check answers as a class. Point out the word *than*, which comes after all the comparative adjectives.
- Ask students to notice what all of the adjectives in the table end in (*–er*). Note: spelling rules are covered in more depth in the Write About It lesson.
- Have students look at the Grammar tip *Watch Out* and point out the irregular adjective *worse*. Ask students *Which adjective in the table is irregular?* (good > better)

Answers

bigger; than; curlier; is; better

C Think and discuss. Then choose.

- Have students work in pairs to discuss when to use comparative adjectives. Encourage them to look at the table in B and the story in A. Check answers as a class.
- Read the options again and have students raise their hands for the one they chose. Confirm their answer and have them circle the correct option in their books.

Answer

1 two

D TRACK 68 TB p. 220 **Listen and say.**

- Play the audio and have students tell you what comparative adjectives they hear (bigger (x 2), worse, longer).
- Play the audio again, pausing after each sentence for students to repeat.
- Play the audio again, this time encouraging students to concentrate on the intonation.
- For ideas on how to vary the drill, see TB p. 22.

E Look and complete.

- Refer students to the picture in their books or enlarge it if you're using the TTL. Point out the name labels, say the names, and have students point to each one. Ask them *Who is the (sister)?* and have students point and say *Carla.*
- Refer students to the example answer and ask them *How old do you think Paul is? How old do you think Helen is?* Say *So Helen is older than Paul.* Highlight that the answer is formed from *old* + *er* + *than* to make the comparison.
- Have students continue the activity individually and then compare answers with a friend.
- To check answers, ask students to read a sentence each. Ask if everyone agrees. Make sure that everyone has remembered to use *than* in every answer. Write the adjectives on the board so everyone can check.

Answers

1 *older than* 2 younger than 3 straighter than
4 curlier than 5 happier than 6 sadder than

F Play *Guess Who!* Look, say, and guess.

- Have students look again at the picture in E. Then point to the example in speech bubbles and read the exchange with a confident student.
- Make another comparative sentence about E (e.g. *She's younger than Stefan*) and have students guess whom you are talking about.
- Have students work in pairs. Tell them to take turns making comparative sentences about E and guessing the answer.

Cool Down

Play *Pass the Whisper!* (see TB p. 26) with sentences from A.

Practice **Resource Bank:** Grammar Printout; **Student's App:** Grammar Practice

Global Citizenship

Lesson Objectives

- to learn short adjectives and nouns: *clean, hard, messy, new, noisy, quiet, soft, thick, building, wall*
- to learn about places in the world and what makes them special
- to practice listening for gist and details

Materials

Audio Tracks 69 to 71; (optional) Audio Track F; (optional) pictures of famous buildings and places around the world (CD)

Opening Question

Ask the opening question: *Which famous places in the world are amazing?* Give students some thinking time and then elicit ideas—amazing nature or amazing cities, buildings, and monuments. Remind students that this is an opinion question, so there are no right or wrong answers.

A TRACK 69 TB p. 220 **Listen to Sara talk about how she likes making things. Where's Sara's favorite place?**

- Have students look at the pictures and say what they can see. Ask *Which picture do you like best? Why? Where do you think the tall tower is?* (in Dubai, UAE)
- Play the audio and have students point to the pictures and words as they hear them.
- Ask the gist question *Where's Sara's favorite place?* and elicit answers. Play the audio again to check.

Answer

Cayan Tower in Dubai

B TRACK 70 TB p. 220 **Listen, say, and number the pictures in A.**

- Play the audio and have students point to the pictures and say the words.
- Play the audio again and have students number the items in the order they hear them.
- Then play the audio again to check answers.

Answers

1 *quiet* 2 noisy 3 building 4 wall 5 new 6 thick
7 messy 8 clean 9 hard 10 soft

International English

Elicit *clean* is American English and *tidy* is British English. Ask if they have heard either of them being used before. Explain that they are both correct. Ask *Which word do we use?*

TRACK F TB p. 220 **Visualization**

- The TTL has a visualization audio track for this vocabulary set (see TB p. 21).

C Play *The Adjectives Game*.

- Tell students that they will play a describing game. Say *a bed, a sofa, and a cat's fur.* As this is an example, also write the words on the board (but tell students afterward that they don't have to write down their words). Elicit the best adjective from A to describe all three (soft).
- Give students some thinking time to look at the adjectives and remember some things they describe. Divide the class into pairs and have them take turns saying their items and guessing the adjectives.
- Ask if any students would like to say their items for the class to guess.

D TRACK 71 TB p. 220 **Now listen to Thomas and Natasha. Number the pictures. Who visited a museum?**

- Listening for the main idea: tell students that they will listen to two children talking about places they've visited in Belgium and Russia. Play the audio and have students number the pictures.
- Ask the gist question *Who visited a museum?* and elicit the answer. Encourage students to justify their answer. Ask *Why do you say that? What do you remember about the museum?* Play the audio again for students to check.

Answers

a 2 b 1 Thomas

E **Listen again. Choose.**

- Listening for detail: have students look at the sentences before they listen again and see if they can remember any of the answers. Then play the audio again and have students circle the answers.
- Check answers by asking students to read the full, correct sentences aloud. Check if the rest of the class agrees. Refer back to the audio where necessary.

Answers

1 *a big lake* 2 buildings 3 a drawing 4 science
5 model

Discussion Questions

- Draw students' attention to the discussion questions: *What are some famous places in your country? How do people feel about them? Why?* Invite opinions and ideas from the class. Students can discuss the questions in pairs or small groups (see **ETB**).
- Return to the original opening question to ask again *What famous places in the world are amazing?*
- Discuss the new information students have learned in this lesson. Ask if they now have any new ideas. Ask *Do you think there are any amazing places in our country?*

Cool Down

Play *Board Race* (see TB p. 25). Stick one of the pictures on the board (or write the name of the place). Students race to write as many related words as they can, including adjectives, colours, etc.

Practice **Student's App:** Vocabulary Practice; Listening Comprehension Practice

Explore Language

Lesson Objectives

- to learn how to use superlatives with short adjectives
- to provide contextualized practice of short adjectives

Materials
Audio Tracks 72 and 73

Warm Up

To prepare students for a lesson on models, brainstorm all the materials that students can use to make models. Ask what people make models of (e.g. planes, trains, cars, buildings, towns) and then elicit all the materials and write them on the board. Ask *Do you make models? What do you make?*

A TRACK 72 TB p. 220 **Listen and read. Why is Lizzy happy?**

- Look at the pictures on p. 80. Ask students *What can you see in the pictures? What models can you see? What materials do you think they are made of?* Draw their attention to the girl. Ask who she is. (Lizzy from Lesson 2)
- Play the audio and have students follow in their books.
- Ask the gist question *Why is Lizzy happy?* and elicit the answer. Play the audio again to check.
- Ask students which model is Lizzy's. (the mountain)

Answer
She has the best model.

B Look at A. Complete.

- Write or project the table on the board.
- Highlight the first sentence, which contains the example answer (smallest). Have students look back at the story to find where that sentence appears.
- Have students work in pairs to complete the blanks in the table. Check answers as a class.
- Point out all these superlative adjectives end in *–est*. Elicit that they always have *the* before them. Note: spelling rules for superlatives are explored in the Write About It lesson.
- Have students look at the Grammar tip *Remember* and point out the irregular adjective *worst*. Ask students *Which adjective in the table is irregular?* (good > best)

Answers
the; *smallest*; noisiest; best

C Think and discuss. Then choose.

- Read the sentence options and have students look at the table in B and draw a conclusion about which option they think is correct.
- Read the options again and have students raise their hands for the one they chose. Confirm the correct answer and have them circle it in their books.

Answer
1 more than two

D TRACK 73 TB p. 220 **Listen and say.**

- Play the audio and have students tell you what superlative adjectives they hear. (best, coolest, thickest, cleanest)
- Play the audio again and have students listen carefully and repeat each sentence, concentrating on pronunciation and intonation.
- For ideas on how to vary the drill, see TB p. 22.

E Look at A. Complete with superlative adjectives.

- Have students look back at the pictures in A. Refer them to the example answer in E and ask *Are any buildings smaller than the shops?* (no) *How do we know?* (smallest) *How do we make the superlative adjective?* (take the normal adjective and add *–est*). Elicit the spelling for *noisiest* encouraging them to use their knowledge of verbs ending in *-y* (Unit 4).
- Have students continue the activity individually. Point out that they should use their own ideas to complete number 6, not just a superlative.
- When students have finished, have them compare their answers with a friend. Then check answers by asking volunteers to read a completed sentence each. Ask if everyone agrees.

Answers
1 *the smallest* 2 the noisiest 3 the coolest
4 the best 5 the tallest 6 Students' own answers

F Look in your book. Find and write.

- Have students look back through the pages of the **Language Book** they've covered so far and choose a page they think is really cool. Ask *What do you think is the coolest page?* Elicit some answers and have students write a full sentence in their notebooks.
- Have students do the same for the other prompts, and then compare ideas with a partner.
- Invite individual students to read their ideas aloud and ask if the other students in the class agree or if they have a different answer.

Answers
1 The coolest page is … 2 The tallest person is …
3 The best activity is … 4 The cutest person is …
5 The smallest picture is …

Cool Down

Have a *Superlatives Quiz*. Divide the class into two teams. Ask them superlative questions based on general knowledge they will know or related to their classroom/friends; for example, *Who is the tallest person in the class? Which is the biggest fruit—a cherry, a banana or a watermelon?* Give a point for correct answers.

Practice **Resource Bank:** Grammar Printout; **Student's App:** Grammar Practice

Take the Stage

Lesson Objectives

- to prepare and give a presentation about making a collage
- to recognize and reproduce /g/ and /k/

Materials
Video; Audio Track 74; (optional) pictures of collages (C)

Warm Up

Have a class brainstorm. Show students a plain piece of paper and have them say all the things they can make with it or use it for, e.g. a paper airplane, a hat—encourage them to get creative! Write their ideas on the board in a colorful word cloud.

A TB p. 234 **Watch and listen. Who does Greta make a picture of?**

- Tell students they will watch a video of a girl named Greta talking about making a picture. Ask what kind of picture they think she will make. Then say *Let's watch and find out.*
- Play the video, then ask the prediction question again: *What kind of picture did Greta make?* (a collage)
- Then introduce the gist question *Who does Greta make a picture of?* Elicit the answer, then play the video again for students to check. Ask further comprehension questions (see **ETB**).
- Ask *Do you think this is an easy picture to make? Would you like to make one?*

Answer
Greta/herself

B Watch again. Check (✔) the phrases you hear.

- Have students read the phrases and draw their attention to the example.
- Play the video again and have students check all the other phrases they hear.
- To check answers, ask students to read a sentence each and say *yes* or *no*. Ask if everyone agrees.
- Have students analyze the phrases, categorizing them as follows: beginning, Greta introduces the talk (1); middle, Greta explains how to make the portrait (2, 3, 4, 5, 7); end, Greta finishes the talk (9). They can write B, M, or E at the end of each phrase.

Answers
1; 2; 3; 4; 5; 7; 9

Pronunciation /g/ and /k/

TRACK 74 TB p. 221 **Listen and say.**

- Demonstrate the **/g/** sound as in *Greta* and the **/k/** sound as in collage and encourage students to copy you.
- Play the audio for students to repeat the sounds and words.
- Say *These are all words Greta says in her presentation. What other words do you know with these sounds?* Elicit ideas (e.g. good, cool) and write them on the board in two sections. Drill all the words at the end.

C Plan. Think of a collage you can make. Choose (✔) or write.

- Tell students that they are going to do a presentation like Greta's about a collage. Show pictures of different collages if you have them. Point out the headings in the plan and ask *What did Greta make?* (a portrait—check students know this means a picture of a person) *What materials did she use?* (colored paper, stickers, scissors, and glue) *What actions did she do?* (draw, cut out, color, use [a pencil, scissors], decorate with [paper shapes, stickers])
- Have them complete the plan with their own ideas for a collage.

D Prepare your presentation. Use your ideas from C and phrases from B.

- Play the video again and have students notice how Greta organizes her presentation. (description, materials needed, how to make it)
- Then have students use the plan they made in C and phrases from B to complete the notes. Provide vocabulary where necessary.
- Have students draw a picture of their collage so they can point to its key features during the presentation.

E Practice with a friend. Then share with your class.

- Have students practice their presentation with a friend as many times as they need to. Remind them to look at the audience and speak slowly and clearly. Tell them to point to their picture to show important parts.
- Invite volunteers to come to the front of the classroom to give their presentation. Encourage the class to give a round of applause after each presentation.

Cool Down

Invite students to say one thing they liked about the presentations they listened to.

Practice Student's App: Speaking Skill Practice; Video

Write About It

Lesson Objectives

- to focus on comparative and superlative endings
- to plan and write a personal profile

Materials

(Optional) Support, Standard, and Challenge writing printouts from the Resource Bank (one per student) (C, D)

Warm Up

Have students look through their **Language Books** and race to find someone with curly hair, someone with straight hair, someone old, someone young, someone who is good at something, and someone who is the best at something.

A Read the personal profile. Circle the comparative adjectives. Underline the superlative adjectives.

- Have students read the text quickly and find the writer's name (*Modelia*) and age (seven). Ask comprehension questions about the profile, e.g. *Does Modelia have a younger brother?* (no, she has an older brother)
- Review the difference between comparative adjectives and superlative adjectives. Refer back to C in Lessons 2 and 4 if necessary.
- Project or write the profile on the board. Highlight the first comparative adjective. (*curlier*) Then ask students to find and circle all the other comparative adjectives, in their books. Ask how many they found. (there are two more after *curlier*)
- Then ask students to underline the superlative adjectives.
- Complete your version of the text on the board for students to check their answers.

Answers

I have brown curly hair. My hair is (curlier) than my brother's. His name is Modifi. He's (older) than me, but my bedroom is (bigger) than his. My favorite activity is dancing. I'm the <u>shortest</u> in my family, but I'm the <u>best</u> dancer.

B Look at A. Write the adjectives in the table.

- Write or project the table on the board. Have students find the stem *short-* in the text in A, and elicit that this is the superlative form. Ask *What are the last three letters?* (est) Point out that *short* is a regular adjective and have them notice the endings for comparative and superlative.
- Have students find the next adjective in the text (bigger). Point out the double g and explain that we add an extra consonant before the *–er/–est* for consonant-vowel-consonant adjectives (like *big*). Have students spell it out and write it in their books.
- Elicit the base adjective *curly* for the next row in the table. Then highlight the superlative ending, curl<u>iest</u>. Point out that the *y* changed to an *i* and explain that this happens to adjectives that end in a *y*. Ask *What's the comparative of curly?* (curlier) Have students spell it out and write it in their books.
- For the fourth row, remind students of irregular comparatives and superlatives. Ask them *What's the adjective that has the comparative* better? (good) Then have them find the superlative form in the text and write it in the table.
- Have students complete the rest of the table individually. Check answers as a class.

Answers

\+ *–er*/+ *–est*: *shorter*, shortest; older, oldest
\+ consonant + *–er*/+ *–est*: bigger, *biggest*; hotter, hottest
– ~~y~~ + *–ier*/–iest: curlier, *curliest*; noisier, noisiest
irregular: *better*, best; worse, worst

C Plan. Think about yourself. Complete.

- Tell students they are going to write their own personal profile.
- Write or project C on the board and do a made-up example with the class, eliciting information from students; for example, Name: Englelia. Age: 8 years old. Hair: short. Activity (something Englelia enjoys or is the best at): running. Adjective (to use with the activity): fast.
- Using this model as a guide, have students complete the information for themselves. Remind them that they will need to use comparative and superlative adjectives when they write their final profile, so they should think about this when choosing the activity and adjective for their plan. Challenge printouts can be handed out now. Monitor and help as necessary.

D Write your character profile.

- Look at your example plan from C. Elicit some sentences you could use to turn this into a personal profile and write them on the board, e.g. *My name is Englelia. I'm eight years old. I have short hair. My hair is shorter than my friend Anna's. My favorite activity is running. I'm the fastest runner in my class.*
- Have students write their own personal profile in their notebooks from the notes they made in C. Encourage them to use A and the example on the board as models. Tell them to make sure they include at least one comparative adjective and one superlative adjective in their profile so that they can say what makes them special. Support printouts can be handed out now.
- Have students write their profile out neatly and draw a picture of themselves on paper or hand out the Standard printouts from the Resource Bank.
- Display the finished profiles around the classroom.

Cool Down

Enjoy each other's work: have students circulate around the classroom, reading their friends' profiles. Before they leave, ask them which profiles they enjoyed reading and why.

Practice **Student's App:** Writing Skill Practice

Think It Over

Lesson Objectives

- to review what has been learned in the unit
- to reflect on the unit and their progress
- to think about learning strategies and how to continue learning at home

Warm Up

This is a chance to review language from the unit and bring the topic back into focus. Ask students what the topic of the unit was (art and creating things).

Play the *Yes/No game* with adjectives and words about art. Students have to point left and say *yes* if the words were in this unit or point right and say *no* if not.

Suggested words: *sculpture* (Y), *curly* (Y), *pyramid* (N), *thick* (Y), *palace* (N), *messy* (Y), *jewelry* (Y), *gold* (N), *mask* (Y), *mustache* (Y), *noisy* (Y), *wall* (Y), *silent* (N)

Read the questions and draw or write your answers.

- Encourage review and reflection of the language and ideas from the unit to help students make connections to past learning experiences.

What did I do?

- Give students a few minutes to look back through the unit at the different activities they did. Ask questions about the unit; for example, *What did you sing about? What did you make? Where did you hear about a museum?*
- Tell students they can draw or write about activities they liked or found interesting, but encourage them not to choose their favorite activity yet. Instead, encourage them to identify something in the unit that they found challenging but which they completed and feel proud of. Alternatively, ask them to choose something that was particularly memorable for them—either because it was interesting, or it was different, or even because it was noisy! You can use L1 to explain these ideas to students.

What did I learn?

- Have students talk to a partner about what they remember from the unit—stories, words, phrases, or people.
- Ask students *Can you find words that you didn't know before? Can you compare two or more things? What new facts did you learn?* Have students talk to a friend.
- Encourage students to draw a picture or write about what they learned.

What was my favorite part?

- Have students look back through the unit and decide what they enjoyed the most. Tell them it can be an activity they found fun, a story they enjoyed reading, or a favorite character. They should try to choose just one and draw a picture or write about it. Explain that when we like something, it is often easier to learn.

How well did I do?

- Tell students to color in the number of masks that best expresses how well they have learned the unit content (i.e. the more they color, the more they feel they have learned). Ask *What do you remember? What do you understand? What do you need to practice more?* Encourage students to look back through the unit to see how much they remember.

What can I do next?

- Brainstorm ideas with the class about what students can do to continue to learn (e.g. use the **Student's App on Navio**; play the game on p. 77 again).
- Encourage students to think about what they can do at home to improve their English, using the four verbs as prompts; for example watch a TV show or video clips in English, practice their presentation in front of family members, share what they have learned with family members, find out more about making collages.
- Ask students to choose one or more activities from the list (watch, practice, share, find out more) that they will do to practice their English.
- Once students have completed the page in their books, have them discuss with a friend what they drew or wrote. Did they choose the same activities or different ones?

Looking Forward

Draw students' attention to the character at the bottom of the page. Ask *Who's this?* and elicit what they remember about him (Joe was looking at models in Lesson 4, p. 80). Tell students that Joe is part of a team. Ask them if they can guess what kind of team and what activity they think his team might be doing. Elicit ideas, then tell students they will find out in the next unit.

Put It Together

To further review and recycle the language in Units 5 and 6, play the game, *Race to the Museum*, on pp. 86–87. See TB p. 210 for teaching notes.

Practice **Resource Bank:** Unit Test; **Student's App:** Vocabulary and Grammar Review

Get Ready to Read

Lesson Objectives

- to activate prior knowledge of art and making things
- to encourage students to observe and interpret through a Think, Pair, Share VTR
- to preview the reading skill of identifying fact and opinion

Materials

(Optional) VTR printout from the Resource Bank (A, B, C); (Optional) some pictures of different ways of making art (e.g. making music, dancing, taking photos) (Transition)

Warm Up

Use this activity to create interest in the topic of making things.

Ask *Do you like art class? What do you do in art class? What do you like doing best? Why?* Have students discuss their ideas in pairs, then invite some students to share their thoughts with the class.

Think, Pair, Share

A Look at the picture. Is this art? Think about it.

- Students are going to do a Think, Pair, Share VTR to explore the image of the inflatable duck.
- Start by asking students to say what they can see in the picture. Encourage them to use adjectives such as colors and shapes to describe what they see. Provide vocabulary where necessary.
- Students will likely find: a (large) yellow duck, (blue) water, (rectangular) buildings/skyscrapers. Students may also notice: a hill, the sky, clouds, a boat, masts, antennae.
- Then write the question *Is this art?* on the board. Give students one or two minutes to think independently about the question so that they form their own ideas. Tell them to place their hands on top of their heads when they are ready.

B Talk with your partner.

- Have students work in pairs to share ideas about whether the duck is art and to think of possible answers together. Encourage them to use questions such as *What do you think?* and *What about you?* and to listen to each other's opinions. Remind students that their ideas will vary and all answers are valid.
- Circulate and encourage students to expand on their ideas by asking *What makes you say that?* Provide vocabulary where necessary.

C Share with the class.

- Bring the class back together and tell them that now they will complete the Share part of Think, Pair, Share. This third step helps students refine their ideas.
- Invite students to share their ideas with the class and encourage them to clarify their thinking. When they have finished making a point, have them ask other students if they agree by saying *What do you think?* Remind them that they don't have to agree.

Here's an example of this part of the routine.

Teacher: What do you think?
Student A: We don't think it's art.
Teacher: Why do you say that?
Student A: Because it's not original. It's just a large rubber duck. What do you think?
Student B: We don't agree. We think it is art because someone made it and put it in the sea.

Transition

Ask *How can people make art?* Brainstorm ideas and write them on the board. Students will initially mention the activities they have done in art class, but encourage them to move beyond this. You could display some pictures around the classroom as a prompt, e.g. someone taking pictures, someone playing a musical instrument, someone dancing. Encourage students to think of different ways of making art.

D Think and discuss. Do you make or create things? What are they?

- Write *at home / at school / another place* on the board and give students time to think about anything they make or create at each of these places. Tell them they can use the ideas on the board from the Warm Up and the previous activity as a prompt. Have them share their ideas in pairs.
- Encourage students to also talk about creative family members and friends who like to create things.
- Ask if any students would like to share their experiences of making and creating things with the rest of the class. Encourage them to see that there are many different ways of making and creating.

E Read and choose. Which of these sentences is <u>not</u> true?

This task is a preview of the reading skill of identifying fact and opinion.

- Check students understand the meaning of the word *sculpture* (taught in Unit 6 of the **Language Book**). Show an image of some sculptures if necessary.
- Ask students to read the sentences and decide which ones are always true and which one may not be true for everyone.
- Read the sentences and have students raise their hands for the one they think is not always true.

Answer

3 The best sculptures are of people.

Now read **The Superstar**

Fiction: *The Superstar—A Story*

Lesson Objectives

- to read a story about a sculpture
- to explore the SEL competency of self-management through setting plans and working toward goals
- to make a personal connection to the reading

Materials

Audio Tracks 34 and 35; (optional) a globe (Words in Context)

Warm Up

Play a TPR game with students. Have students stand behind their chairs and then mime the actions you say; for example, *You're painting a picture. You're making a model. You're cutting out a circle. You're sticking things with glue.*

TRACK 34 TB p. 230 Reading Approach

First Reading: Listen and Engage

- Ask students to open their books and give them a minute to notice the title, the genre, the pictures, and the text. Ask *Who do you think is the main character in this story?* (the man making the sculpture—the sculptor) *Why?* (He is on every page.) Then tell students *Let's read to find out if you're right.*
- Organize students for Circle Time (see TB p. 21) and read them the story. Use a lot of gesture, facial expression, and movement as you read; point to things as you mention them; and use dramatic intonation to portray emotions and to highlight important words and plot points. All of these will help bring the story to life for students. Alternatively, play the audio, or use the Story Player on the TTL, and gesture, show reactions in your face while they listen.
- When you have read the whole story, have students find and point to each of the characters.
- Ask students *Do you like Pablo's sculpture? Why or why not?*
- Then look at the Words in Context.

TRACK 35 TB p. 230 Words in Context

- Play the audio and have students repeat the words.
- Have a race to find the new words in the story. Ask *How many times is each word used?* (*superstar* x 2 [including the title], *assistant* x 1, *fix* x 3, *workshop* x 2)
- Read the story again. Remind students that by **watching what you do and listening to how you read**, they can use storytelling to establish the meaning of new words (see TB p. 13).
- Use these discussion points to confirm the meaning of each word.

superstar Ask students to read what the superstar says on p. 94 and elicit what he is famous for (he works in movies; he is probably an actor, or he could be a director). Ask *Is he famous or very, very famous?* (very, very famous) Ask them to suggest any superstars they know of.

assistant Ask students if the assistant is in the superstar's family (no). Ask *Is she his friend?* (no) *Does she work for him?* (yes) Ask what work they think she does for the superstar.

fix Have students find where Pablo says *I can fix it* on pp. 91–92. Ask *Why does he say it?* (because they aren't happy with the sculpture, so he has to change it) Ask students if they have ever fixed something.

workshop Have students find the word and sentence on p. 92. Ask *Where are they? What does Pablo do there?* (He works—he makes sculptures.)

world Have students find the sentence *I travel all over the world* on p. 94. Ask *Does Pablo go to a few countries or a lot of countries?* (a lot). *Are the countries in one part of the world?* (no, he visits countries in different parts of the world) Invite students to point out some countries Pablo might have visited on a globe.

Second Reading: Analyze the Text and Features

- Play the audio and have students listen and follow the words in their books. Ask them to think about this question while they read: *Do you think the people like the statue at the end of the story?* (no) *Why do you think that?* (their faces in the picture)
- Then discuss the questions in the yellow boxes as a class.
  - **Making Connections** (p. 90): *Why do sculptors make statues of people?* Check understanding of *statue*: a sculpture of a person or animal. Ask students for their ideas. Help them if necessary by asking *Are the people in statues usually famous? Why do we like to remember famous people?* Elicit that making a statue of someone can be a sign of respect.
  - **Making Connections** (p. 91): *Why is it important to have a plan?* Ask students why Pablo needed a plan. (he was doing something complicated and only had a little time; a plan helped him finish it well)
  - **Personalization** (p. 95): *What famous sculptures do you know?* Ask students first if they know of any sculptures in their hometown or in towns they've visited. Then ask if they know any sculptures that are famous around the world.

Third Reading: Interact with the Text

- Play the audio again and have students mime the story while they listen.
- Have students read the story aloud, one sentence each. Encourage them to add the appropriate dramatic intonation!

Cool Down

Ask *What are the most important events in this story?* Have students work in small groups to decide on three.

Explore the Reading

Lesson Objectives

- to understand and analyze *The Superstar* through reading comprehension activities
- to explore the SEL competency of self-management through setting plans and working toward goals
- to recognize and reproduce the *wh–* sound

Materials
Audio Track 36

Warm Up

Play *Who Said It?* (See TB p. 27.)

A Read and number. Put the sentences in order.

- Before students open their books, have a Circle Time discussion about the reading (see TB p. 21). Ask *What's Pablo creating?* (a sculpture of the superstar) *Who comes to look at the statue?* (the superstar's assistant, brother, and mother) *Why don't they like it?* (They think it doesn't look like the superstar.)
- Have students open their books and look at A. Ask individual students to each read a sentence. Ask students if they remember the sentences and point out they are all from the story. Have students look back at the story and decide together which one is the first sentence.
- Have students complete the rest of the activity individually, referring back to the reading to check their answers.
- To check answers, say numbers from 2 to 5 and have a volunteer read the sentence that relates to that number. Ask if everyone agrees and refer back to the reading to resolve any disagreements.

Answers
4, 2, 3, 5, 1

B Think and write. What changes did each person ask Pablo to make?

- Ask students to identify each of the characters in the pictures. (Whitney/assistant, brother, mother)
- Have students look back in their books to find the answer to the first question and elicit that Whitney asked him to make the superstar taller. Help students phrase it by writing it on the board: to make (noun) + comparative (e.g. to make the superstar taller).
- Have students use this model to write the other sentences.
- Check answers by having students raise their hands to give a phrase for each change. Ask if everyone agrees, or if there is an alternative way to say it.

Answers
1 (Whitney asked Pablo) to make the sculpture/him taller.
2 (Mateo's brother asked Pablo) to make the sculpture's/his beard longer and curlier.
3 (Mateo's mother asked Pablo) to make the sculpture's/his arms and hands bigger.

C Think and discuss. Did Pablo's plan help him or not? Why or why not?

This activity gives the opportunity to explore the SEL competency of setting plans and working toward goals.

- Refer students to Pablo's plan at the beginning of the story. Ask *Did the plan help him?* and give students time to think about their answer.
- Then encourage students to discuss their ideas in pairs. Circulate and help with language if necessary.
- Ask for students' ideas. Some will probably point out that everything in the plan had to change, so perhaps the plan wasn't very useful. To present the other side, ask if it was easy for Pablo to make the changes. Ask how easy it would be if there was no plan. Point out that a plan makes it easy to adapt your ideas. It also helps make sure that things are finished on time!
- You can ask students what sorts of things they make plans for and generally how having a plan can help us. They can also think about other things in their lives where a plan could help (e.g. on a busy day with a lot of activities, when doing homework, when planning a route to travel somewhere, when doing an art project, when going shopping).

Phonics *wh–*

TRACK 36 TB. p. 231 **Listen and say.**

- Play the audio and have students listen and look at the words in the phonics box. Ask them what sound all the words have in common (they all start with a /w/ sound) and to notice that they are all written *wh-*.
- Play the audio again and have students repeat, first under their breath and then out loud. Model the mouth shape for them, to help them produce the right sound. Ask a few individual students to repeat each word.
- Ask students to choose their favorite word from the list and to tell a friend.
- Have students find more words in the story starting with *wh–*. Point out the different pronunciation of the *wh* in *who*. Invite students to read the words out loud.

Answers
Whitney; what's; who; Whoops

Cool Down

Ask *Did you enjoy reading* The Superstar? *Why or why not?* Have students discuss their ideas in pairs.

Practice **Resource Bank:** Phonics Printout;
Student's App: Phonics Practice; Reading Comprehension Practice

Get Ready to Read

Lesson Objectives

- to practice the reading skill of identifying facts and opinion
- to activate prior knowledge about getting creative ideas

Materials

Video or Audio Track 24; (optional) pictures of pieces of art to discuss the inspiration behind each one (some simple, e.g. a portrait, and some more complex, e.g. a piece of abstract modern art) (C)

TRACK 24 TB p. 229 **Warm Up**

Use this Warm Up to refresh students' memories about the story in Unit 4, *Where Is She?*

Play the video or audio of *Where Is She?* and have students act out the story. Encourage them to use gestures and facial expressions.

A Read and check (✔) the true sentences.

This lesson practices the skill of identifying fact and opinion.

- Read the first sentence and decide with students if it is true or not. Confirm that there is a check in the box because it is true.
- Do the same with number 2—point out that this is possibly true for the person who said it, but is not true for everyone, so we can't count it as a true sentence. Explain that therefore they should not put a checkmark in that box.
- Have students decide in pairs if the other sentences are true or not.
- Check answers and discuss any that cause confusion.
- Have students read the reading skills box about facts and opinions. Elicit examples to check they understand both terms; for example, *Cats have four legs* (fact—everyone thinks this is true). *Cats are cute* (opinion—only some people think this is true). Have students look again at the sentences in A and decide which are facts and which are opinions. Conclude with students that those with checkmarks are facts and those without are opinions.

Answers

True sentences: *1*; 3 (2, 4, and 5 are opinions)

B Read and underline the opinions.

- Refer students to the example sentence. Ask why number 1 is an opinion. (this person likes the buildings in Barcelona, but some people may not)
- Have students work individually to decide which of the other sentences are opinions and underline them. Then have them discuss their answers with a partner.
- To check answers, read the sentences and have students say *fact* or *opinion*. Discuss any that cause confusion.

Answers

Opinions: *1*; 3; 4; 5

C Think and discuss. When people create, where do they get their ideas? When you create, where do you get your ideas?

- Ask students to remember people they have seen in this unit who create something. (Pablo the sculptor, the superstar (who makes movies), Leonardo da Vinci (mentioned in the first activity of this lesson)
- Ask students to look at the first question *Where do they get their ideas?* Elicit some ideas (possibly from other people who create, from nature, from things around them, from books, etc.), then give students time to think and then discuss more ideas in pairs.
- Bring the class back together and ask what they came up with, writing their ideas on the board in a word cloud. Point out that sometimes ideas seem to come from nowhere, sometimes from nature, sometimes from other creations, sometimes from instructions (like Pablo's statue), and sometimes from dreams!
- If you have brought in some pictures of famous creations (sculptures, paintings, etc.), show these to students one at a time and ask what they think their inspiration was.
- Then ask students to take a minute to read and think about the second question: *Where do you get your ideas?* Ask them to look at the word cloud on the board but to think about whether they have different sources of inspiration, too.
- Then have them discuss their ideas in pairs before coming together to discuss as a class, creating another word cloud on the board.

Cool Down

Write *Fact* on the left side of the board and *Opinion* on the right. Read some sentences about the story *The Superstar* and have students decide if they are facts or opinions. If facts, students say *Fact!* and point to the left. If opinions, students say *Opinion!* and point to the right.

Example sentences: *Pablo makes sculptures.* (fact) *His sculpture isn't very good.* (opinion)

Now read **Visit Gaudí's World**

Nonfiction: *Visit Gaudí's World—* An Informational Text

Lesson Objectives

- to read an informational text about Antoni Gaudí and his works
- to learn through CLIL (architecture): how buildings are designed

Materials
Audio Tracks 37 and 38; Video

Warm Up

Play the *Alphabet Game* with places (see TB p. 25). Tell students they need to think of places in their town (they can be generic such as *hospital* or specific such as *Central Park*) for as many of the letters as possible.

TRACK 37 TB p. 231 Reading Approach

First Reading: Listen and Engage

- Ask students to open their books and give them a minute to notice the title, the genre, the pictures, and the text. Point out that the title talks about Gaudí. Have them point to who they think Gaudí is (the first picture).
- Play the video and ask students to watch and listen carefully. Alternatively, play the audio and have students follow the text in their books. Tell them that at the end you will ask them which is their favorite place.
- When they have watched the whole video, play it again on mute, and this time pause each time a new building or place is shown. Ask students to raise their hands if that was their favorite place. Which place is the most popular with students?
- Then look at the Words in Context.

TRACK 38 TB p. 231 Words in Context

- Play the audio and have students repeat the words.
- Have them race to find the words in the text. Ask *Which word is used more than once? How many times?* (nature x 4)
- Play the video again. Remind students they can **use the images in the video** to help establish the meaning of new words (see TB p. 13). Then, have them discuss their ideas in pairs. They can do this in L1.
- Use these additional discussion points to confirm the meaning of each word.

architect Students may not be able work out the meaning of this word from the video alone. Encourage students to think about what Gaudí did (he designed buildings and other places) and what people who do that are called in students' L1. Ask *Do you think it's an interesting job? Is it difficult?*

nature Have students think about all the buildings Gaudí designed and all the influences mentioned here. Discuss what they have in common (they are all natural, all from outside). Look at every occurrence of the word and confirm that this definition works for all of them.

coral Ask students what the colors remind them of in the picture—*What is in the sea that gave Gaudí an idea?* Point out that sea corals and the walls of Casa Batlló both have the same pink color.

bench Have students identify the picture of the bench in the Park Güell. Ask *What can you do on a bench?* (sit, eat lunch, watch people walk past)

cave Ask *Are caves underground or above ground?* (underground) *Can you draw a cave? Imagine you are in the cave. What can you see/feel?* Encourage them to share their pictures and ideas. Point to the inside of Casa Milà on p. 101. Ask *Do you think it looks like a cave? Why or why not?*

Practice **Student's App:** Video

Second Reading: Analyze the Text and Features

- Play the audio. Have students follow the text in their books. Then discuss the questions in the yellow boxes as a class.
  - **Gist** (p. 98): *Why do Gaudí's buildings look so different?* Encourage students to look at both the text and the pictures again before you elicit ideas. (Answers might include: he designed them to look like different things in nature, he wanted each building to be special.)
  - **Personalization** (p. 99): *To plan his creations, Gaudí made drawings of his buildings. Do you like to draw?* Ask students if they enjoy drawing and how often they draw. Ask *What do you draw? Do you draw to help you plan and get ideas like Gaudí?*
  - **Making Connections** (p. 100): *Gaudí's buildings are UNESCO World Heritage sites! That means they are important for people to see.* Ask if students have heard of UNESCO World Heritage sites before. Create a short list on the board of other such sites that students may know of. Ask why this makes them important to see (because they are special and we can learn something from them—and therefore we must protect them for future generations to see, too).
  - **Making Connections** (p. 101): *Casa Milà's nickname is* The Quarry. *A quarry is a place where people dig out stones.* Ask students if the houses where they live are built of stone or other materials. Ask if they have ever seen a quarry.

Third Reading: Interact with the Text

- Listen to the audio or play the video again. Then put the video on mute and have students use the text to narrate the video. Divide the class into pairs or small groups and have each pair or group narrate one part of the text.

Cool Down

Ask students to think of one interesting fact they learned today. Do a Think, Pair, Share.

Explore the Reading

Lesson Objectives

- to understand and analyze *Visit Gaudí's World* through reading comprehension activities
- to practice the reading skill of identifying facts and opinion
- to learn through CLIL (architecture): how buildings are designed
- to give a personal response to the topic

Materials
Audio Track 37 (WU)

TRACK 37 TB p. 231 **Warm Up**
Play the audio of the text *Visit Gaudí's World* and have students stand up and sit down quickly (or raise and lower their arms if they have limited space) every time they hear a word connected with nature. When the audio is finished, ask them to recall all the nature words they can.

A Read and check (✔). Which of these facts do we learn from the reading?

- Before students open their books, find out what they remember from the reading. Ask *Why is Gaudí famous?* (because of his buildings) *Where are his buildings?* (in Barcelona) *Where did he get his ideas?* (from nature) *What do some of his buildings look like?* (bones, coral, flowers on water, different animals, a stone quarry, a cave)
- Have students watch the video again to check their answers.
- Have students open their books and refer them to the instructions for A and the example answer for the first question. Ask them if this sentence is true. (yes) Then ask students if the information is in the reading and have them find it. (p. 98)
- Ask students if sentence 2 is true and have students look back at the text to decide. (yes) Point out the instructions state they can only check the box if the information is in the text—this activity is not testing general knowledge.
- Have students continue the activity individually and then compare answers with a friend. Have them make a note of the page number where they find each of the answers.
- To check answers, read the sentences and have students raise their hands for the ones they checked.

Answers
1; 3; 5

B Look at the pictures. Where did Gaudí get his ideas from? Match the building to the idea.

This activity allows students to learn something about architecture by exploring how Gaudí created his works.

- Refer students to the sculpture of the lizard on p. 100. Elicit that the idea came from a real lizard and ask students how it looks similar to the animal in b.
- Have students continue the activity individually, using their visual skills and also the reading to match the buildings and ideas together.
- To check answers, ask individual students to say number-letter pairs of matching items. Ask if everyone agrees.

Answers
1 b 2 a 3 e 4 d 5 c

C Think and discuss. Gaudí made his buildings look like nature. What do you want to make your buildings look like?

This is a personalization question to help students understand how buildings are created.

- Ask a student to read the example opinion. Encourage students to brainstorm some ideas on the board for things that buildings could look like.
- Tell students to imagine they are designing some buildings. Ask *What do you want them to look like?* Encourage them to think about shape and size, as well as any unusual features they would like their building to have. Let students know they can choose an idea from the board or think of a different idea.
- Give students time to think and make some notes. Then invite them to share their ideas. Take a class vote for the funniest design.

Cool Down
Ask students to think of one question they would like to ask Gaudí. Have them share their ideas in pairs.

Practice **Student's App:** Reading Comprehension Practice

Think Together

Lesson Objectives

- to make connections between the readings
- to explore the key concept: Why do people make things?
- to reflect on the unit and provide personal thoughts and opinions

Warm Up

Have students look at the Key Concept question at the top of the page: *Why do people make things?* Give them one minute to think about their own answer to the question, then give them three minutes to discuss their ideas with a friend.

Bring the class together and ask some volunteers to share their ideas with the class. Make a spidergram on the board of students' ideas. Use the range of ideas they come up with to point out that the reasons why people make things can be very varied. Some are practical (*I need this*) and some are creative (*I have an idea*). They will discuss these ideas further in A.

A Compare and contrast the creations. Fill in the table.

This activity helps students continue to think more about the Key Concept question for this unit: *Why do people create things?*

- Check students understand the headings for the table by asking some questions; for example, ask if students can think of a different way to say *reason* (*why*, e.g. *What is the reason you like fruit?* = *Why do you like fruit?*), ask what types of creations they have seen in the unit (buildings, park, sculptures), and elicit some ideas about what different materials were used to make them.
- Complete the first line of the table as a whole class.
- Then have students continue the activity individually. While they do this, draw or project the table on the board.
- To check answers, invite students to come to the board and complete one space each. Ask if everyone agrees.

Answers

Pablo's statue: to show how important the superstar is; *sculpture*; stone
Casa Milà: a home for the Mila family; building; *stone, glass, plaster*
Park Güell: somewhere outdoors for people to enjoy; *park*; stone, tiles
Mona Lisa: a portrait for a home; painting; oil, paint, canvas

B Think and discuss. What other creations do you know in your country and around the world? Do a Round Robin.

- Students are going to make connections between creations in their country and in other countries. Set up the class for a Round Robin cooperative learning routine (see TB p. 20).
- Have students share their ideas and knowledge, and count how many creations they remembered.
- Ask students how many creations they had in their group and elicit suggestions from the class. If any are unknown to the others in the class, have the student say a little more about the creation.

C Think and discuss. Why do you think the people made those creations?

- Have students work in their groups again and discuss their favorite creations and why they think they were made. Have them think about practicality versus creativity and any other ideas that arose in the Warm Up, A, and B.
- Ask a student from each group to share their ideas.

My Reading Journal

Imagine you can visit one of the settings in this unit. Which one do you choose? Why?

This task focuses on personalization.

Begin by telling students your choice and why; for example, *I choose Pablo's workshop because I want to see an artist working. Which place from this unit do you want to visit?*

Have students choose where they'd like to go and explain why. Tell them to write their choice in their book and then share it with a friend.

Invite students to share their ideas with the rest of the class.

Answers

Students' own answers

How much did you like the unit? Color the stars.

This question focuses on personalization and giving an opinion.

Have students look back at the unit one more time and decide how much they enjoyed it. Have them color in the number of stars that indicate their level of enjoyment. Ask some students why they colored in that many stars and what they enjoyed most about the unit.

Cool Down

Have students look back at the VTR picture on pp. 88–89. Ask them if they now have any new thoughts on the scene in the picture, why it was created, what it shows, and if it is art or not.

Practice Resource Bank: Unit Test; Student's App: Key Concept Practice

UNIT 7

We're a Team

Unit Overview

Themes

Activities with others

Working together

Synopsis

In this unit, students will find out about team projects in different communities, explore symbiotic relationships in nature, and think about what it means to be a good team member. They will plan and prepare a conversation about team activities and write some team game instructions using target vocabulary and grammar from the unit.

Language Book

Vocabulary

acting, biking, climbing, horseback riding, kayaking, sailing, singing, skating, waterskiing, windsurfing, yoga

p. 144

Explore Language

Telling the Time

p. 145

Global Citizenship

How do people work as a team in different communities?

borrow, club, community, give, help each other, share, take turns, trade, work together

p. 146

Explore Language

Modal Verbs: *Can* for Permissions, Requests, and Offers

p. 147

Talk About It

Conversation: deciding what to do

p. 148

Write About It

Team Game Instructions

Sentence Building: imperatives

p. 149

Think It Over

Review and Reflection

p. 150

Literacy Book

Think Together
What is good about teamwork?
p. 157

Visible Thinking
VTR: See, Think, Wonder
p. 151

Fiction
Story: *It's Mine!*

Words in Context: treasure, password, map, grab, rich, gold, pirate
p. 155

Nonfiction
Informational Text: *Great Teamwork*

Words in Context: hunters, both, Africa, whistles, shrimp, holds on, entrance
p. 152

Reading Skill
Predicting endings
p. 154

Phonics
–ck
p. 156

Language and Literacy Connections

The connecting theme in Unit 7 is different ways to work as a team.

	Language	Literacy
Vocabulary	**Set 1:** activities **Set 2:** working with others	**Nonfiction:** *help each other, share, work together* **Fiction:** *give, take turns*
Grammar	**Telling the Time** It's 5 o'clock. Climbing is at 5 o'clock. **Modal Verbs:** ***can*** **for permissions, requests, and offers** Can we borrow this kayak? Can you go quickly? Can I help you?	Fiction Can you help me open the box? From eight o'clock 'til three thirty.
Skills	**Pronunciation:** /n/ and /ŋ/	**Reading:** predicting endings **Phonics:** *–ck*
International English	*horseback riding / horse riding; biking/cycling; trade/swap*	

Vocabulary

Lesson Objectives

- to learn vocabulary of hobbies and activities: *acting, biking, climbing, horseback riding, kayaking, sailing, singing, skating, waterskiing, windsurfing, yoga*
- to sing a song exploring the importance of teamwork

Materials
Audio Tracks 75 to 78; Video

Warm Up

Introduce the lesson topic by asking students to imagine a perfect day. Ask them to think of activities to do, places to go, people to see, and food to eat. Give them time to imagine their day and then ask for suggestions. Write their answers on the board (write activities with *–ing*).

A TRACK 75 TB p. 221 **Listen and find. Who loves singing?**

- Look at the picture on pp. 88–89. Ask: *Where do you think they are?* (an activity camp) *Does it look like a fun place?* (students' own answers)
- Draw students' attention to the boy in the green T-shirt at the front (the one without a hat). Ask *Who is he?* (Joe from Unit 6)
- Tell students they are going to listen to a conversation about the activities in the activity camp. Play the audio and have students point to the new words and pictures as they listen.
- Ask the gist question *Who loves singing?* and elicit the answer. Play the audio again for students to check.
- Look back at p. 85. Say *Can you answer Joe's question?* Listen again to check. (they are doing a show / acting and singing)

Answer
Padma

B TRACK 76 TB p. 221 **Listen, say, and number the pictures in A.**

- Play the audio and have students point to the pictures and say the words.
- Then play it again and have them number the pictures in order.
- Check answers by playing the audio again.
- Have all students repeat the words one more time, this time with a mime for each word.

Answers
1 *yoga* 2 skating 3 singing 4 kayaking 5 sailing
6 biking 7 acting 8 horseback riding 9 windsurfing
10 climbing 11 waterskiing

International English

Ask students for the two ways to say the activity with horses and the activity with a bike. Elicit which words are American English and which are British English. Point out that both are correct. Ask *Which words do we use?*

C TRACK 77 TB p. 221 **Listen. Close your eyes and visualize.**

- Prepare students for the visualization (see TB p. 21).
- Play the audio, allowing students to visualize the activities and do actions where appropriate as they listen. They say the word after they hear *say*.
- Divide the class into pairs or small groups, play the audio again, and have students share their ideas or do their mimes in pairs.

D **Look and write.**

- Have students look at the equipment in D. Point out these are things used in the activities. Have them look in the picture on pp. 88–89 and decide which item goes with which activity. Elicit the name of the activity associated with the first item (kayaking), then do the second item together (skating). Have students write it in their books and then continue the activity individually.
- To check answers, draw spaces on the board in the same layout as the activity (if you aren't using the TTL) and invite students to take turns filling in answers. Ask if everyone agrees.

Answers
1 *kayaking* 2 skating 3 singing 4 climbing
5 waterskiing 6 biking 7 windsurfing 8 acting
9 horseback riding 10 sailing 11 yoga

E TRACK 78 TB p. 221 **Listen and sing. Then watch and sing.**

- With books closed, write or project the title of the song, ***Teamwork Is Number One***, on the board and ask students what they think it will be about. Ask what *teamwork* is (working or playing together in a team) and what *number one* means here (the most important thing).
- Play the song and have students raise their hands every time they hear one of the new words.
- Have students open their books and look at the song lyrics. Play the song again, pausing after each line for students to repeat.
- Then play the song again and have students sing along.
- Play the song video and encourage students to watch and sing. They can make up actions to do as they sing.

Cool Down

Play *Chain Game* (see TB p. 25). Start the chain by saying *In the picture, children are sailing.* Have the next student continue and say *In the picture, children are sailing … and biking.* Play in small groups.

Practice **Student's App:** Vocabulary Practice; Video

Explore Language

Lesson Objectives

- to learn how to tell the time using the simple present
- to provide contextualized practice of hobbies and activities vocabulary

Materials
Audio Tracks 78 to 80; (optional) Video (WU)

Warm Up

TRACK 78 TB p. 221 Sing ***Teamwork Is Number One*** again and encourage students to do actions.

A TRACK 79 TB p. 221 **Listen and read. Who helps Padma?**

- Project the story on p. 90 on the board or have students look in their books. Ask *What activity can you see?* (climbing) *Do you think it looks difficult?* Ask students if they have ever been climbing. If they haven't, ask them if they would like to do it and elicit reasons why or why not. Reward any students who try to get their point across in English, even if their grammar is incorrect. Encouraging students to have the confidence to try even when they know their message won't be perfect is a very important learning objective for them.
- Draw students' attention to Padma and establish she was also in the previous lesson. Tell students they are going to listen to Padma and Imran going climbing. Play the audio and have students follow the story in their books.
- Ask the gist question *Who helps Padma?* and elicit the answer. Play the audio again to check if necessary.

Answer
Imran

B **Look at A. Complete.**

- Write or project the table on the board.
- Read the question *What time is it?* together and have students find it in the story in A. Then have students answer by looking at the clock. Have students find the answer to the first blank using the pictures and dialogue in A to help. Ask if they can tell you what is different about the way this time is written in A compared with the other times. (*5 o'clock* rather than *5:00*)
- Have students work in pairs to complete the other sentences in the table. Then say the question *What time is it?* and ask students to respond with the complete sentences. Check everyone agrees, then complete the table on the board for students to check their answers.
- Ask students if they can think why we use *at* before the time in the last sentence. Tell them that we use *at* to show when an activity is about to start.
- Have students look at the Grammar tip *Look*, and point out the word *hands* for the pointers of the clock. Ask *Are they called hands in your language?*

Answers
time; 5 o'clock; 5:30; 5:15; at; 5:45

C **Think and discuss. Then choose.**

- Read the options to students and ask them to look at the table in B and the story in A and draw a conclusion about which options they think are correct. Have them discuss their decision with a friend.
- Read the options again and have students raise their hands for the ones they chose. Confirm their answers and have them circle the correct options in their books.
- Draw a clock on the board and then draw in some different times, changing the position of the long and short hands. Ask *What time is it?* for each one and elicit the answer.

Answers
1 minutes 2 hour

D TRACK 80 TB p. 221 **Listen and say.**

- Play the audio and have students tell you what times they hear. (5 o'clock, 12:30, 5:15, 3:45)
- Play the audio again and have students listen and repeat.

For ideas on how to vary the drill, see TB p. 22.

E **Look and complete.**

- Ask students to look at the pictures and identify the three activities. (horseback riding, kayaking, and skating)
- Refer students to the example answer and have them say the question *What time is it?*.
- Have students continue the activity individually, then compare their answers with a friend.
- To check answers, ask students to read a sentence each. Ask if everyone agrees. Write the missing words/times on the board so everyone can check.

Answers
1 *time* 2 What 3 at 5 o'clock 4 at 2:15 5 at 10:45

F **Play a game. Mime and guess.**

- Use your arms as the hands of a clock. Place your arms in the position shown in F and ask students *What time is it?* Have them answer *It's three o'clock*, and check with the example dialogue in F.
- Repeat, moving your right arm to 3:15, 3:30, and 3:45 and ask the question again. Then show different times, changing the hours and minutes, asking each time, *What time is it?*
- Now divide the class into pairs and have them continue the game, taking turns to mime the time and guess.

Cool Down

Play *Pass the Whisper!* (see TB p. 26) with sentences from A, D, and E.

Practice **Resource Bank:** Grammar Printout; **Student's App:** Grammar Practice

Global Citizenship

Lesson Objectives

- to learn vocabulary for working with others: *borrow, club, give, help each other, share, take turns, trade, work together*
- to explore how to work as a team and be a good team member
- to practice listening for gist and details

Materials
Audio Tracks 81 to 83; (optional) Audio Track G

Opening Question

Ask the opening question: *How do people work as a team in different communities?* Check students understand that a community is a group of people who share something—they live, work, or do a hobby together. Tell them their school is an example of a community. Ask which people work together as a team in their school and why it's important that they work as a team.

A TRACK 81 TB p. 221 **Listen to Mr. Muller talk to Zoe and her friends about a garden project. What does Zoe have for the garden?**

- Have students look at the pictures and say what they can see. Ask *Are the people in the pictures alone or with other people?* (with other people) *Are they happy or sad?* (happy)
- Play the audio and have students point to the pictures and words as they hear them.
- Ask the gist question *What does Zoe have for the garden?* Elicit the answer, then play the audio again to check.

Answer
plants and flowers

International English

Elicit which word is American English and which is British English. Drill both words for pronunciation (swap = /swɒp/). Point out that both are correct English and ask *Which word do we use?*

B TRACK 82 TB p. 221 **Listen, say, and number the pictures in A.**

- Play the audio and have students point to the pictures and say the words.
- Play the audio again and have students number the items.
- Then play the audio again to check answers.

Answers
1 *club* 2 give 3 work together 4 take turns
5 community 6 share 7 help each other
8 borrow 9 trade

TRACK G TB p. 221 **Visualization**

- The TTL has a visualization audio track for this vocabulary set (see p. TB p. 21).

C Who do you work in a team with and how? Make a list. Tell your friend.

- Write two columns on the board: *Team* and *What We Do*. Write some examples of situations where you work in a team (a team of teachers, sharing ideas and materials; a family team, preparing food and cleaning).
- Tell students to make a similar list about their own teams. Give them time to think before they write.
- Have them share their ideas with a friend. Ask if their lists were different. Encourage them to add to their lists.

D TRACK 83 TB p. 222 **Now listen to Maia and Bradley. Write the country. Who played on the playground today?**

- Listening for the main idea: tell students they are going to listen to two children from the UK and Myanmar talking about what they did at school today. Elicit what they can see in the pictures. Play the audio and have students label the pictures with the country they hear.
- Ask the gist question *Who played on the playground today?* and elicit the answer. Encourage students to justify their answer. Play the audio again for students to check.

Answers
a Myanmar b UK Maia played on the playground today.

E Listen again. Choose.

- Listening for detail: draw attention to the answer circled in number 1.
- Have students look at the other sentences and see if they can remember any answers. Then play the audio again and have students complete the activity individually.
- To check answers, invite volunteers to read the complete sentences aloud. Ask if the everyone agrees.

Answers
1 *school* 2 books 3 computer 4 dangerous 5 built

Discussion Questions

- Draw students' attention to the discussion questions: *Do you have the same team projects in your community? How can you be a good team member?* Have students discuss the questions in pairs or small groups (see **ETB**).
- Elicit the conclusion that communities are made up of different teams of people helping and supporting each other. Being willing to participate and listening to each other are good traits of good team members.
- Return to the original opening question to ask again *How do people work as a team in different communities?* Ask students if the discussion has given them any new ideas.

Cool Down

Tell students they have a class community project to complete before they go—to clean the classroom and leave it perfect! When they finish, ask if it looks better. Encourage them to give a high five to their team members for a job well done!

Practice **Student's App:** Vocabulary Practice; Listening Comprehension Practice

Explore Language

Lesson Objectives

- to learn how to use *can* for requests, offers, and permission
- to provide contextualized practice of teamwork verbs

Materials

Audio Tracks 84 and 85

Warm Up

With books closed, brainstorm all the activities that students do or know about which involve water. Write all their ideas on the board.

A TRACK 84 TB p. 222 **Listen and read. Why is Imran in the water?**

- Ask students what they can see in the pictures and what activity the friends are going to do (kayaking). Was this on the students' list? Ask who they recognize in the pictures (Imran from Lesson 2).
- Play the audio and have students follow the story in their books.
- Ask them the gist question *Why is Imran in the water?* and elicit the answer. Play the audio again to check. Point out that the answer really comes after he falls in the lake, when they say *Let's try and work together*—they didn't work well enough together.

Answer

They didn't work together. / Alisa went too fast. / He fell in.

B Look at A. Complete.

- Write or project the table on the board.
- Read the first question and have students find it in the story in A. Ask *Do they want something?* (yes) *What do they want?* (to borrow a kayak)
- Have students work individually to complete the other sentences in the table, then allow them time to discuss their answers with a partner. To check answers, elicit the complete questions and sentences, ask if everyone agrees, and write the correct version on the board. Highlight the word order for questions (*can* + subject [e.g. *we, you, I*] + verb) and elicit that in statements the word order changes to subject + *can* + verb.
- Have students look at the Grammar tip *Remember* and point out we never use *to* after *can* or *can't*.

Answers

Permission: *Can*; can
Offers: Can; can
Requests: Can

C Think and discuss. Then choose.

- Give students time to think about their answers, then have them compare in pairs.
- Check answers as a class. Have students notice that this modal verb has three different uses here: to make a request (statement 1); to make an offer (statement 2) and to ask for permission. Check understanding of these concepts in L1 if necessary.

Answers

1 want 2 help

D TRACK 85 TB p. 222 **Listen and say.**

- Play the audio and have students tell you what verbs they hear (borrow, help, use, watch).
- Play the audio again, pausing after each sentence for students to repeat.
- For ideas on how to vary the drill, see TB p. 22.

E Put the words in order.

- Refer students to the example and ask them *Which sentence in B is this like?* (Requests: Can you go quickly?) Confirm that this is someone saying they want something, as described in statement 1 in C.
- Do the second sentence together. Remind them that *can't* is the negative form of *can*. Students should be able to deduce that it's a statement by looking at where the capital letter is and the period and to work out the word order, using the table in B to help.
- Have students continue the activity individually and compare with a friend.
- To check answers, write the correct order on the board so everyone can check their own work.

Answers

1 *Can you help me?* 2 You can't use a pen.
3 Can we borrow cards? 4 Can we work together?
5 We can't run in the classroom.
6 You can take turns to write on the whiteboard.

F Play *You're the Teacher!*

- Have two volunteers read the example mini-dialogue.
- Ask students what other *Can* questions students ask teachers. Take some suggestions and write some key words (not the full questions) on the board. Then elicit some things teachers often say using *You can* … or *You can't* … and write some more key words.
- Divide the class into pairs and have them take turns to be the teacher giving/refusing permission to the student. Have them stay in one role until you say *Change!* and then they switch roles.

Cool Down

Play *Running Sentences* (see TB p. 26) with *can* questions or sentences from this lesson.

Practice **Resource Bank:** Grammar Printout; **Student's App:** Grammar Practice

Talk About It

Lesson Objectives

- to prepare and practice a conversation to decide what to do
- to recognize and reproduce /n/ and /ŋ/

Materials
Video; Audio Track 86

Warm Up

Play *Simon Says* (see TB p. 26) with the activities from this unit (e.g. climbing, waterskiing, sailing, kayaking, biking, horseback riding, windsurfing, skating).

A TB p. 234 **Watch and listen. Why do Jason and Grace choose sailing?**

- Tell students they will watch a video of friends talking about different activities they can do. Ask *Which activity from the Warm Up do you want to do at the weekend? Why?*
- Play the video and ask students to listen for all the activities Jason and Grace talk about. When they have finished, elicit what students heard (climbing, waterskiing, and sailing).
- Then introduce the gist question *Why do they choose sailing?* Elicit the answer, then play the video again to check. Ask further comprehension questions (see **ETB**).

Answer
Because it's a team activity

B **Watch again. Check (✔) the phrases you hear.**

- Have students read the phrases and draw their attention to the example.
- Play the video again and have students check the phrases they hear.
- Then check answers.
- Have students look at these eight sentences and choose two that can be used for making a suggestion (1, 2) and three that can be used for either responding to a suggestion or giving an opinion (3, 5, 8). They can discuss this in pairs. Elicit answers and write them on the board in a table. Explain to students that these categories will be useful later when they are creating their own conversation.

Answers
1; 2; 3; 4; 5; 6; 7

Pronunciation /n/ and /ŋ/

TRACK 86 TB p. 222 **Listen and say.**

- Demonstrate the /n/ sound as in *Jason* and /ŋ/ sound as in *climbing*, and encourage students to copy you.
- Play the audio for students to repeat the sounds and words. Ask what sound the first set of three words have at the end and what sound the second set of three words have.
- Say *These are all words Jason and Grace use in their conversation. What other words do you know with these sounds?* Elicit ideas (e.g. *can*, *sing*) and write them on the board in two columns. Drill all the words at the end.

C **Plan. Think about activities you want to do. Choose and write.**

- Tell students they are going to have a conversation like the one in the video to decide what activity to do.
- Point out the headings in the plan and ask *What activity did Jason and Grace do?* (sailing) *Why did they want to do it?* (because it's a team activity)
- Have students complete the table by choosing three more activities, circling *yes* or *no* to indicate whether they want to do each activity or not, and giving reasons.

D **Prepare your conversation. Use your ideas from C and phrases from B.**

- Project or write the conversation template on the board and fill it in as a demonstration. If you created a table to categorize the phrases from B make sure it is also visible for students to refer to.
- Point to the first green bubble in the dialogue and elicit a suggestion. Continue by pointing to each box and eliciting something appropriate, using the prompts provided and the phrases from B. Remind students to disagree to begin with (by giving a negative opinion), otherwise the conversation will be very short, and to agree at the end by giving a positive opinion.
- Have students prepare their own conversations in pairs, by choosing ideas from C and using the phrases from B.
- Monitor and help with any ideas they find difficult to express.

E **Practice with a friend.**

- Have students practice their conversation as many times as they need to. Remind them to look at their partner while having the conversation.
- Invite volunteers to perform their conversation for the rest of the class. Ask the others to listen and say if they had similar or different ideas.

Cool Down

Play *Disappearing Sentences* (see TB p. 25) with the phrases from today's lesson.

Practice **Student's App:** Speaking Skill Practice; Video

Write About It

Lesson Objectives

- to focus on using imperatives
- to plan and write instructions for a team game

Materials
(Optional) Support, Standard, and Challenge writing printouts from the Resource Bank (one per student) (C, D)

Warm Up

Tell students that this lesson is about games. Have students look back at the Put It Together pages they have completed so far in their **Language Book** (pp. 34–35, 60–61, and 86–87), and consider which game they enjoyed most and why. Take a vote to find out the class's favorite game.

A Read the team game instructions. Circle the imperative verbs.

- Have students open their books and read the text quickly. Ask *What's the name of the game?* (Team Catch) *Do you know this game? Where can you play a game like this?* (outside, on the playground)
- Project the instructions on the board or have students look in their books. Highlight the circled imperative verb in the text (run). Point out that an imperative verb form tells you to do or not do something. It's like a command; it's not a request (as in Lesson 4). Then have students work individually to find all the other imperative verbs and circle them.
- Then check answers.
- Ask which verbs are telling people *Yes, do this!* (Run, Catch, Hold, make, Catch) and which is telling people *No, don't do that!* (Don't stop). Drill the phrases for intonation and then have students practice saying them in pairs.
- Remind students that *I* is a subject and have them remember other words that can be subjects (e.g. *you*, *he*, and names). Ask if they can see subjects in the lines containing imperatives (no). Clarify that when we use a verb to say *Yes, do this* or *No, don't do that!* we don't use a subject.

Answers
Run quickly!; Catch a player.; Hold hands and make a team. ; Don't stop!; Catch more players.

B Write the imperative sentences.

- Refer students to the example answer. Point out the smiley emoji and that the verb is like the *yes* examples in the game instructions—just the infinitive verb. Now point out the sad emoji in number 2 and say that this answer will be like the *no* example in the game instructions. Elicit the answer for number 2.
- Have students complete the activity individually, then invite volunteers to say an answer each and ask if the others agree.

Answers
1 *Sing a song.* 2 *Don't* watch TV. 3 Help your friend.
4 Don't drop the ball. 5 Bounce the ball.
6 Don't move.

C Plan. Think about a team game. Choose or write.

- Tell students they are going to explain how to play a team game. Ask them if they know how to play the games in C (e.g. in a treasure hunt, children follow a series of clues to get to a prize; each clue leads them to an object or a place where they will find the next clue).
- Have students choose a game that they like—they can choose one of the two that are provided or decide on a different game, but it must be a team game. Then have them decide on actions for it, adding in extra verbs where necessary. Challenge printouts can be handed out now.
- Finally, have students write notes explaining why they like the game they have chosen. Remind students that these are notes, so single words or short phrases are fine—they can write full sentences later. Monitor and help with vocabulary as necessary.

D Write your team game instructions.

- Have students write the instructions for their game in their notebooks from the notes they made in C. Encourage them to use the example in A as a model and use bullets for the important instructions. Support printouts can be handed out now.
- Have students write out their final versions neatly on paper or hand out the Standard printouts from the Resource Bank. Allow them time to decorate their game instructions and encourage them to think about whether their picture can help explain parts of the game. Display the finished game instructions around the classroom.

Cool Down

Enjoy each other's work: have students circulate around the classroom, enjoying their friends' instructions and pictures. Write on the board: *a good explanation, a good picture, an interesting game, and the same game as me*

Ask students to look for these four things as they walk around the room. At the end, have students say one thing they enjoyed.

Practice **Student's App:** Writing Practice

Think It Over

Lesson Objectives

- to review what has been learned in the unit
- to reflect on the unit and their progress
- to think about learning strategies and how to continue learning at home

Warm Up

Use this personal-choice TPR task as a chance to review language from the unit and bring the topic back into focus.

Ask students to name as many outdoor activities as they can. Decide with the class on an activity for each corner of the room—so four activities in total.

To check everyone remembers which corner is which, point to the corners and have students say the name of the activity they have assigned to that corner.

Tell students to choose their favorite activity and go and stand in that corner. When they have all chosen an activity, say *Do your activity!* and have students mime doing their chosen activity. Ask which is the favorite activity in the class.

Read the questions and draw or write your answers.

- Give students time to think about and discuss activities in the unit before they complete the questions.

What did I do?

- Give students a few minutes to look back through the unit at the different activities they did. Ask questions about the unit; for example, *What did you sing about? What activities and actions did you do? Where did you hear about a playground?* Encourage students to draw or write about activities they liked or found interesting.

What did I learn?

- Have students talk to a partner about what they remember from the unit—stories, words, phrases, and people.
- Ask students *What words can you find that you didn't know before? Can you make new questions or answers now? What new facts did you learn? Did you learn how to be a better team player?*
- Encourage students to decide on one or two things, among all of the things they just mentioned, that they are proud of or that they will remember because it was interesting or useful or unusual.
- Ask students to draw a picture or write about the thing or things they have chosen.

How did I learn?

- Ask students how they learned the activity words in Lesson 1. Ask *Did you learn with pictures? With actions? By listening, reading, or writing? By discussing ideas? With your friends? With videos? With computers? How do you like learning best? What about the words in Lesson 3? Did you learn using different techniques then? And how did you learn the grammar?*
- Encourage students to think about the pronunciation and spelling of the words they learned in this unit. Ask *What helps you remember how to say/spell these words?*
- Have students draw a picture of a way that they enjoyed learning in this unit or methods that helped them learn.

How well did I do?

- Tell students to color in the number of bikes that best expresses how well they have learned the unit content (i.e., the more they color, the more they feel they have learned). Ask *What do you remember? What do you understand? What do you need to practice more?*

What can I do next?

- Brainstorm ideas with the class about what students can do learn more (e.g. sing the song again, read the stories again, play the game on p. 91 again).
- Encourage students to think about what they can do at home to improve their English, using the four verbs as prompts; for example read a comic or book in English, talk to a family member in English, watch a TV show or video clips in English, find out more about how to play a team game, and so on.
- Ask students to choose one or more activities from the list (read, talk, watch, find out more) that they will do to practice their English.
- Once students have completed the page in their books, have them discuss with a friend what they drew or wrote. Did they choose the same activities or different ones?

Looking Forward

Draw students' attention to the character at the bottom of the page. Ask *Who's this?* and elicit what they remember about her (Susan was helping with the kayaking in Lesson 4, p. 94). Ask if they can guess what other sport she does. Tell students they will have to wait until Unit 8 to find out if they were right!

Practice **Resource Bank:** Unit Test; **Student's App:** Vocabulary and Grammar Review

Literacy

Get Ready to Read

Lesson Objectives

- to activate interest in the topic of teamwork
- to encourage students to observe and interpret through a See, Think, Wonder VTR
- to preview the reading skill of predicting the ending

Materials

(Optional) VTR printout from the Resource Bank (A, B, C)

Warm Up

Use this activity to activate students' imaginations about the unit topic of teamwork.

Write the word *Team* on the board and ask students what they think of when they see this word. Have students brainstorm ideas and write them on the board as a spidergram. Look at the words and ask students if they can make any connections between them.

Show students the unit title, *We're a Team*, and explain that in this unit they'll be learning about different kinds of teams.

See, Think, Wonder

A Look at the picture. What do you see?

- Students are going to do a See, Think, Wonder VTR to explore the image of people working as a team. Ask *What do you see?* and elicit answers.
- Give them a minute to look at the picture. Then elicit one or two examples using the phrase *I (can) see …* before giving them time to share in small groups or pairs. Then bring the groups together for a class discussion.
- Students will likely find: a lot of people, different colors, white pants, a stadium or arena, people taking pictures, a tower of people, flag, musical instruments.

Here's an example of this part of the routine:

Teacher: What do you see?
Student A: (I see) people taking pictures.
Teacher: What else do you see?
Student A: People making a tower.
Teacher: Great. What colors do you see?
Student B: (They're wearing) green T-shirts and white pants.
Student C: (I see) blue, and red, and yellow, too.
Student D: It's (like) a rainbow!

B What do you think?

- Ask students *What do you think?* Give them one minute to think silently about the picture and then share their ideas.
- Answers will vary depending on students' opinions. Remind students to respect each other's thoughts and opinions.

Here's an example of this part of the routine.

Teacher: What do you think?
Student A: (I think) they're trying to make a new record.
Teacher: What makes you say that?
Student A: There are a lot of people in the tower.
Student B: Actually, (I think) they are different in teams.
Teacher: Really? Why do you think that?
Student B: (Because of) their T-shirts

C What do you wonder?

- Ask students *What do you wonder?* Give them one minute to think about the picture silently and then discuss in groups or as a class.

Here's an example of this part of the routine.

Teacher: What do you wonder?
Student A: I wonder where they are.
Teacher: OK. Where do you think they are?
Student A: Maybe in a stadium?
Teacher: I see. What else do you wonder?
Student B: Are they from different countries?
Student C: Are they happy?

Transition

If it hasn't come up in the discussion above, ask students *Do you think these people are working in teams or as one big team?*

Ask students *Do you often work or play in a team? Is working in a team fun? Is it better than working alone?* Conclude that it can be better for certain things, but working alone also has its benefits.

D Think and discuss. What things do you do in a team?

- Ask students for an initial two or three ideas, which will most likely be about sports. Give students a minute to think about other situations where they are in a team—in classes at school, playing on the playground, or at home with the family.
- Have students share their ideas (sports and others) with a friend and then ask for suggestions to share with the class.

E Read and answer. What do you think happens at the end?

This is a preview of the reading skill of predicting the ending.

- Refer students to the picture or enlarge it if you are using the TTL, and have them read the information.
- Ask students what they think happens at the end of the story. Have students raise their hands to give suggestions.
- Then ask them to complete the sentence in their book with the idea they think is best.

Now read **Great Teamwork**

Nonfiction: *Great Teamwork—An Informational Text*

Lesson Objectives

- to read an informational text about working together
- to learn through CLIL (science): exploring symbiotic relationships
- to make a personal connection to the reading

Materials

Audio Tracks 39 and 40; a world map or globe (WU)

Warm Up

Show students a map of the world and have them point out Africa. Explain that Africa is a continent made up of different countries. Ask students to name some countries in Africa, then use the map to discover more countries.

Elicit what students know about Africa—its cultures, languages, animals, history, geography, and so on, and write it on the board.

TRACK 39 TB p. 231 Reading Approach

First Reading: Listen and Engage

- Ask students if they can recall the prediction they made about the reading in the previous lesson.
- Have students sit in a Circle Time formation (see TB p. 21). Sit at the front with your book and read the text slowly, allowing plenty of time to look at the pictures. As you read, give students time to name the things they see on each page.
- Pause after the story about the hunter and the hummingbird and ask students if their prediction from the previous lesson was correct.
- At the end, ask the gist question *Is the reading about friends or enemies?*
- Then look at the Words in Context.

TRACK 40 TB p. 231 Words in Context

- Play the audio and have students repeat the words.
- Have students race to find the new words in the reading. Some of the words appear more than once.
- Tell students they can **use the words around the new words to guess their meaning** (see TB p. 23). Allow students to discuss their ideas in L1.
- Look at each word as a class, using these points to guide the conversation.

hunters Have students find the word *hunter* or *hunters* in two sentences on p. 106. Ask *What do hunters want? What does this hunter want? Are there hunters in your country?*

both Ask *Where do the Boran people and the honey bird live?* Stress the *and.* Ask *How many is "both"?* (two) Look for other instances to confirm this definition.

Africa Ask students to remember what they talked about in the Warm Up. Ask them to look at the pictures and imagine what it's like to live there. Ask *Is this like ancient Egypt?* (no) Elicit how it is different. Come to the conclusion that Africa is a large continent with different climates and landscapes.

whistles Ask *What does the hunter do to call the bird?* Elicit various ways to call someone or something. Demonstrate whistling. Then ask *Can you whistle?* and encourage students to try.

shrimp Ask students to point to the shrimp on p. 108. Ask if they have ever seen a shrimp living in the sea.

holds on Have students look at the last picture on p. 109. Ask *What's the fish doing?* Ask students to demonstrate holding on to something. Ask if they hold on to anything or anyone when they need to be safe.

entrance Ask *Where is the entrance in your house? Show me how you close it.*

Second Reading: Analyze the Text and Features

- Play the audio and have students follow the text in their books.
- Then discuss the questions in the red boxes as a class.
  - **Text Focus** (p. 106): *There are two headings in this reading. Can you find them?* This question helps focus on the text type—it is a factual text organized by headed sections. Ask students what the difference is between a title and a heading. (the title is the name for the whole text, and a heading is the label for part of the text) Have them find the two headings. (*The Honey Hunters* and *Good Friends*)
  - **Making Connections** (p. 107): *Honey birds also help other animals, like honey badgers, find honey. Can you find the badger?* Have students look at p. 107 and find the badger. Alternatively, you could enlarge the image if you are using the TTL. Ask students if there are badgers living in their country. Do they look the same?
  - **Personalization** (p. 109): *Which example of teamwork is your favorite?* Have students take a vote by a show of hands to say which example of teamwork they prefer and why. Allow students to contribute in L1.

Third Reading: Interact with the Text

- Listen to the audio again and have students mime the actions in the text. They can also make any relevant noises (e.g. the whistle and shout of the hunter and the call of the honey bird).

Cool Down

Ask students which story they liked best and why. Have them discuss in pairs.

Explore the Reading

Lesson Objectives

- to understand and analyze *Great Teamwork* through reading comprehension activities
- to learn through CLIL (science): exploring symbiotic relationships
- to explore the SEL competency of relationship skills: exhibiting cooperative learning and working toward group goals

Materials
Audio Track 39

TRACK 39 TB p. 231 **Warm Up**
Play *What Was the Last Word?* (see TB p. 27) with the audio of Reading 1.

A Read the questions. Check (✔) the correct answers.

- Before students open their books, find out what they remember from the reading. Ask *Who is in the teams?* (The Boran hunter and the honey bird; the gobie fish and pistol shrimp) *How do they help each other?* (The honey bird finds the honey, and the Boran hunter gets the honey for them both. The pistol shrimp digs a hole for them both, and the gobie fish looks out for danger and protects the shrimp.) *Where do they live?* (The Boran hunter and honey bird live in Africa. The pistol shrimp and gobie fish live in the sea.) *Why are they a good team?* (because they all do something to help the other team member)
- Project the table on the board or refer students to the table in their books. Have them look at the pictures and identify each character from the reading.
- Refer students to the first question and the example checkmark. Have them find something in the reading that shows the answer is the honey bird (p. 106: *Honey birds know where to find the honey*).
- Have students continue the activity individually, finding proof in the reading for each decision they make. Make sure students are aware that sometimes they should check more than one box.
- To check answers, ask pairs of students to read the question and give the answer. Ask if everyone agrees.

Answers
1 *the honey bird* 2 the hunter
3 the hunter; the honey bird 4 the pistol shrimp
5 the gobie fish 6 the pistol shrimp; the gobie fish

B Read and match.

- Read the first part of number 1 and ask students if they remember why the hunter whistles and shouts. Have students follow the line to find the reason.
- Have students continue the activity individually and then compare their complete sentences with a friend.
- To check answers, ask pairs of students to read the beginnings and endings of the sentences. Ask if everyone agrees.

Answers
1 *d* 2 b 3 e 4 a 5 c

C Read and answer. What makes a good team? Check (✔). Compare with a partner.

This activity allows students to explore the science concept of exploring symbiotic relationships.

- Decide as a class why the first item (sharing ideas) is good for teams (all the people in the team can know everyone's best ideas).
- Give students some time to think and choose what makes for a good team and then compare ideas with a friend.
- Ask students to raise their hands to say one item each that makes for a good team. Encourage them to say why they checked the item (in L1 if necessary). Ask if everyone agrees, then discuss why the ones students haven't checked don't make for a good team.
- Take the opportunity to explore the SEL competency of exhibiting cooperative learning and working toward group goals. You can ask students how working in a team can help us, and how people decide the goals for the team. They can also think about other areas in their lives where teamwork helps.

Answers
1; 2; 5; 6; 7

Cool Down

Put students into groups of eight and have each student draw a picture to illustrate one paragraph of the reading (you can combine paragraphs or have two students working together on a picture, if necessary). Tell students it's a good idea to talk to their teammates who are working on the paragraphs before and after, to make sure their pictures don't overlap. When they have finished, have each group line up holding their pictures in the correct order. Point out they have worked together as a team to recreate the stories.

Practice **Student's App:** Reading Comprehension Practice

Get Ready to Read

Lesson Objectives

- to practice the reading skill of predicting endings
- to activate prior knowledge of and interest in islands
- to make a personal connection to the reading

Materials
Audio Track 34; a short story that students are unlikely to have heard before (CD)

TRACK 34 TB p. 231 Warm Up

Put students in pairs. Play the audio of *The Superstar* (Unit 6, Reading 1) again and have students mime the actions as they listen.

A Read the beginning and the middle of the story. Write an ending.

This activity practices the reading skill of predicting endings, which was previewed on p. 105.

- Enlarge the pictures if you're using the TTL, or have students look at the pictures in their book.
- Ask students what they can see. Ask *Do you recognize the man in red?* (It's Pablo, the sculptor from *The Superstar* in Unit 6). *In the first picture, what can he see on the ground?* (a coin) *In the second picture, what do you think they're talking about?* Ask two students to read the beginning and middle of the story.
- Elicit suggestions from students for what the ending might be.
- Have students write a short ending on the lines provided and then share it with a friend. Ask if any students would like to share their ending with the class.
- Tell students that what they were doing in this task was *predicting*. Direct students to the reading skills box and read the box to students. Ask them if sometimes they can guess the end of a story before they read it all. Ask if they jump to the end of the story to check or if they wait and read everything. Point out that it helps us understand if we can imagine what's coming next.

B Think and discuss. Which ending do you like best? Why?

- Explain to students that 1, 2, and 3 are all possible endings to the story in A. Read the three endings while students listen and follow in their books.
- Allow some time for students to think which ending they like best.
- Ask students who like ending 1 to stand on the left of the classroom, ending 2 in the middle, and ending 3 on the right. Have students share with their group why they like that ending.
- Ask someone from each group to explain why they chose that ending. Ask if any students would like to change their minds.
- Ask students which ending they think is most surprising in B. Ask if they have read or watched any stories with a surprise ending and if they guessed the ending before it happened.

C Read page 112. What do you think happens at the end of the reading?

- Project p. 112 on the board or have students read it in their books. Ask *Who are they?* (pirates) *Where are they?* (on a beach/island) *What do they want?* (treasure)
- Ask students to think about whether the pirates are going to get what they want at the end of the story. Then ask them to decide what they think happens at the end. Do a Think, Pair, Share.
- Tell students that they will have to wait until the next lesson to see whose ending is most accurate!

Cool Down

Read students the beginning and middle of a short story they're unlikely to have heard before (this can be in L1). Pause and encourage students to discuss in pairs how they think the story will end. Read the end of the story and have a show of hands to see who guessed correctly.

Now read **It's Mine!**

Fiction: *It's Mine!—A Story*

Lesson Objectives

- to read a story about pirates and teamwork
- to explore the SEL competency of relationship skills: exhibiting cooperative learning and working toward group goals

Materials

Audio Tracks 41 and 42; Video; pictures of a pirate, an island, and treasure chest (either drawings or downloaded from the internet) in the middle of a large piece of paper (WU)

Warm Up

Draw pictures of a pirate, a desert island, and a closed treasure chest in the middle of three large pieces of paper (one drawing on each piece of paper). Divide the class into three groups and do a Chalk Talk activity (see TB p. 20).

Then have students look quickly at the story on pp. 112–117 and see which of their ideas they can find.

TRACK 41 TB p. 231 Reading Approach

First Reading: Listen and Engage

- Ask students to recall their prediction about the ending from the previous lesson.
- Play the audio while students follow the text in their books.
- At the end of p. 113, pause the audio and ask *Are they nice pirates? Why or why not?* Accept any answers if students can provide justification for their opinion.
- At the end of the story, ask if anyone's predictions about the ending were correct.
- Then look at the Words in Context.

TRACK 42 TB p. 231 Words in Context

- Play the audio and have students repeat the words.
- Have students race to find the words in the reading. Ask *Which word is used the most times?* (*treasure* x 6). Check whether they also found two instances of *password*, *map*, and *rich*.
- Remind students that they can **use the pictures to help establish the meaning of new words**. Have them discuss ideas with a partner, using L1 if necessary.
- Use these discussion points to confirm the meaning of each word.

treasure Ask students to find the word twice on the first page of the story. Students may already be familiar with this word from earlier tasks. Ask *What are the pirates looking for?* Have students find and point to the treasure on p. 115.

password Ask *What is the password?* (teamwork) *Do you or your family use passwords? What for?*

map Refer students to the sentence and the picture on p. 114. Ask *What's on the map?* (an arrow and an X telling them where to dig to find the treasure)

grab Ask students to mime how they think the pirates took the map. Ask *Is it nice to grab?*

rich Ask students *What's inside the box? Do you think the pirates had much money before? Do they have much money now?* Ask what the opposite of rich is. (poor)

gold Have students point to the picture of the gold. Ask *Is there anything gold in our classroom? What things are made of gold?*

pirate Students should already be familiar with this word from earlier tasks. Ask students *What do pirates do? Are they good people? Why or why not? Is it a nice life?*

Second Reading: Analyze the Text and Features

- Play the video to help students consolidate the story. Before they watch ask *Why do the pirates lose the treasure?* (because it's too heavy for the boat) Check answers at the end.
- Play the video again on mute. Pause at each key point in the story and ask students what emotion they think the pirates are feeling at that point from the expression on their faces. Ask students to make a face to demonstrate that emotion.
- Discuss the words in the yellow boxes as a class.
  - **Making Connections** (p. 112): *Parrots are very intelligent. They can copy sounds and words.* Ask students if they have ever heard a parrot speaking. Ask *What does it sound like? Do you think they understand what they're saying?* Ask students if they know how long parrots live (50–70 years, on average).
  - **Detail** (p. 113): *Close your book. Can you remember the password?* Have students turn their books over and try to remember and then spell the password.

Third Reading: Interact with the Text

- Play the audio again and have students follow in their books, at the same time raising their hands when the pirates are working well as a team and lowering their hands when they are not.
- Then divide the class into four groups: one group for each pirate and one for the parrot. Play the audio or the video again and have each group join in with the lines for their character.

Cool Down

Have students make a new password by choosing a word from the story and either write it backward or change some letters for numbers that look similar (e.g. *5* for *S* or *1* for I). Have them give the password to a friend to "solve."

Practice Student's App: Video

Explore the Reading

Lesson Objectives

- to understand and analyze *It's Mine!* through reading comprehension activities
- to learn about good story endings and teamwork
- to explore the SEL competency of relationship skills: exhibiting cooperative learning and working toward group goals
- to give a personal reaction to the story
- to recognize and reproduce the –*ck* digraph

Materials

(Optional) Video (A); Audio Track 43

Warm Up

Play the *Yes/No Game* (see TB p. 27).

Suggested sentences: *The pirates are looking for treasure.* (yes) *The parrot can speak.* (yes) *The password is k-r-o-w-m-e-a-t.* (no) *The pirates always help each other.* (no) *The treasure is under the ground.* (yes) *The pirates take the treasure home.* (no) *They like being pirates.* (yes)

A Read and number. Put the events in order. Retell the story.

- Before students open their books, find out what they remember from the story. Ask *Where does the story happen?* (on an island) *What do they need to unlock the box?* (a password) *Who has the password?* (the parrot) *Why don't they get the treasure?* (because it falls out of the boat)
- Have students watch the video again to check their answers to the questions. Alternatively, have students read it in their books.
- Have six volunteers read aloud one sentence each from A. Then refer students to the example answer and ask whether students agree that this is the first thing that happens in the story. Then decide number 2 as a class.
- Have students continue the activity individually and then compare their answers with a friend.
- To check answers, ask students to volunteer to read the next sentence in order. Ask if everyone agrees, and refer back to the reading to check if necessary.
- Put students into pairs and have them take turns reading the sentences in order to retell the story.

Answers

5; 3; 2; 4; *1*; 6

B Read and choose.

- Have students read the four endings and give them some time to decide which is the true ending from the story.
- Have students compare their answer with a friend.
- Elicit the answer, then refer back to the reading to decide together why the others are not correct.
- Review students' earlier predictions about the story's ending. Ask if they predicted the pirates would get the treasure or not at the beginning of the story. Have them circle *Yes* or *No*. Ask some students to explain why they thought they would/wouldn't (in L1 if necessary). This question links to the SEL competency of cooperating and working together—maybe the students saw they didn't cooperate and decided they wouldn't get the treasure!

Answers

1 c 2 Students' own answers

C Think and discuss. Did the pirates work together? Were they a good team? Why or why not?

- Connect this to the unit's SEL competency (cooperative learning and working toward group goals) by asking students to look back at the story and raise their hands to suggest one thing the pirates did well together and one time they didn't work well together. Write one suggestion for each on the board in two columns with the headings *Good teamwork* and *Bad teamwork*.
- Have students work individually to find more examples.
- Have students compare ideas with a partner and decide together if the pirates are a good team.
- Ask students what they decided and ask them why they think that.
- Ask *Do things work better when they help each other?* (yes) Ask students if they think they are better at working in a team than the pirates.

Phonics –*ck*

TRACK 43 TB. p. 232 **Listen and say.**

- Play the audio and have students look at the words in the phonics box. Ask them what sound all the words have in common (they all have **/k/** at the end, which is written –*ck*).
- Play the audio again and have students repeat, first in a high voice, then in a low voice.
- Ask students to choose their favorite word from the list and to tell a friend.
- Have students find more words in the story ending with –*ck*. Invite students to read the words out loud.
- Play *Silly Sentence* (see TB p. 26); for example, *Quick, quick! Unlock the clock!*

Answers

unlock; back; quick; o'clock

Cool Down

Play *Disappearing Sentences* (see TB p. 25). Choose four simple sentences from the reading; e.g. *Listen to the parrot at the top of the tree. / Can you say that again, please? / Let's help each other. / Let's look for treasure on another island.*

Practice **Resource Bank:** Phonics Printout; **Student's App:** Phonics Practice; Reading Comprehension Practice

Think Together

Lesson Objectives

- to make connections between the readings
- to explore the key concept: What is good about teamwork?
- to reflect on the unit and provide personal thoughts and opinions

Warm Up

Ask students to think about the question at the top of this lesson's page: *What is good about teamwork?* Write or project this question on the board. Elicit ideas from students based on what they have read and discussed. Remind students that there are no incorrect answers.

A Read and write *Yes* or *No*. Then compare with a partner.

- Before students look at the activity, ask them what teams they can remember from this unit (the people building a human tower/pyramid in the VTR picture, the hunter and honey bird, the gobie fish and pistol shrimp, the pirates). Ask which they think is the best and which is the worst team.
- Draw or project the table on the board. Decide the answer to number 1 as a class. Then have students continue the activity individually.
- To check answers, read each sentence and the answer options and have students raise their hands for their choices. Check everyone agrees, using the readings to resolve disagreements, and complete the table on the board.

Suggested Answers

1 yes; yes; no
2 yes; yes; yes
3 yes; yes; no
4 yes; no/yes; no

B Think and discuss. Are these good teams? Why or why not? Do a Think, Pair, Share.

Students are going to make evaluations about successful teams.

- Set the class up for a Think, Pair, Share cooperative learning routine (see TB p. 20).
- Project the three pictures as large as possible on the board or refer students to the pictures in their books. Ask them what teams they can see (1, horse and rider; 2, actors in a play; 3, boy waterskiing and [they can imagine] person driving the boat).
- Ask students to consider whether these are good teams. Do a Think, Pair, Share routine and encourage students to give reasons for their answers.

Practice **Resource Bank:** Unit Test; **Student's App:** Key Concept Practice

My Reading Journal

Pick a reading and change the ending. How does this change the story?

This task focuses on the skill of predicting and understanding how the beginning of a story relates to the ending.

Tell students an idea for an alternative ending to the story of the shrimp and the fish (e.g. *at the end of the day, the fish eats the shrimp and looks for a new helper*). Ask students if they think it is a good ending for the reading. Ask them how it changes what they read before—maybe the shrimp is scared of the fish?

Have students imagine an alternative ending for either the story of the hunters and the honey birds, the fish and the shrimp, or the pirates. Have them think about how it changes the story—did the pirates finally learn to be a team? Did the birds get tired of helping the hunters? Have them compare their ideas with a friend.

Ask if any students would like to read their new ending and share their ideas with the class.

Example Answer

The pirates work together and put the treasure in the boat. They leave the island together. They are all very rich and happy.

Color the coins to rate each reading in this unit.

This task focuses on personalization.

Have students decide how much they liked each reading and color the coins accordingly.

Say the name of each reading and call out *1, 2, 3, 4, 5* and have students raise their hands to show how they rated the readings.

Invite students to say why they liked or didn't like the readings.

Answers

Students' own answers

Cool Down

Have students look back at the picture on pp. 104–105. Ask them if they now have any more ideas about what it shows. Ask what important thing it shows about teamwork. (the people in the pyramid are relying on each other not to fall down—they are trusting one another)

UNIT 8

You're My Hero

Unit Overview

Themes

Sports and attributes

Real and fictional heroes

Synopsis

In this unit, students will learn about a famous athlete, find out about different heroes around the world, and think about personal heroes. They will plan, prepare, and play a superhero game and write a hero profile using target vocabulary and grammar from the unit.

Language Book

Vocabulary

gymnastics, race, tennis, track and field, volleyball, difficult, exciting, patient, popular, strong

p. 160

Explore Language

Comparatives: Long Adjectives

p. 161

Global Citizenship

Who are heroes around the world?

beautiful, brave, friendly, helpful, intelligent, interesting, mean, selfish, thoughtful

p. 162

Explore Language

Superlatives: Long Adjectives

p. 163

Talk About It

Conversation: taking turns and playing games

p. 164

Write About It

A Hero Profile

Sentence Building: *I think, because*

p. 165

Think It Over

Review and Reflection

p. 166

Literacy Book

Think Together
What makes a hero?
p. 173

Visible Thinking
VTR: See, Think, Wonder
p. 167

Fiction
Play: *A New Hero*

Words in Context: City, Mayor, job, robber, X-ray
p. 171

Nonfiction
Biography: *In First Place*

Words in Context: Olympic Games, hurt, comfortable, barefoot, medal
p. 168

Reading Skill
Understanding characters
p. 170

Phonics
tr–
p. 169

Language and Literacy Connections

The connecting theme in Unit 8 is different kinds of heroes.

	Language	Literacy
Vocabulary	**Set 1:** sports and long adjectives **Set 2:** attributes	**Nonfiction:** *difficult, race, strong* **Fiction:** *helpful*
Grammar	**Comparatives: Long Adjectives** It's more exciting than homework. **Superlatives: Long Adjectives** Dave is the most helpful student.	**Nonfiction** One of the most famous Olympic marathon runners was a man named Abebe Bikila. He was more comfortable. **Fiction** He is the most helpful hero!
Skills	**Pronunciation:** /oʊ/ and /aʊ/	**Reading:** understanding characters **Phonics:** *tr–*
International English	*track and field / athletics; math/maths*	*trash/rubbish; math/maths*

Vocabulary

Lesson Objectives

- to learn sports vocabulary: *gymnastics, race, tennis, track and field, volleyball*
- to learn and practice long adjectives: *difficult, exciting, patient, popular, strong*
- to sing a song about a sports hero

Materials
Audio Tracks 87 to 90; Video

Warm Up

Play the *Alphabet Game* with sports (see TB p. 25).

A TRACK 87 TB p. 222 **Listen and find. Does Mom win?**

- Project the picture from pp. 100–101 on the board or have students look at it in their books. Ask students to say what they can see in the picture. Ask questions to guide them: *Where are they?* (a sports stadium) *What event are they at?* (a sporting event, perhaps a tournament, because there are a lot of sports being played at the same time)
- Draw students' attention to the woman wearing purple, who is running a race at the bottom of the picture. Establish that she is Susan from the previous unit.
- Refer students back to the question they were asked at the end of Unit 7: *What sport does Susan do?* Elicit answers based on the picture (running). Ask if any of the students' predictions were correct.
- Tell students they are going to listen to a conversation between people watching the sports in the picture. Play the audio and have students point to the new words and pictures as they listen.
- Ask the gist question *Does Mom win?* and elicit the answer. Play the audio again for students to check.

Answer
No, she comes in third.

B TRACK 88 TB p. 222 **Listen, say, and number the pictures in A.**

- Play the audio and have students point to the pictures and say the words.
- Then play it again and have them number the pictures in order.
- Check answers by playing the audio again and pausing after each number for students to say the word.
- Have all students repeat the words one more time, this time with a mime for each word.

Answers
1 *tennis* 2 popular 3 strong 4 exciting 5 difficult 6 patient 7 track and field 8 race 9 volleyball 10 gymnastics

International English

Elicit that *track and field* is American English and *athletics* is British English. Drill for pronunciation. Then ask *Which do we use?*

C TRACK 89 TB p. 222 **Listen. Close your eyes and visualize.**

- Prepare students for the visualization (see TB p. 21)
- Play the audio, allowing students to visualize the sports and adjectives and do actions where appropriate as they listen. They can say the word after they hear *say*.
- Divide the class into pairs or small groups, play the audio again, and have students share their ideas or do their mimes in pairs.
- Then ask students if they had similar ideas.

D Look and write.

- Draw or project the table on the board. Discuss the example answers together, and then have students work individually to classify the other words as sports or adjectives.
- To check answers, invite students to come to the board and write a word each. Ask if everyone agrees.

Answers
Sports: *tennis*, track and field, race, volleyball, gymnastics
Adjectives: *popular*, strong, exciting, difficult, patient

E TRACK 90 TB p. 222 **Listen and sing. Then watch and sing.**

- With books closed, write or project the song title on the board: *Who's Your Hero?* Ask students *Who's your hero?* Elicit some ideas.
- Tell students they are going to listen to the song and they should raise their hands every time they hear a word from B. Play the audio once all the way through.
- Have students open their books and look at the song lyrics. Play the song again, pausing after each line for students to repeat.
- Then play the song again and have students sing along. You could have half the class sing the first verse and half sing the second verse, then switch.
- Play the song video and encourage students to watch and sing. They can make up actions to do for each of the sports as they sing.

Cool Down

Play *Back Spelling* with the vocabulary from this lesson. Have students stand up in pairs and spell out the new vocabulary on each other's back for their partner to guess.

Practice **Student's App:** Vocabulary Practice; Video

Explore Language

Lesson Objectives

- to learn how to make comparatives with long adjectives
- to provide contextualized practice of vocabulary of sports and long adjectives

Materials
Audio Tracks 90 to 92

TRACK 90 TB p. 222 **Warm Up**
Sing ***Who's Your Hero?*** again and encourage students to do some actions for the sports.

A TRACK 91 TB p. 222 **Listen and read. Who's the hero?**

- Project the story on p. 102 on the board or have students look in their books. Ask *What can you see?* Ask students if they recognize the boy and tell them that it is the boy who was cheering on his mom in the previous lesson. Tell them his name is Bob.
- Ask what they think the relation is between Bob and the man (father and son), and what they think they are talking about (heroes).
- Play the audio and have students follow the story in their books. Ask if their predictions were correct.
- Then ask the gist question *Who is the hero?* and elicit the answer. Play the audio again to check.

Answer
The Human Elephant

International English

Ask students to notice the spelling difference between *math* and *maths*. Elicit which is American English and which is British English and drill both for pronunciation. Ask *Do you know what math/maths is short for?* (mathematics) *Which do we use?*

B Look at A. Complete.

- Write or project the table on the board. Read the first sentence, saying *mmm* for the blanks on either side of *exciting*. Have students find the sentence in the story and fill in the blanks.
- Have students complete the other sentences in the table.
- Check answers by asking students to read the completed sentences and ask if everyone agrees. Complete the table on the board and have students repeat each sentence.
- Ask students what words to use before and after the adjective to show a difference (more … than).
- Have students look at the Grammar tip *Look* and ask if they can remember adjectives that end in *–er* to show a difference (e.g. bigger, longer, hotter). Ask if they know why the adjectives in this table are different (if not, tell them they'll find out soon).

Practice **Resource Bank:** Grammar Printout; **Student's App:** Grammar Practice

Answers
more; *exciting*; than; popular; difficult

C Think and discuss. Then choose.

- Write *strong* and *difficult* on the board. Drill the pronunciation of both. Repeat them both again while clapping in time to the syllables and have students do the same. Ask *How many claps?* (one and three) Point out that each clap represents a syllable.
- Read the options in C. Give students time to think about their answers, then have them compare their ideas in pairs.
- Read the options again and have students put their hands on their shoulders for the answers they chose. Have them circle the correct options.

Answers
1 two 2 two or more syllables

D TRACK 92 TB p. 222 **Listen and say.**

- Play the audio and have students tell you what adjectives they hear (exciting, popular, difficult, patient).
- Play the audio again and have students listen and repeat.
- For ideas on how to vary the drill, see TB p. 22.

E Put the words in order. Do you agree (✔) or disagree (✘)?

- Refer students to the example sentence and elicit the three words that show a difference between the two things (*more difficult than*).
- Ask them to raise their hands if they agree with the sentence—point out the students with their hands raised will put a checkmark after the sentence and those with their hands down will put an 'X'.
- Have students continue the activity individually and then compare answers with a friend. Tell them to say *I agree* or *I disagree* to specify whether they have checked the box. Then check answers.

Answers
1 *Gymnastics is more difficult than volleyball.*
2 Track and field is more exciting than basketball.
3 Tennis is more popular than table tennis.
4 Karate is more dangerous than swimming.

F Choose and say.

- Ask two students to read the example dialogue. Find out which speaker they agree with.
- Give students time to make three sentences they think are true. Have them take turns sharing their ideas with a friend and each responding by agreeing or disagreeing.

Cool Down

Play *Pass the Whisper!* (see TB p. 26) with sentences from A or E.

Global Citizenship

Lesson Objectives

- to learn vocabulary of attributes: *beautiful, brave, friendly, helpful, intelligent, interesting, mean, selfish, thoughtful*
- to explore what makes a hero
- to practice listening for gist and details

Materials

Audio Tracks 93 to 95; (optional) Audio Track H

Opening Question

Ask the opening question: *Who are heroes around the world?* Encourage students to first think about who are heroes to them, and in their country. Do they think that people in other countries know about the same heroes? Do they have different heroes? Give students some time to think, then elicit ideas.

A TRACK 93 TB p. 223 **Listen to Felipe talk about his hero. Who's his hero?**

- Have students look at the pictures and say what they can see. Ask *Are the pictures of people or of things?* (of people) Say *Point to one picture showing a person doing a good thing. Point to one showing a person doing a bad thing.* (Have students point but not say the words yet.)
- Play the audio and have students point to the pictures and words as they hear them.
- Ask the gist question *Who's his hero?* Elicit the answer. Then play the audio again to check.

Answer

his cousin, Paco

B TRACK 94 TB p. 223 **Listen, say, and number the pictures in A.**

- Play the audio and have students point to the pictures and say the words.
- Play the audio again and have students number the items.
- Then play the audio again to check answers. Pause after each number and nominate students to say the adjective,

Answers

1 *thoughtful* 2 friendly 3 interesting 4 mean
5 selfish 6 brave 7 beautiful 8 intelligent
9 helpful

TRACK H TB p. 223 **Visualization**

The TTL has a visualization audio track for this vocabulary set (see TB p. 21).

C **Play *Back Spelling*. Guess the words your friend is spelling.**

- Students are going to write words, letter by letter, on each other's backs with their finger. As an example, call out a word from A and have students hold up their index finger and write it in the air as you spell it out (e.g. *brave, b-r-a-v-e*). Then have students write the word on their friend's back.
- Have students take turns choosing a word and writing it on their friend's back. If their friend guesses incorrectly, have him/her write the word again.

D TRACK 95 TB p. 223 **Now listen to Mónica and Shayma. Number the pictures. Whose hero is strong?**

- Listening for the main idea: tell students they are going to listen to two people from Tunisia and Cuba talking about their heroes. Elicit what they can see in the pictures. Play the audio and have students number the pictures.
- Ask the gist question *Whose hero is strong?* and elicit the answer. Encourage students to justify their answer. Play the audio again for students to check.

Answers

a 2 b 1 Shayma's hero is strong.

E **Listen again. Choose the correct name.**

- Listening for specific information: have students look at the sentences and see if they can remember any answers. Then play the audio again and have students complete the activity individually.
- To check answers, invite volunteers to read a sentence each, followed by the name of the person it is about.

Answers

1 *Mónica* 2 Mónica 3 Shayma 4 Shayma
5 Mónica

Discussion Questions

- Draw students' attention to the discussion questions: *Who are your heroes from your country? Why are they heroes?*
- Ask students who they think are heroes in their country. Give them some time to remember people (people from history or people alive today) and why they are heroes. Have students discuss the questions in pairs or small groups (see **ETB**).
- Elicit the conclusion that heroes do lots of different things, and it isn't always about being strong or brave.
- Return to the original opening question to ask again *Who are heroes around the world?* Ask if the lesson has given them any new ideas. Ask if the heroes they have named in their country are also heroes around the world. Ask *Are you surprised that heroes can be different around the world?*

Cool Down

Play *Chain Game* (see TB p. 25) in groups. Start the chain by saying *My dad is my hero because he is thoughtful.* Have the next student say, for example, *My dad is my hero because he is thoughtful … and brave.*

Practice **Student's App:** Vocabulary Practice; Listening Comprehension Practice

Explore Language

Lesson Objectives

- to learn how to make superlatives with long adjectives
- to provide contextualized practice of long adjectives

Materials

Audio Tracks 96 and 97

Warm Up

Divide the class into teams. Say an adjective from Unit 6 (e.g. *curly, straight, clean, hard, messy, new, noisy, quiet, soft, thick*) and have the teams write down the superlative form. At the end, ask students to spell their answers. Award points for correct spelling.

A TRACK 96 TB p. 223 **Listen and read. Why is the teacher intelligent?**

- Ask students what they can see in the pictures. Ask *Where are they?* (at school) *What is happening?* (They are giving out prizes.) *How do you think the people feel?* Draw students' attention to the man giving the prizes. Ask *Who is it?* (It's Bob's dad from Lesson 2.)
- Play the audio and have students follow the dialogue in their books.
- Ask the gist question *Why is the teacher intelligent?* and elicit the answer. Play the audio again to check.

Answer

Because she teaches everything.

B Look at A. Complete.

- Write or project the table on the board.
- Point out the example answer (intelligent) and have students find the sentence in the text. Have students complete it in their books.
- Have students work in pairs to complete the other blanks in the table. Check answers as a class.
- Ask students if they can remember other adjectives they used before to say why one thing or person was special and different from all the others (e.g. smallest, cutest, tallest).
- Have students look at the Grammar tip *Look* and ask if they know why we use *most* and not *–est* with these adjectives. Have them think about the comparative adjectives with *more* and try to draw a conclusion.

Answers

the; most; helpful; *intelligent*; interesting

C Think and discuss. Then choose.

- Read the options for students and ask them to look at the table and draw a conclusion about which options they think are correct. Have students discuss their ideas in pairs and circle the answers in their books.
- To check answers, read the options again and have students raise their hands for the ones they chose.

Answers

1 more than two 2 two or more syllables

D TRACK 97 TB p. 223 **Listen and say.**

- Play the audio and have students tell you what adjectives they hear (helpful, thoughtful, interesting, dangerous).
- Play the audio again, pausing after each sentence for students to repeat.
- For ideas on how to vary the drill, see TB p. 22.

E Choose and write.

- Write the first sentence on the board, including the example answer. Ask students what name they think you should put in this sentence to make it about someone in their class. Elicit some suggestions.
- Have students complete the other sentences individually by choosing a different adjective from the box each time and then compare their answers with a friend.
- To check answers, ask volunteers to read a sentence each and explain their answer. Ask if anyone else would like to share their sentences.

Answers

Students' own answers

F Choose and say.

- Have two students read the example dialogue.
- Elicit one or two more suggestions from the class. Then give students time to think of a minimum of three more sentences.
- Divide the class into pairs and have them exchange their ideas. Remind them to say *Me, too!* or *I agree!* if their opinion is the same and to say *I disagree* if they have a different opinion.
- Bring the class back together and ask if there were any ideas that the pairs disagreed about, and ask the pair to repeat what they said for the rest of the class.

Cool Down

Play *Running Sentences* (see TB p. 26) with superlative sentences from this lesson.

Practice **Resource Bank:** Grammar Printout; **Student's App:** Grammar Practice

Talk About It

Lesson Objectives

- to prepare and practice a conversation about taking turns and playing a game
- to recognize and reproduce /oʊ/ and /aʊ/

Materials
Video; Audio Track 98

Warm Up

Tell students that this lesson is about superheroes. Ask students to call out the names of superheroes and write them on the board. Now have them think of an adjective that describes that hero's most important characteristic. Invite students to come and write an adjective next to the names. If adjectives are repeated, ask students if there is another adjective they can use for one of the heroes.

A TB p. 235 **Watch and listen. What is Lara's superhero's name?**

- Ask students *Do you like playing games? What games do you play with your friends?* and elicit ideas. Tell them they will watch a video about friends taking turns to play a game.
- Introduce the gist question *What is Lara's superhero's name?* Elicit some possible ideas and then play the video to find out. Ask students if they would like to play this game. Ask further comprehension questions; for example, *How many superheroes do they have each?* (six) (see **ETB**).

Answer
Fun Fifi

B Watch again. Check (✔) the phrases you hear.

- Have students read the phrases and draw their attention to the example.
- Now play the video again and have students check the phrases they hear.
- Ask students to read a sentence each and say *yes* or *no*. Ask if everyone agrees.

Answers
1; 2; 3; 4; 7; 8

Pronunciation /oʊ/ and /aʊ/

TRACK 98 TB p. 223 **Listen and say.**

- Demonstrate the **/oʊ/** sound as in *go* and the **/aʊ/** sound as in *how* and encourage students to copy you.
- Play the audio and have students repeat each word. Ask students to say the sound the first set of three words have in common and then the sound of the second set of three words.
- Say *These are all words Lara and Sam use in their conversation.* Ask students what other words they know with these sounds (e.g. hero, cow). Ask for suggestions and write them on the board in two columns. Drill all the words at the end.

C Plan. You're going to play the Superhero Game. Choose adjectives for the cards.

- Let students know that they are going to play the game they saw the children play in the video with their own superhero cards.
- Tell them to start by writing adjectives for their superheroes like Lara and Sam did. Have them write the adjectives from the box (and only these adjectives) in the order they want for each superhero. Remind them not to share their answers with anyone else.

D Now, play the game. Use your cards from C and phrases from B.

- Show the video again to remind students how to play the game.
- Divide the class into pairs and ask how they start the game. (You go first. Choose an adjective.) Ask *What happens next?* (Each person chooses a superhero for the other person to play.) *Who wins?* (the person whose superhero has the higher number for the adjective)
- Have students play the game in pairs using their superhero cards from C and phrases from B. Remind them to write down the score in their notebooks, like Lara does in the video. Monitor and help as necessary.

Cool Down

Ask students *Did you enjoy playing this game? Who was your favorite character?* Have them draw a picture of their favorite character, highlighting the character's strongest characteristic according to the cards they made. Invite students to tell the class why this character was their favorite; for example, *My favorite character is Top Tanya because she's brave.*

Practice **Student's App:** Speaking Skill Practice; Video

Write About It

Lesson Objectives

- to focus on sentence building with *I think …, because* to give opinions
- to plan and write a hero profile

Materials

(Optional) Support, Standard, and Challenge writing printouts from the Resource Bank (one per student) (C, D)

Warm Up

Play *Running Spelling* (see TB p. 26) with key vocabulary from the text *My Grandpa* in A. (Students don't need to look at the text to play the game.)

Suggested words: *awesome, volleyball, difficult, better, stories, funny, kindest, best*

A Read the hero profile. Underline *I think* and the word after it. Circle *because*.

- Have students look at the pictures in A and read the text quickly. Ask questions to check general understanding: *Who is the text about?* (the writer's grandpa) *Why is he awesome?* (because he can do a lot of things) *Does the writer think he's a good grandpa?* (Yes, he thinks he's the best.) Ask *Is this grandpa like your grandpa?*
- Project the profile on the board. Have students find the first *I think* in the text. Ask what the next word is (*he's*). Then have them find and underline the other instances of *I think* and the word after in the text in their books. Elicit the word after *I think* in each case. Point out it can be any subject (*you, we, my mom*, etc.).
- Have students find and circle *because* in the text. Ask what happens in the sentences before the word *because* (there is an opinion). Elicit that *because* tells us *why* someone has the opinion.
- Ask students which words we use to give our opinion (tell them they can look at A to check). Elicit that we use *I think* when we want to give our opinion.

Answers

I think he's the most awesome person because he can do a lot of things.
I think he plays better than my dad.
I love his stories because they're funny.
I think he's the kindest person because he takes care of me.

B Match.

- Have a volunteer read number 1 and its matching second half. Ask if this sentence is a fact or an opinion (opinion). Explain that all of these sentences are opinions.
- Have students complete the activity individually.
- To check answers, ask individual students to read a completed sentence. Ask if everyone agrees.

Answers

1 d 2 a 3 c 4 b

C Plan. Think about your hero. Choose and complete.

- Tell students they are going to write about their own hero. Ask if they think a hero is always a famous person and elicit that a hero can be a family member or a friend who is special or who does something special.
- Project or write the spidergram in C on the board and do an example with the class: *Who: My uncle Jamie. Personality: intelligent, interesting. Why?: He makes fantastic sculptures with metal and wood. Activities: He plays the drums.* Point out that this is a plan. They can complete the spidergram in note form; they don't need to use full sentences.
- Give students a minute to decide who their hero is and then have them complete the spidergram, adding extra information where they can. Challenge printouts can be handed out now. Monitor and help with vocabulary as necessary.

D Write a hero profile.

- Have students write a hero profile in their notebooks from the notes they made in C. Encourage them to use the example in A as a model and remind them to include opinions and reasons. Support printouts can be handed out now.
- Have students write out their final versions neatly on paper or hand out the Standard printouts from the Resource Bank. Allow them time to draw their hero. Display the finished profiles around the classroom.

Cool Down

Enjoy each other's work: have students circulate around the classroom, enjoying their friends' hero profiles. Write four things on the board that students should look for: *a good text, an interesting person, a good example of an opinion, and a good picture.*

When they have had time to circulate, ask students to point to the work where they noticed each of the four things.

Practice **Student's App:** Writing Practice

Think It Over

Lesson Objectives

- to review what has been learned in the unit
- to reflect on the unit and their progress
- to think about learning strategies and how to continue learning at home

Warm Up

This is a chance to review language from the unit and bring the topic back into focus.

Have students open their books to the first lesson of Unit 8. Face in the same direction as the students and "write" one of the words in the air with your finger. Have students raise their hands when they know what it is. Repeat if necessary. Confirm their answer and ask them for an example of how the word was used in the unit. Repeat with the vocabulary in the Global Citizenship lesson.

Read the questions and draw or write your answers.

- Explain to students that they can choose to either write a few words or sentences or they can draw a picture.

What did I do?

- Give students a few minutes to look back through the unit at the different activities they did. Ask questions about the unit; for example, *What did you sing about? What activities and actions did you do? What games did you play? What did you describe?*
- Tell students they can draw or write about activities they liked or found interesting, but encourage them not to choose their favorite activity yet. Instead, encourage them to identify something in the unit that they found challenging but which they completed and feel proud of. Alternatively, ask them to choose something that was particularly memorable for them—because it was interesting, or it was different, or even because it was noisy! You can use L1 to explain these ideas to students.

What did I learn?

- Have students talk to a partner about what they remember from the unit—stories, words, phrases, and people.
- Ask students *Can you find words that you didn't know before? Can you make new sentences? What new facts did you learn?*
- Encourage students to draw a picture or write about what they learned.

What was my favorite part?

- Have students look back through the unit and decide what they enjoyed the most. Tell them it can be an activity they found fun, a story they enjoyed reading, a favorite character, or a favorite sport. They should try to choose just one and draw a picture or write about it. Explain that when we like something, it is often easier to learn.

How well did I do?

- Tell students to color in the number of gymnasts that best expresses how well they have learned the unit content (i.e., the more they color, the more they feel they have learned). Ask *What do you remember? What do you understand? What do you need to practice more?* Encourage students to look back through the unit to see how much they remember.

What can I do next?

- Brainstorm ideas with the class about what students can do to continue to learn (e.g. sing the song again, play the game on p. 105 again).
- Encourage students to think about what they can do at home to improve their English, using the four verbs as prompts; for example, sing a popular song in English, practice vocabulary and grammar by doing activities on the **Student's App on Navio**, play *Superheroes!* with family members, and share what they have learned about heroes with family members.
- Ask students to choose one or more activities from the list (sing, practice, play, share) that they will do to practice their English.
- Once students have completed the page in their books, have them discuss with a friend what they drew or wrote. Did they choose the same activities or different ones?

Looking Forward

Draw students' attention to the character at the bottom of the page. Ask *Who's this?* and elicit what they remember about her (she is Matilde, and she talked about her teacher Jane in Lesson 4, p. 106). Ask students to make predictions about where Matilde might be visiting in Unit 9. Then tell them they will find out in the next unit!

Put It Together

To further review and recycle the language in Units 7 and 8, play the game, *Give Me a Clue!*, on pp. 112–113. See TB p. 211 for teaching notes.

Practice **Resource Bank:** Unit Test;
Student's App: Vocabulary and Grammar Review

Get Ready to Read

Lesson Objectives

- to activate prior knowledge about obstacles and heroism
- to encourage students to observe and interpret through a See, Think, Wonder VTR
- to preview the reading skill of understanding characters

Materials

(Optional) VTR printout from the Resource Bank (A, B, C)

Warm Up

Use this activity to create interest in the topic of heroes.

Ask students to remember the names of heroes they know from books, TV shows, or movies. Build a list on the board and ask if they have anything in common. Leave this list on the board to refer to later (in D).

See, Think, Wonder

A Look at the picture. What do you see?

Students are going to do a See, Think, Wonder VTR to explore the image of a family having a party.

- Give them a minute to look at the picture. Then elicit one or two examples of what they see before giving them time to share their ideas in small groups or pairs.
- Students will likely find: a family (their clothes, hair), houses/buildings, trees, leaves, party hats, cats, birds, a nest, balloons, presents, a picnic, food, birthday cake, plates, candles, fruit, a ladder, grass, a curtain, sky, clouds.

Here's an example of this part of the routine.

Teacher: What do you see?
Student A: (I see) some people.
Student B: I see balloons and a cake.
Teacher: Great. What shapes do you see?
Student C: The plates are circles.
Student D: Some windows are rectangles, but that window's (a) square.

B What do you think?

- Ask students *What do you think?* Give them one minute to think silently about the picture and then share their ideas. Students' ideas may vary here, but remind them that all answers are valid.

Here's an example of this part of the routine.

Teacher: What do you think?
Student A: (I think) it's a party.
Student B: Yes, (I agree,) and I think it's a birthday party.
Teacher: Really? Why do you think that?
Student B: I see presents and a cake with candles.

C What do you wonder?

- Ask students *What do you wonder?* Give them one minute to think about the picture silently and think of questions they have about the picture.

Here's an example of this part of the routine.

Teacher: What do you wonder?
Student A: I wonder why she isn't in the group.
Teacher: Good question. Why do you think?
Student B: Maybe she's a neighbor.
Teacher: Great. What else do you wonder?
Student C: Why does the boy have leaves in his hair?

Transition

Point out the title of the unit *You're My Hero*. Ask students *Who could be the hero in this picture?* (Example answers: the dad if he has just rescued the boy from the tree; the boy if he was getting the cat out of the tree; the Mom because she is very busy, but she baked the delicious cake)

D Think and discuss. What makes someone a hero?

- Have students look at the list of heroes on the board from the Warm Up. Ask *What special qualities does each one have?*
- Ask *Do these qualities make someone a hero? Is there anything extra or different needed?* Have students discuss what makes a hero in pairs.

E Look at the pictures in the reading. Who is the main character? Which adjectives do you think describe him? Think and check (✔).

This is a preview of the reading skill of understanding characters.

- Have students look at the pictures on pp. 122–125 (or project them on the board) and decide which person is the main focus of the pictures (a man, whose name they won't yet know, but he looks like an athlete).
- Look at the first word together and ask students if they think the man is strong (probably, if he is a good athlete) and check the box. Then ask if they think he is funny. (we don't know from the pictures; point out it may be true, but we can't check it if the pictures don't tell us) Have students continue individually and then compare with a friend.
- Read the adjectives and ask students to raise their hands for the ones they chose. Ask some students why they checked the adjectives—point out there are no right or wrong answers here.

Suggested Answers

strong, brave, tall

Now read **In First Place**

Nonfiction: *In First Place— A Biography*

Lesson Objectives

- to read a biography about a famous marathon runner
- to learn through CLIL (history): finding out about important people
- to make a personal connection to the reading

Materials

Audio Tracks 44 and 45 (optional) picture of the Olympic flag (Words in Context)

Warm Up

Tell students you will say the names of some sports or games (and mime them to help students understand). Then ask if they have tried any of the sports and if they liked them.

Suggested sports: *running, soccer, gymnastics, swimming, tennis, volleyball*

TRACK 44 TB p. 232 Reading Approach

First Reading: Listen and Engage

- Have students look quickly at the title of the text, the genre, the layout, and the pictures on all four pages. Ask them what they think they will read about today (a winning runner).
- Play the audio and have students follow the text in their books. Ask them to think about this question as they read: *Why is the man in the pictures special?* (He won running races in the Olympic Games.)
- Then look at the Words in Context.

TRACK 45 TB p. 232 Words in Context

- Play the audio and have students repeat the words.
- Have them race to find the words in the reading. Say *Three of the words are used twice—which ones?* (*hurt*, *comfortable*, and *medal*)
- Review the different strategies we can use to understand new words in a text (see TB p. 13), then have students discuss the words in pairs.
- Use these additional discussion points to confirm the meaning of each item.

Olympic Games Have students look at the picture on p. 122. Elicit that it's a sports stadium. Guide them to figure out that it's an event with lots of different sports, including running. Show the picture of the Olympic flag and explain that the rings and colors represent continents and countries united.

hurt Ask *Did you ever have new shoes? How do your feet feel the first time you wear them—good or bad? Is* hurt *positive or negative?* (negative) Ask students to mime Abebe Bikila wearing his shoes (saying *ouch!*)

comfortable Ask *Do comfortable shoes feel good?* (yes) *How did Abebe Bikila's shoes feel?* (bad—they weren't comfortable)

barefoot Point out that *barefoot* is made up of two words: *bare* and *foot*. Ask *Is "barefoot" with or without shoes?* (without)

medal Ask if they can see the medal in the picture on p. 125 and have a student point to it. Ask *Do you have a medal? What for?*

Second Reading: Analyze the Text and Features

- Ask students *Is this a real story?* (yes) *What is it about?* (the life of a famous person) Ask if students know what we call texts written about the life of a person (a biography). Explain that usually biographies talk about the life of a person in the order it happened.
- Give students time to read the text silently by themselves. Ask them to make a note of every date they come across. When they have finished reading, ask if the dates are in order (yes: 1932, 1960, 1964).
- Then discuss the questions in the green boxes as a class.
  - **Fact** (p. 122): *Every four years, the world's best athletes compete at the Olympic Games.* Explain that the Olympic Games is the most important competition for many sports and because it is only held every four years, sports people train for a long time and have to be really good to compete in it. Ask students if they know when the last Olympic Games was. Together, work out how old students would have been then. Ask *Do you know when the next Olympic Game is? Where is it?*
  - **Personalization** (p. 123): *How do you think Bikila felt when he joined the Olympic team?* Ask students to imagine how they would feel if they were a last-minute replacement for another athlete. Would they feel confident?
  - **Critical Thinking** (p. 124): *Why do you think some people laughed at Abebe Bikila?* Ask students what made Abebe Bikila different from the other marathon runners (he didn't wear shoes). Ask if they can think of why this might make people laugh (maybe because it looked funny or strange).
  - **Making Connections** (p. 125): *Abebe Bikila was the first person to win the Olympic marathon twice in a row.* Clarify the meaning of *twice in a row*—he won the marathon gold at one Olympics and then again at the next Olympics. Ask students *Do you know any other runners who won two gold medals?*

Third Reading: Interact with the Text

- Have students be the narrators of the text, each student reading one sentence at a time. Have the others mime the actions as they hear them spoken.

Cool Down

Ask students to recall one interesting fact they learned from today's lesson. Give them time to think and then have them tell their partner.

Explore the Reading

Lesson Objectives

- to understand and analyze *In First Place* through reading comprehension activities
- to learn through CLIL (history): finding out about important people
- to make a personal connection to the reading

Materials
Audio Track 44

TRACK 44 TB p. 232 Warm Up

Play *What's the Next Word?* (see TB p. 27) with the *In First Place* audio from the previous lesson.

A Read and write *True* or *False*.

- Before students open their books, have a Circle Time discussion (see TB p. 20) about the reading. Ask *Where was Abebe Bikila born?* (Ethiopia) *What big race did he win?* (the Olympic marathon) *Why was it difficult for him?* (It was a tough race.) *Why did some people laugh at him?* (because he didn't wear shoes) *How many times did he win?* (twice)
- Refer students to question 1 and the example answer. Ask them if they can find something in the reading that shows it is false (p. 122, first sentence).
- Have students continue the activity individually.
- To check answers, read the sentences and have students raise their hands for those they think are true. Ask why the others are false. Check everyone agrees, referring back to the reading when necessary.

Answers
1 *False* 2 True 3 False 4 False 5 True 6 True

B Put the events in order.

- Project the activity on the board or refer students to the sentences in their book. Point out these are the main events of the story. Elicit the event that happened first (Abebe took the other runner's place).
- Have students continue individually to number the rest of the events in the correct order.
- Check answers by asking students to read a sentence each. Write the numbers on the board and ask if everyone agrees.

Answers
3, 4, *1*, 6, 2, 5

C Think, write, and discuss. How do you think Abebe Bikila felt?

- Have students look at the adjectives in the box. Ask them to read all three sentences and then give them time to decide which adjectives they feel best describe how Abebe Bikila felt at each stage.
- Point out that often more than one answer is possible. Have them complete the sentences individually. Encourage them to think of reasons for their answers.
- To check answers, ask a student to read their completed first sentence. Then ask if anyone had anything different. Elicit all options from the class, then discuss if they are all viable.

Suggested Answers
1 scared; sad 2 surprised; brave 3 thankful; happy

D Think and discuss. What other famous people from history do you know?

- Explore the CLIL history objective of finding out about important people. Ask students if they've read a biography before and who it was about. If they studied Level 1, remind them they read a biography about Margarete Steiff, who made the first teddy bear. Ask students to think about other famous people they know about from class, books, or movies. Discuss who they were, where/when they lived, and what they did. Have students make a list in pairs or small groups.
- Then ask *Why do you think we remember these people from the past? How are these people important to us today?*
- Bring the class together to share ideas. You could also ask *Are there famous people today who will be important in the future?*

Cool Down

Play *Disappearing Words* (see TB p. 25) with the 15 words students tell you they consider the most important words in the reading.

Practice **Student's App:** Reading Comprehension Practice

Get Ready to Read

Lesson Objectives

- to practice the reading skill of understanding characters
- to activate prior knowledge about who heroes are and what makes them

Warm Up

Play the *Yes/No Game* (see TB p. 27) with sentences from *In First Place* and *It's Mine!* (Unit 7).

Suggested sentences: *The marathon is a long swimming race.* (no) *Abebe Bikila was from Ethiopia.* (yes) *Abebe Bikila was in the army.* (yes) *He didn't like his shoes, so he found a better pair.* (no) *Abebe Bikila won three gold medals.* (no) *He is a hero to many people.* (yes)

The pirates didn't find the treasure. (no) *The pirates were bad at teamwork.* (yes) *The pirates asked a parrot for help.* (yes) *The pirates wanted to share the treasure.* (no) *The pirates lost the treasure.* (yes)

A Look, think, and discuss. What kinds of characters are they? How can you describe them?

- This lesson practices the reading skill of understanding characters, which they previewed in Lesson 1. Refer students to the pictures in their book or project them on the board.
- Ask students who the characters are and if they remember the stories that they are from. (If they have done the Warm Up, this should be easy.) Ask them what kind of people the pirates and Abebe Bikila are. Ask students to raise their hands to give suggestions. Write *Pirates* and *Abebe Bikila* on opposite sides of the board and make a spidergram with the suggestions.
- Refer students to the reading skills box. Have students read the information about characters. Ask *Which character in A is real? Which characters are made up?*
- Ask students which other characters they can remember from other readings in the book. Ask *Were they real or made up?*

Suggested Answers

Pirates made up, not kind, selfish Abede Bikila real, brave, interesting, strong

B Match the characters to the sentences.

- Have students look at the pictures and read the names. Ask *Who are they?* (maybe superheroes) Tell them that they are characters from the next reading.
- Have students read the four the sentences and then encourage them to look at the pictures again and match the first picture together and write a number in the box.
- Have students continue the activity individually and then compare answers with a friend.
- To check answers, say the names of the characters and have a volunteer say the number. Say *What gives you the answer in the picture?* and have the volunteer come to the front and point to the relevant part of the picture. Check everyone agrees.
- Ask *What do you think the reading is about?* Confirm that it is about heroes (or superheroes) but don't give anything else away yet.

Answers

1 c 2 a 3 b 4 d

C Think and discuss. Does a hero need to be someone famous? Does a hero need to be a grown-up?

- Read the questions to the class. Then ask two students to read the example answers in the speech bubbles. Ask students if they think these are good answers.
- Ask them for their initial reactions to get the class thinking. After two or three reactions from the class, do a Think, Pair, Share routine. Remind students that they must try to say why they think what they do.

Cool Down

Look at the pictures of the characters in B again and have students discuss in pairs what they think the characters will be able to do with their abilities.

Now read **A New Hero**

Fiction: *A New Hero—A Play*

Lesson Objectives

- to read a play about heroes
- to explore the SEL competency of responsible decision-making by identifying problems when making decisions and generating alternatives
- to make a personal connection to the reading

Materials
Video; Audio Tracks 46 and 47

Warm Up

Introduce the topic by talking about superheroes and their characteristics and abilities. Say *Name a superhero who can fly.* Repeat with other characteristics, e.g. *is like an animal; is from another planet.*

TRACK 46 TB p. 232 **Reading Approach**

First Reading: Listen and Engage

- Project on the board the list of characters on the first page of the play or refer students to the page in their books. Have them say each character's name aloud. Ask which ones they know from the previous lesson.
- Play the video or audio all the way through. Have students raise their hands each time they see (or hear) a new hero.
- At the end, ask students the gist question *Who or what is the Mayor looking for?* (a new hero, to make the city a better place)
- Then look at the Words in Context.

TRACK 47 TB p. 232 **Words in Context**

- Play the audio and have students repeat the words.
- Have them race to find the words in their books.
- Remind students to **use the words around the new words to guess their meaning and to look for clues in sentences near the new words** (see TB p. 23).
- Then use these discussion points to confirm the meaning of each word.

City Ask if students think the people live in a small place or a big place. Point out that a bank is the type of place you find in a city. Ask what other places there are in a city.

Mayor Have students find the Mayor in the pictures. Ask *Is a mayor an important person? What does a mayor do in a city?*

job Ask *What is the job in the story? Is it an interesting job?* Ask some students *What jobs do your parents do?*

robber Have students find the word in the sentence on p. 128 and identify the robbers in the picture. Ask *Where are they?* (a bank) *What do robbers take from this place?* (money) *Are they good or bad people?* (bad)

Practice Student's App: Video

X-ray Looking at the picture on p. 132, ask *What can you see with an X-ray? Have you ever had an X-ray? Why is it useful, do you think?*

Second Reading: Analyze the Text and Features

- Ask students *What kind of text is this?* (a play) *How do we know?* Elicit that in a play each character's lines are written next to their name. Point out the lines spoken by a narrator on p. 128. Explain that the Narrator provides background information. Ask if they can find any other information provided by the Narrator (p. 130).
- Play the audio and have students follow the text in their books.
- Then discuss the questions in the green boxes as a class.
  - **Gist** (p. 128): *Who is the hero in this play?* Have students find the names of all the candidates for the city hero in the story (Allie Gator, Helicopter Harri, Otto Octopus, and Bob) and then say who the real hero is (Bob). Ask students *Are you a hero like Bob? What everyday things do you do to make you a hero?*
  - **Critical Thinking** (p. 132): *How do "little things" make a place better or worse?* Ask students to find the part of the story that talks about little things, and find what Bob says about them (beginning of p. 132: *Little things add up*). Ask students what he means (a lot of little, good things all together make a big, good change). Ask if a lot of little, bad things can also make a big, bad change.
  - **Personalization** (p. 133): *Which of these heroes do you like best?* Have students look back at the story and decide on their favorite hero. Say the names of the heroes and have students raise their hands for their favorite. Appoint one student as the vote counter to see who wins.

International English

Ask students to find the trash in the picture and point out the British English word *rubbish*. Then have them find the American English *math* in the text. Point out in British English it ends in -s. Both words are an abbreviation of *mathematics*. Say that both ways are correct. Ask *Which word do we use?*

Third Reading: Interact with the Text

- Play the video (or listen to the audio) again and have students mime the actions in the play.
- Divide the class into six groups. Give each group a character: Mayor, Assistant, Bob, Allie Gator, Helicopter Harri, and Otto Octopus. Play the video again and have students join in chorally with their character's lines. Then mute the video and have students provide the dialogue.

Cool Down

Play *What Was the Last Word?* (see TB p. 27) with key phrases from the reading.

Explore the Reading

Lesson Objectives

- to understand and analyze *A New Hero* through reading comprehension activities
- to explore the SEL competency of responsible decision-making: identifying problems when making decisions and generating alternatives
- to give a personal reaction to the reading
- to recognize and reproduce the *tr–* blend

Materials

Video (WU); Audio Track 48

TB p. 235 Warm Up

Play *Who Said It?* (see TB p. 26) with the characters from *A New Hero*. Have students watch the video before you confirm their answers.

Suggested sentences: *I snap my teeth at robbers* (Allie Gator). *I fly around the city saving cats* (Helicopter Harri). *I have eight strong arms to help people* (Otto Octopus). *I pick up trash in the park* (Bob). *I can see through anything* (Bob). *I can't find my keys!* (Allie Gator) *I can start tomorrow* (Bob).

A Think and answer. What makes Bob a hero? Check (✔).

- Before students open their books, find out what they remember about the reading from the previous lesson. Ask *Where does the story happen?* (Rockham City) *How many people want to be the city's new hero?* (four) *Why doesn't the mayor think Bob is a hero?* (because he's a kid) *What special ability does Bob have?* (He has X-ray glasses.) *When can Bob start?* (tomorrow)
- Refer students to sentence number 1 and have them notice the example. Ask them to find something in the story that shows this is correct. (top of p. 131)
- Have students continue the activity individually and find something in the reading that gives the answer for each one.
- Check answers. Ask if everyone agrees and refer back to the reading to resolve any disagreements.

Answers

1, 3, 5, 6

B Draw and write. Create another hero at the Mayor's office. What does your hero do in the city?

- Draw or project the template on the board and do an example with the class; e.g. Traffic Light Tim can control traffic lights to help the cars move quicker (draw a figure with a cape, emitting rays from his gloves, aimed at traffic lights that are now green). Elicit what Traffic Light Tim does in the city and write a short text in the relevant space.
- Allow students some time to think and invent another possible hero and write a profile—point out that the hero's powers can be something amazing or something very simple—as long as it helps people!
- Have students share their ideas with a friend and say what their hero does in the city.
- Ask if any students would like to show and tell the class about their hero.

C Think and discuss. Imagine you are the Mayor. Who do you want to be the hero of Rockham City? Why did you choose that hero?

- Read the question and have one student read the example answer. Ask students if they agree.
- Give students some time to decide who they think is the best hero for Rockham City (including their own invented hero) and why. Encourage them to think about the pros and cons of each hero, before making a decision. Ask students to back up their answers with reasons.
- Have students compare ideas in groups and then ask if anyone would like to share their ideas with the rest of the class. Try asking *What makes you say that?* to elicit a deeper response. Ask if the other students agree, and encourage them to use phrases such as *I don't think so* and *Yes, I agree with you.*
- Use the activity to explore the SEL competency of identifying problems when making decisions and generating alternatives. Ask students *What does the mayor do when she has a problem in the story?* (She looks for a solution.) *Does she do it on her own, or does she ask other people to help?* (She invites other people to help.) *Does she listen to other people's opinions?* (Yes, she listens and can change her ideas.) Discuss that this is a healthy way to approach problems—to listen to advice from others and to change your plan if necessary.

Phonics tr–

TRACK 48 TB p. 232 **Listen and say.**

- Play the audio and have students listen and look at the words in the phonics box. Ask them what sound all the words have in common (they all start with **/tr/**).
- Play the audio again and have students first whisper the words and then say them aloud. Ask a few individual students to repeat each word.
- Ask students to choose their favorite word from the list and to tell a friend.
- Have students find more words in the reading beginning with *tr–* and invite them to read them out loud.

Answers

trees; trouble; trash; try; true

Cool Down

Ask students if they like the character of X-Ray Bob. Have them discuss their opinions in pairs and encourage them to give reasons.

Practice **Resource Bank:** Phonics Printout;
Student's App: Phonics Practice; Reading Comprehension Practice

Think Together

Lesson Objectives

- to make connections between the readings
- to explore the key concept: What makes a hero?
- to reflect on the unit and provide personal thoughts and opinions

Warm Up

Have students look at the Key Concept question at the top of the page: *What makes a hero?* Give them one minute to think about their own answer to the question, then give them three minutes to discuss their ideas with a friend.

Bring the class together and ask some students to share their ideas with the class. Make a spidergram on the board to hold all of the students' ideas. Discuss if everyone's idea of a hero is the same. Ask if only special people can be heroes.

A Think and write. Abebe Bikila and the heroes from *A New Hero* come to your class. What questions do you want to ask them?

- Elicit from the whole class one possible question to ask Abebe Bikila and one to ask a hero from *A New Hero* (elicit their names: Allie Gator, Helicopter Harri, Otto Octopus, and Bob). Write them on the board and then give students some time to think.
- Have students write four more questions and include who they are for (they can write two questions for the same person if they want). Have students compare their ideas with a friend. Remind them that there are no right or wrong answers.
- Then ask for example questions from individual students. Have the others raise their hands if they also wrote the same question.

Answers
Students' own answers

B Think and discuss. What are heroes like? What do they do? Do a Numbered Heads Together routine.

- Students are going to share ideas about heroes. Set the class up for the Numbered Heads Together cooperative learning routine (see TB p. 20). Try to ensure students who were paired together in the Warm Up work in different groups now if possible.
- Encourage students to share with their group the ideas they came up with in the Warm Up, then work together to create a combined group answer to the questions in B.
- Tell students that for the first question you would like them to use adjectives to describe the character of a hero. For the second question, they should give examples of things heroes do.
- Give some time for discussion, then follow the Numbered Heads Together collaborative strategy to check ideas for each question.

My Reading Journal

Imagine you are making a movie. Choose *In First Place* or *A New Hero*. Which do you choose? Why?

This question asks students to make a critical choice.

Ask students to think which story would make a better movie—the story about Abebe Bikila or the city heroes. Have them choose and complete the sentence in their books.

Have students share their ideas with a friend. Ask students to raise their hands for the story they chose and ask some students why they chose it. Allow them to read from their books but encourage them to expand on their answers verbally, by asking follow-up questions. Allow other students who chose the same movie to help them answer if necessary.

Answers
Students' own answers

Abebe Bikila won the gold medal at the Olympics. Which medal do you give this unit? Circle one.

This question focuses on personalization.

Have students decide how much they enjoyed this unit and give it a medal accordingly.

Call out bronze, silver, gold and have students raise their hands to show what medal they gave.

Why did you choose that medal?

Ask some students what they liked or didn't like about the unit and why they chose the medal.

Answers
Students' own answers

Cool Down

Have students look back at the VTR picture on pp. 120–121 or project it on the board for students to study. Ask them if they now have any more ideas about what the picture shows and what the boy in the picture might have done. Ask *Do you think he is a hero? Why?*

Practice **Resource Bank:** Unit Test; **Student's App:** Key Concept Practice

UNIT 9

Do You Live Here?

Unit Overview

Themes

Dream homes

Castles and protection

Synopsis

In this unit, students will think about different castles around the world, learn the names for different parts of a castle, and talk about emotions. They will plan and prepare a presentation about their dream house and write a picture story, using target vocabulary and grammar from the unit.

Language Book

Vocabulary

attic, balcony, basement, bathtub, cabinet, castle, closet, fridge, lamp, stairs, stove, tower

p. 176

Explore Language

Simple Past: Regular and Irregular Verbs

p. 177

Global Citizenship

Why do people visit castles?

angry, annoyed, bored, excited, frightened, happy, proud, sad, surprised, tired

p. 178

Explore Language

Simple Past: *There Was / There Were*

p. 179

Take the Stage

Presentations: describing your dream house

p. 180

Write About It

A Picture Story

Sentence Building: sequencers

p. 181

Think It Over

Review and Reflection

p. 182

Literacy Book

Think Together
Why did people build castles?

p. 189

Visible Thinking
VTR: Think, Pair, Share

p. 183

Nonfiction
Informational Text: *Amazing Castles*

Words in Context: emperors, wooden, round, secret, passages, bakery, stables

p. 187

Fiction
Fable: *The Clever King*

Words in Context: clever, grumpy, automatic, drawbridge, moat, sticky, crown

p. 184

Reading Skill
Scanning for specific information

p. 186

Phonics
br–

p. 188

Language and Literacy Connections

The connecting theme in Unit 9 is castles as homes.

	Language	Literacy
Vocabulary	**Set 1:** around the home **Set 2:** emotions	**Fiction:** *castle, excited, sad, stairs, tower* **Explore the Reading:** *angry* **Nonfiction:** *castle, tower*
Grammar	**Simple Past: Regular and Irregular Verbs** We visited him. I didn't visit a museum. He found me. I didn't find him. **Simple Past: *There Was / There Were*** There was a kitchen. There weren't any TVs.	**Fiction** Once upon a time, there was a grumpy dragon king. He lived alone in an old castle. **Nonfiction** He built high stone walls and he made the lake bigger. Many years ago, there was a kitchen and a bakery for making bread.
Skills	**Pronunciation:** /s/ and /ð/	**Reading:** Scanning for specific information **Phonics:** *br–*
International English	*stove/cooker; bathtub/bath*	

Vocabulary

Lesson Objectives

- to learn vocabulary of rooms, furniture, and appliances: *attic, balcony, basement, bathtub, cabinet, castle, closet, fridge, lamp, stairs, stove, tower*
- to sing a song exploring why castles are scary

Materials
Audio Tracks 99 to 102; Video

Warm Up

Play *Board Race* (see TB p. 25). Teams have two minutes to write as many items from the picture on pp. 114–115 as they can.

A TRACK 99 TB p. 223 **Listen and find. What does Arni do?**

- Have students look at the picture. Ask *What rooms can you see?* Ask if they recognize the girl (she's Matilde from the previous unit). Refer students back to the question they were asked at the end of Unit 8. Say *Can you answer Matilde's question now?* Elicit answers based on the picture (she's visiting a castle). Ask if any of the students' predictions were correct.
- Point out that *castle* is one of the new words on the page. Tell students they are going to listen to a conversation between a brother and sister, Arni and Matilde, visiting the castle. Play the audio and have students point to the words or pictures.
- Ask the gist question *What does Arni do?* and elicit the answer. Play the audio again for students to check.

Answer
He closes the door.

B TRACK 100 TB p. 223 **Listen, say, and number the pictures in A.**

- Play the audio and have students point to the new words and repeat them.
- Then play the audio again and have them number the pictures in order. Look at the example together (closet). If necessary, pause the audio after each word to give students time to write their answers.
- Check answers by playing the audio again and pausing after each number for students to say the word. Continue the audio to confirm each answer.
- Have all students repeat the words one more time, this time raising their hands if their home has the item and lowering their hands if it doesn't.

Answers
1 *closet* 2 basement 3 balcony 4 fridge 5 cabinet 6 bathtub 7 attic 8 stairs 9 stove 10 tower 11 lamp 12 castle

International English

Elicit which are the American words and which are the British words. Drill them for pronunciation. Point out that they are all correct, then ask *Which word do we use?*

C TRACK 101 TB p. 223 **Listen. Close your eyes and visualize.**

- Prepare students for the visualization (see TB p. 21).
- Play the audio, allowing students to visualize the descriptions and do actions where appropriate as they listen. They can say the word after they hear *say.*
- Divide the class into pairs or small groups, play the audio again, and have students share their ideas.

D **Look and write.**

- Have students look at the table in D, and have a volunteer read the column headings.
- Ask students why *stairs* are a place, not a thing (they're a part of the house). Elicit one more word for each column and then have students add the rest of the words individually. While they are doing this, draw or project the table on the board.
- To check answers, invite students to come to the board and write a word. Ask if everyone agrees.

Answers
Places: *stairs*, castle, tower, basement, balcony, attic
Things: *closet*, fridge, stove, bathtub, lamp, cabinet

E TRACK 102 TB p. 224 **Listen and sing. Then watch and sing.**

- With books closed, project or write the title of the song, ***In the Scary Castle***, on the board and ask students what can be scary in a castle. Ask *What makes you scared?*
- Play the song and have students raise their hands every time they hear one of the new words.
- Have students open their books to look at the lyrics. Play the song again and stop after each line for students to repeat. Check that they have understood that each verse adds a line on the front of the verse before. Tell them this is a good memory challenge!
- Then play it again and have students sing along. You could split the class into four groups and have each group sing one verse, then rotate.
- Play the song video and encourage students to watch and sing. They can make up actions for each of the appliances or animals as they sing.

Cool Down

Play *Draw It!* (see TB p. 25) with the vocabulary from this lesson.

Practice **Student's App:** Vocabulary Practice; Video

Explore Language

Lesson Objectives

- to review how to use the simple past with regular and irregular verbs
- to provide contextualized practice of vocabulary of rooms, furniture, and appliances

Materials

Audio Tracks 103 and 104

Warm Up

Project the story from p. 116 on the board or have students look in their books. Ask if they recognize the boy (it's Arni from the previous lesson). Ask students *What can you see? What do you think they're talking about?*

A TRACK 103 TB p. 224 **Listen and read. What game did Hilda play?**

- Tell students they are going to listen to Arni and his friend Hilda talking about a visit to a castle. Play the audio and have students follow the story in their books.
- Ask the gist question *What game did Hilda play?* and elicit the answer. Ask *Did she find her cousins?* (No, they found her.) Play the audio to check if necessary.

Answer

hide-and-seek (she looked for her cousins)

B **Look at A. Complete.**

- Write or project the table on the board.
- Read the first sentence, including the example answer (visited), and have students find it in the story. Draw students' attention to *visited* and ask what kind of word it is (a verb). Draw a line on the board with *past* written on the left end of the line and *now* on the right. Say *We visited them. When? Now or in the past?* and have students point to *past.*
- Have students work in pairs to complete the other sentences in the table. Check answers as a class.
- Ask students what word we use to make questions and negatives in the past (*did*). Ask them how regular verbs end in the past (*–ed*) and how irregular verbs end (a lot of different ways!).
- Have students look at the Grammar tip *Remember* and point out that *did* does all the work for past questions and negatives—the main verb stays in its infinitive form.

Answers

Visited; found; didn't find; Did

C **Think and discuss. Then choose.**

- Read the options. Give students time to think about their answers, then have them compare their ideas in pairs.
- Read the options again and have students put their hands on their ears for the answer they chose. Have them circle the correct option.

Answer

1 past

D TRACK 104 TB p. 224 **Listen and say.**

- Play the audio and have students tell you what verbs they hear (*visited, [didn't] play, saw, [did you] go*).
- Play the audio again and have students listen and repeat.
- For ideas on how to vary the drill, see TB p. 22.

E **Read and complete.**

- Refer students to the sentences. Point out that each number is a mini-dialogue with a question and an answer. Point out the example answer in number 1 (did you go). Elicit the answer for the second part of number 1 and elicit why (regular positive verbs end in *–ed*).
- Have students continue the activity individually, then compare answers with a friend.
- To check answers, ask pairs of students to read questions and answers aloud. Ask if everyone agrees. Write the verbs on the board so everyone can check spelling.

Answers

1 *did; go;* visited 2 Did; climb; didn't
3 Did; see; played 4 did; play; didn't find

F **Play *True or False*. Write sentences. Then ask and answer.**

- Write three sentences on the board about your previous weekend, two true and one false; for example, *I went to the grocery store. I visited a museum. I saw a movie.* Tell the class that two are true and one is false, and they need to ask questions to find out.
- Elicit a question students could ask; for example, *Did you go to the grocery store?* Give the answer *Yes, I did. It's true!* or *No, I didn't! It's false!* Elicit questions for the other two sentences. Then have students make a conclusion: *You went to the grocery store and you saw a movie, but you didn't visit a museum.*
- Give students some time to make three sentences to show their partner (remind them not to mark them true or false, as their friend will see!). Then have students work in pairs to show each other their sentences and ask questions to find the true ones.
- Bring the class back together and ask some volunteers to tell the class what their partner did and didn't do.

Cool Down

Play *Pass the Whisper!* (see TB p. 26) with sentences using simple past verbs from this lesson.

Practice **Resource Bank:** Grammar Printout; **Student's App:** Grammar Practice

Global Citizenship

Lesson Objectives

- to learn vocabulary of emotions: *angry, annoyed, bored, excited, frightened, happy, proud, sad, surprised, tired*
- to explore why people visit castles
- to practice listening for gist and details

Materials
Audio Tracks 105 to 107; (optional) Audio Track 1

Opening Question

Ask the opening question: *Why do people visit castles?* Tell students to think about themselves—*Why would you like to visit a castle?* Elicit some ideas. Tell students they will learn about some castles and why people visit them in this lesson.

A TRACK 105 TB p. 224 **Listen to Shane talk about a castle visit. Did he have fun there?**

- Have students look at the pictures and say what they can see. Ask *Where is the boy?* (on a castle wall—in a window) *How many are happy faces?* (two, plus the boy—proud, excited, and happy) Have them copy each of the happy expressions.
- Play the audio and have students point to the pictures and words as they hear them.
- Ask the gist question *Did he have fun there?* and elicit the answer. Play the audio again to check.

Answer
Yes, he did.

B TRACK 106 TB p. 224 **Listen, say, and number the pictures in A.**

- Play the audio and have students point to the pictures and say the words.
- Play the audio again and have students number the items. Then play the audio again to check answers.

Answers
1 *happy* 2 excited 3 tired 4 proud 5 sad
6 surprised 7 angry 8 frightened 9 bored
10 annoyed

TRACK 1 TB p. 224 **Visualization**

The TTL has a visualization audio track for this vocabulary set (see TB p. 21).

C **Play *What Am I Feeling?* Mime and guess.**

- Choose a sentence from the listening. Write it on the board. Say it with two or three of the emotions in A and have students identify the emotion.
- Divide the class into pairs or small groups and have students continue the game, taking turns to speak and to guess.

D TRACK 107 TB p. 224 **Now listen to Min-Seo and Boris. Write the country. Which castle has four towers?**

- Listening for main idea: tell students they are going to listen to two children from South Korea and Bulgaria talk about old buildings they've visited. Play the audio and have students write the name of the country under each picture.
- Ask the gist question *Which castle has four towers?* and elicit the answer. Encourage students to justify their answer. Play the audio again for students to check. Then ask *What else do you remember about the buildings?*
- Play the audio again for students to check.

Answers
a Bulgaria b South Korea Baba Vida Castle (in Bulgaria) has four towers.

E **Listen again. Write *True* or *False*.**

- Listening for detail: draw attention to the first statement and the example answer *True*.
- Have students look at the other sentences and see if they can remember any answers. Then play the rest of the audio and have them complete the activity individually.
- To check answers, ask students to read sentences and say if they are true or false. Ask if the others agree. If they are false, ask the class to say why.

Answers
1 *True* 2 False (It has four towers.) 3 True 4 True
5 False (The king lived there many years ago.)

Discussion Questions

- Draw students' attention to the discussion questions: *Are there any castles in your country? What can you learn from them?* Have students discuss the questions in pairs or small groups (see **ETB**).
- Bring the class back together and ask students what they learned when they visited a castle. They may mention specific things like who lived there and when, or what it is used for now.
- Guide students to the conclusion that castles can help us understand our history and the past. Discuss why people built castles in the past and we don't build many castles today.
- Return to the original opening question to ask again *Why do people visit castles?* Help students make a link between why people go and what people learn in castles; that is, people go because they can learn.

Cool Down

Play *Chain Game* (see TB p. 25). Start the chain by saying *Yesterday I was bored!* Have the next student say, for example, *Yesterday I was bored … and frightened.*

Practice **Student's App:** Vocabulary Practice; Listening Comprehension Practice

Explore Language

Lesson Objectives

- to review how to use *there was* / *there were* (simple past)
- to provide contextualized practice of vocabulary of emotions

Materials

Audio Tracks 108 and 109

Warm Up

Play *Apple Tree* (see TB p. 25) with the emotions vocabulary from the previous lesson

A TRACK 108 TB p. 224 **Listen and read. Does the castle have a TV?**

- Project the picture on p. 120. Ask students *What can you see in the picture? What are they doing?* (visiting a castle) Ask if they recognize the guide. (Rolf featured in Lesson 2 as Hilda's uncle) Point to the girl wearing purple and tell students her name is Carol. Ask *How do you think Carol feels?* (She looks worried.)
- Play the audio and have students follow the story in their books.
- Ask the gist question *Does the castle have a TV?* Elicit the answer, then play the audio again to check.

Answer

no

B **Look at A. Complete.**

- Write or project the table on the board.
- Read the first and second sentences and have students find the second one (with the answer *were*) in the text. Ask *How many kitchens?* (three) *Then or now?* (then) Then have students work in pairs to complete the other sentences in the table.
- Check answers by eliciting the complete sentences and completing the table on the board.
- Ask students when we use *there was* (singular) and when we use *there were* (plural). Ask what word comes after the plural question and the negative (*any*).
- Have students look at the Grammar tip *Watch Out* and have them pronounce the two phrases to hear the difference.

Answers

were; There; weren't; Was; *there*; there

C **Think and discuss. Then choose.**

- Read the sentence and answer options and ask students to look at the examples in the table in B and draw a conclusion about which option they think is correct. Have them discuss their decision with a friend and circle an option in their books.
- Read the options again and have students raise their hands for the one they chose. Confirm their answer.
- Ask students what we use to describe things in the present and elicit *There is* / *There are*.

Answer

1 past

D TRACK 109 TB p. 224 **Listen and say.**

- Tell students they are going to listen to four statements or dialogues. Ask them to decide how many are positive and how many are negative. (two are positive; two are negative)
- Play the audio again and have students listen and repeat.
- For ideas on how to vary the drill, see TB p. 22.

E **Look and complete.**

- Have students read the dialogue in A again (or project it on the board) and also look at the picture next to E. Refer students to the example and ask them to find the four lamps in the picture. Point out that the answers are about the castle in the past, so the answers will be in the simple past.
- Have students continue the activity individually and then compare their answers with a friend. Have them point to the picture to show the positive answers each time.
- To check answers, ask students to read a completed sentence each. Ask if everyone agrees.

Answers

1 *There were* 2 There weren't 3 There was
4 There wasn't 5 Were there 6 there were

F **Play a memory game. Close your book. Ask and answer with a friend.**

- Explain to students that they will study the picture in E, then close their books and ask and answer questions to see how much they can remember. Have two students read the example dialogue. Ask if the example is plural or singular (plural), then elicit a singular example; for example, *Was there a table? Yes, there was. / No, there wasn't.*
- Give students 30 seconds to memorize as much detail as they can from the picture. Then have them turn their books over.
- Have students take turns asking and answering about the picture. If necessary, allow them to check quickly to see if their answers are correct.

Cool Down

Play *Running Sentences* (see TB p. 26) with sentences from this lesson.

Practice **Resource Bank:** Grammar Printout;
Student's App: Grammar Practice

Take the Stage

Lesson Objectives

- to prepare and practice a presentation about a dream house
- to recognize and reproduce /s/ and /ð/

Materials
Video; Audio Track 110

Warm Up

Play *Board Race* (see TB p. 25). Tell students the theme is "the house" and they have two minutes to remember and write on their side of the board as many words connected with the house—its rooms and contents, not activities—as they can remember.

A TB p. 235 **Watch and listen. Where's the tennis court?**

- Tell students they will watch a video of a boy named Sam talking about his dream home. Ask students *What's a dream house? A perfect house or a horrible house?* (perfect)
- Play the video and tell students to stand up if they see something they like.
- Introduce the gist question *Where's the tennis court?* and elicit the answer. Play the video again to check. Ask further comprehension questions, e.g. Is the house real? (no) (see **ETB**).

Answer
in the backyard

B Watch again. Match.

- Have students read the phrases and draw their attention to the example.
- Play the video again and have students match the phrases.
- To check answers, ask students to read a complete sentence each. Ask if everyone agrees.
- Have students analyze the phrases and help them notice that the phrases on the left mostly list things that are in Sam's house and the ones on the right mostly explain why he wants these things. Have students identify the two words that Sam uses to give reasons for having the different things in his dream house (he uses *because* and *so*). Tell students that when they write their own presentation, they will be able to use *because* and *so* to explain their reasons, too.

Answers
1 b 2 c 3 d 4 e 5 f 6 a

Pronunciation /s/ and /ð/

TRACK 110 TB p. 224 **Listen and say**

- Demonstrate the /s/ sound as in *Sam* and the /ð/ sound as in *this* and encourage students to copy you.
- Play the audio and have students repeat each word. Ask students to say the sound the first three words have in common and then to say the sound the second three words have in common.
- Say *These are all words Sam says in his presentation. What other words do you know with these sounds?* Elicit ideas (e.g. *stairs, they*) and write them on the board in two columns. Drill all the words at the end.

C Plan. Think about your dream house. Choose (✔) and complete.

- Let students know they are going to plan a presentation like Sam's about their dream house. Tell them they can be as imaginative as they like.
- Draw or project the plan in C on the board. Have a volunteer read aloud the six rooms. Then ask *What other rooms can we have?* (e.g. game room, home theater)
- Look at the second question and have a volunteer read the options aloud. Then ask *What other things can we have in the rooms?* (e.g. basketball hoop, slide)
- Point out the *Why?* and explain that they will have to write some reasons for the things they choose.
- Give your own example first and build it on the board; for example, *What dream rooms do you have? Living room, bedroom, library. What do you want in your rooms and yard? TV, big sofa, a lot of books, a fishpond. Why? I love reading, I want to be comfortable, and I like fish!*
- Have students complete their own plan. Point out that they can talk about rooms and items on the list or think of their own ideas. Monitor and help with vocabulary if needed.

D Prepare your presentation. Use your ideas from C and phrases from B.

- Have students use their plan from C and the phrases from B to write a presentation about their dream house. Remind them to use *because* and *so* to give reasons for their choices.
- Give them time to draw their dream house to use in their presentation.

E Practice with a friend. Then share with your class.

- Have students practice their presentation in pairs as many times as they need to. Remind them to look at their partner while giving the presentation and to point out features in their drawing of a dream house.
- Invite volunteers to perform their presentation for the rest of the class. Ask the others to listen and say if they had similar or different ideas.

Cool Down

After students have watched some of the presentations, ask them which dream house they would like to live in. Have a class vote.

Practice **Student's App:** Speaking Skill Practice; Video

Write About It

Lesson Objectives

- to focus on sequencers: *one day, first, then, finally*
- to plan and write a picture story

Materials

(Optional) picture books to show students (WU); Support, Standard, and Challenge writing printouts from the Resource Bank (one per student) (C, D)

Warm Up

Ask students to think about their favorite picture book, what it's about, and why they like it. Give them time to think and then have them compare books with a partner. Ask if they know the book their partner talked about and, if not, if they'd like to read it. You can also show students some picture books if you have brought some from home or from the library.

A Read the picture story. Underline the beginning phrases for each picture.

- Tell students they are going to read a picture story. Have them look at the pictures, read the text quickly, and say what it is about. (a boy who finds a castle with his friend Ron) Ask *What was happening?* (a party) *Do you think it's a good story?*
- Project the text on the board or have students look in their books. Have students find the beginning phrase for the first part of the story. (*One day*)
- Then have students find and underline the other beginning paragraph phrases in the story. Elicit that sequencers can guide the reader and tell us the order things happened.

Answers

One day, I saw an old castle in the forest. I was surprised. My friend Ron wanted to look inside.
First, we ran to the big door and we opened it. There was music inside!
Then, we walked into the huge hallway. We heard laughing.
Finally, we climbed the tall tower and saw … a party!

B Look at A. Complete with sequencers. Put the sentences in order.

- Point out the example answer in the first sentence and have students find it in A. Have students work in pairs to complete the other sentences in B with the correct sequencers from A. Then tell them to write in the numbers to show the sentence order.
- Ask volunteers to read the sentences in the correct order. Point out the comma after *first, then,* and *finally.*

Answers

1 *Finally*; 4 2 Then; 3 3 First; 2 4 One day; 1

C Plan. Think about this story. Make a list of verbs and adjectives.

- Tell students they are going to write their own picture story based on the pictures in C. Ask *What can you see in the pictures? Do you think it looks like a good story?*
- Write the numbers 1–4 on the board (or project the pictures, leaving space under each to write).
- Ask what verbs students can use for the first picture (e.g. climb, see) and what adjectives (big, old). Ask them what emotions they think the girl might be feeling. Elicit a lot of suggestions and write these on the board under picture number 1.
- Have students think of their favorites and write them next to the number 1 in their notebooks or on a sheet of paper.
- Have students think of verbs and adjectives for the other pictures and compare ideas with a friend. Point out it's OK if they have slightly different words—some people will tell the story differently. Challenge printouts can be handed out now.

D Write your picture story.

- Have students write their story based on the actions and descriptions they chose in C. Remind them to use sequencers to make the order of their story clear. Support printouts can be handed out now.
- After reflection, students should be encouraged to write a clean, corrected version on the Standard printout from the Resource Bank. Point out that a well-presented story is easier and more enjoyable to read.
- Encourage them to color in the artwork on the printout (telling them that they can choose different colors from the pictures on the lesson page if they wish).

Cool Down

Invite students to read out their picture stories to the class.

Practice Student's App: Writing Practice

Think It Over

Lesson Objectives

- to review what has been learned in the unit
- to reflect on the unit and their progress
- to think about learning strategies and how to continue learning at home

Warm Up

Play *Simon Says* (see TB p. 26) with the emotions vocabulary from Lesson 3; for example, *Simon says be angry! Simon says be surprised!*

Read the questions and draw or write your answers.

- Allowing students to make a personal response will help them retain knowledge and engage with the new material.

What did I do?

- Give students a few minutes to look back through the unit at the different activities they did. Ask questions about the unit; for example, *What did you sing about? What activities and actions did you do? What did you talk about?*
- Encourage students to draw or write about activities they found interesting.

What did I learn?

- Have students talk to a friend about what they remember from the unit—stories, words, phrases, and people.
- Ask students *Can you find words that you didn't know before? Can you make new questions or answers? What new facts did you learn?*
- Encourage students to draw a picture or write about what they learned.

How did I learn?

- Ask students *Did you learn with pictures? With actions? By listening, reading, or writing? By discussing ideas with your friends? With videos? With computers? How do you like to learn?*
- Encourage students to think about the pronunciation and spelling of the words they learned in this unit. Ask *What helps you remember how to say/spell these words?*
- Have students draw a picture of a way that they enjoyed learning in this unit.

How well did I do?

- Tell students to color in the number of faces that best expresses how well they have learned the unit content (i.e., the more they color, the more they feel they have learned). Ask *What do you remember? What do you understand? What do you need to practice more?*

What can I do next?

- Brainstorm ideas with the class about what students can do to continue to learn (e.g. sing the song again, read the stories again, or play the game on p. 120 again).
- Encourage students to think about what they can do to improve their English at home, using the four verbs as prompts; for example, read a comic or book in English, share what they have learned about castles with family members, watch a TV show or video clips in English, and play a memory game with family members.
- Ask students to choose one or more activities from the list (read, share, watch, play) that they will do to practice their English.
- Once students have completed the page in their books, have them discuss with a friend what they drew or wrote. Did they choose the same activities or different ones?

Looking Forward

Draw students' attention to the character at the bottom of the page. Ask *Who's this?* (Carol) and elicit what they remember about her (she was visiting a castle in Lesson 4 on p. 120). Ask if they can guess the answer to her question *Where am I going with my family?* Then tell them they will find out in the next unit.

Practice **Resource Bank:** Unit Test;
Student's App: Vocabulary and Grammar Review

Get Ready to Read

Lesson Objectives

- to activate prior knowledge about castles and protection
- to encourage students to observe and interpret through a Think, Pair, Share VTR
- to preview the reading skill of scanning for specific information

Materials

(Optional) VTR printout from the Resource Bank (A, B, C)

Warm Up

Write the word *beach* in the middle of the board and ask students to brainstorm all the things they do on the beach. Write their ideas around the word. Make sure the activity *making a sand castle* is included. Read out the activities and have students raise their hands for their favorite. Ask some students why they like that activity.

Think, Pair, Share

A Look at the picture. Does anyone live there? Think about it.

Students are going to do a Think, Pair, Share VTR to explore the image of the sand castles.

- Start by asking students to say what they can see in the picture. Encourage them to use adjectives such as colors and shapes to describe what they see in the picture. Provide vocabulary where necessary.
- Students will likely find: a (sand) castle, beach, sea/water, rocks, buildings, windows, roofs, people, walls, stairs.
- Students may also notice: towers, turrets, tools (for building the sand castle), (plank of) wood, bucket, horses.
- Ask students to think about the castle and point out the question *Does anyone live there?* Ask them to think about what it is for. Give students one or two minutes to think independently about the question so that they form their own ideas. Tell them to place their hands on top of their heads when they are ready.

B Talk with your partner.

- Point out the examples on the page and have two students read them aloud. Ask students *Do you agree with this idea?*
- Have students work in pairs to share ideas about the castle—not just about who lives there, but also about why it was built. Remind students that their ideas will vary and all answers are valid.
- Circulate and encourage students to expand on their ideas by asking *What makes you say that?* Provide vocabulary where necessary.

C Share with the class.

- Bring the class back together and invite students to share their ideas with the class. Encourage them to clarify their thinking. Remind them that they don't have to agree.

Here's an example of this part of the routine.

Teacher: (Student A), what do you and your friend think?
Student A: I think that it took a long time to build.
Teacher: Why do you think that?
Student A: (Because) it's very big. (Student B) thinks that a crab or a sea animal lives there.
Teacher: How interesting. Why do you think that, (Student B)?
Student B: (Because) crabs live in the sand.
Teacher: Great. (Student C), what do you and your friend think?
Student C: We think that no one lives there—it's just for decoration.

Transition

- Ask *Have you ever built a sand castle at the beach? Was it big, like the one in the picture? Have you ever visited a real castle? Did you like it? / Would you like to? Do you know any famous castles? Where are they?*

D Think, write, and discuss. What do you know about castles? What do you want to find out about them?

- Draw or project the table on the board. Elicit things they already know about castles (e.g. what they are made of, whether they are big or small) and write it in the *Know …* column.
- Have students work individually to complete the table. Then have them compare with a friend.
- Elicit ideas from the class. Write their ideas and questions in the table on the board (and save these lists for the end of the unit). Ask if anyone can answer another student's questions.

E Read page 138 quickly. Answer these questions.

This is a preview of the reading skill scanning for specific information.

- Have students read p. 138 (or project it on the board) and say if they think it will be a good story.
- Have students read the questions and identify what they are looking for in question 1 (*Where*, so a place) and in question 2 (*What*, so a thing).
- Then have students find the answers to the questions in E as quickly as possible, telling them not to read every word but to look specifically for the answers to these questions.
- Check answers as a class.

Answers

1 He lived in a castle
2 He didn't want anybody in his castle.

Now read **The Clever King**

Fiction: *The Clever King—A Fable*

Lesson Objectives

- to read a fable about a king and his castle
- to explore the SEL competency of self-management by regulating emotions such as impulses, aggression, and self-destructive behavior

Materials
Video; Audio Tracks 49 and 50

Warm Up

Project the first page of the story on the board or refer students to the page in their books. Tell students they are going to read a story about dragons. Ask *What do you know about dragons? Do you know any stories or movies about dragons?* Have students discuss ideas in pairs.

TRACK 49 TB p. 232 Reading Approach

First Reading: Listen and Engage

- Play the video and allow students to watch it all the way through. Alternatively, have them listen to the audio and follow the text in their books.
- Play the video (or audio) again, this time pausing after each addition to the castle (the drawbridge, the cameras, and the glue) to ask *How does the king keep his castle safe?*
- Then look at the Words in Context.

TRACK 50 TB p. 232 Words in Context

- Play the audio and have students repeat the words.
- Play the video again. Remind students they can **use the actions in the video to help establish the meaning of new words** (see TB p. 23). Have them share their ideas in pairs.
- Then use these questions to confirm the meaning of each word.

clever Refer students to the word in the king's chant. Ask if the king thinks he had a good idea. Ask if they can think of another adjective that means almost the same as *clever.* (intelligent)

grumpy Ask students to find the word at the beginning of the text and read the first paragraph. Ask *If he wasn't friendly, what sort of person was he?* Then say *Can you make a grumpy face?*

automatic Look at *drawbridge* first, then return to this. Ask *If the drawbridge is automatic, does the king need to do anything?* Ask if they know anywhere with automatic doors (e.g. a library or museum) or automatic locks (e.g. their parents' car).

drawbridge Ask students if they can see the drawbridge in the picture. Ask if they can see how it works.

moat Have students point to the moat in the picture. Ask *What is usually in a moat?* (water) *How did they make the moat?* (by digging) *What is a moat for?* (to stop people from getting in)

sticky Ask *How does glue feel when you touch it? What other things are sticky?* (e.g. foods, drinks, stickers)

crown Have students point to the crown in the picture. Ask *Who wears a crown?* (a king or queen) Have students mime putting on a crown and walking around carefully and regally, looking very important.

Second Reading: Analyze the Text and Features

- Play the audio and ask students to follow the text in their books.
- Then discuss the questions in the yellow boxes.
  - **Critical Literacy** (p. 138): *Why does the king make changes to his castle?* Ask students for their ideas. If necessary, prompt them by asking if they think the king wanted to make friends or if he wanted to make people scared of him. (make them scared) Ask *Do you think it worked?*
  - **Text Focus** (p. 139): *Listen to the word castle in the story. Can you hear the t?* Play the beginning of the story again. Ask students if they heard the *t*. Confirm it is not pronounced and drill the word. Ask *Do you know any other words like this?* (e.g. *listen, whistle*)
  - **Making Connections** (p. 140): *Many castles had big doors that came down when the drawbridge went up.* Ask students why they think castles were built like this. (to stop people getting in, to keep the people inside safe)
  - **Text Focus** (p. 141): *Adding* super- *is like adding* very, very. *How sticky is the glue?* Elicit that the glue is very, very sticky. Then ask students what you can call a car that is very, very fast. (a super-fast car)
  - **Critical Literacy** (p. 141): *How do you think the king feels?* Ask students to say how they think the king feels when his crown falls off (worried, surprised), when he can't get it out of the glue (annoyed), and when he can't get back into the castle (sad, annoyed, angry). Ask if they think the other dragons will help him. (probably not, because he wasn't nice to them!)
  - **Text Focus** (p. 143) Some words sound like noises, for example, beep. Can you find two more in the story? Have students find the words and make the noises. (clunk x 2 and creak x 3)

Third Reading: Interact with the Text

- Divide the class into two groups and have them read the story chorally—with one group saying the lines that are spoken (and thought on p. 138) by a character, and the other being the Narrator.

Cool Down

Have students close their books and see if they can sing the song the king has playing from his castle without looking at the words!

Practice **Student's App:** Video

Explore the Reading

Lesson Objectives

- to understand and analyze *A Clever King* through reading comprehension activities
- to explore the SEL competency of self-management by regulating emotions
- to make a personal connection to the reading

Materials
Video; Audio Track 49

TB p. 236 Warm Up

Play *What's the Next Word?* (see TB p. 27) with the video from Reading 1.

A Think and complete the story map.

- Before students open their books, find out what they remember. Use the five *W* questions: *Where did the king live?* (in a castle) *What changes did the king make to his castle?* (He made an automatic drawbridge, put cameras up, and filled the moat with glue.) *Why did he do that?* (to have the castle for himself; to stop people from coming in) *Who did he want to keep out?* (the other dragons) *When did his crown fall in the moat?* (when he looked down)
- Have students watch the video again to ensure that the story is completely fresh in their memory.
- Draw or project the story map on the board. Elicit the title of the story from the class and write it at the top of the story map.
- Clarify the other headings with them (setting: where it happens; solution: how to put a problem right).
- Have students complete the map in their book and compare with a friend.
- Invite students to come to the board and complete one item at a time. Ask if everyone agrees.

Answers
Title: *The Clever King*
Characters: dragon king, dragons
Setting: a castle
Problem: the dragon king didn't want anybody in his castle
Solution: the dragon king made an automatic drawbridge, put cameras on the towers, and put sticky glue in the moat

B Read and choose the answer.

- Ask students to look at all the words in blue. Ask *What type of word are they?* (adjectives / describing words) Discuss any words students don't understand.
- Refer students to the example answer and ask them to find the place in the reading where this answer is found (p. 138).
- Elicit the answer to number 2 from the class and have them locate a justification in the story (pp. 139–140).
- Have students continue the activity individually.
- Ask students to read the completed sentences. Check if everyone agrees and refer back to the reading to resolve any confusion.

Answers
1 *grumpy* 2 unfriendly 3 clever 4 great 5 sad

C Think and discuss. What makes you grumpy? What can you do to feel better?

This activity explores the SEL competency of the unit (regulating emotion such as impulses, aggression, and self-destructive behavior).

- Start by looking at the story. Ask students *What is the king like?* (grumpy, unfriendly) *How does he behave toward the dragons?* (He isn't nice—he pushes them away.) *Does his behavior hurt him?* (Yes, he gets locked out of his own castle.)
- Refer students back to the question: *What makes you grumpy?* Give an example yourself first: *I'm grumpy when I'm hungry!*
- Give students some time to think about what makes them grumpy and then share their ideas with a friend. Ask if they can find three things they have in common. Circulate and help with vocabulary.
- Ask students to share the things they found in common with their friend.
- Ask *What do you do when you feel grumpy? Does it affect other people? Is this a good thing? How can we change it?*
- Remind students of your example *I'm grumpy when I'm hungry. What can I do to feel better?* and elicit suggestions.
- Have students work with their friend again to come up with ways to feel better when they feel grumpy. Then ask for volunteers to share ideas.

Cool Down

Play *Disappearing Sentences* (see TB p. 25) using the 15 words from the story that students consider the most important.

Practice **Student's App:** Reading Comprehension Practice

Get Ready to Read

Lesson Objectives

- to practice the reading skill of scanning for specific information
- to activate prior knowledge about countries with castles

Warm Up

Ask some questions about the readings in earlier units and have pairs race to find the answers. The first pair to find all the answers should raise their hands.

Suggested questions: *Where does X-ray Bob live?* (Rockham) *Who lives with the gobie fish?* (pistol shrimp) *Who does Jannah give her glasses to?* (an old woman) *When did Peruggia steal the Mona Lisa?* (1911) *What color are the potatoes in* The First Harvest? (pink) *Who invents a smart eraser?* (Clara)

A Read the questions. Then read quickly and find the answers.

This lesson practices the reading skill of scanning for specific information, which was previewed in Lesson 1.

- Have students read the questions first and then the information, and raise their hands as soon as they find the answers to both questions. Tell them to do this as quickly as possible.
- Read the questions and have students say the answers. Check everyone agrees.
- Ask students if they read all the information in the sentences or just the information they needed for the answer. Point out that sometimes, to be quicker, they just need to find pieces of information, not to read everything. Then clarify that of course they can choose to read the whole text properly later, to enjoy it or to get more detailed information.
- Read the information in the reading skills box and have students follow. Point out this technique of scanning is useful because often we only need a little information from a big text.

Answers

1 India 2 450 years old

B Scan *Amazing Castles*. Choose one of the castles. Fill in the card.

- Have students quickly scan the article on pp. 146–149 and count the number of castles (there are three). Have students choose one and complete the information with the name, age, and place. Remind them they don't need to read all the information about the castle, just the pieces to fill in the card.
- To check answers, read the name of each castle in turn and ask a student who chose that castle to say their answers.

Answers

Leeds Castle / about 900 years old / Great Britain;
Nakhal Fort / more than 1,500 years old / Oman;
Brézé Castle / about 500 years old / France

C Think and discuss. Can you name countries with castles in them?

- Ask *Do you know any castles in your country? Where are they? What are their names?* Then ask students to raise their hands to say the name of a country they think has castles. Ask students if they have visited any castles in other countries and encourage them to say what they remember about them.

Cool Down

Divide the class into small teams and tell each group to take a piece of paper. Give students two minutes to think of as many words to do with castles as they can. They can name places, they can use simple words like *old*, or they can use new vocabulary from the story (and from Unit 9 of the **Language Book** if they have studied it). The winning team is the one with the most words. For this activity, don't worry too much about correct spelling; it's more important that students feel able to communicate their ideas.

Now read **Amazing Castles**

Nonfiction: *Amazing Castles—* An Informational Text

Lesson Objectives

- to read an informational text about castles
- to learn about architecture: exploring castle designs
- to make a personal connection to the reading

Materials

Audio Tracks 51 and 52; (optional) a world map (WU)

Warm Up

Tell students that in this lesson they are going to look at castles in three countries: Great Britain, Oman, and France. Show students where the countries are on a map, then have students brainstorm anything they know about the countries. They can mention places, food, languages, people, culture, and history. Write all of the words in three word clouds on the board.

TRACK 51 TB p. 232 Reading Approach

First Reading: Listen and Engage

- Have students sit in a Circle Time formation (see TB p. 21). Sit at the front with your book. Show the title, *Amazing Castles*, then have them look quickly at pp. 146–149 and say which castle they think looks most interesting.
- Read the text aloud to students and point to the pictures. Pause after each castle and ask *Can you see a (drawbridge/window/moat/tower)?*
- Then look at the Words in Context.

TRACK 52 TB p. 233 Words in Context

- Play the audio and have students repeat the words.
- Have students race to find the words in the reading. Ask if any of the words appears more than once (secret x 2).
- Tell students that you will read the story to them again and they should first try to **use storytelling to establish meaning of the words** (see TB p. 24).
- Read the story aloud again, then give students time to try other strategies for the words they still don't know. Have them discuss their ideas in pairs.
- Then use these discussion points to ensure every word is clear to students.

emperors Ask *Who lives in castles like these?* Elicit that important people who run the country live in them. Ask *Is an emperor like you and me or like a king?* (a king) Elicit any countries or movies they know with an emperor.

wooden Ask students to look at the castle on p. 146. Ask *What is the drawbridge is made of? What was the Dragon King's door made of? Which is stronger, a castle with wooden walls or stone walls?* Ask *Is there anything wooden in the classroom? What about at home?*

round Have students look at the tower in the picture and ask them what's special about it. Then ask if they can show you any other round objects in the classroom.

secret Ask *If you have a secret, do you talk to your friends about it?* Mime zipping your mouth shut to demonstrate that you don't talk about secrets. Then ask *Is it difficult to keep a secret?*

passages Ask *How did people get to the secret rooms? How do you think they entered the secret passages?*

bakery Ask *What did they make in the bakery? What is this called in your language? Do you sometimes go to the bakery? What do you buy?*

stables Ask *What animal lives in stables?* (horses)

Second Reading: Analyze the Text and Features

- Play the audio and have students follow the text in their book.
- Then discuss the questions in the yellow boxes.
  - **Detail** (p. 146): *Which castle is a family home today?* Have students practice the reading skill of scanning the text to find the answer to this question (Brézé Castle). You could turn it into a race and have students put their hands on their head when they've found the answer. Once everyone has found it, invite a student to answer. Ask students if anyone lives in Leeds Castle now (no). Ask them why they think that is.
  - **Text Focus** (p. 147): *The names of kings and queens sometimes use Roman numbers.* I = 1, II = 2, III = 3, IV = 4, and V = 5. Point out to students how the names and numbers are spoken (e.g. *Edward the first*). Write some other names on the board and ask students how we say them; for example, Henry IV (*Henry the fourth*), Felipe V (*Felipe the fifth*), and Louis XIV (*Louis the fourteenth*—X = 10).
  - **Making Connections** (p. 148): *The word* fort *means strong in Latin.* Ask students if this type of castle has a name in their own language and what it means.
  - **Personalization** (p. 149): *Which castle do you like most? Why?* Take a vote by a show of hands for students' favorite castle. Ask some students why they voted for each castle.

Third Reading: Interact with the Text

- Listen to the audio again and have students decide which castle they would like to live in. Ask *Do you think they were nice places to live? Why or why not?* (Students may need to use L1 to answer this.)

Cool Down

Have students tell a partner one interesting fact they learned about castles in the lesson.

Explore the Reading

Lesson Objectives

- to understand and analyze *Amazing Castles* through reading comprehension activities
- to practice the reading skill of scanning for information
- to learn through CLIL (science): architecture and designing a castle
- to recognize and reproduce the *br–* blend

Materials
Audio Track 53

Warm Up

Call out phrases about different parts of a castle and have students do a mime for each one; for example, *The moat is full of water. The drawbridge goes up and down. The walls are tall and thick. The windows are small. The towers are very high.*

A Look at the picture. Match and write.

- Find out what students remember from the reading in the previous lesson. Ask four *W* and *How* questions: *Where are the three castles?* (Great Britain, Oman, and France) *Who lives in them now?* (A family lives in Brézé Castle, but nobody lives in the others.) *How did King Edward I make his castle stronger?* (He built stone walls and made the lake bigger.) *When is the goat market at Nakhal Fort?* (every Friday) *Why is Brézé Castle special?* (It has another castle under it.)
- This activity allows students to connect adjectives to parts of a castle. If possible, project the diagram for A on the board. Ask students to look at the drawing of the castle and say which word goes with *tall*. Remind them to follow the line to see what part of the castle it is pointing to. Ask *What's the tallest thing in the picture?* (towers)
- Have students continue the activity individually and then compare answers with a friend.
- To check answers, have individual students read pairs of words. Ask if everyone agrees.

Answers
tall towers; small windows; strong door; deep moat; thick walls

B Scan the article and find the information. Check (✔) the correct answers.

- Refer students to the first question and the example answer. Point out that scanning for an important word that was in the question is a quick way to find the answer you need from a long text. Help them decide that *island* is the key word in this question, then ask them to scan the reading to find that word (p. 147: *It is on an island in the middle of a lake*). Confirm that it is part of the Leeds Castle information and notice the check is in that column.
- Guide students to decide what the key worcs are in the other questions (2 rock; 3 family; 4 moat; 5 market; 6 rooms/underground) and have students continue the activity individually, seeking out these key words in the article. Ask them to underline the part of the text that justifies their answer, then check the correct column.
- Check answers and encourage students to find something in the text to justify each answer. If students think that Leeds Castle has a moat too, accept that the lake is like a moat.

Answers
1 *Leeds Castle* 2 Nakhal Fort 3 Brézé Castle
4 Brézé Castle 5 Nakhal Fort 6 Brézé Castle

C Think and discuss. Imagine you can build your own castle. What do you want to use to build it?

- This activity explores the CLIL science objective and develops creative thinking and allows students to learn more about architecture. Ask students to first name all the materials they can imagine to build a castle. When they have named a few (e.g. stone, wood, brick), encourage them to get creative! If they need help getting started, ask them what the castle on the opening page of the unit is made of (sand). Then have them read the example on the page (cheese).
- Write the materials they suggest on the board and then give students some time to decide what to build their castle with. Encourage them to think about the two aspects of architecture, art and science, when doing this. Tell students they can choose more than one material. Encourage them to think about what the towers will be built of, the doors, the moat, and so on.
- Have students compare their ideas in pairs and ask if any pairs would like to share their ideas with the class.

Phonics *br–*

TRACK 53 TB. p. 233 **Listen and say.**

- Play the audio and have students listen and look at the phonics box. Ask them what sound all the words have in common. (/**br**/)
- Play the audio again and have students first repeat the words under their breath and then aloud. Ask a few individual students to repeat each word.
- Have students find more words in the reading beginning with *br–* and invite students to read them out loud.

Answers
Britain; Brézé; bridge; bread

Cool Down

Play *Silly Sentence* (see TB p. 26) with the *br–* words; for example, *They have bread for breakfast in Britain!*

Practice **Resource Bank:** Phonics Printout;
Student's App: Phonics Practice; Reading Comprehension Practice

Think Together

Lesson Objectives

- to make connections between the readings
- to explore the key concept: Why do people build castles?
- to reflect on the unit and provide personal thoughts and opinions

Materials

Large pieces of paper (WU)

Warm Up

Have students look at the Key Concept question at the top of the page: *Why did people build castles?* Give them one minute to think about their own answer to the question, then have them discuss their ideas in small groups. Answers could include: to stay safe, to see who was coming to attack, to keep other people out, to show you were important, to be more powerful, to have a big place to live. Give each group a piece of construction paper and have students nominate one person from each group to write down their ideas. Stick the paper up on the walls for students to refer to later in the lesson.

A Look at your table on page 137. What did you learn about castles?

- Project or draw the (empty) table from p. 137 on the board. Ask students if they can remember what they wrote in the *I Know* column at the beginning of the unit. Have them look back at p. 137 and see if they remembered correctly what they wrote.
- Have them share some of their ideas again.
- Ask students if they found the answer to any of their questions in this unit and if they learned anything else (give them time to look at the readings again). If any of their questions remain unanswered, ask where they think they can find the answer.
- Have them complete the sentences about what they learned and compare their ideas with a friend. Remind them they can refer to their Warm Up ideas. Tell them that what they write here can correspond to what they wrote in Lesson 1 but it doesn't have to—they can write about anything that they learned.
- Ask if they now know more about why people build and live in castles.

B Think and discuss. Which castle is the strongest? Why? Do an Inside–Outside Circle.

- Students are going to evaluate the strongest castle of the four in the unit and justify their answers. Set the class up for an Inside–Outside Circle cooperative learning routine (see TB p. 20).
- Give students some time to decide what makes each castle strong , which one is the strongest and why. Remind students that there is no right or wrong answer—this is an opinion exercise.
- Begin the routine. Encourage students to react to what each partner says, with phrases such as *That's interesting* and *I agree* and *Really? Why?*
- When the routine is finished, ask some volunteers to tell the class what they heard from their partners. Tell them to mention the most interesting points.
- Then take a class vote to decide which is the strongest castle.

My Reading Journal

Was there a funny part in this unit? Write or draw about it.

This question encourages students to reflect on the unit.

Ask students if they found any part of the unit funny. Encourage them to go back to the readings, the activities, and the images and say what they thought was funny.

Have students draw a picture of the funny part and/or write a sentence about it. Give a model first of something you found funny (e.g. *I thought it was funny when the dragons went somewhere else for their picnic!*) and draw a quick picture of it on the board.

Have students share their ideas, drawings, and sentences with a friend and see if they agree.

Ask if any students would like to share their ideas and/or drawings with the class.

Answers

Students' own answers

Choose adjectives to describe the unit.

This question focuses on personalization.

To clarify the meaning of the adjectives, do a mime of someone reading a text with each of the qualities of the adjectives given. Encourage students to join in with you.

Then ask students to decide which adjective(s) they choose to describe the unit and compare with a friend.

Call out the adjectives and have students raise their hands for the one(s) they chose. Ask some students why they chose each adjective.

Answers

Students' own answers

Cool Down

Have students look back at the picture on pp. 136–137. Ask them if they now have any more ideas about what the picture shows or if they can name more parts of the castle. Ask if they can think of a reason why someone built that castle.

Practice **Resource Bank:** Unit Test; **Student's App:** Key Concept Practice

UNIT 10

Are We There Yet?

Unit Overview

Themes

Journeys and the weather

Famous journeys

Synopsis

In this unit, students will read a book about famous journeys, find out how different children around the world travel to school, and talk about their own school journeys. They will plan and prepare a conversation about a future trip and write an email using target vocabulary and grammar from the unit.

Language Book

Vocabulary
airport, boat, country, journey, passport, plane, station, suitcase, ticket, traffic
p. 192

Explore Language
Future Plans: *Going to* Statements
p. 193

Global Citizenship
How does weather change journeys to school around the world?
cloudy, foggy, lightning, rain, rainbow, snow, storm, sunny, thunder, windy
p. 194

Explore Language
Prepositions of Movement: *Through / Around / Up / Down / Under / Over*
p. 195

Talk About It
Conversation: buying a ticket
p. 196

Write About It
An Amazing Journey Email
Text Type: emails
p. 197

Think It Over
Review and Reflection
p. 198

Literacy Book

Think Together
Why do people travel?
p. 205

Visible Thinking
VTR: See, Think, Wonder
p. 199

Nonfiction
Biography: *The Thirty-Year Journey*
Words in Context: travelers, caravans, camped, dangers, robbed, ruler
p. 203

Fiction
Story: *Young Nicholas*
Words in Context: ship, land, branch, captain, mast
p. 200

Reading Skill
Identifying the sequence of events
p. 202

Phonics
sw–
p. 204

Language and Literacy Connections

The connecting theme in Unit 10 is how and why we travel.

	Language	Literacy
Vocabulary	**Set 1:** journeys **Set 2:** weather	**Fiction:** *boat, journey* **Nonfiction:** *lightning, storm*
Grammar	**Future Plans: *Going to* Statements** Grandma's going to take us. **Prepositions of Movement: *Through / Around / Up / Down / Under / Over*** Through the forest. Under the bridge. Down the steps.	**Fiction** I'm going to win that prize. Tomorrow, I'm going to get the prize. **Nonfiction** Ibn Battuta traveled through the desert with caravans.
Skills	**Pronunciation:** /r/ and /w/	**Reading:** identifying the sequence of events **Phonics:** *sw–*
International English	*country/countryside; round-trip/return*	

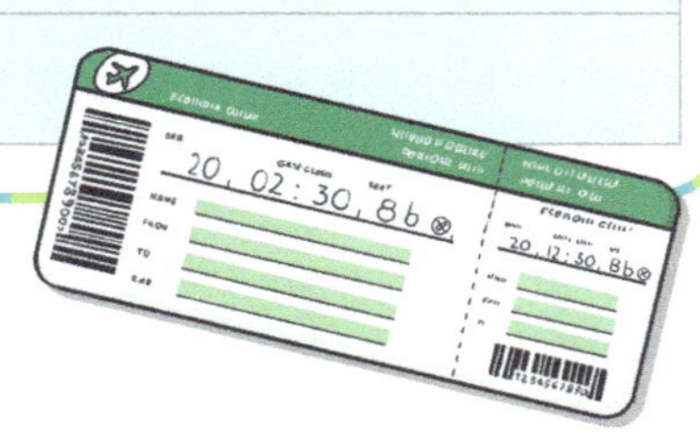

Vocabulary

Lesson Objectives

- to learn vocabulary of journeys: *airport, boat, country, journey, passport, plane, station, suitcase, ticket, traffic*
- to sing a song about journeys around the world

Materials
Audio Tracks 111 to 114; Video

Warm Up

Play the *Alphabet Game* with means of transportation (see TB p. 25).

A TRACK 111 TB p. 225 **Listen and find. When is the family's trip?**

- Ask students to say what they can see in the picture. Ask *Where is this?* (in a city) *What places can you see?* (library, hospital, café, cinema, sea/lake, park) *Is this similar to your town?*
- Ask students if they recognize anyone in the picture. Help them spot Carol from Unit 9 (she's running for a train at the bottom of p. 126).
- Tell students they are going to listen to Carol's family talking as they prepare to go on vacation. Play the audio and have students point to the words or pictures.
- Ask the gist question *When is the family's trip?* and elicit the answer. Play the audio again for students to check.
- Refer students back to the question they were asked at the end of Unit 9. Say *Can you answer Carol's question now?* Listen again to check. (She's going to her aunt Connie's) Ask students if any of their predictions were correct.

Answer
tomorrow

B TRACK 112 TB p. 225 **Listen, say, and number the pictures in A.**

- Play the audio and have students say the words.
- Then play it again and have them number the pictures in order.
- Check answers by playing the audio again.
- Have all students repeat the words one more time, saying *yes* or *no* after each to indicate if they have used these things or been to these places.

Answers
1 *plane* 2 station 3 suitcase 4 boat 5 traffic
6 passport 7 airport 8 journey 9 ticket 10 country

International English

Have students find the *country* in the picture. Point out that in British English it is called the countryside. Drill the pronunciation of both words. Remind them both are correct, then ask *Which word do we use?*

C TRACK 113 TB p. 225 **Listen. Close your eyes and visualize.**

- Prepare students for the visualization (see TB p. 21).
- Play the audio, allowing students to visualize the descriptions and do actions where appropriate as they listen. They can say the word after they hear *say*.
- Divide the class into pairs or small groups, play the audio again, and have students share their ideas or do their mimes in pairs.

D **Look and write.**

- Draw or project the table on the board. Look at the first heading. Ask *Do you get ready before or after you go on a trip?* (before) Point to the example answer (suitcase) and establish that you pack a suitcase to get ready to go on vacation.
- Then point to the second column and tell students that "Getting there" means moving from one place to another. Explain that under this heading we can list both methods of transportation (like a plane) and things we experience on the journey (like traffic).
- Then have them look at the heading and the example answer (station) in the last column. Establish with students that a station is a place.
- Have students work individually to classify the other words into the three categories, then discuss their answers with a friend.
- To check answers, invite students to come to the board and write a word each in the table. Ask if everyone agrees.

Answers
Getting ready: *suitcase*, passport, ticket
Getting there: *plane*, boat, traffic, journey
Places: *station*, airport, country

E TRACK 114 TB p. 225 **Listen and sing. Then watch and sing.**

- With students' books closed, project or write the title of the song on the board, *Let's Go on a Journey*. Have a student read it aloud, then ask students *Would you like to go on a journey?*
- Play the song all the way through and have students raise their hands every time they hear one of the new words.
- Have students open their books to look at the lyrics. Play the song again and stop after each line for students to repeat.
- Then play the audio again and have students sing along.
- Play the song video and encourage students to watch and sing. They can make up actions as they sing.

Cool Down

Play *Mime It!* (see TB p. 26) with words from the lesson (e.g. *in the airport, showing a passport*).

Practice **Student's App:** Vocabulary Practice; Video

Explore Language

Lesson Objectives

- to learn how to use *going to*
- to provide contextualized practice of transportation and travel vocabulary

Materials

Audio Tracks 102 (WU), 115 and 116

Warm Up

TRACK 102 TB p. 224 Sing *In the Scary Castle* again (Unit 9) and encourage students to do some actions.

A TRACK 115 TB p. 225 **Listen and read. Who is the family visiting?**

- Project the story on p. 128 on the board or have students look in their books. Ask if they recognize Dad (he's Rolf from Unit 9), the son (he's Nathan from Lesson 4 in Unit 6), and the daughter (she's Elena from Units 2 and 3). Ask *Where are they?* (at the airport) *What time is it?* (It's nighttime.) *How do you think they feel?* (They look tired!)
- Tell students they are going to hear the family talking about their journey. Play the audio and have students follow in their books.
- Ask the gist question *Who are they visiting?* and elicit the answer. Ask *Are the children happy or sad to see Grandma?* Play the audio again to check.

Answer

Grandma

B **Look at A. Complete.**

- Write or project the table on the board.
- Draw students' attention to the example *Grandma's* and have them find it in the story. Have them fill in the missing words after *going*.
- Have students work independently to complete the other sentence in the table. Invite a student to read the completed sentence and ask if everyone agrees.
- Check understanding by asking students if these sentences are about possible ideas or definite plans (definite plans). Ask students if they can find other *going to* sentences in the dialogue. (*We're going to stay somewhere better. / We're going to go by bus. / We're going to travel by boat. / You're going to look for Grandma.*) Highlight or elicit that we use *be* + *going to* + verb to talk about plans.
- Have students look at the Grammar tip *Watch Out* and remind them not to forget *to* after *going*—and the verb *be* before!

Answers

's; to; take; aren't

Practice **Resource Bank:** Grammar Printout; **Student's App:** Grammar Practice

C **Think and discuss. Then choose.**

- Read the sentence and answer options for students and ask them to look at the table in B and the dialogue in A and draw a conclusion about which option they think is correct. Have them compare with a friend and circle their answer in their book.
- To check answers, read the options again and have students raise their hands for the one they chose. Confirm the correct answer.

Answer

1 future

D TRACK 116 TB p. 225 **Listen and say.**

- Play the audio and have students tell you what verbs they hear. (*find, visit, swim, see*)
- Play the audio again and have students listen and repeat.
- For ideas on how to vary the drill, see TB p. 24.

E **Put the words in order.**

- Refer students to the example sentence and have a volunteer read it aloud. Point out *going to*. Tell them all the sentences are *going to* sentences. Remind them of the "*going to* + infinitive" rule in C.
- Have students continue the activity individually and then compare answers with a friend.
- To check answers, ask volunteers to read sentences aloud. Ask if everyone agrees, and refer back to the table in B to resolve queries. Write the sentences on the board so everyone can check spelling.

Answers

1 *Dad's going to buy the plane tickets.*
2 Aunt Jane isn't going to drive us.
3 You're going to need your passport.
4 I'm going to sleep on the journey.
5 We aren't going to eat at the airport.

F **Play a chain game. Then write.**

- This is a version of *Chain Game* (see TB p. 25). Have two students read the example start to the game in the speech bubbles. Point out that each student must repeat what the others have said, and add a new activity of their own. They must think of a definite plan and use *going to*.
- When the game is finished, point out the written example on the page. Tell students they should write down all the activities they can remember from the game using *going to* sentences. Then have them compare with a partner to see if they remembered all the activities.

Cool Down

Play *Running Sentences* (see TB p. 26) with sentences from this lesson.

Global Citizenship

Lesson Objectives

- to learn vocabulary of weather: *cloudy, foggy, lightning, rain, rainbow, snow, storm, sunny, thunder, windy*
- to explore how weather can change the journey to school
- to practice listening for gist and details

Materials
Audio Tracks 117 to 119; (optional) Audio Track J

Opening Question

Ask the opening question: *How does weather change journeys to school around the world?* Give students time to think, then elicit ideas and encourage them to say in what way it could change; for example, a different method of transportation or a different route. Make notes on the board and keep them for reference at the end of the lesson. Tell students they will learn about some unusual journeys to school in this lesson.

A TRACK 117 TB p. 225 **Listen to Daan talk to his dad about his journey to school. How is Daan going to travel there?**

- Have students look at the pictures and ask *Which picture is most like today's weather? Which picture do you like best?* Explain they will listen to a conversation about Daan's journey to school.
- Play the audio and have students point to the pictures and words as they hear them. Ask the gist question *How is Daan going to travel there?* Elicit the answer, then repeat the audio to check.

Answer
by car

B TRACK 118 TB p. 225 **Listen, say, and number the pictures in A.**

- Play the audio and have students listen and say the words.
- Then play it again and have them number the pictures in order.
- Then play the audio again to check answers.
- Have students repeat the words chorally, and for each word have them raise their hands if they like that kind of weather and lower it if they don't.

Answers
1 *sunny* 2 rainbow 3 storm 4 thunder 5 windy
6 foggy 7 cloudy 8 lightning 9 snow 10 rain

TRACK J TB p. 225 **Visualization**

The TTL has a visualization audio track for this vocabulary set (see TB p. 21).

C What do you think the weather is like now around the world? Make a list. Tell your friend.

- Elicit names of countries and write them on the board. Have students choose five or six countries and imagine what the weather is like there today. Give some examples; for example, *I think it's snowing in Finland. And it's windy in Argentina!*
- Have students write their chosen countries in their notebook, plus notes about the weather in each one.
- Then have them share their ideas with a friend. Ask if any students had the same ideas.

D TRACK 119 TB p. 226 **Now listen to Dakila and María. Write the country. Who lives on the side of a valley?**

- Listening for main idea: tell students they are going to listen to two children from The Philippines and Columbia talking about their journey to school. Play the audio and have students write the country below each picture.
- Ask the gist question *Who lives on the side of a valley?* and elicit the answer. Encourage students to justify their answer. Play the audio again for students to check.
- Ask *What else does this person say about the valley?* (She lives on one side, and her school is on the other side.)

Answers
a The Philippines b Colombia
María lives on the side of a valley.

E Listen again. Check (✔).

- Listening for detail: have students look at the sentences and see if they can remember any answers. Then play the audio and have them complete the activity individually.
- To check, ask pairs of students to read questions and answers aloud. Ask if the others agree.

Answers
1 *the country* 2 sunny 3 two hours 4 fun 5 zip line

Discussion Questions

- Draw students' attention to the discussion questions: *Is your journey to school the same or different? How can the weather change it?*
- Have students discuss the questions in pairs or small groups (see **ETB**).
- Guide students to conclude that these children really want to get to school!
- Return to the original opening question to ask again *How does weather change journeys to school around the world?* Show them the notes you made earlier. Ask if the lesson and the discussion have given them any new ideas.

Cool Down

Play *Pass the Whisper!* (see TB p. 26) with sentences about the weather.

Practice **Student's App:** Vocabulary Practice; Listening Comprehension Practice

Explore Language

Lesson Objectives

- to learn how to use prepositions of movement
- to provide contextualized practice of nature words

Materials
Audio Tracks 120 and 121

Warm Up

Tell students you will give directions from this classroom to different places in the school. Use simple directions such as *turn left/right* and *go straight*. Use gesture the first few times to help students understand. At the end of each set of directions, ask *Where are we?*

A TRACK 120 TB p. 226 **Listen and read. Where's Grandma's house?**

- Project the story on p. 132. Ask students who they can see in the pictures and what they think they are talking about. They should recognize Elena, Nathan, and Rolf from the dialogue in Lesson 2. Ask who they think the lady is. (Elena and Nathan's grandma) Ask what places in nature they can see. (forest, mountains, river)
- Play the audio and have students follow the story in their books.
- Ask the gist question *Where's Grandma's house?* and elicit the answer. Play the audio again to check.

Answer
on the other side of the river

B Look at A. Complete.

- Write or project the table on the board.
- Draw students' attention to the completed example (*through the forest*) and have them find it in the story. Ask *Who says it?* (Grandma)
- Draw some trees on the board. Mime walking through the trees with your fingers and say *Is this through the forest?* (yes) Then mime walking around the forest and repeat *Is this through the forest?* (no)
- Have students work in pairs to complete the other phrases in the table. Elicit the complete phrases and write the correct version on the board for students to check their answers.
- To check understanding, draw a bridge, a mountain, and steps on the board and use your fingers to show "walking" around, over, up, down, and under. Students call out the name of the correct preposition each time.
- Draw students' attention to the Grammar tip *Look* and have them find the verb used with all the phrases in the story (walk).

Answers
through the forest; around the mountain
over that bridge; under the bridge
up the steps; down the steps

Practice **Resource Bank:** Grammar Printout; **Student's App:** Grammar Practice

C Think and discuss. Then choose.

- Have students read the sentence and the answer options and ask them to draw a conclusion independently. Then have them compare ideas with a friend and circle one of the options.
- Read the answer options again and have students raise their hands for the one they chose. Confirm the correct answer.

Answer
1 movement

D TRACK 121 TB p. 226 **Listen and say.**

- Tell students they are going to listen to four sentences. Play the audio and have students tell you which prepositions of movement they hear. (*through, around, under, up, over*)
- Play the audio again and have students listen and repeat.
- For ideas on how to vary the drill, see TB p. 22.

E Look and complete.

- Have students look at the picture of the island and say what features they can see.
- Direct students to the example answer for number 1 (*through*) and have students point to where the forest is in the picture.
- Then have students look at the picture to complete the other directions individually.
- To check answers, have students read a sentence each. Ask if everyone agrees.

Answers
1 *through* 2 over 3 around 4 up 5 under

F Play *Find the Treasure*. Give directions.

- Tell students they are going to move the treasure on the map in E to a new location, then direct a partner to the treasure.
- Give students example directions: *Start at the airport and go between the castle and the lake. Then go around the mountain. Go over the bridge and through the forest. Turn right.* Ask *Where's the treasure now?* (on the beach)
- Have students plan a route on the map. Remind them to decide on a start and finish point. Divide the class into pairs and have them give directions to their partner and then ask *Where's the treasure?*
- Ask if any students would like to say their directions for the class to follow.

Cool Down

Play *Running Sentences* (see TB p. 26) with sentences from A and E.

Talk About It

Lesson Objectives

- to prepare and practice a conversation about buying a ticket
- to recognize and reproduce /r/ and /w/

Materials

Video; Audio Track 122

Warm Up

Name some places in your students' country—some near their home or school, others farther away, and some very far away. Ask *What's the best way to travel to [. . .]?* and help students reach a consensus for each place. Write each means of transportation on the board as they are suggested.

A TB p. 235 **Watch and listen. Where do Rob and Greta want to travel?**

- Tell students they will watch a video of two conversations where Rob and then Greta buy tickets for a journey. Ask where they think Rob and Greta might be going.
- Play the video and have students answer the question *Where do Rob and Greta want to travel?* Ask *Who wants to go to Rain Town?* (Rob) *Who wants to go to Sun City?* (Greta) Then ask further comprehension questions (see **ETB**).

Answer

Rain Town (Rob) and Sun City (Greta)

B Watch again. Number the phrases.

- Have students read the phrases and draw their attention to the example in each conversation.
- Play the video again and have students number the other phrases.
- To check answers, ask students to read a sentence each in the correct order. Ask if everyone agrees.
- Have students analyze the phrases, categorizing them as phrases said by the customer (a, b, h) and phrases said by the ticket seller (c, d, e, f, g).

Answers

Conversation 1: a 2 b 4 c 3 d 1
Conversation 2: e 2 f 3 g 4 h 1

International English

Explain that these are both words to describe a journey that is there and back (use gestures to illustrate this). Elicit *round-trip* is American English and *return* is British English. Point out that both words are correct, then ask *Which do we use?*

Pronunciation /r/ and /w/

TRACK 122 TB p. 226 **Listen and say.**

- Demonstrate the **/r/** sound as in *rain* and the **/w/** sound as in *would* and encourage students to copy you.
- Play the audio and have students repeat each word. Ask students to say the sound the first three words have in common and then to say the sound the last three words have in common.
- Say *These are all words used in the video to buy tickets. What other words do you know with these sounds?* Elicit ideas (e.g. *river, windy*) and write them on the board in two sections. Drill all the words at the end.

C Plan. Think about your trip. Choose (✔) and write.

- Let students know they are going to plan a trip. Highlight the categories in the table and ask if they can remember the questions the ticket seller asked.
- Read the options for transportation and have students close their eyes and imagine themselves on each one. Ask *Where are you going when you close your eyes?* This can be their *place*. Remind them they must be specific about a city—a country isn't exact enough!
- Encourage students to choose or write answers for the other categories in the table.

D Prepare your conversation. Use your ideas from C and the phrases from B.

- Give students time to complete the template for the conversation in their books.
- Have students work in pairs and read each other's conversations. Ask them to look back at their plan. Have they included all six categories? If not, where can they add information? Have their friend help them find a place to insert it.

E Practice with a friend.

- Have students work in pairs to practice both of their conversations. Suggest that they start with one, perfect it, then move on to the other. After they have practiced a few times, encourage them to try saying the conversations without using the written version.
- Invite pairs to perform one of their conversations for the class. Ask students to listen and see if anyone chose a similar destination, transportation, or time.

Cool Down

Give students a minute to look back through their books at all the conversations and presentations they have planned and practiced in Level 2. Brainstorm some of the things they think they do better now or that they find easier than at the start of the year (e.g. looking at the audience, speaking slowly and clearly, writing a plan, speaking without using notes). Have students choose one they think is true for them and tell a friend.

Practice Student's App: Speaking Skill Practice; Video

Write About It

Lesson Objectives

- to focus on the features of an email
- to plan and write an amazing journey email

Materials

Support, Standard, and Challenge Writing printouts from the Resource Bank (one per student) (C, D)

Warm Up

Ask students if they have ever sent an email, and if so, who they sent it to. Ask what they said in the email and if they got an answer. If not, ask who their parents send emails to and why.

A Read the email. Who is it to? What's the subject of the email? Circle.

- Have students look at the picture, read the email quickly, and say why the person is writing (to talk about her vacation). Ask *Where is Isabel's hotel?* (in a rainforest) *What's her plan for tomorrow?* (see some animals—maybe a crocodile) *Would you like to be on this vacation?*
- Have students find who the email is to and what the subject is. Have them circle the answers and raise their hands to share with the class.

Answers

To: harry@globalstage.com / Hi Harry
Subject: My Amazing Journey

B Look at A. Complete.

- Refer students to the example sentence and have them find an equivalent sentence in A.
- Have students complete numbers 2–4 by finding the corresponding part of the email in A. Write or project the incomplete version on the board (including number 1).
- To check answers, invite students to come to the board and write an answer each. Ask if everyone agrees.

Answers

1 *To:* 2 Subject: 3 Hi / Hello 4 Write soon / Bye

C Plan. Think about an amazing journey. Complete.

- Draw or project the spidergram on the board. Tell students they are going to plan an email that describes an amazing journey they have been on. Tell them it doesn't have to be real—they can make something up, and it can be as exciting and exotic as they like!
- Have students help you complete the spidergram with an example. Encourage them to suggest a place you are visiting, an adjective to describe the journey and experiences, the transportation you are using, more information on the route (e.g. over a bridge, up a mountain), and what you're going to do tomorrow (e.g. going shopping, going to the zoo, going swimming in a lake).
- Have students fill in the spidergram with their own journey. If they want more space, have them use their notebooks. Monitor and help as necessary. Challenge printouts can be handed out now.

D Write an Amazing Journey email.

- Have students write their email based on the plan they made in C. Remind them that the email must include the typical email information and ways of starting and finishing, all used in A and B. Support and Standard printouts can be handed out now.
- Have students exchange their work with a friend and peer-correct. You can put a checklist of things to correct on the board (e.g. spelling, use of vocabulary, punctuation).

Cool Down

Play *Correct the Teacher* (see TB p. 25) with a version of the email in A.

Suggested version:

Hi Harry,

How are you? I'm staying in a <u>bathroom</u> in a <u>hospital</u>. The journey was <u>boring</u>!

We ran to our <u>bathroom</u> because you can't <u>sleep</u> in a <u>hospital</u>. First, we <u>swam</u> to the <u>kitchen</u> and over a long <u>table</u>. I didn't like it because the <u>door</u> was big. Then, we <u>jumped</u> around a <u>doctor</u>, through the <u>garden</u>, and up a <u>tower</u>.

Tomorrow we're going to see some <u>movies</u>. I want to see a <u>dinosaur</u>!

Write <u>never</u>,

Isabel

Practice **Student's App:** Writing Practice

Think It Over

Lesson Objectives

- to review what has been learned in the unit
- to reflect on the unit and their progress
- to think about learning strategies and how to continue learning at home

Materials

Certificate templates downloaded from the internet (one for each student) (C, D)

Warm Up

This task is a chance to review language from the unit and bring the topic back into focus.

Do a class brainstorm. Write the word *journey* in the middle of the board and invite students to come to the board and write all the words connected with journeys that they can remember from the unit. Have them look back through the unit to get ideas.

Read the questions and draw or write your answers.

- Encourage review and reflection of the language and ideas from the unit to help students make connections to past learning experiences.

What did I do?

- Give students a few minutes to look back through the unit at the different activities they did. Ask questions about the unit; for example, *What did you sing about? What activities and actions did you do? What did you talk about?*
- Tell students they can draw or write about activities they liked or found interesting, but encourage them not to choose their favorite activity yet. Instead, encourage them to identify something in the unit that they found challenging but which they completed and feel proud of. Alternatively, ask them to choose something that was particularly memorable for them—either because it was interesting, or it was different, or even because it was noisy! You can use L1 to explain these ideas to students.

What did I learn?

- Have students talk to a partner about what they remember from the unit—stories, words, phrases, and people.
- Ask students *Can you find words that you didn't know before? Can you make new questions or answers? What new facts did you learn?*
- Encourage students to draw a picture or write about what they learned.

What was my favorite part?

- In this activity, students will think about the activities they enjoyed. Have students look back over the unit to remember the activities they did. Ask *Which is your favorite activity?* Alternatively, they could choose a favorite character, place, or text. They should try to choose just one thing and draw a picture and/or write about it. Explain that when we like something, it is often easier to learn and remember.

How well did I do?

- Tell students to color in the number of weather pictures that best expresses how well they have learned the unit content (i.e. the more they color, the more they feel they have learned). Ask *What do you remember? What do you understand? What do you need to practice more?* Encourage students to look back through the unit to see how much they remember.

What can I do next?

- Brainstorm ideas with the class about what students can do to continue to learn (e.g. sing the song again, read the stories again, look at vacation websites in English, or write an email in English to a friend or family member).
- Encourage students to think about what they can do at home to improve their English, using the four verbs as prompts; for example, sing other songs in English, practice vocabulary and grammar by doing activities on the **Student's App on Navio**, talk about they have learned with family members, and find out more about weather and journeys.
- Ask students to choose one or more activities from the list (sing, practice, talk, find out more) that they will do to practice their English.
- Once students have completed the page in their books, have them discuss what they drew or wrote with a friend. Did they choose the same activities or different ones?

Reflection

Have students look at the characters at the bottom of the page. Ask *Who are they?* Have them discuss what they remember about them in pairs. Draw students' attention to the speech bubble and say *What do you think you're going to learn in Level 3?* Elicit ideas on topics, vocabulary, and so on.

Cool Down

Prepare certificates for students before the lesson. You can find templates online. Hold a graduation ceremony to celebrate the end of the course.

Put It Together

To further review and recycle the language in Units 9 and 10, play find the differences, *Day by Day*, on pp. 138–139. See TB p. 210 for teaching notes.

Play 2

To further review and recycle the language in Units 6, 7, 8, 9, and 10, have students practice and perform the play, *King Grandpa's Treasure*, on pp. 142–143. See TB p. 212 for teaching notes.

Practice **Resource Bank:** Unit Test; End-of-year Test; **Student's App:** Vocabulary and Grammar Review

Get Ready to Read

Lesson Objectives

- to activate prior knowledge of journeys and why we travel
- to encourage students to observe and interpret through a See, Think, Wonder VTR
- to preview the reading skill of identifying the sequence of events

Materials

(Optional) VTR printout from the Resource Bank (A, B, C)

Warm Up

Use this activity to engage students and prepare them for the VTR activity.

Ask students to think about journeys they made in the last year, how they went, and where they went. Give a couple of examples to start them thinking: *I went to the shops in the city center by car* and *I went to visit my aunt and uncle on the other side of the country by train.*

Give students time to think and then have them raise their hands to say some of the journeys they can remember. Make a list of the modes of transportation on the board.

Remind students that this activity is not about checking grammar and vocabulary, so it doesn't matter if they make mistakes.

See, Think, Wonder

A Look at the picture. What do you see?

Students are going to do a See, Think, Wonder VTR to explore the image of travelers at a busy train station.

- Ask students *What do you see?* and elicit answers.
- Give them a minute to look at the picture. Then elicit one or two examples using the phrase *I (can) see …* before giving students time to share the rest of their ideas in small groups or pairs.
- Students will likely find: travelers/passengers, a train, giraffes, a briefcase and suitcases, backpacks, students, teachers, parents, paintings, ball, books, pencils, uniform.

Here's an example of this part of the routine.
Teacher: What do you see?
Student A: I (can) see a lot of people.
Student B: There are school children.
Teacher: What else do you see?
Student C: Some giraffes.
Student D: The giraffes are in a train.

B What do you think?

- Ask students *What do you think?* Give them one minute to think silently about the picture and then share their ideas with a partner.

Here's an example of this part of the routine.
Teacher: What do you think?
Student A: I think they go to the same school.
Teacher: What makes you say that?
Student A: They're wearing the same clothes.
Student B: Yes (definitely), and she's a teacher.

C What do you wonder?

- Ask students *What do you wonder?* Give them one minute to think about the picture silently and think of questions they have about the picture. Then share ideas as a class.

Here's an example of this part of the routine.
Teacher: What do you wonder?
Student A: I wonder where the giraffes are going.
Teacher: Where do you think?
Student B: Maybe they're going to a new zoo?
Student C: I wonder where the children are going.

Transition

Ask students if they have been on a steam train like this. Ask *Where did you go? Did you enjoy it?*

D Think and discuss. Did you ever go on a long trip?

- Give students an example of a long trip; for example, *I went to the mountains on vacation with my family. We went there by car, and it took us five hours!*
- Give students some time to remember a long trip they have made. Then have them share their ideas with a friend.
- Instead of reporting back their own stories, ask if any students heard an interesting story from their partner.

E Look, think, and number. What events do you see? What order do you think they happen?

This activity is a preview of the reading skill of identifying the sequence of events.

- Have students look at the pictures or project them on the board. Tell them that these are pictures from the reading they will read next.
- Tell students that they are going to use the pictures to imagine what happens in the story. Ask *Where is the boy in the first picture? Who is he? Who do you think the man is in the second picture? What is the boy doing in the third picture?* Then ask *What do you think happens in the story?*
- Have students think about the order of the pictures in the story. To check answers, call out numbers *1, 2, 3* and point to the pictures each time. Have students raise their hand when you say the number they chose for the picture. Ask them to explain why they chose that order.

Now read Young Nicholas

Fiction: *Young Nicholas—A Story*

Lesson Objectives

- to read a diary-based story about a young sailor
- to explore the SEL competency of self-management by displaying grit, determination, or perseverance
- to make a personal connection to the reading

Materials
Audio Tracks 54 (A) and 55

Warm Up

Write the following words from the reading on the board: *journey, water, boat, win, finally, excited.* Tell students that the story contains all these words and ask them what they think it will be about. They can also think about the pictures they viewed in Lesson 1 (E) to help them predict.

TRACK 54 TB p. 233 Reading Approach

First Reading: Listen and Engage

- Project the reading, page by page, on the board or have students look quickly at pp. 154–157 in their books and say what they will read about today. (a journey on a boat) Ask *Did this story happen now or in the past?* (in the past) *How do you know?* (the pictures—their clothes and the boat)
- Have students listen to the audio and follow the text in their books.
- Then look at the Words in Context.

TRACK 55 TB p. 233 Words in Context

- Play the audio and have students repeat each word.
- Have students race to find the words in the reading. Tell them that some words are used more than once and they must find all instances. Ask *Which word is used the most? (land* × 8)
- Remind students they can use various strategies to help them figure out the meanings, e.g. pictures, words around the new word (see TB p. 23). Give students time to discuss in pairs.
- Discuss ideas, and use these additional points to confirm the meaning of each item.

ship Ask students if they can find another word for ship in the reading. (boat) Ask *What do you think it was like to live on a ship in 1769? Where does Nicholas sleep and eat?*

land Have students point out some of the places where land is used in the reading. Ask which context helped them. Ask *Why does the captain want to find land?*

branch Ask *What is in the water? Where does it come from?* (a tree)

captain Have students point to the captain. Ask *What does the captain do?* (He makes all the decisions on the ship—he is the boss.) *Why is he dressed differently from the other people?* (so he can be recognized, to have respect)

mast Ask *What does a mast do on a ship?* (It holds the sails that catch the wind.) Ask *Why is Nicholas climbing the mast?* (so he can see a long way)

Second Reading: Analyze the Text and Features

- Have students read the text chorally. Remind them to think about the feelings of the speakers as they read and to change their intonation to suit.
- Then discuss the questions in the pink boxes as a class.
  - **Making Connections** (p. 154): *How does the tree branch tell him land is close?* Ask students for their ideas. Point out that branches and other things (like coconuts) come from land. They can sometimes cross oceans, but it is more probable that they mean land is near.
  - **Personalization** (p. 157): *Did you ever look really hard for something?* Ask students if they can remember looking really hard for something—a face they know in a crowd or a picture, a place on a map, or a landmark when out traveling.

Third Reading: Interact with the Text

- Listen to the audio again and have students act out the story. If you can, project the story on the board as they listen—the pictures and text will help them with their acting.

Cool Down

Have students suggest things in the reading they would like to do and things they definitely would not like to do. Ask *Why do/don't you want to do that? Why did Nicholas do it?* and have students discuss in pairs.

Explore the Reading

Lesson Objectives

- to understand and analyze *Young Nicholas* through reading comprehension activities
- to explore the SEL competency of self-management by showing grit, determination, or perseverance
- to recognize and reproduce the initial *sw–* blend

Materials

Audio Tracks 54 (A) and 56

Warm Up

Play *What Was the Last Word?* (see TB p. 27) with the reading from the previous lesson.

A Read and answer.

- Have a Circle Time discussion to find out what students remember from the story (see TB p. 21). Ask *Where did Nicholas live?* (on a ship) *What did he find?* (land) *Why did he try so hard?* (because he wanted to win the captain's prize) *When did the story happen?* (1769)
- Have students read the story again if they are unsure of some of the answers.
- Refer students to the example question and answer. Have them find the name of the ship in the story (p. 154, paragraph 1). Have students try to remember the pronunciation of *Endeavour* from the audio—then say it for them and have them repeat it: /ɪnˈdevə(r)/.
- Have students continue the activity individually and then compare answers with a friend.
- Check answers. Ask if everyone agrees and refer back to the reading to resolve any queries or disagreements.

Answers

1 *The name of the ship was Endeavour.*
2 They were looking for (new) land.
3 Nicholas saw the branch in the water.
4 Nicholas climbed the mast so he could see a long way.
5 Nicholas won the prize.

B Think and complete the table.

- Draw or project the table on the board. Remind students that the *effect* is what happened or changed. Ask if they can remember what the *cause* is (why that thing happened or changed).
- Refer students to the first cause, *The ship was close to land,* and ask them to look back at the story to find the effect of this. Elicit *A branch floated near the boat* (p. 155).
- Have students look back at the story and complete the other two rows.
- To check answers, invite students to come and complete a space each. Ask if everyone agrees.

Answers

	Cause	Effect
1	*The ship was close to land.*	A branch floated near the boat.
2	Nicholas climbed the mast.	*Nicholas saw land.*
3	*Nicholas found land first.*	Nicholas won the prize.

C Think and write. Imagine you are Nicholas. How do you feel?

- Use the reading to explore the SEL competency of the unit (display grit, determination, or perseverance).
- Ask students *Do you think life was difficult as a sailor hundreds of years ago? What problems did they have? Why do you think they traveled so far? What qualities did you need to be an explorer? Did Nicholas show any special qualities?* (Yes, he was brave and tried very hard to get what he wanted.) *Why didn't he give up?* (because he wanted the prize)
- Ask them if they have ever been in a difficult situation where they didn't give up. Ask *How did you feel at the time and at the end?*
- Ask students to suggest possible adjectives that can describe how Nicholas feels. Encourage them to think about more than *happy*—remind them he works very hard, he did something very difficult, he has a place named after him, and so on. Write the adjectives on the board. Have students write sentences about how Nicholas feels and why and then compare with a friend.
- Ask students for their suggestions and write two or three different versions on the board.

Phonics sw–

TRACK 56 TB p. 233 **Listen and say.**

- Play the audio and have students listen and look at the words in their book. Ask them what sound all the words have in common (/sw/).
- Play the audio again and have students first say the words under their breath and then aloud. Ask a few individual students to repeat each word.
- Have students find more words in the reading beginning with *sw–* and ask them to read them out loud.

Answers

swept; swaying; swim

Cool Down

Say *At the end of the story, Nicholas wins a prize. What do you think he wins?* Have students discuss their ideas in pairs.

Practice **Resource Bank:** Phonics Printout; **Student's App:** Phonics Practice; Reading Comprehension Practice

Get Ready to Read

Lesson Objectives

- to practice the reading skill of identifying the sequence of events
- to activate prior knowledge of the difficulties of travel

Warm Up

Play the *Yes/No Game* (see TB p. 27) with sentences about the story *Young Nicholas*.

Suggested sentences: *Nicholas lived on the ship.* (yes) *Every day he cleaned the sailors' clothes.* (no) *He took a branch from the water and showed it to the captain.* (no) *The captain offered a prize to the first person to see land.* (yes) *Nicholas climbed to the top of a table.* (no) *He could see very far from the top of the mast.* (yes) *Nicholas saw land and got the prize.* (yes)

A Read and number. Put the events in order.

This lesson practices the reading skill of identifying the sequence of events. This skill was also covered in Unit 1, p. 17, with a sequence of instructions.

- Ask students if they remember the sequence of instructions to play a game on a tablet: *First, press on. Next, type password. Then, press play. Finally, play the game.*
- Refer students to the example sentence and have students find the related sentence in the reading. (on p. 154: *Everyone is looking for land*)
- Have students continue to order the other sentences individually and then compare answers with a friend.
- To check answers, ask volunteers to read the next sentence in the sequence. Ask if everyone agrees, and refer to the reading when necessary.
- Have students read the reading skills box about the sequence of events.
- Write another little story on the board with the events in the wrong order: *I'm here now. I woke up. I came to school. I had breakfast.* Ask students to tell you the correct order, and to point out the beginning, middle, and end of the story. Ask if they think yours is a good story!

Answers

1 *The men looked for new land.*
2 Nicholas saw a branch in the water.
3 "The first man to find land wins a prize," said the captain.
4 Nicholas climbed to the top of the mast.
5 "I see land!" said Nicholas.

B Look and number. What is the sequence of events?

- Have students look at the pictures or project them on the board. Tell them that these are from the story they will read next. Ask them what is happening in the pictures. Ask what general event they think the pictures show. (a journey)
- Ask students what is happening in the picture that has been labeled as number 1 (he is getting things ready for the journey) and elicit which one they think is number 2. Then have students continue individually.
- Hold up your book (or point to the pictures on the board) and ask *What's number 1, 2, 3, 4, 5?* and move your finger across the pictures. Have students say *yes* when you are pointing at the correct picture for the number. Check everyone agrees. Ask students where they think he is going in the last picture.

Suggested Answers

4, *1*, 3, 2, 5

C Think and discuss. Do you think the journey looks easy? Why or why not?

- Have students read the example answer. Tell them to think about whether they agree with it.
- Ask them for two more reasons why they think the journey looks easy or difficult and write them on the board. (*Easy* is more difficult to see—point out he doesn't have to buy tickets or wait in line. The boat will take him where he wants to go, the horse carries his things to the boat, and he doesn't have to walk or ride.)
- Give students some time to decide on their answer to the question and then have them discuss ideas with a friend. They can use the ideas discussed as a class, or they can use some of their own. Circulate and help with vocabulary as necessary.
- Then ask for suggestions and ask students to justify their answers.

Cool Down

Have students imagine being Young Nicholas and act out his life on the boat. Have them think about whether it was easy or hard, busy, or relaxed. Remind students that Nicholas was only 11 years old.

Now read **The Thirty-Year Journey**

Nonfiction: *The Thirty-Year Journey—A Biography*

Lesson Objectives

- to read a biography about a legendary traveler
- to learn through CLIL (history): finding out about important people
- to make a personal connection to the reading

Materials

Video; Audio Tracks 57 and 58

Warm Up

Do a class brainstorm. Write in the middle of the board the theme *transportation with no motor.* Ask students to think of as many modes of transportation as possible with no motor. (horse, bike, boat, skateboard, etc.) Count the number of different means of transportation students came up with.

TRACK 57 TB p. 233 Reading Approach

First Reading: Listen and Engage

- Project the first two pages of the story on the board or have students look at pp. 160–161 in their books. Ask students to notice the title, text, genre, pictures, and characters on the page. Ask them *What can you see?* Have some students name—or point to—something that they think is interesting in the pictures.
- Play the video. Ask students to listen and watch for some of the things Ibn Battuta found hard about traveling. (he was robbed, he had to run for his life, there were big storms)
- Help students notice that it was Ibn Battuta who they saw preparing for his journey in the previous lesson. Ask *In the previous lesson, did you say his journey was easy or difficult? What do you think now? What do you think were the best and the worst parts of his journey?*
- Then look at the Words in Context.

TRACK 58 TB p. 233 Words in Context

- Play the audio and have students repeat the words.
- Have students race to find the words in the reading. Ask *Do any of them appear more than once?* (only *caravan*, twice)
- Tell students they can **look for links to words they already know to help establish the meaning of new words.** Then, if any of them don't link well to another word, **try another strategy** (see TB p. 23). Discuss *traveler* as an example—if they know the word *travel*, can they guess what a traveler is? (someone who travels)
- Give students time to think, then discuss in pairs. Then use these discussion points to confirm the meaning of each word.

travelers Ask what a *traveler* does. Ask if they know someone they would call a traveler (i.e., someone who travels a lot).

caravans Ask: *Is Ibn Battuta alone or with people in this picture?* (with people) Establish that this big group of people is traveling together on horses—this is a caravan. Ask why it is good to travel in a big group (for safety).

camped Ask students where you sleep when you camp (in a tent). Elicit that this is the verb in the simple past.

dangers Point out that the sentences after the word *danger* give examples of it. Ask *Can these sentences help us decide what danger is?*

robbed Ask *What do you think the men in the picture are going to do?* Remind students of the word *robbery,* which they learned in Unit 4, *Where Is She?* Ask *What happened to Ibn Battuta when he was robbed? What did he lose?* (everything but his clothes)

ruler Check if students know what a rule is. Name some school rules. Ask *Who is the ruler? Is he important? What other words do you know for* ruler? (king, queen, emperor)

Second Reading: Analyze the Text and Features

- Play the audio and have students follow the text in their books.
- Then discuss the questions in the pink boxes as a class.
  - **Text Focus** (p. 160): *What words describe the main character?* Possible answers include brave, adventurous, determined, curious, and crazy!
  - **Text Focus** (p. 162): *What do you think* run for his life *means?* Ask students what is happening in the picture on p. 162. Ask what they would do in this situation. Ibn Battuta ran—why? (because he wanted to save his life)
  - **Making Connections** (p. 164): *Ibn Battuta traveled over 120,000 km.!* Ask students how many times around the world they think 120,000 km. would go. (about three times)
  - **Personalization** (p. 165): Rihla *means journey in Arabic. Have you ever taken a journey?* Ask students how to say *journey* in their own language. Is it similar to English or Arabic? Then discuss any interesting journeys students have been on.

Third Reading: Interact with the Text

- Divide the class into six groups. Play the audio again and ask each group to read one paragraph each. The whole class can join in with the final line (*Today, to remember …*).

Cool Down

Ask students to tell their partner one new thing they learned from the reading.

Practice **Student's App:** Video

Explore the Reading

Lesson Objectives

- to understand and analyze *The Thirty-Year Journey* through reading comprehension activities
- to practice the reading skill of identifying a sequence of events
- to learn through CLIL (history): finding out about important people
- to give a personal reaction to the story

Materials
Video

TB p. 236 **Warm Up**

Play the video of the story of Ibn Battuta from the previous lesson on mute, and have students call out all the events they see in the story. Pause if necessary to give them time to explain.

A Look and number. Put the events in order.

- Review other aspects of the reading by asking *Why did Ibn Battuta travel?* (He wanted to learn about the world.) *What problems did he have?* (He was robbed, and there was bad weather.) *When did he travel?* (in the 1300s) *How do we know about his journey today?* (He wrote a book.)
- Have students look at A in their books. Ask what they can see happening in the pictures. Ask them to look back at the story and find the first event in the story/pictures. Have them write number 1 in the box and then have them complete the others in the order they appear in the story.
- Have students compare with a friend and say what happened in each picture.
- Hold up your book and point to the pictures and have students say the correct number. Check everyone agrees.

Answers

(from left to right) 2, 3, 4, 1

B Read and match. How do you think Ibn Battuta feels?

- Have students look at the adjectives and act out feeling each emotion.
- Have them read the first statement. Ask students how they think Ibn Battuta felt when he left home to start his journey. Ask them to imagine they are going on long journey. Say *How do you feel?* Elicit he is probably excited to start a journey he planned.
- Have students look at the adjectives and decide in which situation he felt this way. There are different ways to answer these questions, but tell students that they must use each adjective once, so they should do some critical thinking and choose what they feel is the most suitable adjective in each case. Have students compare their ideas and explain their choices in pairs.
- To check answers, have pairs of students say the phrases and the matching adjective. Ask if everyone agrees. Encourage discussion of alternative answers.
- Use the reading to explore the SEL competency of displaying grit, determination, or perseverance. Ask students *Why do you think Ibn Battuta traveled so much? What qualities did he need to travel so far and for so long? Could you do this?* Point out that when something is very important to us, we must use all our determination to get what we want.

Suggested Answers

1 excited 2 happy 3 scared 4 proud

C Think and write. Why does Ibn Battuta keep traveling for 30 years? Write three reasons.

- This activity links to the CLIL history objective of finding out about famous people. Elicit one or two ideas from the class to start their thinking. Write their example answers on the board; for example, *Because he always wanted to see something new.*
- Have students think of three more reasons, write them down, and then share their ideas with a partner.
- Ask students to give their suggestions and write all their ideas on the board in a spidergram. Discuss how varied they are, and that we don't actually know his real reasons. Tell them that perhaps his book would help us learn more!

Cool Down

Play *Pass the Whisper!* (see TB p. 26) with sentences from the reading.

Suggested sentences: *He went on a journey that took 30 years! / Some caravans had thousands of people. / He traveled through Africa and into parts of Europe.*

Practice **Student's App:** Reading Comprehension Practice

Think Together

Lesson Objectives

- to make connections between the readings
- to explore the key concept: Why do people travel?
- to reflect on the unit and provide personal thoughts and opinions

Materials

(Optional) map of the world (B), a picture of a compass, or the compass on a map (My Reading Journal)

Warm Up

Write or project the Key Concept question *Why do people travel?* on the board. Ask students to think back on the two readings they have studied in this unit and on the activities they have completed. Elicit ideas; for example, *They travel to new places* (e.g. Ibn Battuta), *they travel to be the first person to go to a new country* (e.g. Captain Cook), *or they travel because it's their job* (e.g. the cabin boy, Young Nicholas, or the other sailors).

A Work with a group. Make a Venn diagram about Nicholas and Ibn Battuta.

- Draw or project the Venn diagram on the board and ask students what each of the areas are for. (information only about Nicholas on the left, information only about Ibn Battuta on the right, and things they have in common in the middle)
- Ask students for one example of each.
- Divide the class into small groups and have students look back at the readings to find more things the travelers have in common and more differences between them.
- Invite students to write their ideas on the board. Ask if everyone agrees.

Suggested Answers

Nicholas: worked as a cabin boy, was a child when he traveled, traveled only at sea, was from England, lived in the 1700s;
Ibn Battuta: traveled with a caravan, was robbed, traveled mostly on land, traveled for 30 years, was from Morocco, wrote a book;
Both: displayed grit, determination, or perseverance; traveled on a ship

B Think and write. Imagine you're going on a journey like Nicholas and Ibn Battuta. Where do you want to go? Why?

- Tell students your own idea for a journey; for example, *I want to go to Africa because there are awesome animals there.*
- Give students some time to think about what journey they would like to go on and why. You could project a map of the world on the board to help students imagine different possibilities.
- Have students write down their ideas, and ensure that they complete the *because* section so that they are ready for the next step in C.

C Think and discuss. Where do you want to travel? Why? Do a Three-Step Interview and talk about it.

Students are going to discuss where they would like to travel and give reasons, using their notes in B.

- Set the class up for the Three-Step Interview cooperative learning routine (see TB p. 20).
- Write the questions on the board. Divide the class into four groups. Have students pair up with a student from a different group and take turns to ask and answer the questions.
- After students have reported back to their original group, invite them to share some of the things they have learned about other students.

My Reading Journal

For each compass direction, write down a fun fact from the unit. Can you find four things you found interesting?

This task focuses on personalization.

Ask students if they recognize the drawing with N, E, S, W and where they might see it. (on a compass or a map) Show students a picture of a compass if possible.

Elicit two or three ideas that they found interesting or fun in the unit. Remind them that there are no right or wrong answers—this is an opinion task.

Give students some time to find and write down four interesting things they learned.

Have them share their ideas with a friend and see if they had any ideas in common.

Answers

Students' own answers

How can you learn more about famous journeys?

This question focuses on ways that students can extend their knowledge.

Elicit some ideas from the class (e.g. from books, from the internet, from movies, from history lessons) and write them on the board.

Have students choose their favorite and complete the sentence in their books.

Answers

Students' own answers

Cool Down

Have students look back at the VTR picture on pp. 152–153. Project it on the board for students to study. Ask them if they now have any more ideas about what the picture shows, where the train might have come from, or where it might be going.

Practice **Resource Bank:** Unit Test; End-of-year Test; **Student's App:** Key Concept Practice

Lemonade for Everyone

Lesson Objectives

- to review vocabulary from Units 1 and 2, focusing on gadgets, places in school, food, drink, and containers
- to review grammar from Units 1 and 2, focusing on the simple present with adverbs of frequency, the present progressive, and quantifiers
- to practice communication and fluency skills

Warm Up

Have students do a group mime to review the present progressive. Divide the class into two teams or more if you have a big class—big groups of up to about ten students work well for this activity. Tell each student to think of an activity that they do regularly. (e.g. playing video games, brushing their teeth) Give students time to discuss their activities so that they all do different things. Both (or all) teams can do this preparation at the same time.

Team A then has 20 seconds to mime doing their chosen activities, all at the same time, while Team B watches and tries to identify what they are doing.

Team A stops miming, and Team B then has 20 seconds to explain as many of the activities they can remember Team A doing as possible; for example, *Wati is watching TV.*

The teams then swap roles and Team B mimes while Team A watches. The team that identifies the most activities is the winner.

Tell a Story

Students are going to do an activity where they build up a story from pictures.

- Tell students they're going to make a chain story. Before they begin telling the story, point out the words in the box at the bottom of p. 35. Say the words and have students call out numbers of pictures that the words could refer to. Also point out the names of the characters labeled in picture 1: Henry, Leo, and the teacher, Miss Tea.
- Ask two students to read the example dialogue in the speech bubbles and have the class suggest ways to complete what Henry says, based on what they see in picture 2.
- Have students work in pairs. One student describes what is happening in picture 1. The other student repeats what their friend said and makes another sentence about picture 2. Students can help each other make sentences—this is a collaborative activity. They keep taking turns, repeating what their friend said and adding a new sentence until the story is complete.
- Circulate and help as necessary. Encourage them to use the present progressive, adverbs of frequency (*always*, *sometimes*, etc.), and quantifiers (*a lot of*, *many*, *much*, etc.) where they can.

Here is an example:

Speaker 1: Henry and Leo are using computers in the language lab.
Speaker 2: Henry and Leo are using computers in the language lab. Henry says, "I always have three bottles of water."
Speaker 1: Henry says, "I always have three bottles of water." Leo says, "I always have three bottles of lemonade!"
Speaker 2: Leo says …

- At the end of the activity, ask them to say sentences from the story. Then have pairs turn their books over and work together to try to remember the story in order.

Suggested Answers

1 Henry and Leo are using computers in the language lab.
2 Henry says, "I always drink water."
3 Leo says, "I often drink lemonade."
4 Henry and Leo are playing soccer on the playground.
5 Mrs. Tea says, "How many bottles of water do you have?"
6 Henry says, "I have three bottles of water."
7 Leo says, "I don't have much water. I have some lemonade."
8 Now, everyone has lemonade!

International English

Point out that the word *lemonade* means different things in different countries. In the USA, it is a soft lemon drink made from lemon juice, water, and sugar, usually served in a glass pitcher. In the UK, it is a fizzy drink that usually comes in a can or a bottle. Ask students if they have had similar drinks. What are these called in their country?

Cool Down

Play a variation of *I Spy …* with the pictures on pp. 34–35 (see TB p. 25). When they guess the item you were thinking of, have them make a sentence about what is happening with that item in the picture. For example, for *computers*, they might say *Henry and Leo are using a computer.*

Have students continue the game in pairs.

Explore The Island

Lesson Objectives

- to review vocabulary from Units 3 and 4, focusing on nature, animals, action verbs, and regular verbs
- to review grammar from Units 3 and 4, focusing on simple past of *be* and regular verbs
- to practice communication and fluency skills

Materials

A set of question cards from the Resource Bank (one set per group of four students); a Spinner and Counters printout from the Resource Bank (one spinner per group; one counter per student)

Warm Up

Brainstorm all the different things you can do on an island—activities, what you can see, what you can eat and drink, and so on. Elicit students' suggestions and write them on the board. Ask students if they think an island is a good place to live or to visit for a vacation.

How to Play

- Have students make their spinners or prepare them before the class.
- Tell students they are going to play a board game in which they move around an island and answer questions.
- Put students in pairs or small groups of up to four. Have them choose one book to use as the board and put it in the middle of the table.
- Have students find and say the names of the starting points on the board: *Desert Home*, *Waterfall Home*, *Forest Home*, *Beach Home*. Tell each player to choose a home to start from. Give each student a counter and tell them to color it to match their home (yellow, blue, green, or red).
- To start, each player takes turns choosing a card and answering the question (*What is it?* or *What are they?* for vocabulary and *What happened?* or *Complete the Sentence* for past actions). If students answer correctly, they spin the spinner and move around the board. If they land on a *Take a card* space, they choose a question card and say the answer. If the answer is correct, they stay on the space. If it is wrong or they can't answer it, they go back to their original space. If they land on the same space as another player, that person goes back to his/her starting point.

Here is an example:
Student A: (takes card)
Student B: *What happened?*
Student A: *They packed the bag.*
Student B: *Yes! You can stay.*

Playtime Practice

Have students work in their pairs to write extra question cards to use in the game. They can then change groups and play the game again with a new group, using the new question cards they made with their previous partner.

Cool Down

Have students draw a picture of a situation in their game and label it with what happened. They can then share their pictures in small groups and describe what happened. Display the pictures on the wall or scan them and include them in students' digital portfolios.

Race to the Museum!

Lesson Objectives

- to review vocabulary from Units 5 and 6, focusing on body parts and adjectives, fossils and ruins, art nouns and adjectives, and short adjectives
- to review grammar from Units 5 and 6, focusing on comparatives and superlatives with short adjectives
- to practice communication and fluency skills

Materials

A Spinner and Counters printout from the Resource Bank (one spinner per group; one counter per student)

Warm Up

Brainstorm all the things we can see in museums and write students' ideas on the board. Then have a class vote to decide on the best thing to see in a museum.

How to Play

- Have students make their spinners or prepare them before the class.
- Tell students they are going to play a board game called *Race to the Museum!* The goal of the game is to get to the museum, but to get there they have to make a sentence every time they stop on a space.
- Put students in pairs or small groups. Give each student a counter and have them color it a different color from the other student(s) in their pair or group. Have them choose one student's book to use as the board and put it in the middle of the table.
- Project the game board using the TTL if possible. Have students find the start point (labeled *Start*) and the finish point (the museum).
- Point out *Miss a turn* and *Go back X spaces*. Ask students what happens here. (If students land on a *Miss a turn* space, they don't play in the next round. If they land on a *Go back* space, they have to count back from where they are to move backwards.)
- Students spin the spinner and move around the board. Each time they stop, they use the picture and prompt on the space to make a sentence.
- The winner of the game is the first person to get to the museum.

Here is an example:

Student A: Five! One, two, three, four, five. Scary, dinosaur, elephant, tiger. Ah! A tiger is scarier than an elephant, but a dinosaur is the scariest!

Student B: Good answer!

Student A: Your turn.

Student B: Three. One, two, three. STOP! Dig here. MISS A TURN. Oh, no! I can't play next time! Your turn …

- When students finish, ask them if they had difficulty with any of the sentences. Invite students to say some of the sentences they made in the game and ask if others also made the same sentence.

Cool Down

Use sentences from the game to play *Running Sentences* (see TB p. 26). You can use sentences from the spaces (e.g. *Where did she go on vacation? What did they drink?*) or sentences from the answers (e.g. *A lion is noisier than a snake*).

Give Me a Clue!

Lesson Objectives

- to review vocabulary from Units 7 and 8, focusing on hobbies, activities, describing words, and working with others
- to review grammar from Units 7 and 8, focusing on using *can* for permission
- to practice communication and fluency skills

Materials

A Spinner and Counters printout from the Resource Bank (one spinner per group; one counter per student)

Warm Up

Play the *Alphabet Game* with hobbies and activities (see TB p. 25).

How to Play

- Have students make their spinners or prepare them before the class.
- Tell students they are going to play a board game in which they read a clue and say a word every time they stop on a space.
- Put students in pairs or small groups. Give each student a counter and have them color it a different color from the other student(s) in their pair or group. Have them choose one student's book to use as the board and put it in the middle of the table.
- Students start on the Start space (bottom left) and are aiming to get to the Finish space (top right). They take turns spinning the spinner and moving their counter around the board. If they land on a space with a clue, they say the answer, which begins with the large pink letters in the bottom right-hand corner. If the answer is correct, they stay on the space. If it is wrong or they can't answer it, they go back to their original space.
- Ask students what they think happens if they land on a space with a wall and rope (they use the rope to climb up to the space at the top of the wall) and what happens if they land on a kayaking space (they kayak down to the space at the bottom of the river).
- The winner of the game is the first person to get to the *Finish* square.

Here is an example:

Student A: Five! One, two, three, four, five. Some people think math is … D. Ah! Difficult!

Student B: Good answer!

Student A: Your turn.

Student A: Two. One, two. This person smiles and is kind. He is … F. I'm not sure … Oh! Friendly!

Answers

1 climbing	14 selfish
2 friendly	16 popular
3 traded	20 horseback riding
5 difficult	21 intelligent
6 singing	23 tennis
8 skating	24 exciting
10 track and field	26 volleyball
11 took turns	27 borrow
12 thoughtful	28 brave

Cool Down

Play *Physical Spelling* (see TB p. 26) using key words from the game.

Day by Day

Lesson Objectives

- to review vocabulary from Units 9 and 10, focusing on rooms, furniture, appliances, emotions, travel and transportation, and weather
- to review grammar from Units 9 and 10, focusing on the simple past, *there was / there were*, *going to*, and prepositions of movement
- to practice communication and fluency skills

Warm Up

Have students turn to a clean page in their notebooks. Tell them you will describe a picture to them and they should draw what you describe. After you finish, have everyone hold up their picture for the others to see.

Note: the picture you are describing is one of the ones in the game, but students won't know that yet!

Suggested description: *There's a town with a big castle. I can see a playground across from the castle and a train station behind the playground. There are some cars on the road. It's sunny, but there are some dark clouds. Maybe there will be thunder!*

How to Play

- Students are going to play a game in which they work with a partner to find the differences between sets of pictures by asking questions and describing.
- Tell students to decide who is A and who is B and have them turn over the other side of the double page so they can see only their own pictures. Tell them they must not look at each other's pictures. Point out that they each have two scenes: one from yesterday and one from today. Their challenge is to make statements and ask questions to find the differences. Tell them they need to find eight differences. They should circle the differences when they find them.
- Ask students who are looking at picture A what the first question is on their page and elicit a short dialogue to show how to find the answer.

Here is an example:

Student A: Was there a storm yesterday?

Student B: Yes, there was. I can see lightning! In this picture, the dog next to the castle is sleeping today.

Student A: Ah! In this picture, the dog is awake.

- Have students take turns asking and answering or describing until they find eight differences.
- When students have had time to find as many differences as they can, give them a chance to look at one another's pictures and see what their partner was describing. They can also find things they may have missed.
- To check answers, invite pairs to describe a difference they found and ask if everyone agrees.

Answers

In Picture B:

Yesterday:

The girl and the boy running up the steps were frightened (not excited).

There was no chameleon climbing up the castle wall.

The man at the station didn't have a suitcase.

The woman ran to the airport (not the station).

Today:

The dog is happy/awake (not tired/sleeping).

There is a rain cloud in the sky.

There is a closet on the road, not a fridge.

The man walking around the playground is going to throw a ball back to the kids on the playground (not trip over it).

Cool Down

Have students compare their pictures from the Warm Up to the pictures in their **Language Book**. Have them say what is similar and different between their picture and the pictures in the book.

Adventures on Purple Mountain

Materials

Audio Track 123; small cards numbered 1–7 to designate roles; simple props: an open book for a laptop, a pencil case for a cell phone, school bags for backpacks, a bag for Mario's food (the food can be mimed); alternatively, provide some craft materials to make props

CHARACTERS

Narrator	Rafa
Sean	Mario
Resham	Mom
Ellie	

Warm Up

Do a visualization activity to prepare students for the play. Say *You are climbing a mountain. You climb up and up and up. You are at the top! You look down. What can you see? What can you hear? What can you smell?*

TRACK 123 TB p. 229 Listen and Engage

- Have students read the title of the play. Ask *Where are they going?* (Purple Mountain) Ask *Is an adventure exciting or boring?* (exciting) Encourage students to predict what the adventure might be.
- Have students look at the character list. Ask *How many characters are there?* (six plus the Narrator) Ask *Which characters from the list are in the pictures?* Encourage students to figure out that the pictures show the children (so, not Mom or the Narrator).
- Play the audio and have students listen and follow in their books. Ask them if they can point to Mario (eating) and Sean (he has the cell phone).
- Point to the words in light blue italics and ask *Did you hear these words?* (no) *Why not?* Elicit that these are stage directions that tell the actors what is happening.

Interact

- Play the audio again and encourage students to listen and invent some actions (e.g. walking up the mountain, eating a cupcake, eating potato chips). Ask them to think about how the children feel when they are lost and hear a noise.
- Play the audio again and have students repeat each line—first without the actions and then with actions.

Practice, Prepare, and Perform

- Tell students they are going to practice the play to perform to an audience. You may decide to have them perform it to another class in the school, a group of teachers, or to their parents.
- Divide the class into groups of ten or more. Give seven students in the group a number from one to seven. Explain that the rest of the students in the group are the Chorus. Tell students that this time, all number ones are the Narrator, twos are Sean, threes are Resham, fours are Ellie, fives are Rafa, sixes are Mario, and sevens are Mom.
- Play the audio and have students mime their own character's actions. Encourage students in the Chorus to invent actions to show walking up and down a mountain and encouraging Mario to walk faster.
- Give students time to practice their parts. They can read the lines from their books.
- If you can, allow students ten minutes to practice the play every day. When they have memorized their lines, have them incorporate simple props into their performance. You can suggest the props listed in *Materials* above, or you could encourage students to make their own props in a craft session.
- Encourage students to come up with ideas about what they can do to make the play more real. For example, in the forest scene, students who have a Chorus role could stand around the actors with their arms raised like trees.
- Keep costumes simple by allowing students to wear their own clothes.
- Designate some students to be in charge of welcoming the audience and showing them to their seats and others to introduce the play.
- Stand at the side of the stage and prompt any students who have forgotten their lines.

Cool Down

After the performance, congratulate students and ask them if they enjoyed performing the play. Review all the different things they had to do to prepare and write them on the board (e.g. *practicing the lines, thinking of actions for the characters, creating the props and scenery*). Ask students to put the things in order from what found most difficult to what they found easiest. Invite pairs to share their answers and encourage them to give reasons.

King Grandpa's Treasure

Materials

Audio Track 124; small cards numbered 1–8 to designate roles; simple props: a classroom cupboard, a model boat or a picture of a boat, a model castle or a picture of a castle, a poster of a painting (or other subject), a (big) box, a model plane (or a picture of a plane), a medal or a paper/card circle colored gold

CHARACTERS

Narrator	Princess Mom
King Grandpa	Young Prince Eric
Queen Grandma	Sofia, Eric's friend
Prince Dad	Ramón, Eric's friend

Warm Up

Ask students to remember their three favorite memories—tell them it can be a trip, a celebration, a competition, a show, anything they like. Have students share their ideas with a partner and then ask if they had any choices in common.

TRACK 124 TB p. 230 Listen and Engage

- Have students read the title of the play. Ask *What treasure do kings usually have?* Encourage students to predict what King Grandpa's treasure might be.
- Have students look at the character list. Ask *How many characters are there?* (seven plus the Narrator)
- Play the audio and have students listen and follow in their books. Have them find and point to Grandpa, Dad, Mom, Grandma, and the three children.

Interact

- Play the audio again and encourage students to listen and invent some actions (e.g. going down to the basement, looking in cabinets, carrying the box of treasure).
- Play the audio again and have students repeat each line—first with no actions and then with actions.

Practice, Prepare, and Perform

- Tell students they are going to practice the play to perform to an audience. You may decide to have them perform it to another class in the school, a group of teachers, or to their parents.
- Divide the class into groups of 11 or more. Give eight students in each group a number from one to eight. If students had a Chorus role in the previous play, make sure they take a number card this time. Tell students that this time, all number ones are the Narrator, twos are King Grandpa, threes are Queen Grandma, fours are Prince Dad, fives are Princess Mom, sixes are Young Prince Eric, sevens are Sofia, and eights are Ramón. Students without a card are the Chorus.
- Play the audio and have students mime their own character's actions. Encourage students in the Chorus to invent movements for looking for the treasure and working together.
- Give students time to practice their parts. They can read the lines from their books.
- If you can, allow students ten minutes to practice the play every day. When they have memorized their lines, have them incorporate simple props into their performance. You can suggest the props listed in *Materials* above, or if you have time, encourage students to make their own props during a craft session. Students who have a Chorus role in the play can be in charge of deciding which props are needed.
- Keep costumes simple by having students wear their own clothes, but bring in something to wear as a crown if they are one of the royal characters. Alternatively, you could have students make crowns during a craft session.
- Designate some students to be in charge of welcoming the audience and showing them to their seats and others to introduce the play.
- Stand at the side of the stage and prompt any students who have forgotten their lines.

Cool Down

After the performance, congratulate students and ask them if they enjoyed performing the play. Review all the different things they had to do to prepare and write them on the board (e.g. *practicing the lines, thinking of actions for the characters, creating the props and scenery*). Do a Think, Pair, Share routine: ask students to think about the thing they liked the best, then share with a partner. Invite pairs to share their answers and encourage them to give reasons.

Audio Scripts
Language Book

Language Review

TRACK 1

Language Review

A Listen and number. Who's Frank?

1 **Zara:** Hi Sam. What are you doing here?
Sam: Hi Zara. I'm having a picnic with my family. Look! Those are my grandparents sitting in the chairs.
2 **Sam:** Grandma has the hat with the flower.
3 **Sam:** And Grandpa is wearing a blue sweater.
4 **Zara:** Oh yes. I see. And so are those your parents? Your mom and dad?
5 **Sam:** That's right. Mom has the yellow jacket.
6 **Zara:** Ooh! I like your mom's brown boots!
7 **Sam:** She likes them too. And Dad loves those red shorts. He always wears them.
Zara: (laughs)
8 **Zara:** Aww! Are those the twins with your Mom?
Sam: Yes.
9 **Zara:** I love their little sneakers!
Sam: I know. They're great.
10 **Zara:** Sam! Did you bring your pet to the park?
Sam: Frank the Frog … umm Yes. How do you know? … Uh-oh!

TRACK 2

Language Review

A Listen and choose.

1 **Zara:** How many sisters do you have?
Tom: Five.
2 **Zookeeper 1:** Where's the crocodile?
Girl 1: There! In the lake.
3 **Boy:** What are they doing?
Zookeeper 2: They're running away!
4 **Old Lady:** Whose frog is this?
Sam: That's mine. Thank you!
5 **Girl 2:** When does the zoo open?
Girl 2's Dad: After lunch.

Unit 1

TRACK 3

Unit 1, Vocabulary

A Listen and find. Where's Luke?

Zara: Hi, Clara!
Clara: Hey there Zara! What's that noise?
Zara: That's Grandma and Bobby. They're playing tennis on the TV in the living room.
Clara: Is it a video game?
Zara: Yes.
Grandma: Woo-hoo! This is a great game!
Clara: Grandma's happy! (laughing) Are you using your laptop now?
Zara: Yes! I love it! The keyboard is really big.
Clara: Can you see me on your screen?
Zara: Yes, I can. It's really big, too.
Clara: Cool! Where's Penny?
Zara: She's in the dining room, playing on her tablet.
Mom: Zara. Where's my mouse?
Zara: I don't know, Mom.
Mom: Penny …. PENNY!
Penny: Uh!
Mom: Where's my … Who's under the table? Oh, Luke, you have my mouse… And Grandpa's alarm clock!
Grandpa: Zara. Can you help me with the cookies?
Zara: Sure, Grandpa. Bye, Clara. It's cookie time!
Clara: OK. Bye!

TRACK 4

Unit 1, Vocabulary

B Listen, say, and number the pictures in A.

1 computer
2 TV
3 cell phone
4 tablet
5 mouse
6 video game
7 keyboard
8 alarm clock
9 screen
10 laptop
11 radio

TRACK 5

Unit 1, Vocabulary

C Listen. Close your eyes and visualize.

Computer. Does your family have a computer? Which room is it in? Say "computer".
TV. Do you have a TV in your house? Where is it? Say "TV".
Cell phone. Mime talking on a cell phone. Who are you talking to? Say "cell phone".
Tablet. Imagine you're using a tablet. What are you doing? Say "tablet".
Mouse. Imagine you're using a mouse. Move it, then click something. Say "mouse".
Video game. What's your favorite video game? Why do you like it? Say "video game".
Keyboard. Put your fingers on a keyboard. Type your name. Say "keyboard".
Alarm clock. It's your alarm clock. Get up! Say "alarm clock".
Screen. Think about screens in your house. Where are they? Say "screen".
Laptop. Think of a laptop. Open it. Close it. Say "laptop".
Radio. Imagine you can hear a radio. What can you hear? Say "radio".

TRACK 6

Unit 1, Vocabulary

E Listen and sing. Then watch and sing.

Living in a Modern World

Chorus

Living in a modern world,
With a lot of cool technology.
Living in a digital world.
It's so easy for you and me.

With my computer, yeah, yeah,
I can learn about the world.
And for music, yeah, yeah,
I can listen to the radio.

Chorus

I use my tablet, yeah, yeah,
To watch movies and play games, too.
And when I'm lonely, yeah, yeah,
I use a cell phone to talk to you.

Chorus (x 2)

TRACK 7

Unit 1, Explore Language

A Listen and read. Who does Grandpa email?

Luis: Grandpa, are you OK?
Grandpa: My friend Sidney never answers his phone!
Luis: You can email him. I often email my friends.
Grandpa: I don't know, Luis. I rarely use the computer.
Luis: I can help. How often do you use this tablet?
Grandpa: That's Grandma's. We sometimes watch movies together on weekends.
Luis: OK. What do you want to say?
Grandpa: ANSWER - YOUR - PHONE!

TRACK 8

Unit 1, Explore Language

D Listen and say.

1 How often do you use this tablet?
2 How often does she play video games?
3 We sometimes watch TV after school.
4 They rarely listen to the radio.
5 You never use an alarm clock.

TRACK 9

Unit 1, Global Citizenship

A Listen to Teddy talk to Olivia about his school. Does Teddy's school have technology?

Teddy: Excuse me. Are you our new exchange student?
Olivia: Yes, that's right. My name's Olivia.
Teddy: Great! Hi, Olivia, I'm Teddy. Welcome to our school!
Olivia: Thanks!
Teddy: This is the language lab. We learn on the computers here.
Olivia: Oh, wow!
Teddy: Come on. This is the cafeteria. We eat lunch here.
Olivia: What's in that room?
Teddy: The gym. We play basketball in there. Let's go to our classroom.
Olivia: OK. This hallway is very long.
Teddy: Here we are. Our classroom.
Olivia: Wow! There's technology everywhere! What's that white box there?
Teddy: That's the projector. We use it all the time. Sometimes we use it to watch videos on the whiteboard.
Olivia: Are those tablets on the teacher's desk?
Teddy: Yes. We study with them, too!
Olivia: Cool! We don't have computers at my school.
Teddy: Really? How do you learn, then?
Olivia: We use books!
Teddy: Oh, yes! We have books, too!

TRACK 10

Unit 1, Global Citizenship

B Listen, say, and number the pictures in A.

1 whiteboard
2 playground
3 bookcase
4 language lab
5 gym
6 classroom
7 hallway (British English: corridor)
8 cafeteria
9 projector

TRACK A

Unit 1, Global Citizenship

Listen. Close your eyes and visualize.

Whiteboard. Is there a whiteboard in your class? Mime writing on the whiteboard. Say "whiteboard."
Playground. You're standing on the playground. What can you hear? Say "playground."
Bookcase. Imagine a library with lots of bookcases. Are they big or small? Say "bookcase."
Language lab. Shh. You're in a language lab. Put on your headphones and listen. Say "language lab."
Gym. Think about your school gym. What sports do you do there? Say "gym."
Classroom. Think of your classroom. Where is your desk? Say "classroom."
Hallway. You're walking in the hallway. Where are you going? Say "hallway."
Cafeteria. It's lunchtime and you're in a cafeteria. Who is sitting with you? Say "cafeteria."
Projector. Imagine a projector in the classroom. Where is it? Say "projector."

TRACK 11

Unit 1, Global Citizenship

D Now listen to Olivia and Akash. Number the pictures. Who uses technology at school?

1 **Akash:** My name is Akash. I live in a village in Bangladesh. We don't have a school, but we do have lessons. We all go to a big room in the village. There isn't a teacher in the room, but there's a TV, a projector and a big screen. The teacher's in, a different place, but we can see her on the screen, and we can speak to her and ask her questions. I love her lessons.
2 **Olivia:** I'm Olivia. I go to a fantastic school in the UK. We don't have computers or laptops, and at home I don't watch TV or play video games. At school, we use books for learning, we make things with our hands and we play outside. Sometimes I want to watch TV, but usually I'm happy reading, sewing, or playing outside.

TRACK 12

Unit 1, Explore Language

A Listen and read. Who sends Dad a message?

Dad: Are you talking to me?
Mom: Shh! No, I'm not. I'm talking to Luis on my cell phone.
Dad: Oh, he's sending messages to me. He says he's doing his homework.
Mom: Hey, Luis! Are you listening to me?
Luis: Sure, Mom. I'm talking and doing my homework at the same time.

TRACK 13

Unit 1, Explore Language

D Listen and say.

1 I'm talking to Luis.
2 I'm not using my tablet.
3 What are they doing?
4 They aren't sitting in the language lab.
5 Are they playing video games? Yes, they are.

TRACK 14

Unit 1, Take the Stage, Pronunciation

Listen and say.

/eɪ/ name
/e/ help
/eɪ/ name Grace great
/e/ help instead when

Unit 2

TRACK 15

Unit 2, Vocabulary

A Listen and find. What's Lucy making?

Erin: Hello, Mrs. Jonas
Mrs. Jonas: Hello, Erin. You have some nice fruit, Toby.
Toby: Cherries and apples from Grandpa's garden. And big, red tomatoes. I can give you six tomatoes for your nice yellow corn.
Mrs. Jonas: Good idea! Is that a big purple eggplant?
Toby: Yes.
Mrs. Jonas: Yum! Your eggplant for my green peas?
Toby: OK. Look, Mom! Corn and peas.
Erin: Wonderful, Toby. I like peas.
Toby: Pink cupcakes! Hello! I have four tomatoes. Can I have two cupcakes, please?
Mrs. Kneed: Which cupcakes do you like?
Toby: The cupcakes with the red cherries.
Mrs. Kneed: Here you are.
Toby: Thanks. Look! Two cupcakes, Mom.
Erin: There's Mr. Bell. Can you get a pineapple?
Toby: OK. Hello, Mr. Bell. Can I have a pineapple for three tomatoes, please?
Mr. Bell: Certainly.
Toby: Lucy! What juice are you making?
Lucy: Orange juice. But I can make tomato juice, too.
Toby: Tomato juice? Great! Oh, no! I have no more tomatoes!

TRACK 16

Unit 2, Vocabulary

B Listen, say, and number the pictures in A.

1 tomato
2 chicken
3 spinach
4 corn
5 fruit
6 eggplant (British English: aubergine)
7 cupcake (British English: fairy cake)
8 sausage
9 pineapple
10 peas
11 cherry
12 rice

TRACK 17

Unit 2, Vocabulary

C Listen. Close your eyes and visualize.

Tomato. Imagine tomatoes growing in the garden. What color are they? Say "tomato."
Chicken. Think of a delicious chicken dinner. How does it smell? Say "chicken."
Spinach. Do you like spinach? What color is it? Say "spinach."
Corn. Mime eating some yellow corn. Do you eat from left to right, or right to left? Say "corn."
Fruit. Think of some fruit in a bowl. What type of fruit can you see? Say "fruit."
Eggplant. Imagine a big purple eggplant. What color is it inside? Say "eggplant."
Cupcake. Ooh! There are some cupcakes on the table. Count them. Say "cupcake."
Sausage. You can see a plate of hot sausages. Mime eating one with a knife and fork. Say "sausage."
Pineapple. You're holding a big pineapple. What does it feel like? Say "pineapple."
Peas. You can see a lot of green peas on a plate. Can you count them? Say "peas."
Cherry. Imagine cherries on a cake. Take one of the cherries and eat it. Say "cherry."
Rice. Do you like rice? What food do you eat with rice? Say "rice."

TRACK 18

Unit 2, Vocabulary

E Listen and sing. Then watch and sing.

It's Market Day!
Chorus (x 2)

It's market day! Hooray! Hooray!
It's market day today!

There are tomatoes and peas.
Some spinach? Yes, please!
Look! Cupcakes with cherries on top!

Chorus (x 2)

There's chicken and rice.
Those sausages look nice!
And cupcakes with cherries on top!

Chorus (x 2)

There are eggplants and corn.
Pineapples and more!
And yes! Cupcakes with cherries on top!

TRACK 19

Unit 2, Explore Language

A Listen and read. What fruit does Mr. Bell have?

Ling: Hi, Mr. Bell. Mom says we need a lot of different fruit. We want fruit salad for a picnic.
Mr. Bell: Hmm, I don't have much fruit here in my fruit cart.
Ling: Ooh … are those cherries?
Mr. Bell: Let's see … Yes, they are.
Ling: Great! Oh, you don't have many cherries left.
Mr. Bell: That's OK. You take them.
Ling: Oh, thank you!
Mr. Bell: You're welcome. Now … I know I have some pineapples.
Ling: Wow! You have a lot of pineapples.

TRACK 20

Unit 2, Explore Language

D Listen and say.

1 You don't have many cherries.
2 He doesn't have much fruit.
3 He has a lot of pineapples.
4 We need a lot of rice.

TRACK 21

Unit 2, Global Citizenship

A Listen to Basilio talk to his mom about lunch. What does he have in his lunchbox?

Mom: Basilio, here's your lunchbox. You have a salad and some rice. Do you want a carton of juice?
Basilo: Um, can I have some lemonade, please?
Mom: No, but you can have a bottle of water … and some fruit.
Basilo: Dragon fruit again? I like the taste. But I don't like the color – it's pink!
Mom: But we have this big bowl of it from our garden! It grows so well here in Mexico, and now we have so much of it!
Basilo: OK … ooh can I take that box of chocolates?
Mom: No, Basilio, that's a present for Grandma.
Basilo: Oh yeah. OK. What about a bag of potato chips?
Mom: Hmm. You don't often have potato chips, so … OK.
Basilo: Yes! Thanks, Mom! I love potato chips.

TRACK 22

Unit 2, Global Citizenship

B Listen, say, and number the pictures in A.

1 a box of
2 a bag of
3 a bowl of
4 a bottle of
5 a can of
6 a carton of
7 lemonade
8 soup
9 potato chips (British English: crisps)

TRACK B

Unit 2, Global Citizenship

Listen. Close your eyes and visualize.

A box of. Think of chocolates in a box. Open it. How many chocolates are there? Say "a box of chocolates."
A bag of. You're holding a big bag of apples. Can you carry it? Say "a bag of apples."
A bowl of. What do you eat from a bowl? Mime eating soup from a bowl. Say "a bowl of soup."
A bottle of. Imagine you're drinking water from a small bottle. Is it cold? Say "a bottle of water."
A can of. Mime opening a can of soda. Drink from the can. Say "a can of soda."
A carton of. Open the fridge. There's a carton of milk in the fridge. Say "a carton of milk."
Lemonade. Imagine drinking lemonade. How does it taste? Say "lemonade."
Soup. You're eating soup. What flavor is it? Say "soup."
Potato chips. Think about eating potato chips. How do they sound? Say "potato chips."

TRACK 23

Unit 2, Global Citizenship

D Now listen to Vania and Precious. Write the country. Who eats fruit for breakfast?

1 **Vania:** Hello. My name is Vania and I'm from Indonesia. My favorite fruit is green outside and yellow inside. It's the durian. We call it "the king of fruit". Some people don't like durian because it smells bad, but I love it! You can eat it in different ways. Every summer, my mom buys a big box of durians and makes ice cream. It's delicious. You can also have durian chips. Yum!
2 **Precious:** Hi. I'm Precious and I come from Botswana. I love this melon: it's a kiwano melon. I think it's beautiful, too. The outside is orange and the inside is green and juicy. I often have a bowl of kiwano melon and other fruit for breakfast because it gives me energy. And I sometimes eat it at school for lunch.

TRACK 24

Unit 2, Explore Language

A Listen and read. What food does Elena have?

Mom: Oh, no! We don't have any lunch.
Grandpa: Elena, how much food do we have?
Elena: Let's see … We have these sandwiches.
Grandpa: And how many apples do we have?
Elena: We have this big bag of apples. There are…six.
Ling's little sister: Mom! We're ready for lunch.
Mom: Oh, dear!
Grandpa: We have some food. Come and eat with us!
Ling's little sister: Thank you!

TRACK 25

Unit 2, Explore Language

D Listen and say.

1 How much food do we have?
2 How many tomatoes do you have?
3 We don't have any spinach.
4 He has some sausages.

TRACK 26

Unit 2, Talk About It

Pronunciation Listen and say.

/l/ let's
/r/ Rob
/l/ let's online lemonade
/r/ Rob carrots rice

Unit 3

TRACK 27

Unit 3, Vocabulary

A Listen and find. Where's Ivan going?

Guide: OK everyone, look at this map of our walk. We're here now, on the beach, and … do you see those trees over there?
Kids' chorus: Yes!
Guide: That's the forest. We go in there for our walk. Then, we go up this very tall mountain here.
Ivan: Oh, is that a glacier?
Guide: Yes, Ivan. It's cold up there.
Elena: What's that, behind those trees?
Guide: Oh, that's the desert, Elena. It's very hot over there. Now, on the way down, we walk in this valley between the mountains. There's a big, blue lake.
Ivan: Can we swim there?
Guide: You can, but the water is very cold. Then, we walk next to the river back to that beach. We can have lunch in the café and look at the ocean. Is everybody ready to go?
Kids: Yes!
Guide: Hey! Where are you going, Ivan?
Ivan: To the café. This is a quick way there.

TRACK 28

Unit 3, Vocabulary

B Listen, say, and number the pictures in A.

1 river
2 mountain
3 waterfall
4 valley
5 beach
6 ocean
7 glacier
8 desert
9 lake
10 forest
11 island

TRACK 29

Unit 3, Vocabulary

Listen. Close your eyes and visualize.

River. Think about a river. Draw it with your hand in the air. Say "river."
Mountain. Mime walking up a mountain. How do you feel? Say "mountain."
Waterfall. Imagine you're standing under a waterfall. Listen to the water. Say "waterfall."
Valley. You're in a valley. Wow! Look up at the mountains around you. Say "valley."
Beach. You're walking on the beach with no shoes. What can you feel? Say "beach."
Ocean. You're at the beach looking at the ocean. Do you want to swim in it? Say "ocean."
Glacier. Think about a glacier. Mime walking on it. Say "glacier."
Desert. Think about the desert. Is it hot or cold? Say "desert."
Lake. Imagine you are in a boat on a lake. What can you see? Say "lake."
Forest. You're in a forest. What can you see in the trees? Say "forest."
Island. You're on the beach. Look! There's an island. Is the island big or small? Say "island."

TRACK 30

Unit 3, Vocabulary

E Listen and sing. Then watch and sing.

It's a Wonderful World

Chorus

Nature is a wonderful thing.
It's a wonderful world we're living in.
With changing nature everywhere,
It's a wonderful, wonderful world!

Up in the mountains it's very cold.
There are a lot of valleys and waterfalls.
Glaciers can change to beautiful lakes.
It's a wonderful, wonderful world!
Out in the desert it's very hot.
And you need to drink a lot.
Forests can change from green to red.
It's a wonderful, wonderful world!

Chorus

TRACK 31

Unit 3, Explore Language

A Listen and read. Where's Ivan?

Nita: Wow! The lake is beautiful.
Guide: Yes! It wasn't a lake millions of years ago. It was a glacier.
Guide: Hey, Nita! Where's Ivan?
Nita: I don't know. He was on the beach with us.
Guide: Yes. Then we were in the forest.
Nita: What was that?
Ivan: Boo!
Nita: Arrgh!
Ivan: Ha ha! It's me, I was behind the tree!
Nita: We weren't scared, Ivan!

TRACK 32

Unit 3, Explore Language

D Listen and say.

1 I was behind the tree.
2 He wasn't on the mountain.
3 You were on the island.
4 They weren't on the beach three days ago.

TRACK 33

Unit 3, Global Citizenship

A Listen to Sebastian learn about animals. Who is losing hair and skin right now?

Sebastian: Is that penguin OK?
Keeper: Yes, but it can't swim at the moment.
Sebastian: Why not?
Keeper: It's losing its feathers. Humboldt penguins here in Chile do this every year so they can grow new ones.
Sebastian: That's weird!
Keeper: Not really, Sebastian. Other birds in other countries do that too. White swans lose their feathers in the fall. When this happens they can't fly. It's the same for ducks and their different colored feathers.
Sebastian: So, it's just birds then?
Keeper: No, other animals do it, too. Do you know chameleons, those animals that look like lizards? You know, they have scales and their color changes when they feel happy and sad?
Sebastian: Oh! Yes, I know.
Keeper: Well, they lose their scales so they can grow. And snakes lose their scales too. The scales look long and thin, just like a snake.
Sebastian: Eww!
Keeper: All animals do it. You are losing hair and skin right now.
Sebastian: Noooooooo! Reeeeally?

TRACK 34

Unit 3, Global Citizenship

B Listen, say, and number the pictures in A.

1 penguin
2 swan
3 duck
4 bear
5 chameleon
6 snake
7 feathers
8 scales
9 fur

TRACK C

Unit 3, Global Citizenship

Listen. Close your eyes and visualize.

Penguin. Imagine a penguin. Watch it walk. Say "penguin."
Swan. Think of a swan. What color is it? Say "swan."
Duck. You see a duck with brown and white feathers. Is it flying? Say "duck."
Bear. Think of a big, strong bear. Roooaaarrr! Say "bear."
Chameleon. You can see a chameleon. Where is it? Say "chameleon."
Snake. Imagine being a snake. Move like a snake. Say "snake."
Feathers. Think of a bird? What color are its feathers? Say "feathers."

Scales. Think of an animal with scales. What animal is it? Say "scales."
Fur. Think of an animal with fur. Feel the fur. Say "fur."

TRACK 35

Unit 3, Global Citizenship

D Now listen to Ingi and Kulap. Write the country. Which animal is now red and blue?

1 **Ingi:** Hi! I'm Ingi. I live near a glacier in Iceland, and you can see Arctic foxes there. They're really cool! They have brown fur in the summer. But when Iceland is cold and white in the winter, the foxes grow thick white fur. It helps them hide and keeps them warm.

2 **Kulap:** Hello from Thailand! My name's Kulap. I really like fish, and my favorite is the betta fish. Their scales change color from baby to adult, and the adults are really beautiful! We have some pet fish at home. One is a betta fish. His name is Toto, and now he's red and blue.

TRACK 36

Unit 3, Explore Language

A Listen and read. Why are the leaves brown now?

Nita: Hi Ravi. How's Charlie?
Ravi: Umm … I don't know. I can't see him!
Nita: Oh, no!
Ravi: He was here yesterday.
Nita: OK. Where was he yesterday? Was he on those brown leaves?
Ravi: No, he wasn't. Hmm … those leaves weren't brown before.
Nita: Were they green?
Ravi: Yes, they were.
Nita: You see, they were new yesterday. Now they're old.
Ravi: Oh! Look! There he is!
Nita: Where? Oh! Silly Charlie!

TRACK 37

Unit 3, Explore Language

D Listen and say.

1 Where was he this morning?
2 Was he at the animal park? Yes, he was.
3 Were you at school yesterday? No, I wasn't.
4 What color were the fish? They were orange.

TRACK 38

Unit 3, Talk About It, Pronunciation Listen and say.

/ɑr/ park
/ʌ/ summer
/ɑr/ park Lara are
/ʌ/ summer Gus love

Unit 4

TRACK 39

Unit 4, Vocabulary

A Listen and find. Who wins the Spelling Bee?

Ravi: Hi, Alfred. Hi, Chen. What are you doing with that big book?
Chen: Shh! I need to study, Ravi.
Alfred: Chen wants to compete in the Spelling Bee. It's after this dance show.
Ravi: Oh, I like the music.
Chen: Shh!
Emcee: Good job, dancers! Let's clap again for them, everyone. OK, now the Spelling Bee.
Chen: Oh!
Alfred and Ravi: You can do it, Chen!
Emcee: Chen. You start. Your word is mountain.
Chen: Mountain. M-O-U-N-T-A-I-N. Mountain.
Emcee: Correct.
…
Chen: Alfred and Ravi, look! I'm first!
Ravi: Yay!
Alfred: Good job, Chen!
Ravi: That's a big trophy! Can I carry it for you?
Chen: Yes. Oh, careful Ravi! Don't drop it.
Ravi: Whoops!
Alfred: Ow! (laughing, but in pain) My toe!
Ravi: Sorry, Alfred!

TRACK 40

Unit 4, Vocabulary

B Listen, say, and number the pictures in A.

1 dance
2 clap
3 compete
4 bake
5 carry
6 trip
7 drop
8 start
9 study

TRACK 41

Unit 4, Vocabulary

C Listen. Close your eyes and visualize.

Dance. Imagine a dance show. How many people are dancing? Say "dance."
Clap. The show is finished. Clap your hands. Say "clap."
Compete. You are competing in a race. Who else is in the race? Say "compete."
Bake. Imagine you are making cupcakes. Put them in the oven to bake. Say "bake."
Carry. Imagine carrying your school bag. How many books are in it? Say "carry."
Trip. Imagine a book on the floor. Be careful! Don't trip! Say "trip."
Drop. You have an egg in your hand. Imagine you drop it! Say "drop."
Start. Think about a running race. Ready? Start! Say "start."
Study. You have a test. What are you studying? Say "study."

TRACK 42

Unit 4, Vocabulary

E Listen and sing. Then watch and sing.

It's OK

It's time for the Spelling Bee.
But I still need to study!
Oh no, I don't think I can win.
Oh no, it's time to begin!

It's OK.
It's fine.
You can do it, friend of mine!

It's time for the cake sale, hurry!
But that's a lot to carry.
Oh no, you can't carry those plates.
Oh no, don't trip and drop the cakes!

It's OK.
It's fine.
You can bake them again in time!

It's OK.
It's fine.
You can do it, friend of mine! (x 2)

TRACK 43

Unit 4, Explore Language

A Listen and read. Who was lucky?

Judy: Did you compete in the baking competition?
Alfred: Yes, I did. I competed with my brother. We baked 25 cupcakes.
Judy: That's a lot of cupcakes!
Alfred: That was the problem!
Judy: Why?
Alfred: I carried the cupcakes in a tower, but I tripped and I dropped it.
Judy: Oh, no!
Alfred: But … I didn't drop all of the cupcakes.
Judy: You were lucky!
Alfred: Yes, but I did drop some!

TRACK 44

Unit 4, Explore Language

D Listen and say.

1 We baked 25 cupcakes.
2 I carried my backpack.
3 They didn't dance in the competition.
4 My dad didn't study English at school.

TRACK 45

Unit 4, Global Citizenship

A Listen to Kadir talk to his brother about his first day at school. When does Kadir start school?

Kadir: Haluk! I want to go to school with you.
Haluk: But I finish school on Friday for the holidays. And you start school in September, Kadir.

Kadir: Oh… Haluk! Was your first day at school scary?
Haluk: Oh no! It was great! You know, at some schools in Turkey, we all give flowers to our teacher on our first day. My teacher was Miss Badem and she loved them. She was very happy and she smiled a lot. On our first day, we learned the alphabet, we painted pictures, and we practiced writing.
Kadir: Is the school big?
Haluk: No, but the playground is big. We play clapping games and bounce balls. It's fun!
Kadir: Oh good! … I don't want to wait for September! Can I go to school today?
Haluk: (sigh!)

TRACK 46

Unit 4, Global Citizenship
B Listen, say, and number the pictures in A.

1 travel
2 pack
3 practice
4 learn
5 bounce
6 play
7 wait
8 smile
9 finish
10 move

TRACK D

Unit 4, Global Citizenship
Listen. Close your eyes and visualize.

Travel. How do you travel to school? Do you take the bus? Say "travel."
Pack. Think about packing your backpack for school. What do you put in it? Say "pack."
Practice. Imagine singing a song. Practice singing it again and again. Say "practice."
Learn. Think about listening to your teacher. What are you learning about? Say "learn."
Bounce. You're holding a basketball in your hands. Bounce your ball 3 times. Say "bounce."
Play. Think about a game you play. Who do you play with? Say "play."
Wait. Imagine you're at the train station. Sit and wait for your train. Say "wait."
Smile. Think of something happy. Smile! Say "smile."
Finish. It's time to finish school. Is it the morning or the afternoon? Say "finish."
Move. Close your eyes and stand on one leg. Did you move? Say "move."

TRACK 47

Unit 4, Global Citizenship
D Now listen to Hiroko and Wati. Write the country. Who starts school in July?

1 **Hiroko:** Hello. My name is Hiroko. In Japan we start school in April, and today was my first day. First, we went into the gym for a big ceremony with the principal. He said that we must study hard and be good students. There are 35 students in my class, and I have two new friends now: Akiko and Takayoshi.
2 **Wati:** Hello. This is Wati, and I'm from Indonesia. Today is my sister's first day at school. We start school in July and in our school all our new students are put in groups with older students. Together, we do things to help the school and make new friends.

TRACK 48

Unit 4, Explore Language
A Listen and read. Where do Anna's friends live?

Dad: Did Anna pack her backpack?
Mom: Yes, she did. Let's go!
Dad: It's OK, Anna. I'm sad, too.
Mom: In our old house, did we ride our bikes?
Anna: No, we didn't.
Mom: Because we lived on that big hill. Did you study in your bedroom?
Anna: No, I didn't.
Dad: Because your bedroom was small. Did your friends come and play in the yard?
Anna: No, they didn't.
Mom: Because your friends live *here*!

TRACK 49

Unit 4, Explore Language
D Listen and say.

1 Did Anna pack her backpack? Yes, she did.
2 Did they go to the park? Yes, they did.
3 Did you play soccer yesterday? No, I didn't.
4 Did you travel by train? No, we didn't.

TRACK 50

Unit 4, Take the Stage, Pronunciation
Listen and say.

/d/ and /t/ traveled
/ɪd/ started
/d/ and /t/ traveled practiced helped
/ɪd/ started visited wanted

Unit 5

TRACK 51

Unit 5, Vocabulary
A Listen and find. What's David's favorite dinosaur?

David: Wow! This is amazing! Look at the dinosaurs! Come on, Anna and Els! This one is huge!
Anna: Yeah! It's body is as big as a house! But its head is really small.
David: It was a plant eater.
Els: It has a really long tail. Oh! Look at that egg. It's a baby dinosaur! It's tiny!
Anna: Aw! So, cute!
…
Mother: Josie! Don't walk on that! It's dangerous!
Anna: Look up there! That one has huge wings! What's it called, David?
David: It's a pter….ano….ptera…. It's a big flying dinosaur with a big mouth!
Els: Pteranodon!
David: Yeah. And, read this! It was a meat eater!
Anna: Oh!
David: Look over there! My favorite! Tyrannosaurus-Rex.
Anna: T-Rex. The really scary one! Look at those teeth! Uhh! Definitely a meat eater.
David: Yeah! It was the king of the dinosaurs! Scary but really cool!

TRACK 52

Unit 5, Vocabulary
B Listen, say, and number the pictures in A.

1 wings
2 dinosaur
3 huge
4 tiny
5 body
6 claws
7 slow
8 dangerous
9 tail
10 scary

TRACK 53

Unit 5, Vocabulary
C Listen. Close your eyes and visualize.

Wings. Imagine you have wings. Mime flying. Say "wings."
Dinosaur. Think of your favorite dinosaur. Is it big or small? Say "dinosaur."
Huge. Imagine you are carrying something huge. Open your arms wide. Say "huge."
Tiny. Imagine a tiny mouse. What noise does it make? Say "tiny."
Body. Where's your body? Move it. Say "body."
Claws. Imagine you have claws. What animal are you? Say "claws."
Slow. Think of a slow animal. What is it? Say "slow."
Dangerous. Think about climbing a tree very high. Is it dangerous? Say "dangerous."
Tail. Think of an animal with a long tail. What animal is it? Say "tail."
Scary. Think about a scary animal? What is it? Say "scary."

TRACK 54

Unit 5, Vocabulary
E Listen and sing. Then watch and sing.

King of the Dinosaurs

Chorus

T-Rex, T-Rex,
King of the dinosaurs,
T-Rex, T-Rex,
Roar! Roar! Roar!

It had a huge body and a great big head,
Its mouth was full of scary teeth.
It had a long tail, two short arms,
And claws on its fingers and feet.

Chorus

It wasn't fast, but it wasn't slow,
It walked on its two back legs.
It didn't have wings—it wasn't a bird.
But it started life as an egg.

Chorus (x 2)

TRACK 55

Unit 5, Explore Language

A Listen and read. Did the dinosaur eat meat?

Presenter: This dinosaur had a huge body and a long tail.
David: Oh, yes! We went to the dinosaur exhibition before this. I saw it there, Jannah.
Presenter: It ran on two feet.
Jannah: Ooh, David! These dinosaurs were fast!
Presenter: It had big claws and big teeth.
Jannah: Wow!
Presenter: It didn't eat plants. It ate meat!
David and Jannah: Help!

TRACK 56

Unit 5, Explore Language

D Listen and say.

1 I saw it there.
2 We didn't see its claws.
3 They didn't go to the lake.
4 Some dinosaurs ate meat.

TRACK 57

Unit 5, Global Citizenship

A Listen to Paz, talk about a museum near her town. What was very dirty there?

Paz: Hi, my name's Paz, and I live in Chile in a place where people have found a lot of dinosaur bones. They've found leg bones and back bones—there are so many bones they can make skeletons and see what dinosaurs really looked like in the past. Near my town, there is a museum where you can try digging in the ground just like real scientists. You can find a lot of different bones and talk to the scientists about what they were in the past. When I went they also had pottery there, like old bowls, cups and jugs. I found a bowl. It was very dirty and it was broken in two parts because it was very old. My friend found a fossil of a fish. These things are both thousands of years old. It's amazing!

TRACK 58

Unit 5, Global Citizenship

B Listen, say, and number the pictures in A.

1 find
2 skeleton
3 jug
4 broken
5 bones
6 fossil
7 dig
8 build
9 pottery

TRACK E

Unit 5, Global Citizenship

Listen. Close your eyes and visualize.

Find. You find candy in the kitchen. How do you feel? Say "find."
Skeleton. Imagine a dinosaur skeleton. Was it a big dinosaur or a small one? Say "skeleton."
Jug. Think about a jug of milk. Take it and pour the milk on your cereal. Say "jug."
Broken. Imagine you have a broken toy. Why is it broken? Say "broken."
Bones. Think about your hands. Feel your bones. Say "bones."
Fossil. You can see a fossil in a stone. What does it look like? Say "fossil."
Dig. Mime digging. How do you feel? Say "dig."
Build. Imagine you're building something. What is it? Say "build."
Pottery. Imagine an old jug, a bowl, and a plate. What color are they? Say "pottery."

TRACK 59

Unit 5, Global Citizenship

D Now listen to Karol and Rashid. Number the pictures. Who lives in an old city?

1 **Karol:** Hello. I'm Karol, and I'm from Poland. Yesterday, my school went to a fantastic museum in Biskupin. There was a model of a very old town. There were houses and a square. You can imagine people living there. We saw old bowls, jugs, and animal bones, too. It was great!
2 **Rashid:** My name's Rashid and I'm from Pakistan. I live in the old city of Taxila. It's nearly 2,000 years old! Archeologists found a lot of interesting things there, like broken pottery and skeletons! My dad's an archeologist, and he works at the Taxila Museum. Sometimes, I go and dig with him. It's great!

TRACK 60

Unit 5, Explore Language

A Listen and read. What were the interesting shapes?

Harold Digger: Look, Jannah! Yesterday, we used this digital scanner.
Jannah: Really? What did you see?
Harold Digger: We saw these interesting shapes.
Jannah: Wow! Did you dig there?
Harold Digger: Yes, we did. We dug for hours.
Jannah: What did you find?
Harold Digger: We found three cans and an old plate.
Jannah: Oh! What did you learn from that?
Harold Digger: We learned that dinosaurs liked to have parties!
Jannah: Oh, Dad!

TRACK 61

Unit 5, Explore Language

D Listen and say.

1 What did you see?
2 What did they think?
3 Did you dig? Yes, we did.
4 Did she find a skeleton? No, she didn't

TRACK 62

Unit 5, Take the Stage, Pronunciation

Listen and say.

/oʊ/ nose
/ɔr/ Ecuador
/oʊ/ nose slow
/ɔr/ Ecuador dinosaur

Unit 6

TRACK 63

Unit 6, Vocabulary

A Listen and find. What color are Mr. Pocassi's eyes?

George: Hello, Mr. Pocassi. This is my Uncle Harold. He has some fossils for you.
Mr. Pocassi: Oh, thank you, Uncle Harold! What wonderful shapes! George, show your uncle your work.
George: OK. This is my painting of some flowers.
Harold: That's great! I love the colors!
George: And that drawing next to the window is of my dad.
Harold: With the straight hair?
George: No, with the mustache! And I made a great sculpture. Come this way.
Harold: Is this your sculpture, George? The girl with the black hair?
George: Yes. It's my sister.
Harold: Oh, yes. I can see that. It's very good!
George: Look at my mask over here, Uncle Harold.
Harold: Which one is it?
George: It has green eyes, red curly hair, and a long beard.
Harold: That's a great mask, George!
George: (whispers) It's Mr. Pocassi!
Harold: (whispers) I know. It looks just like him!

TRACK 64

Unit 6, Vocabulary

B Listen, say, and number the pictures in A.

1 box
2 drawing
3 curly
4 beard
5 straight
6 sculpture

7 mustache (British English: moustache)
8 painting
9 jewelry (British English: jewellery)
10 mask

TRACK 65

Unit 6, Vocabulary

C Listen. Close your eyes and visualize.

Box. Look! There's a box. Open it. What's inside? Say "box."
Drawing. You're doing a drawing. Hold your pencil and draw a flower. Say "drawing."
Curly. Think of someone with curly hair. What color is their hair? Say "curly."
Beard. Imagine you have a beard. Touch your beard. Say "beard."
Straight. Imagine brushing your hair. Is it straight? Say "straight."
Sculpture. Think about a sculpture you know. What is the sculpture of? Say "sculpture."
Mustache. Imagine you have a mustache. Where is it? Say "mustache."
Painting. Imagine you're at a museum. Look at a painting on the wall. Do you like it? Say "painting."
Jewelry. Imagine you are wearing some beautiful jewelry. Is it on your fingers or around your neck? Say "jewelry."
Mask. You can see a mask. Is it an animal or a person? Put it on your face. Say "mask."

TRACK 66

Unit 6, Vocabulary

E Listen and sing. Then watch and sing.

Get Creative
Chorus
Get creative! Have some fun!
Get creative, everyone!
Get creative! Have some fun!
Get creative, everyone!

Don't sit there and watch TV.
Make a painting, play with me.
Do a drawing, bake a cake.
There are a lot of things to make.

Chorus

Don't sit there and wait all day.
Make some jewelry, that's the way!
Make a sculpture with a box.
Make a toy with old socks.

Chorus (x 2)

TRACK 67

Unit 6, Explore Language

A Listen and read. Who did Lizzy paint?

George: Hey, Lizzy! Look at my drawing of Dad. I did it at Art Club.
Lizzy: Hmm. It doesn't look like him. The hands are bigger than Dad's. The hair is curlier than Dad's.
My painting is better than yours. Look!
George: Let me see. Oh! It's … great. What is it? A train? A lion?
Lizzy: No. I painted Dad, too!
George: Oh!

TRACK 68

Unit 6, Explore Language

D Listen and say.

1 The hands are bigger than Dad's.
2 The sculpture is bigger than the mask.
3 His drawing is worse than my painting.
4 My uncle's mustache is longer than my teacher's.

TRACK 69

Unit 6, Global Citizenship

A Listen to Sara talk about how she likes making things. Where's Sara's favorite place?

Sara: I got a great new video game for my birthday. I love making things, and in this game you can make a whole world! First, I put soft grass on the ground, so it's nice to walk on. Then, I built a house with walls, so it's safe inside. Then, I made a lot of different buildings, and it became a town.
Dad wasn't happy because the game was noisy. He came into my room and said, "Be quiet Sara!"
So I showed him the game, and now he's helping me. We're making an interesting building for the center of the town. My favorite place in the world is the Cayan Tower in Dubai. I saw it with my cousins last year. It's very, very tall. I want our building to look the same. Dad is helping me, and the world is getting bigger.
I like making things in the video game. I don't need paper, glue and paints, so my room isn't messy now; it's clean!

TRACK 70

Unit 6, Global Citizenship

B Listen, say, and number the pictures in A.

1 quiet
2 noisy
3 building
4 wall
5 new
6 thick
7 messy
8 clean (British English: tidy)
9 hard
10 soft

TRACK F

Unit 6, Global Citizenship

Listen. Close your eyes and visualize.

Quiet. Shhh! You're in a quiet place. Listen. What can you hear? Say "quiet."
Noisy. Imagine a very loud sound. What is it? Say "noisy."
Building. Think of a special building in your town. Is it a big building or a small building? Say "building."
Wall. Imagine a wall in your living room. What's on the wall? Say "wall."
New. Imagine you have some new shoes. Look at them. What color are they? Say "new."
Thick. Mime holding a thick book. What book is it? Say "thick."
Messy. Think of a messy room. Why is it messy? Say "messy."
Clean. Think about your bedroom. Is it clean? Say "clean."
Hard. Imagine sitting on the floor. How does it feel? Say "hard."
Soft. Imagine sitting on a soft sofa. How do you feel? Say "soft."

TRACK 71

Unit 6, Global Citizenship

D Now listen to Thomas and Natasha. Number the pictures. Who visited a museum?

1 **Natasha:** My name is Natasha. Last year I visited Russia with my parents and we went to Kizhi Island. It's in the center of a big lake and it has a lot of interesting old buildings. They are called Karelian houses, and their walls are all made from wood from local trees. They are so beautiful I did a drawing for my history project.
2 **Thomas:** Hi! I'm Thomas. I love science and I love making things. We went to Belgium on a school trip and saw an awesome museum called the Atomium. The silver balls are rooms and the tubes are hallways. It's so amazing! It looks like an atom. It looked so amazing I made a model of it from paper and cardboard.

TRACK 72

Unit 6, Explore Language

A Listen and read. Why is Lizzy happy?

Joe: Look at all these amazing models, Nathan!
Nathan: Wow! Which do you like best, Joe?
Joe: I like those shops. They're the smallest buildings.
Nathan: And they're the cutest! This fair is the noisiest place.
Joe: Yeah, but it's the coolest!
Nathan: Look at Lizzy! That's the best model.
Joe: Wow! Her mountain is the tallest model here.
Nathan: And she has the biggest smile!

TRACK 73

Unit 6, Explore Language

D Listen and say.

1 They're the smallest buildings.
2 This model city is the coolest city.
3 This wall is the thickest wall in the house.
4 Our classroom is the cleanest room in the school.

TRACK 74

Unit 6, Talk About It, Pronunciation Listen and say.

/g/ Greta
/k/ collage
/g/ Greta going glue
/k/ collage color cut

Unit 7

TRACK 75

Unit 7, Vocabulary

A Listen and find. Who loves singing?

Sally: Hello guys, and welcome to Camp Active. I'm Sally. You're going to have so much fun. Red team, today you're climbing or horseback riding.
Girl 1: Cool, we're on the red team. Let's go climbing together.
Boy 1: OK. But I want to go horseback riding tomorrow. I love horses.
Sally: Off you go! Stay together. Don't get lost. Blue team, you're at the lake today. Do you like boats?
Children: Yeah!
Sally: Well, you can go sailing and you can go kayaking. Or you can be behind the boat and learn waterskiing.
Boy 2: But I can't waterski.
Girl 2: Don't worry. We can learn together. Come on! Let's go.
Sally: Green team. You're inside today, with me. We're doing a show. I hope you like acting or singing.
Joe: Oh, no! I'm terrible at singing! Can I do yoga instead?
Padma: Aw, come on, Joe! I love singing.
Joe: Then Padma, can you sing really loudly so nobody can hear me?
Padma: Haha! OK, Joe
Joe: Great teamwork! High-five!

TRACK 76

Unit 7, Vocabulary

B Listen, say, and number the pictures in A.

1 yoga
2 skating
3 singing
4 kayaking
5 sailing
6 biking (British English: cycling)
7 acting
8 horseback riding (British English: horse-riding)
9 windsurfing
10 climbing
11 waterskiing

TRACK 77

Unit 7, Vocabulary

C Listen. Close your eyes and visualize.

Yoga. Imagine you're doing yoga. Are you standing or sitting? Say "yoga."
Skating. Imagine you're skating. Careful! Don't fall. Say "skating."
Singing. Sing a song. What are you singing? Say "singing."
Kayaking. You're in a kayak on the water. Mime kayaking. Say "kayaking."
Sailing. Imagine you're sailing. Are you on a lake or on the ocean? Say "sailing."
Biking. Mime riding your bike. Where are you biking? Say "biking."
Acting. Mime acting in a play. Is your character happy or sad? Say "acting."
Horseback riding. You're riding a horse. Move up and down. Say "horseback riding."
Windsurfing. Imagine you're windsurfing. Where are you? Say "windsurfing."
Climbing. Mime climbing a tree. How do you feel? Say "climbing."
Waterskiing. Mime waterskiing. Is it quick or slow? Say "waterskiing."

TRACK 78

Narrator: Unit 7, Vocabulary

E Listen and sing. Then watch and sing.

Teamwork Is Number One

Chorus
What do you do as a team, team, team?
What do you do for fun?
We're all good at different things,
But teamwork is number one!

I'm good at acting.
I'm good at singing.
Together we can do a show!
I like windsurfing.
Can you teach me?
Yes! Together we can go, go, go.

Chorus

I'm good at biking,
And horseback riding.
Together we can ride fast or slow.
I like skating.
Can you teach me?
Yes! Together we can go, go, go.

Chorus

TRACK 79

Unit 7, Explore Language

A Listen and read. Who helps Padma?

Imran: Padma, dinner is at 5:45. What do you want to do?
Padma: Well, it's five o'clock, now.
Imran: Great! Climbing is at five o'clock. Let's go!
Padma: Imran! I don't like it!
Imran: You're doing really well.
Padma: What time is it?
Imran: It's 5:15. Not far now!
Imran: You can do it, Padma!
Padma: What time is it now?
Imran: It's 5:30.
Other Kids: That's it, Padma!
Imran: You did it!
Padma: Thanks, everyone! What time is it now?
Other Kids: Dinner time!

TRACK 80

Unit 7, Explore Language

D Listen and say.

1 What time is it? It's 5 o'clock.
2 What time is it? It's 12:30
3 I have a singing class at 5:15.
4 They don't go sailing at 3:45.

TRACK 81

Unit 7, Global Citizenship

A Listen to Mr. Muller talk to Zoe and her friends about a garden project. What does Zoe have for the garden?

Mr. Muller: Hello, everyone from Kids Club USA.
A group of children and teenagers: Hello!
Mr. Muller: Thank you for coming to work with us today on our garden project for our community. It's a garden for all our older neighbors, and we want it to look beautiful for them! Now, I have some paint and brushes to paint the fence with, but there aren't many, so please share them. Zoe, can you and your friends pick up the leaves, please?
Zoe: Yes, OK. We can do that.
Mr. Muller: You can take turns carrying the bag. It's quicker when you work together as a team.
Zoe: Mr. Muller, we have these plants and flowers; we want to give them to the community for the garden.
Mr. Muller: Oh, they're beautiful, Zoe! Thank you. Can you put them over there next to the paint please? Oh, it's great when we all help each other!

TRACK 82

Unit 7, Global Citizenship

B Listen, say, and number the pictures in A.

1 club
2 give
3 work together
4 take turns
5 community
6 share
7 help each other
8 borrow
9 trade (British English: swap)

TRACK G

Unit 7, Global Citizenship

Listen. Close your eyes and visualize.

Club. Are you in a club? What do you do in the club? Say "club."
Give. It's your friend's birthday. Give them a gift. Say "give."
Work together. Think about when you work together. Who do you work together with? Say "work together."
Take turns. Imagine playing a board game. Whose turn is it? Say "take turns."
Community. Think about your community. Who are you thinking about? Say "community."

Share. Do you share your toys? Who do you share them with? Say "share."
Help each other. When do you and your friends help each other? How? Say "help each other."
Borrow. Imagine you need an eraser. Ask your friend. Now give it back. Say "borrow."
Trade. Trade your banana for your friend's apple. Say "trade."

TRACK 83

Unit 7, Global Citizenship

D Now listen to Maia and Bradley. Write the country. Who played on the playground today?

1 **Bradley:** Hi! Bradley here, from the UK. I did a really good project at school. My friends and I wrote some books with children in another school! We didn't see the other children, but we shared our ideas by talking on the computer and writing emails. We drew the pictures, too. The book's fantastic!

2 **Maia:** I'm Maia and I'm from Myanmar. Today I played on the playground at my school. Before, it was very dangerous because there was no fence, and there are a lot of cars on the street. But everyone in the village worked together and built a fence around the school, so now we can play outside! Yay!

TRACK 84

Unit 7, Explore Language

A Listen and read. Why is Imran in the water?

Alisa: Susan, can we borrow this kayak, please?
Susan: Yes, you can use it for the next hour.
Imran: Alisa, can I help you carry it?
Alisa: Thanks! Can you go quickly, please?
Imran: No. Can you go slowly, please?
Alisa: I can help you get out of the water.
Imran: Thanks. Let's try and work together this time.

TRACK 85

Unit 7, Explore Language

D Listen and say.

1 Can we borrow this kayak?
2 Can I help you? Yes, you can.
3 You can use crayons and paints.
4 They can't watch TV after 8 o'clock.

TRACK 86

Unit 7, Talk About It, Pronunciation

Listen and say.

/n/ Jason
/ŋ/ climbing
/n/ Jason mountain open
/ŋ/ climbing morning sailing

Unit 8

TRACK 87

Unit 8, Vocabulary

A Listen and find. Does Mom win?

Ella: That was a great volleyball game!
Bob: Oh, it was so exciting when the player tripped and the other team got a point…
Ella: Yeah!
Bob: Is it Mom's race now?
Ella: No, it's at 3:15. Just wait.
Bob: What time is it now, Ella?
Ella: Three o'clock. Be patient. Let's watch the track and field events. There's running, throwing, and jumping.
Bob: Oh, the throwing is good! Look at the man in the chair. He's so strong!
Ella: Wow! Yeah. And look, there's the long jumper, Javier Kato. He's really popular. A lot of people like watching him. He's my hero.
Bob: Why is he so popular?
Ella: Not many people can jump like that. It's really difficult. Oh, look! There's Mom now. The race is starting, Bob.
Bob and Ella: Come on, Mom! Go! Go! Go!
Bob: Yay! She's third. That was Mom's fastest time!

TRACK 88

Unit 8, Vocabulary

B Listen, say, and number the pictures in A.

1 tennis
2 popular
3 strong
4 exciting
5 difficult
6 patient
7 track and field (British English: athletics)
8 race
9 volleyball
10 gymnastics

TRACK 89

Unit 8, Vocabulary

Listen. Close your eyes and visualize.

Tennis. Hold a tennis ball in your hand. Mime playing tennis. Say "tennis."
Popular. Which sport does everyone like to play in your school? Why is it popular? Say "popular."
Strong. Imagine an elephant carrying a tree. Is it strong? Say "strong."
Exciting. You're watching an exciting movie. What movie is it? Say "exciting."
Difficult. Think of something you find difficult? Why is it difficult? Say "difficult."
Patient. You're having a party tomorrow. You're excited, but you have to wait. Say "patient."
Track and field. Imagine you're doing sports. Are you running, jumping, or throwing? Say "track and field."
Race. You're running a race. Are you winning? Say "race."
Volleyball. Imagine you're playing volleyball. What do you have in your hand? Say "volleyball."
Gymnastics. Imagine you're doing gymnastics. Can you stand on your head? Say "gymnastics."

TRACK 90

Unit 8, Vocabulary

E Listen and sing. Then watch and sing.

Who's Your Hero?

Chorus
Who's your hero?
Is it a sports hero?
Who's your hero?
Shout out the name. (x 2)

Do they play tennis,
Soccer, or volleyball?
Do they do gymnastics,
Or play basketball?

Chorus (x 2)

Who's my sports hero?
It's difficult to say.
Sports are so exciting,
In many different ways.
Chorus (x 2)

TRACK 91

Unit 8, Explore Language

A Listen and read. Who's the hero?

Dad: That looks exciting. Is it your homework?
Bob: No, it's more exciting than homework. I'm making a poster about my hero.
Dad: Oh, so who's your hero?
Bob: It's a secret.
Dad: Hmmm. Is he popular?
Bob: He's more popular than my favorite actor.
Dad: Is he strong?
Bob: He's stronger than … an elephant.
Dad: Oh, this is difficult.
Bob: Yes, it's more difficult than my math homework!
Dad: Is it me?
Bob: Noooo! Look! It's The Human Elephant!
Dad: Oh!

TRACK 92

Unit 8, Explore Language

D Listen and say.

1 It's more exciting than homework.
2 Gymnastics is more popular than track and field.
3 Tennis is more difficult than volleyball.
4 My mother is more patient than me.

TRACK 93

Unit 8, Global Citizenship

A Listen to Felipe talk about his hero. Who's his hero?

Felipe: My cousin Paco is older than I am, and he's really friendly—always smiling. He studies math. He's very intelligent. Paco is really good at playing the guitar. Now, he's teaching me to play, too; he's so helpful. Sometimes, he sends me books about music. He knows I like interesting music, especially music from our country, Spain. Sometimes, I was mean to my little sister. I got angry and I pulled her hair, and I was a bit selfish. I just didn't like her playing with any of my toys. But Paco is always kind and thoughtful to her. Now, I try to do the same. I want to be just like my cousin! He's my hero.

TRACK 94

Unit 8, Global Citizenship

B Listen, say, and number the pictures in A.

1 thoughtful
2 friendly
3 interesting
4 mean
5 selfish
6 brave
7 beautiful
8 intelligent
9 helpful

TRACK H

Unit 8, Global Citizenship

Listen. Close your eyes and visualize.

Thoughtful. Imagine a thoughtful person. How is this person thoughtful? Say "thoughtful."

Friendly. Think about someone you know who is friendly. Who is it? Say "friendly."

Interesting. You're in an interesting class. What are you learning about? Say "interesting."

Mean. Think about a mean character in a story. What does this person do? Say "mean."

Selfish. Are you selfish sometimes? How do you feel? Say "selfish."

Brave. Imagine you're climbing a tree to help a cat. Do you feel brave? Say "brave."

Beautiful. Imagine a beautiful place. What can you see? Say "beautiful."

Intelligent. Think of an intelligent friend. What are they good at? Say "intelligent."

Helpful. You are being helpful at home. What are you doing? Say "helpful."

TRACK 95

Unit 8, Global Citizenship

Now listen to Mónica and Shayma. Number the pictures. Whose hero is strong?

1 **Mónica:** Hi! My name is Mónica and I'm from Cuba. I like reading, so my hero is Margarita Engle. She writes fantastic books about brave and interesting people. My favorite book is *Drum Dream Girl*. It's about a girl who wants to play in a boys' drum band because she loves playing drums. A lot of her stories are about people in Cuba.

2 **Shayma:** Hello! I'm Shayma. I love track and field. I go running every day. I want to be a runner like Abderrahim Zhiou. He's from my country, Tunisia. He can't see very well, so it's difficult for him, but he's a really strong and quick runner. He has a lot of medals from races, too. He is my hero.

TRACK 96

Unit 8, Explore Language

A Listen and read. Why is the teacher intelligent?

Mr. Perez: The first school award is for … Dave Lee. He is the most helpful student. Good job, Dave! Now, our best teacher. Let's listen to Matilde and Dave.

Matilde in video: I think she's the most thoughtful teacher.

David in video: English is the most interesting class. Her activities are really fun.

Matilde in video: I think she's the most intelligent teacher because she teaches everything.

Mr. Perez: The best teacher is Jane.

Jane: Thank you very much. I'm the happiest teacher, too!

TRACK 97

Unit 8, Explore Language

D Listen and say.

1 He's the most helpful student.
2 Our most thoughtful student is Sarah.
3 This is the most interesting book in the library.
4 Which sport is the most dangerous?

TRACK 98

Unit 8, Talk About It, Pronunciation

Listen and say.

/oʊ/ OK
/aʊ/ how
/oʊ/ OK go so
/aʊ/ how now wow

Unit 9

TRACK 99

Unit 9, Vocabulary

A Listen and find. What does Arni do?

Dad: OK. Arni and Matilde, you can look around the castle but don't run, and don't touch anything!

Arni and Matilde: Yes, Dad.

Dad: Come back here at half past twelve for lunch.

Arni: OK. Let's go up the stairs.

Matilde: This is a bedroom. Look at that huge bed. And look at this closet! They had a lot of clothes! Where are you Arni?

Arni: In the bathroom.

Matilde: Get out of the bathtub!

Arni: Let's go to the tower!

Matilde: OK.

Arni: Look, Matilde! We can go out on to the balcony.

Matilde: Wow! You can see everything!

Arni: Look at the little people down there! Hello-o! Come on! Let's go down to the basement!

Matilde: Ooh! It's scary! I can't see.

Arni: Wooooooo!

Matilde: Very funny, Arni! Here's a lamp. I can see now. Arnie, don't close the door!

Arni: Ha ha! Oh, no! I can't open the door! Help!

Matilde: Help!

TRACK 100

Unit 9, Vocabulary

B Listen, say, and number the pictures in A.

1 closet (British English: wardrobe)
2 basement
3 balcony
4 fridge
5 cabinet (British English: cupboard)
6 bathtub (British English: bath)
7 attic
8 stairs
9 stove (British English: cooker)
10 tower
11 lamp
12 castle

TRACK 101

Unit 9, Vocabulary

C Listen. Close your eyes and visualize.

Closet. You're in your bedroom. Open the closet door. What can you see? Say "closet."

Basement. Imagine you're going down into the basement of a castle. Is it scary? Say "basement."

Balcony. You are standing on the balcony of a tall house. What can you see? Say "balcony."

Fridge. Think about your fridge at home. Is there any milk in the fridge? Say "fridge."

Cabinet. You can see a cabinet in the kitchen. Open the door. What can you see? Say "cabinet."

Bathtub. Think of a bathtub. Get in the bathtub. Is the water hot or cold? Say "bathtub."
Attic. Imagine you are in an attic at the top of a castle. Is it dark? Say "attic."
Stairs. Mime walking on the stairs. Are you going up or down? Say "stairs."
Stove. Can you see a stove? What is on the stove? Can you smell it? Say "stove."
Tower. Think of a tower. How tall is it? Are you standing at the top or the bottom? Say "tower."
Lamp. Imagine a lamp. Turn it on. Turn it off. Say "lamp."
Castle. Imagine a big castle. How old is it? Say "castle."

TRACK 102

Unit 9, Vocabulary

E Listen and sing. Then watch and sing.

In the Scary Castle

In the scary castle,
There's a mouse in the fridge,
A spider in the bathtub,
And noises everywhere!

In the scary castle,
There's a bird in the closet,
A mouse in the fridge …

In the scary castle,
There's a bat on the stove,
A bird in the closet …

In the scary castle,
There's a skeleton in the attic,
A bat on the stove …

Wooooahhhhhhh!

TRACK 103

Unit 9, Explore Language

A Listen and read. What game did Hilda play?

Arni and Hilda: Hahaha! (laughing).
Arni: Castles are so exciting, Hilda!
Hilda: I know! My Uncle Rolf and my cousins live in a castle.
Arni: Wow! Really?!
Hilda: Yes, we visited them last year. It was really fun.
Arni: What did you do?
Hilda: We played a game. I looked for my cousins in every room!
Arni: Did you find them?
Hilda: No, I didn't find them. They found me!

TRACK 104

Unit 9, Explore Language

D Listen and say.

1 We visited him.
2 We didn't play board games.
3 I saw the tower from the lake.
4 Did you go there?

TRACK 105

Unit 9, Global Citizenship

A Listen to Shane talk about a castle visit. Did he have fun there?

Shane: Hello, I'm Shane, and I live in Bunratty in Ireland. We have a castle right in our village. It's called Bunratty Castle. We had a special meal there. I was so excited because it was like living in the past! We dressed up in old clothes. My dad was annoyed because his pants were too short and he looked funny. Then, we went into a huge dining room and we sat at a long table with a lot of other people. There was music and dancing. My baby sister, Mary, was a bit frightened when a man came to our table and started laughing and shouting. But he was an actor! I was very proud of her because she didn't cry. And I was really surprised because she liked the food, too. Mom was happy because we all had so much fun. We were sad when we had to go home, but Mary was very tired.

TRACK 106

Unit 9, Global Citizenship

B Listen, say, and number the pictures in A.

1 happy
2 excited
3 tired
4 proud
5 sad
6 surprised
7 angry
8 frightened
9 bored
10 annoyed

TRACK 1

Unit 9, Global Citizenship

Listen. Close your eyes and visualize.

Happy. Smile. When are you happy? Say "happy ."
Excited. It's your birthday and you're having a party. Are you excited? Say "excited."
Tired. It's time to go to bed. Mime being tired. Say "tired."
Proud. Your teacher puts your poster on the wall. Are you proud? Say "proud."
Sad. Imagine a sad person. Why are they sad? Say "sad."
Surprised. You're hiding behind a door. Jump out. Is your friend surprised? Say "surprised."
Angry. Make an angry face. Why are you angry? Say "angry."
Frightened. It's night time and you hear a noise. Mime being frightened. Say "frightened."
Bored. You have nothing to do. How do you feel? Mime being bored. Say "bored."
Annoyed. Are you sometimes a little bit angry with your brother or sister or friend? When? Say "annoyed."

TRACK 107

Unit 9, Global Citizenship

D Now listen to Min-Seo and Boris. Write the country. Which castle has four towers?

1 **Boris:** Hi! My name is Boris and I'm from Bulgaria. Last week I was really excited because my school visited Baba Vida Castle. It's a very old castle with four big towers and very thick walls. It's a museum, so you can see how people lived in the past. In the summer, there are concerts and theater performances, too.
2 **Min-Seo:** Hello. I'm Min-Seo. Gyeongbok Palace, in South Korea, is a really famous old building. And it's huge! It has 500 buildings and thousands of rooms. There are two different museums inside that people can visit today. Many years ago the king lived there, and he had a lot of people to take care of him. There was a big wall all around it, because people were frightened and wanted to stay safe.

TRACK 108

Unit 9, Explore Language

A Listen and read. Does the castle have a TV?

Rolf: Come into this room. It was the great hall.
Carol: Wow! It's huge.
Rolf: There weren't any TVs or computers, but the children weren't bored.
Carol: What did they do?
Rolf: They danced and sang. They watched plays and played music. They were happy.
Carol: Where was the kitchen?
Rolf: Well, there were three kitchens. They were down the stairs, in the basement.
Carol: Was there a bathroom?
Rolf: No, there wasn't.
Carol: Oh, no! I need the bathroom.
Rolf: It's OK, there's a bathroom here now!

TRACK 109

Unit 9, Explore Language

D Listen and say.

1 There was a kitchen.
2 There weren't any TVs.
3 Were there any towers? Yes, there were.
4 Was there a TV? No, there wasn't.

TRACK 110

Unit 9, Take the Stage, Pronunciation

Listen and say.

/s/ Sam
/ð/ this
/s/ Sam so swimming
/ð/ this the there

Unit 10

TRACK 111

Unit 10, Vocabulary

A Listen and find. When is the family's trip?

Dad: Time to go, everybody. We have a long trip to Aunt Connie's house! Do you have your suitcases?

Mom and Carol: Yes.

Dad: Do you have our passports, Mom?

Mom: Yes, I have them here.

Dad: OK. Everybody get in the car.

Carol: Um, Dad? Do you have the train tickets?

Dad: Oh, no! Quick! Carol! Get the tickets! Thanks! OK. Let's go!

Mom: Look at all the cars! The traffic is terrible!

Nathan: Hey, Carol!

Carol: Look! In that taxi! It's Elena and Nathan! Hey, Elena!

Elena: Hi! We're going to the airport to catch our plane!

Carol: We're going to the station. Bye!

Nathan: Have fun!

Elena: Have a good time!

Mom: Phew! We're here!

Dad: Everybody out! OK. Do you have your suitcases?

Mom and Carol: Yes.

Dad: And the passports, Mom?

Mom: Yes!

Carol: Do you have the tickets, Dad?

Dad: YES! Let's go!

Carol: Hello, Mr. Digger! Hi, Jannah!

Harold Digger: Hello, Carol!

Jannah: Are you on our train, Carol?

Carol: I don't know!

Station master: Tickets, please!

Dad: Here you are.

Station master: Sorry, Sir. But, these tickets are for tomorrow.

Mom and Carol: Oh, no!

TRACK 112

Unit 10, Vocabulary

B Listen, say, and number the pictures in A.

1 plane
2 station
3 suitcase
4 boat
5 traffic
6 passport
7 airport
8 journey
9 ticket
10 country (British English: countryside)

TRACK 113

Unit 10, Vocabulary

C Listen. Close your eyes and visualize.

Plane. Imagine a plane flying in the sky. Point to it. Say "plane."
Station. You're at the station. How many trains can you see? Say "station."
Suitcase. Mime carrying a big suitcase. What's in it? Say "suitcase."
Boat. Mime standing on a boat. Can you feel it moving? Say "boat."
Traffic. Think about sitting in a car with a lot of traffic all around you. What can you see? Say "traffic."
Passport. You're holding a passport. Open it and look inside. Say "passport."
Airport. Imagine an airport. What can you see? Say "airport."
Journey. You're going on a journey. Are you traveling by bus, car, or train? Say "journey."
Ticket. You have a ticket in your hand. Where are you going? Say "ticket."
Country. Imagine you are in the country. Look around. What can you see? Say "country."

TRACK 114

Unit 10, Vocabulary

E Listen and sing. Then watch and sing.

Let's Go on a Journey

Chorus

Let's go on a journey around the world
By land or sea or air.
I want to see different countries,
And make new friends everywhere. (x 2)

I want to see the country from a bus,
And walk by a lake and climb a tree.
I want to look at mountains from a plane.
Do you like the idea? Come with me!

Chorus

I want to see an island from a sandy beach,
And go on a boat on the sea.
I have my passport, ticket and suitcase.
Do you like the idea? Come with me!

Chorus

TRACK 115

Unit 10, Explore Language

A Listen and read. Who is the family visiting?

Nathan: That was a long journey.

Elena: Where's the hotel, Dad?

Rolf: Oh, we aren't going to stay in a hotel.

Elena: Really?

Rolf: We're going to stay somewhere better than a hotel. First, we're going to go by bus to the lake. And from the lake we're going to travel by boat.

Nathan: That's a lot of traveling!

Rolf: And after the boat…

Elena: Yes?

Rolf: You're going to look for Grandma.

Nathan: Grandma?

Rolf: And Grandma's going to take us to her new house.

Nathan and Elena: Hooray!

TRACK 116

Unit 10, Explore Language

D Listen and say.

1 Grandma's going to take us.
2 She's going to visit the castle in August.
3 He isn't going to swim next week.
4 They aren't going to see the country tomorrow.

TRACK 117

Unit 10, Global Citizenship

A Listen to Daan talk to his dad about his journey to school. How is Daan going to travel there?

Daan: Hooray! It's sunny today. I'm going to go to school on my bike.

Dad: Really? I know we love riding bikes here in Holland, but I think it's cold outside.

Daan: Oh, it is a bit cloudy and gray now. That's OK. I'm going to wear a sweater.

Dad: It's windy, too. Look at the trees moving.

Daan: Hmm. Maybe I need a coat.

Dad: And remember, it rains a lot.

Daan: (determined) Don't worry, I'm going to wear a hat.

Dad: Can you hear that? Is that thunder? And did you see the lightning?

Daan: (Sigh!)

Dad: That's a bad storm, Daan. I'm going to drive you to school today.

Daan: (defeated) OK. Thanks, Dad!

TRACK 118

Unit 10, Global Citizenship

B Listen, say, and number the pictures in A.

1 sunny
2 rainbow
3 storm
4 thunder
5 windy
6 foggy
7 cloudy
8 lightning
9 snow
10 rain

TRACK J

Unit 10, Global Citizenship

Listen. Close your eyes and visualize.

Sunny. Imagine the sun on your face. Is it hot or cold? Say "sunny."
Rainbow. It's not raining now; you can see a rainbow. Count the colors. Say "rainbow."
Storm. Think about a storm. What can you hear? What can you see? Say "storm."
Thunder. Listen. You can hear thunder. How do you feel? Say "thunder."
Windy. It's a windy day. Act out being a tree on a windy day. Say "windy."
Foggy. Imagine it's a foggy day. What can you see? Say "foggy."

Cloudy. Look up at the sky. It's cloudy. What shapes are the clouds? Say "cloudy."
Lightning. It's dark and there's lightning in the sky. Draw lightning with your finger. Say "lightning."
Snow. Imagine you're walking in the snow. Is it difficult to walk? Say "snow."
Rain. Imagine you're in the rain. How does it feel? Say "rain."

TRACK 119

Unit 10, Global Citizenship

D Now listen to Dakila and María. Write the country. Who lives on the side of a valley?

1 **Dakila:** Hello. I'm Dakila and I come from the Philippines. I live in the country, and every day, I have a very long journey to school. I walk down the mountain and through the forest. Some days I walk really slowly because it's sunny and hot. The journey is two hours long, but I love school, especially math. And my friends, of course.

2 **María:** I'm María and I'm from Colombia. My journey to school is really fun! I live on one side of a valley and my school is on the other side of the valley. I go there by zip line. I have to carry my little brother. It's very quick, and it's exciting because I feel like I'm flying. But sometimes, when it's windy or foggy, it's a little scary.

TRACK 120

Unit 10, Explore Language

A Listen and read. Where's Grandma's house?

Grandma: Hello, my dears! Let's go to my house.
Nathan: Great! Where's your car?
Grandma: No car. We're going to walk. First, we walk through the forest.
Nathan: I can't see your house!
Grandma: We're going to walk around the mountain. Look! My house is on the other side of the river.
Nathan: Oh! Are we going to walk over that bridge?
Grandma: Yes, we walk up the steps and then over the bridge. Surprise! Welcome!

TRACK 121

Unit 10, Explore Language

D Listen and say.

1 Let's walk through the forest.
2 We need to walk around the mountain.
3 Let's go under the bridge.
4 You walk up the steps and over the bridge.

TRACK 122

Unit 10, Talk About It, Pronunciation

Listen and say.

/r/ rain
/w/ would
/r/ rain round sorry
/w/ would one Wednesday

Play 1 Units 1-5

TRACK 123

Adventures on Purple Mountain

Narrator: Sean is using his laptop.
Resham: Hi, Sean! What are you doing?
Sean: Hello, Resham and Ellie. I'm reading about Purple Mountain. It's really beautiful!
Ellie: Let's go there today!
Sean: Great idea, Ellie! Mom! We want to go to Purple Mountain. Is that OK?
Mom: OK. But take my cell phone with you.
Sean: Thanks! Let's tell Mario and Rafa.
Narrator: The friends arrived at Purple Mountain.
Sean: Everybody ready?
All: Yes!
Sean: Let's go!
Chorus: *We're walking up the mountain.*
Up, up we go ...
Rafa: You're walking very slowly. Come on, Mario!
Ellie: What are you eating?
Mario: A cupcake.
All: A cupcake?
Mario: I didn't have my breakfast! I'm hungry!
Sean: Come on!
Ellie: What are you eating now, Mario?
Mario: Some potato chips.
Rafa: How much food do you have?
Mario: A bag of potato chips, a box of cookies, and a bag of cherries. And, I had a cupcake.
Resham: You're very hungry!
Sean: Look down there! There's a lake.
Ellie: And look at the river. You can see it go all the way to the ocean!
Rafa: This is a great place!
Sean: Let's go.
Chorus: *We're walking up the mountain.*
Up, up we go.
You're walking very slowly.
Come on, Mario!
Resham: Oh, look! There's a forest.
Narrator: The friends were lost in the forest!
Rafa: Where are we?
Sean: This is a little scary!
Resham: Call your mom!
Sean: The cell phone isn't working!
Ellie: Listen! Can you hear that noise in the trees?
Resham: What is it?
Rafa: Is it a dangerous animal?
Sean: Is it a bear?
Ellie: It's coming! Oh, no!
Mario: Hi, everyone!
Resham: It's you, Mario!
Mario: What's the matter?
Sean: We don't know where we are!
Ellie: And we can't get home.
Mario: Yes, we can. Look!
Rafa: We can follow your food crumbs!
Resham: Great, Mario!
Chorus: *We're walking down the mountain.*
Down, down we go.
We're following the crumbs!
Thank you, Mario!

Play 2 Units 6-10

TRACK 124

King Grandpa's Treasure

Narrator: It was summer. Sofia and Ramón went to Eric's castle on vacation, but Eric's family wasn't happy.
Eric: Hi. Can you help us?
Sofia: Yes. What's the matter?
King Grandpa: It's my treasure.
Queen Grandma: We don't know where it is.
Ramón: We can look for it.
Prince Dad: Yes, but our castle has a lot of rooms!
Eric: Let's work in teams. We can look in different rooms.
Princess Mom: That's a great idea! Let's go.
Chorus: *We're looking for the treasure*
And we're working together!
Narrator: King Grandpa and Prince Dad went down to the basement.
Prince Dad: It's messy. I'm scared.
King Grandpa: Me, too!
Prince Dad: I'm going to look in the cabinets.
King Grandpa: Did you find my treasure?
Prince Dad: No, I didn't. Sorry. But I found my boat.
King Grandpa: Ooh!
Chorus: *We're looking for the treasure*
And we're working together!
Narrator: Queen Grandma and Princess Mom climbed the tower.
Queen Grandma: This was my playroom. I played here with my cousins.
Princess Mom: I can't see the treasure here. What's that small building?
Queen Grandma: It's a model castle. I built it for your birthday.
Princess Mom: Thank you! It's wonderful.
Chorus: *We're looking for the treasure*
And we're working together!
Narrator: Eric, Ramón, and Sofia went to the king's bedroom.

Eric: This is the biggest bedroom in the castle.
Sofia: These paintings are beautiful.
Eric: This is the most famous painting.
Narrator: Ramón touched the painting. It opened, and there was a secret room.
Ramón: Oops, Sorry!
Eric: This is exciting!
Sofia: Come on!
Ramón: What's this big box?
Eric: That's King Grandpa's treasure!
Sofia: Hooray! Can you help me carry it?
Ramón: Yes, we can.
Chorus: *We're looking for the treasure*
And we're working together!

Narrator: Eric, Sofia, and Ramón carried the treasure into the Great Hall.
Ramón: We found your treasure!
Eric: It was in a secret room.
All: Great job!
King Grandpa: Thank you so much.
Sofia: What's the treasure?
King Grandpa: Look! These are my favorite things.
Everyone: Oooohhhh!
Ramón: Why is that treasure?
Queen Grandma: Because they're the most important things from his life.

King Grandpa: I traveled on this plane! And I ran in this race!
Prince Dad: It's like my boat!
Princess Mom: And my model castle!
Eric: It's 2 o'clock.
Princess Mom: Let's eat lunch.
King Grandpa: And after, I'm going to tell you about my trips!
All: With your treasure!
Chorus: *We have the treasure*
And we're working together!

Literacy Book

Phonics Review

TRACK 1

Phonics Review

A Listen and say. Then look at the pictures and write the words with the long *a* sound.

cake
plane
rain
table
grapes
paint
baby
plate

TRACK 2

Phonics Review

B Listen and say. Then choose the words with the long e sound.

1 bed
tree
red
2 pretty
teeth
net
3 hen
leg
green
4 sweet
pen
chef
5 nest
eat
peg
6 bee
desk
egg
7 these
elephant
help
8 mess
get
leaf

TRACK 3

Phonics Review

C Listen and say. Then complete the words with the long *u* sound.

1 glue
2 cute
3 juice
4 Tuesday
5 blue
6 fruit
7 soup
8 room

TRACK 4

Phonics Review

D Listen and say. Choose the letters that make the long *i* sound. Then complete the table.

1 Friday
2 kind
3 nine
4 bike
5 ice
6 lion
7 climb
8 drive

TRACK 5

Phonics Review

E Listen and say. Then complete the sentences using a word with the long *o* sound.

1 soap
2 goat
3 bowl
4 boat
5 yellow
6 toe
7 hippo
8 sofa

TRACK 6

Phonics Review

A Listen and choose the correct word with *sh*.

1 On the beach, we find shells.
2 There is a fish in the sea.
3 Put on your shoes.
4 Remember to wash your hands before lunch.
5 Please shut the door.
6 Her shirt is yellow.
7 I brush my teeth in the morning.
8 His hair is very short.

TRACK 7

Phonics Review

B Listen and say. Use *st* or *ch* to complete the words. Then match.

stick
chair
strawberries
check
star
chicken
storm
child

TRACK 8

Phonics Review

D Listen and say. Then listen again and write the words starting with *pr* or *fr*.

1 fries
2 free
3 prince
4 front
5 pretty
6 friend
7 present
8 frog
9 prize

Unit 1

TRACK 9

Unit 1, Fiction, *The After-School Inventor*

Clara: My name is Clara Doodle. I invent things after school.
I have a lot of new ideas and some of them are cool.
Here are my rain glasses and my umbrella pen.
OK. Some ideas are not so good …
… but I always try again!
…

Clara: When I have an idea, I always make a plan.
I draw and change, and change and draw.
I do the best I can. Here's my smart eraser.
It tells me when I'm wrong.
And my alarm clock pillow wakes me with a song.

Pillow: Goooood morning, Clara!

Clara: This is my special mirror. It changes what I see.
When I click this button, I see the back of me. But something's not quite right! It's changing all my clothes.
Oh, no! I have long purple hair and a big long nose.
Mom says my room's a mess, but I don't like to clean.

Mom: What a mess!

Clara: Here's my new invention … it's a big clean-up machine.

TRACK 10

Unit 1, *The After-School Inventor*, Words in Context, Find these words in the reading. What do you think they mean?

invent
try again
change
mirror
mess
invention
machine

TRACK 11

Unit 1, Explore the Reading, Phonics, Listen and say.

/cl/ climb clue cloud close clap

TRACK 12

Unit 1, Nonfiction, *My Good Ideas Book*

One. Get started. Write your ideas down. A lot of them! Choose a good one.
You need: ideas, time, a notebook, a pencil
When you have a problem, look for a solution.
My pencils always roll off the table. How can I stop them?
I can shape them like hexagons.
Look at animals and plants. They can give you good ideas. … Use old things to make something new. …
Two. Work on your idea. Draw a picture of your idea. Drawing helps you to see your idea. When you see a problem, you can change it.
These are some of da Vinci's drawings.
Make a model of your idea. Use your model to test your idea.
Three. Improve your idea. Show your idea to your friends and family. Listen to what they say and maybe change your idea.

Karl Benz: What do you think?

Bertha: No horses. Good idea!

Friend: Only three wheels?

Don't give up! Try again … and again … and again!

TRACK 13

Unit 1, *My Good Ideas Book*, Words in Context, Find these words in the reading. What do you think they mean?

problem
solution
hexagon
improve
parachute
model

Unit 2

TRACK 14

Unit 2, Nonfiction, *Chuseok: Korea's Harvest Festival*

Who can weave the most cloth? Two teams have a contest to find out. They weave and weave for a whole month!
It is the night of the full moon. The king comes. "This team wins!" he says. The prize is a big feast for both teams.
Some people say this is the beginning of the *Chuseok* holiday.
Today, the festival of *Chuseok* is still an important holiday in Korea. It is at the end of summer. It lasts three days. People always go home. They spend time with their families. They want to celebrate and give thanks for the harvest.
…
Everyone has a feast a big feast on *Chuseok*. There are many kinds of food. People make special rice cakes called *songpyeon*.
Some people buy new clothes to wear on *Chuseok*. There are dances and games.
Chuseok is also a time for Koreans to remember their ancestors. Families have a special ceremony. They bow and offer food from the harvest. This shows they care about their family. *Chuseok* is all about being thankful.

TRACK 15

Unit 2, *Chuseok: Korea's Harvest Festival*, Words in Context,
Find these words in the reading. What do you think they mean?

weave
cloth
contest
festival
harvest
ancestors

TRACK 16

Unit 2, Fiction, *First Harvest*

Narrator: Harvest time is here. The family works hard on the farm. They dig up vegetables. They pick fruit.

Dad: "I'm worried. It's hard for plants to grow here. There isn't much water,"

Narrator: says Dad.

Dad: "I don't believe it! These carrots are beautiful,"

Narrator: says Dad.
There are pink potatoes and purple corn. There are tomatoes with red and green stripes. There is red pineapple. There are orange peas.

August: "We have a lot of food!"

Narrator: says August

Dad: "And we worked hard for it,"

Narrator: says Dad.

Dad: "Thank you!"

…

Mom: "How can we celebrate?"

Narrator: asks Mom.

Ruth: "I know, let's get everyone together. We can have a feast!"

Narrator: says Ruth.

Dad: "That's a great idea,"

Narrator: says Dad.

Dad: "This is our very first harvest, after all."

Mom: "I want to make an apple pie,"

Narrator: says Mom.

Mom: "You two can help."

…

Ruth: "Can we go outside and play first?"

Narrator: asks Ruth.

Ruth: "Please?"

Dad: "Oh, all right,"

Narrator: says Dad.

Mom: "Check your space suits before you go,"

Narrator: Mom says.

Mom: "And make sure you have a lot of air."

August and Ruth: "We will!"

Narrator: say August and Ruth.

TRACK 17

Unit 2, *First Harvest*, Words in Context

Find these words in the reading. What do you think they mean?

pick
worried
grow
believe
stripes

TRACK 18

Unit 2, Explore the Reading, Phonics Listen and say.

/st/ fast last lost best test

Unit 3

TRACK 19

Unit 3, Fiction, *The Bear and I*

I'm from a land of wind and cold,
With fields of ice and snow.
My story starts when I was young,
Many years ago.
My fishing hole was in the ice,
Each morning, fish were there.
But one day I was face to face,
With a giant arctic bear.
The polar bear was twice my size,
Its fur was the color of the snow.
When it was busy with my fish,
It was my chance to go.
From that day on, for many years,
The bear was my enemy.
It was often near my fishing hole,
It was hungry, just like me.
...
After many warm winters,
The ice on the sea was thin.
One morning, the bear was near me,
Crack! The bear and I fell in.
It was difficult to swim
In a trap of ice and sea.
But we were in the trap together,
The bear was not my enemy.
From that day on, it was clear,
Things change as years go by.
There is danger in this changing world,
For the bear and I.
Today the ice is melting,
And I am getting old,
But I hope to see the bear once more,
Living in the cold.

TRACK 20

Unit 3, *The Bear and I*, Words in Context

Find these words in the reading. What do you think they mean?

hole
twice
enemy
thin
trap
melting

TRACK 21

Unit 3, Explore the Reading, Phonics, Listen and say.

/ng/ sing long reading bang spring

TRACK 22

Unit 3, Nonfiction, *Clean Cars*

Cars are everywhere! We use them to go shopping, go to school, and go on vacation.
A lot of cars use gasoline for energy.
Gasoline comes from oil in the ground.
Gasoline cars are fast, but they are noisy and make the air dirty. Dirty air is bad for animals, plants, and people. It changes our climate, too.
...
Not long ago, most cars were gasoline cars.
Now some cars use biofuels. Biofuels come from plants like corn, but these plants need big fields and a lot of water. These cars make the air only a little dirty. Like gasoline cars, they go fast, but they aren't very quiet.
They are very noisy.
Today, there are clean cars that don't use gasoline or biofuel.
These cars use electricity, just like a TV or a lamp. They are fast and quiet. They are clean, but they are expensive.
...
Other cars use air for energy. They are not very expensive. They are quiet and clean, but they are small and slow.
Solar cars use energy from the sun. Some of them are fast. There are even races!
They are not noisy or dirty, but they can be expensive. Not many people have them.
Clean cars are one way to have a clean world.

TRACK 23

Unit 3, *Clean Cars*

Words in Context, Find these words in the reading. What do you think they mean?

gasoline
energy
oil
noisy
electricity
expensive

Unit 4

TRACK 24

Unit 4, Nonfiction, *Where is She?*

In 1503, Leonardo da Vinci painted the Mona Lisa.
In 1911, Vincenzo Peruggia walked into the Louvre Museum in Paris. Peruggia had a plan. He wanted to steal the painting.
Peruggia dressed like a museum worker.
He waited for the other workers to leave and lifted the painting off the wall. He put it under his clothes and walked out of the museum!
On the way out, he took the painting out of the frame. He rolled it up and hid it again.
He walked out the door.
...
The next day, someone wanted to see the Mona Lisa. But there was only an empty space on the wall. A museum worker called the police.
Soon, the Mona Lisa was in the news all over the world. Everyone learned about the robbery. People lined up to see the empty space on the wall! The Mona Lisa was famous.
For two years, the police couldn't find the painting. Where was the Mona Lisa?
...
In 1913, Peruggia tried to sell the Mona Lisa.
The man looked at the painting and then called the police. They arrested Peruggia.
At last, the Mona Lisa returned home to the Louvre. Because of the robbery, the Mona Lisa is one of the most famous paintings in the world!

TRACK 25

Unit 4, *Where is She?*, Words in Context

Find these words in the reading. What do you think they mean?

plan
steal
lifted
robbery
arrested

TRACK 26

Unit 4, Fiction, *The Angry Mountain*

That evening, I played on the beach by Papa's boat. Then the loud noises started.
It sounded like thunder. Under my feet, the ground moved. Then it stopped. It was the mountain. Mount Tambora was angry again.
I wanted to see more, so I climbed a tree. I looked out at Mount Tambora. Fire went up into the sky. There was fire everywhere.
I needed to find Mama and Papa.
The village streets were full of people. Dogs barked, people shouted. No one knew what to do. Some people went inside and locked their doors. A big cloud filled the sky.
...
"We must leave," said Mama. Papa packed up our things. We carried our things and ran to our boat. Ash and stones fell down from the sky. It was so dark. We couldn't see the mountain anymore.
The small boat bounced up and down over large waves. More sounds of thunder came from the mountain. Mama hugged me close.
I tried to sleep, but my dreams were full of scary things.
The next morning, at sunrise, we looked back at the island, and I cried. Nothing was left of our home—just ash and stones.

Then we saw a ship on the sea. We waved and it saw us. We were finally safe. Our home was gone, but we had each other.

TRACK 27

Unit 4, *The Angry Mountain*, Words in Context

Find these words in the reading. What do you think they mean?

thunder
bark
ash
dream
sunrise

TRACK 28

Unit 4, Explore the Reading, Phonics

Listen and say.

/nd/ end stand wind send find hand

Unit 5

TRACK 29

Unit 5, Fiction, *The Time Book*

It was time for Jannah to go to bed. *Just one more story*, she thought. *What's this? I don't remember this book. It looks interesting.*

On the book, there was a picture of an old street with a lot of people. She saw a girl. *That girl looks like me!* she thought. *How strange!*

She opened the book.

"Oh! Where am I?" asked Jannah. She was in a very old city.

"Look!" said an old woman next to her. "The pharaoh is coming."

...

"I want to see the pharaoh," said the woman. Then Jannah saw the huge chariot.

"Look out!" she shouted.

"Oh, thank you," said the woman. "I can't see very well."

"Try my glasses," said Jannah.

"Glasses?"

"Yes, they help you see. Put them in front of your eyes."

The old woman was surprised. "Now I can see everything. There's the pharaoh!"

...

"Who's that girl?" asked the pharaoh.

"What strange clothes. Stop her!"

"Oh, no! They're coming," said the old woman. "Run!"

Jannah was scared. *Did I do something wrong?* She thought. She turned and ran.

"Wait!" shouted a guard. Jannah ran through the ancient city. The streets were hot and dark. Suddenly, there was a hand on her shoulder.

"Wake up, Jannah," said her mom.

Jannah sat up in bed. She looked at the book. "That's strange," she said. "The picture looks different."

"... and where are my glasses?"

TRACK 30

Unit 5, *The Time Book*, Words in Context

Find these words in the reading. What do you think they mean?

strange
pharaoh
chariot
surprised
scared
ancient

TRACK 31

Unit 5, Nonfiction, *Time Capsules*

Do you want people in the future to know about your life right now? One way you can do this is to make a time capsule. It's like giving a present from the past.

Many different things can go inside a time capsule. People put letters, pictures, and objects in them. Kids put cool things like movies, music, video games, and toys in time capsules. They put them in the ground. In the future, other people can dig and find them.

This time capsule is from 1795. People didn't find it until 2014. It was under a building in Massachusetts, USA. It had coins and newspapers in it.

More than forty years ago, people put time capsules in two spacecraft called Voyager 1 and Voyager 2. There are no people on the spacecraft, but each one has a gold disc. The gold disc is a time capsule. It says *hello* in 55 different languages.

On the disc, there are also sounds of the sea, wind, thunder, and rain. There are the songs of birds, whales, and people. It also has photos of people, animals, and places on Earth.

Voyager 1 and Voyager 2 went into space in 1977. Now, they are billions of kilometers from Earth. They are still in space today.

TRACK 32

Unit 5, Time Capsules, Words in Context

Find these words in the reading. What do you think they mean?

future
objects
newspapers
spacecraft
disc
Earth

TRACK 33

Unit 5, Explore the Reading, Phonics

Listen and say.

/nt/ point plant front invent student

Unit 6

TRACK 34

Unit 6, Fiction, *The Superstar*

Pablo: "Hi, can I help you?"
Narrator: asked Pablo.
Whitney: "Hi, I'm Whitney. Mr. Mateo Martinez, you know, the Superstar, I'm his assistant. Can I see the sculpture, please?"
Narrator: asked Whitney.
Whitney: "Remember, it has to be finished before the celebration on Friday."
Her phone rang.
Whitney: "Excuse me,"
Narrator: she said and answered it. Whitney wasn't happy.
Whitney: "Oh, no, no. I don't like it. Mr. Martinez isn't going to like it, either."
Pablo: "What's wrong?"
Narrator: asked Pablo. He looked at his plan.
Pablo: "It looks just like him."
Whitney: "The sculpture is too short. Mateo's taller than that,"
Narrator: she said.
Pablo: "No problem. I can fix it,"
Narrator: said Pablo. The next day, Mateo's brother came to see the sculpture.
Brother: "It's not bad,"
Narrator: he said.
Brother: "But my brother's beard is longer and curlier."
Pablo: "Don't worry. I can fix it,"
Narrator: said Pablo. Later, Mateo's mother came to the workshop.
Brother: "My son's arms and hands need to be bigger,"
Narrator: she said.
Pablo: "Bigger?"
Narrator: asked Pablo.
Brother: "Much bigger,"
Narrator: she said. All week, it was noisy in Pablo's workshop. Finally, he finished the sculpture. Mateo came to see the sculpture.
Superstar: "Thank you,"
Narrator: he said.
Superstar: "I travel all over the world for my movies, but I always love coming home!" "Who is *that*?"
Narrator: asked Mateo.
Pablo: "It's you,"
Narrator: said Pablo.
Superstar: "But it doesn't look like me! My beard is too long, I'm too tall, and my hands are huge! Please fix it!"
Pablo: "Whoops! OK, but we need a new plan,"
Narrator: said Pablo,
Pablo: "... or maybe the old one."

TRACK 35

Unit 6, *The Superstar*, Words in Context
Find these words in the reading. What do you think they mean?

superstar
assistant
fix
workshop
world

TRACK 36

Unit 6, Explore the Reading, Phonics
Listen and say.

/wh/ whale wheel where whisper why

TRACK 37

Unit 6, Nonfiction, *Visit Gaudí's World*

The city of Barcelona in Spain has some of the world's greatest buildings. They look like they are from a children's storybook.

They are the work of the famous architect Antoni Gaudí (1852–1926). Gaudí designed buildings and studied nature for ideas.

In 1904, a man named Josep Batlló asked Gaudí to make him a new home. Gaudí's plan was to use round shapes and the colors of nature.

The front of the building looks like bones. The colors Gaudí used are the colors of coral from the sea. The walls look like flowers on water.

...

Gaudí also wanted to create somewhere for people to enjoy nature. In Park Güell, there is a famous sculpture in the shape of a lizard. There are stone walls that look like tree trunks. There is a bench in the shape of a sea snake.

Gaudí's plan for Casa Milà was for the building to look like nature, too. The front of the building looks like a stone quarry. Inside, part of the building looks a little like a cave. The building was home for the Milà family.

Join people from all over the world. Come and see the buildings of Antoni Gaudí.

TRACK 38

Unit 6, *Visit Gaudí's World*, Words in Context, Find these words in the reading. What do you think they mean?

architect
nature
coral
bench
cave

Unit 7

TRACK 39

Unit 7, Nonfiction, *Great Teamwork*

The Honey Hunters

The Boran people and the honey bird both live in Africa. Both like honey, but both have a problem. The Boran hunters don't know where the honey is. Honey birds know where to find the honey, but they can't get it out of the bees' nests.

The people and the honey birds help each other and work together. When a Boran hunter wants honey, he whistles and shouts. When a hungry honey bird is near, it answers with a special call.

The bird flies through the forest and the hunter follows.

When they are near a bees' nest, the bird sings in a different way. This tells the hunter where the bees and honey are. The hunter takes the honey from the nest, but he always leaves some for the bird to say *thank you*. ...

Good Friends

The gobie fish and the pistol shrimp are two very different animals, but they both need help. The gobie fish cannot dig, but the pistol shrimp can. The shrimp digs a hole in the sand where they both live.

The shrimp cannot see very well, but the fish can. When the shrimp is looking for food, it holds on to the fish. The fish watches for danger. It moves its tail to tell the shrimp that danger is near. The shrimp hides.

At night, the shrimp closes the entrance with sand. The fish and the shrimp sleep in the safe hole. They share their home.

TRACK 40

Unit 7, *Great Teamwork*
Words in Context, Find these words in the reading. What do you think they mean?

hunters
both
Africa
whistles
shrimp
holds on
entrance

TRACK 41

Unit 7, Fiction, *It's Mine*

Purplebeard: Can you two help me, please?
Pinkbeard: The treasure is on this island.
Greenbeard: Yes, but where?
Purplebeard: Look, there's a box!
Pinkbeard: I saw it first!
Greenbeard: No, I did! I can't read. What does it say?
Pinkbeard: To unlock this box, there is no key ...
Purplebeard: ... listen to the parrot at the top of the tree.
Pinkbeard: Look! There's the parrot!
Greenbeard: Come back!
Purplebeard: Ha! The treasure is mine!: Can you help me open the box?
Parrot: TEAMWORK!
Pinkbeard: What's the password?
Parrot: TEAMWORK!
Greenbeard: Maybe *teamwork* is the password! The treasure's mine!
Purplebeard: No way!
Greenbeard: T-E-A ... Oh, no! I can't remember. Can you help?
Purplebeard: T-E-A-M-W. I can't remember.
Pinkbeard: I know, it's O-R-K. Look, it's a map.
Greenbeard & Purplebeard: Give it to me!
Pinkbeard: Don't grab!
Greenbeard: Oh, no!
Pinkbeard: Let's share the map.
Purplebeard: Let's help each other. Look! The treasure's there.
Pinkbeard: I saw it first!
Greenbeard: It's mine!
Pinkbeard: It's mine now.
Purplebeard & Greenbeard: Wait!
Parrot: TEAMWORK!
Pinkbeard: I need help.
Greenbeard: Let's take turns.
Purplebeard: Good idea.
Pinkbeard & Greenbeard: We're rich! Greenbeard: No, I'm rich.
Pinkbeard: It's all mine.
Purplebeard: The gold is mine.
Pinkbeard: Let's work together. Quick! Put it into the boat.
Purplebeard: It's very heavy.
Greenbeard: Goodbye.
Pinkbeard: Come back!
Purplebeard: Wait for me.
Pinkbeard: Watch out!
Greenbeard: I can't swim!
Pinkbeard: Oh, no! The treasure! Let's look for treasure on another island.
Purplebeard: Good idea.
Pinkbeard, Greenbeard, Purplebeard:
From eight o'clock 'til half past three
We sail across the big blue sea
From four o'clock 'til half past ten
We sail across the sea again
Yes, it's a pirate's life for me.

TRACK 42

Unit 7, *It's Mine*, Words in Context
Find these words in the reading. What do you think they mean?

treasure
password
map
grab
rich
gold
pirate

TRACK 43

Unit 7, Explore the Reading, Phonics
Listen and say.

/ck/ sock black backpack neck duck

Unit 8

TRACK 44

Unit 8, Nonfiction, *In First Place*

In the Olympic Games, the marathon is a very long and difficult running race. It is 42 kilometers long. One of the most famous Olympic marathon runners was a man named Abebe Bikila.

Bikila was born in Ethiopia in 1932. He was the son of a shepherd. As a young man, he joined the army. In the army, he learned to run well and win races.

In 1960, one of the runners on the Ethiopian team hurt his foot. He could not go to the Olympics. At the last minute, Bikila took his place.

Bikila did not have comfortable shoes. His shoes made his feet hurt. Bikila decided to run barefoot so he was more comfortable.

…

At the start of the race, people didn't know his name. Some people wondered who he was. Some people laughed when they saw Bikila did not have shoes.

It was a tough race, but Bikila was strong. After a while, there were only two runners in front of him. With one kilometer left in the race, Bikila pushed himself. Soon, the brave runner was in first place.

Bikila kept running. He crossed the finish line and won the gold medal! Then everyone knew his name. No one laughed at him.

In the 1964 Olympic Games, Bikila ran the marathon with shoes. He won the gold medal a second time.

Abebe Bikila is a great athlete and a hero for people around the world.

TRACK 45

Unit 8, *In First Place*, Words in Context

Find these words in the reading. What do you think they mean?

Olympic Games
hurt
comfortable
barefoot
medal

TRACK 46

Unit 8, Fiction, *A New Hero*

Narrator: Rockham City wants a new hero. They want someone to make the city a better place. The Mayor and her assistant meet people for the job.

Assistant: Hello, welcome to the Mayor's office.

Allie Gator: Hi, I'm Allie Gator.

Mayor: Hello, what do you do?

Allie Gator: I snap my teeth at robbers.

Mayor: Very good. Next! How do you help our city?

Harri: I'm Helicopter Harri and I fly around saving cats in trees.

Mayor: Well done. Next!

Otto: I'm Otto Octopus. I have eight strong arms to help people who are in trouble.

Mayor: Wow!

Narrator: A young boy knocks on the door. He looks small and shy.

Assistant: Who are you?

Bob: My name is Bob.

Mayor: You're a kid. What makes you a hero?

Bob: On my way home from school, I pick up trash in the park.

Mayor: Hmm.

Bob: I help people carry their shopping bags, even though they can be heavy.

Mayor: I see …

Bob: I always help my neighbor with his homework. In school, I find math really hard, but I try my best.

Mayor: But those are small things.

…

Bob: Little things add up. Oh, and I have these X-ray glasses. I can see through anything!

Allie Gator: I can't find my keys!

Bob: There they are.

Allie Gator: Thank you so much. This kid is a true hero!

Helicopter Harri: Oh, yes!

Otto: He is the most helpful hero!

Mayor: You're right! X-Ray Bob is just the person this city needs. The job is yours!

Bob: I can start tomorrow.

Mayor & Assistant: Great!

Bob: Just as soon as I finish my homework.

TRACK 47

Unit 8, *A New Hero*, Words in Context

Find these words in the reading. What do you think they mean?

city
mayor
job
robber
X-ray

TRACK 48

Unit 8, Explore the Reading, Phonics

Listen and say.

/tr/ tractor train travel trip treasure

Unit 9

TRACK 49

Unit 9, Fiction, *The Clever King*

Once upon a time, there was a grumpy dragon king. He lived alone in an old castle, and he wasn't very friendly.

"I don't want anybody in my castle," he thought. "Hmm, I have an idea."

First, he made an automatic drawbridge. When dragons came near his castle, the bridge went up. *Creak!* The king was very pleased.

"Ha, ha!" he shouted from the window.

I have the best castle. I'm a clever king. You can try and try but you can't come in!

"We don't want to come in," said the dragons, and they went away.

…

Next, he put cameras on the towers. When any dragons came near his castle, an alarm sounded, *beep-beep-beep*. The doors closed, *clunk*. The bridge went up, *creak*. And an automatic message said,

I have the best castle. I'm a clever king. You can try and try but you can't come in!

"Let's have our picnic somewhere else," said the dragons.

Then the king filled the moat with super-sticky glue.

He went to the top of the tower and looked down. He was very excited.

Ha, ha! I have the best …

But just then, his crown fell off. It fell down … down … down … onto the bridge … and into the glue.

…

The king ran down the stairs … across the bridge … and he tried to pull his crown out of the glue.

Suddenly he heard the alarm.

Beep-beep-beep.

The doors went *clunk*.

The bridge went *creak*.

Then he heard,

I have the best castle. I'm a clever king.
You can try and try but you can't come in!

The king felt sad. He didn't feel clever anymore.

TRACK 50

Unit 9, *The Clever King*, Words in Context

Find these words in the reading. What do you think they mean?

clever
grumpy
automatic
drawbridge
moat
sticky
crown

TRACK 51

Unit 9, Nonfiction, *Amazing Castles*

Castles are big, strong buildings. Important people like kings, queens, and emperors built castles to keep their families safe.

Leeds Castle is in Great Britain. It is about 900 years old. It is on an island in the middle of a lake. The first castle on the island was small. It had wooden walls. King Edward I made the castle stronger. He built high stone walls, and he made the lake bigger. It was his favorite castle. Nobody lives in the castle now.

Nakhal Fort is more than 1,500 years old. It is in Oman. It is high up on a rock. It

has stone walls and a round tower in the middle. Today, there is a museum inside the fort, and every Friday there is a goat market inside the castle walls.
From the top of the tower, visitors can see in all directions. They can see the valley, the mountains, and the palm trees.
Brézé Castle is in France. It is about 500 years old. It has a bridge and a big moat, but there's no water in it. Inside the castle there are a lot of rooms to live in. A family still lives in the castle now.
But this castle has a secret …
Under the castle, there is another castle. This is the oldest part of the castle. It is nearly 1,000 years old. There are secret passages and rooms in the rock. Many years ago, there was a kitchen and a bakery for making bread. There were stables for the horses. There was even an ice room for keeping food cool. Nobody lives there now, but people can visit it.

TRACK 52

Unit 9, *Amazing Castles*, Words in Context
Find these words in the reading. What do you think they mean?
emperors
wooden
round
secret
passages
bakery
stables

TRACK 53

Unit 9, Explore the Reading, Phonics
Listen and say.
/br/ brother breakfast brown Brazil brain

Unit 10

TRACK 54

Unit 10, Fiction, *Young Nicholas*
October sixth, 1769
Dear Diary,
My name's Nicholas. I live on a ship called the *Endeavour*. We're on a journey at sea. We left England a long time ago. Everyone is looking for land. I love the water, but I miss land. I think the other sailors do, too. Everything is blue here.
I'm a cabin boy. Every day, I clean the boat. Today, I swept the cabins and scrubbed the deck. Then I saw something swaying in the water. I looked closer. It was a tree branch! I wanted to pull it out, but I couldn't get it. I knew land was close, so I ran to tell the captain.
When I found him, he was talking to his men. "Hear this!" he said. "The first man to find land wins a prize. I'll also name a place after him!"
I'm going to win that prize, I thought. *I'm going to find land.*
It was windy and I climbed up slowly. I kept my eyes on the top of the mast. *Come on, Nicholas!* I thought.
At last, I reached the top. From here, I could see a very long way.
I looked and looked. I didn't give up. I needed to find land.
Finally, I saw something. It was very small and far away. My heart started beating faster. I wanted to jump in and swim. There it was—land!
"Land!" I shouted down to the others. "I see land!"
Tomorrow, I'm going to get the prize. I'm so excited!
Yours truly,
Nicholas

TRACK 55

Unit 10, *Young Nicholas*, Words in Context
Find these words in the reading. What do you think they mean?
ship
land
branch
captain
mast

TRACK 56

Unit 10, Explore the Reading, Phonics
Listen and say.
/sw/ sweater swan swing swap sweet

TRACK 57

Unit 10, Nonfiction, *The Thirty-Year Journey*
Ibn Battuta was one of the world's greatest travelers. He was born in Morocco in 1304. Ibn Battuta left his home when he was 21 years old. He went on a journey that took 30 years! He wanted to learn about the world. He saw more of the world than anyone else in his time. When he started his journey, Ibn Battuta was all by himself.
Later, Ibn Battuta traveled through the desert with caravans. They rode their animals, cooked, and camped together. Some caravans had thousands of people. They were almost like a moving town.
…
Traveling in those days was hard. There were many dangers on the road. Once, Ibn Battuta was robbed and left with only his clothes. Sometimes, he had to run for his life!
Traveling by ship was hard, too. There were big storms with thunder and lightning.
…
Ibn Battuta wanted to see everything. He traveled through deserts, across seas, and over mountains. He traveled through Africa and into parts of Europe. He also went to the Middle East and India. He even went to Southeast Asia and China.
He missed his home and went back to Morocco. The ruler of Morocco wanted to hear all about his journey. Ibn Battuta told his stories to a writer, and together they wrote a book called *Ar-Rihla*. In the book, Ibn Battuta describes all the people and places he saw. The book gives us a good idea of life in those days.
Today, to remember him and his great journey, there is a place on the moon called Ibn Battuta.

TRACK 58

Unit 10, *The Thirty-Year Journey*, Words in Context
Find these words in the reading. What do you think they mean?
travelers
caravans
camped
dangers
robbed
ruler

Video Scripts

Language Book

The video scripts for the songs in the **Language Book** are exactly the same as for the audio scripts and the text on the page.

Unit 1

PRESENTATION

Technology Is Great

Grace: Hello, my name's Grace. Today, my presentation is about laptops. They can help you with school projects. You can use a laptop to find information. I often go online and learn about different things. You can also use a laptop to plan a presentation. These are my ideas for today. I sometimes use a notebook instead – when I don't have my laptop! A laptop is great for pictures. I always draw pictures on it for presentations. A laptop is useful because it has a screen, a keyboard, and a mouse—everything you need! Thank you.

Unit 2

CONVERSATION

Let's Go Shopping

Dad: Let's do the online shopping, Rob.
Rob: OK, Dad.
Dad: We need some milk.
Rob: How many cartons?
Dad: Three.
Rob: How about some lemonade?
Dad: OK. One bottle. And we need some carrots.
Rob: How many carrots?
Dad: Let's get three bags of carrots. What would you like for dinner?
Rob: Hmmm … I'd like … chicken, please.
Dad: Get one chicken, then.
Rob: Can we have some pineapple after?
Dad: Of course. Get one pineapple, too.
Rob: What about cereal?
Dad: Oh, yes. Let's get two boxes.
Rob: OK. Do we need any rice?
Dad: No, we need some pasta. Let's get three bags of pasta.
Rob: Anything else?
Dad: No, that's it.

Unit 3

CONVERSATION

I Love Animals

Gus: This Safari Park is so cool, Lara!
Lara: I know! I was here last summer.
Gus: Really?
Lara: Yes. Oh, Gus, look at the penguins. They're so big. And they're black and white. They were gray and small before.
Gus: *Wow!*
Lara: They were just babies then.
Gus: Oh, I see. I love penguins!
Lara: Me, too.
Gus: What about those gray seals? Are they the same?
Lara: Ooh! No, they're not. They were white and small before. They were babies, too.
Gus: Cool!
Lara: Let's see the insects over there. I think they have caterpillars.
Gus: Really? I don't like caterpillars.
Lara: Me, neither. But, look! Now they're butterflies!
Gus: Amazing

Unit 4

PRESENTATION

My Big Event

Gus: Hello. I'm Gus. I want to tell you about an important event in my life. This event is my first trip to another country. It happened last summer and I was with my family. We traveled by plane to France. We started our vacation in Paris and visited a lot of interesting places. It was good because I wanted to learn about a new country. It was difficult because I didn't speak French. But I practiced and my dad helped me. Most of the time I was happy because I like traveling with my family. Thank you for listening.

Unit 5

PRESENTATION

My Dinosaur

Flo: Hi. I'm Flo and I'm going to talk about the Floraptor. The Floraptor lived in Ecuador, about 73 million years ago. It wasn't a big dinosaur. It was like a swan, my favorite animal. It wasn't like a lizard. It had a big head but a small body and a very long tail, like a snake. It had feathers like a bird, but it didn't fly. It didn't have wings. It was very scary. It had a big mouth and a huge nose! And, what did it eat? It ate other dinosaurs! It had scary claws, and it walked on two legs. It was very slow. It was a cool dinosaur!

Unit 6

PRESENTATION

How Do You Make It?

Greta: Hello, my name's Greta. I'm going to show you how to make a collage. My collage is a portrait of me. I have short hair, two blue eyes, two ears, a small nose, and a big mouth. First, choose your materials. You can choose pencils, crayons, different colored paper, or stickers. You need scissors and glue. Next, use a pencil (or a crayon) and draw your face. Then, use the scissors and cut out your face shape. You can decorate it with the paper shapes or stickers. My collage has different colored paper for my face, hair, and neck. And stickers for my eyes. Finally, you can color your nose and mouth. Here's my portrait.

Unit 7

CONVERSATION

What Can We Do?

Grace: What can we do on Sunday, Jason?
Jason: I don't know, Grace.
Grace: Hmm! I know, let's do an outdoor activity.
Jason: OK. How about mountain climbing?
Grace: Um, I'm not sure about climbing. I don't like heights.
Jason: The water sports center is open on Sunday. Do you like watersports?
Grace: I love them. Let's look at the timetable.
Jason: OK. What do you want to do?
Grace: Is there anything on Sunday morning?
Jason: We can go waterskiing or sailing at 10 o'clock. Which do you prefer?
Grace: I prefer sailing because it's a team activity. We can call Al and Ben, and they can come, too.
Jason: That's a great idea!

Unit 8

CONVERSATION

Let's Play Superheroes!

Lara: Do you want to play the superhero game?
Sam: Cool! OK. How?
Lara: Like this. These are our superheroes.
Sam: Thanks.
Lara: Now, we need to choose adjectives for each number.
Lara: Oh, wait. Don't let me see yours!
Sam: OK.
Lara: Ready?
Sam: Yes. OK.
Lara: You go first. Choose an adjective.
Sam: Umm … "brave."
Lara: OK.
Lara: Now, you choose a superhero for me.
Sam: Right … um … You play "Fun Fifi."
Lara: OK. And you play … "Super Sam."
Lara: Now, what score does Super Sam have for "brave"?
Sam: Umm … 9.
Lara: Ooh, that's high.
Sam: What score does "Fun Fifi" have?
Lara: She has … 6 for "brave." So, you win this round.
Sam: Wow! Great. Is it your turn?
Lara: Yes, it's my turn now.
Sam: This is fun!
Lara: Yes! OK, next I choose "intelligent"…

Unit 9

PRESENTATION

My Dream House

Sam: Hello, I'm Sam. I'm going to talk about my dream house. This is my tower. It´s huge! My bedroom is in the attic. I can see everything! There are a lot of toys so I can share with all my friends. And in my bathroom, I don't have a bath. I have a swimming pool because I love swimming. This is the kitchen. It has a big table so I can eat with all my family. And, there's an enormous fridge because I love cold juice! In the backyard there's a tennis court because I want to be a tennis player. I need to practice every day. I love my dream house.

Unit 10

CONVERSATION

Tickets, Please!

Ticket seller: Good afternoon. How can I help you?
Passenger: I'd like a ticket to Rain Town, please.
Ticket seller: Would you like a one-way ticket or a round-trip?
Passenger: One-way, please.
Ticket seller: OK, that's 10 dollars. Thank you. Here you are.
Passenger: Thank you.
Ticket seller: You're welcome.
Ticket seller: Good morning. How can I help you?
Passenger: I'd like a round-trip ticket to Sun City for next week, please.
Ticket seller: Of course. What day would you like to travel?
Passenger: On Wednesday.
Ticket seller: Sorry, there are no trains to Sun City on Wednesday.
Passenger: Are there any trains on Thursday?
Ticket seller: Yes there are. In the morning or in the afternoon?
Passenger: In the afternoon, please
Ticket seller: OK, that's twenty dollars. Thank you. Here you go.
Passenger: Thank you.
Ticket seller: You're welcome. Have a nice trip.
Passenger: Thank you. Goodbye.

Literacy Book

The video scripts for the **Literacy Book** reading texts (fiction and nonfiction) are mostly the same as for the audio scripts and on the pages of the book. Occasionally, some narrator's lines have been cut to work better with the animation; these altered scripts are shown here.

Unit 1

NONFICTION

My Good Ideas Book

Audio Script Track 12 TB p. 232

Unit 2

FICTION

First Harvest

Narrator: Harvest time is here. The family works hard on the farm. They dig up vegetables. They pick fruit.

Dad: "I'm worried. It's hard for plants to grow here. There isn't much water,"

Narrator: says Dad.

Dad: "I don't believe it! These carrots are beautiful."

Narrator: There are pink potatoes and purple corn. There are tomatoes with red and green stripes. There is red pineapple. There are orange peas.

August: "We have a lot of food!"

Narrator: says August.

Dad: "And we worked hard for it. Thank you!"

Mom: "How can we celebrate?"

Narrator: asks Mom.

Ruth: "I know, let's get everyone together. We can have a feast!"

Narrator: says Ruth.

Dad: "That's a great idea,"

Narrator: says Dad.

Dad: "This is our very first harvest, after all."

Mom: "I want to make an apple pie. You two can help."

Ruth: "Can we go outside and play first? Please?"

Dad: "Oh, all right."

Mom: "Check your space suits before you go. And make sure you have a lot of air."

August and Ruth: "We will!"

Unit 3

NONFICTION

Clean Cars

Audio Script Track 22 TB p. 234

Unit 4

NONFICTION

Where Is She?

Audio Script Track 24 TB p. 234

Unit 5

FICTION

The Time Book

It was time for Jannah to go to bed. *Just one more story,* she thought. *What's this? I don't remember this book. It looks interesting.*

On the book, there was a picture of an old street with a lot of people. She saw a girl. *That girl looks like me!* she thought. *How strange!*

She opened the book.

"Oh! Where am I?" asked Jannah. She was in a very old city. "Look!" said an old woman next to her. "The pharaoh is coming. I want to see the pharaoh," said the woman. Then Jannah saw the huge chariot.

"Look out!"

"Oh, thank you, I can't see very well."

"Try my glasses."

"Glasses?"

"Yes, they help you see. Put them in front of your eyes."

The old woman was surprised.

"Now, I can see everything. There's the pharaoh!"

"Who's that girl?" asked the pharaoh.

"What strange clothes. Stop her!"

"Oh, no! They're coming. Run!"

Jannah was scared. *Did I do something wrong?* she thought. She turned and ran.

"Wait!" shouted a guard.

Jannah ran through the ancient city. The streets were hot and dark. Suddenly, there was a hand on her shoulder.

"Wake up, Jannah," said her mom.

Jannah sat up in bed. She looked at the book.

"That's strange. The picture looks different ... and where are my glasses?"

Unit 6

NONFICTION

Visit Gaudí's World

Audio Script Track 37 TB p. 235

Unit 7

FICTION

It's Mine

Audio Script Track 41 TB p. 236

Unit 8

FICTION

A New Hero

Audio Script Track 46 TB p. 237

Unit 9

FICTION

The Clever King

Audio Script Track 49 TB p. 237

Unit 10

NONFICTION

The Thirty-Year Journey

Audio Script Track 57 TB p. 238